About the book

This excellent book is further testimony to one of the most remarkable phenomena of English literary history—the lasting world-wide interest in the works and personality of a man who in his lifetime found little sympathy for either except in a small circle of intimate friends . . . Yet once his poems caught proper attention long after his death they rapidly acquired a permanent place in the upper regions of English literature.   THOUGHT

Dr. Pick's excellent selection . . . for admirers of the poetry who are new to the prose Dr. Pick's excellent anthology will be a wonderful revelation of 'the whole man.'
                    THE TIMES LONDON LITERARY SUPPLEMENT

A Hopkins Reader is a fine introduction to a poet's poet—and to an intellectual Christian who cut a bright, if often steep, path of his own in searching the love of God.   TIME

This generous gathering of poems, letters, journal entries, and even a sampling of Hopkins' drawings has to be one of the best buys of the literary year. The collection was first published more than a decade ago. This revised and enlarged paperback edition provides 18 additional poems, that is, all of Hopkins' mature poetry, an increased number of letters, and an entirely new section of notes on the poetry.   LOS ANGELES TIMES

Professor Pick has made an admirable and useful selection from Gerard Manley Hopkins' many letters, notebooks, and journals—originally published between 1936 and 1938, and long out of print—as well as from the poetry. The material, even in its cut form, is astonishingly rich, and it is required reading for anyone interested in Hopkins either as a unique human being or as a poetic innovator.   THE NEW YORKER

This selection from the Poems, Notebooks, and Letters has long been needed, because the bulk and expansiveness of the various volumes have kept them from general attention. A notable feature of Professor Pick's excellent introduction is his concentration on the poetic and technical features of Hopkins' art, suggesting that there is no longer any need to explain or defend Hopkins the Catholic priest.   COMMONWEAL

With the publication of John Pick's excellent reader, the poetry of Gerard Manley Hopkins comes forth from the cells of scholars and poets to be shared by the wider public which it deserves. It could hardly be done under better auspices, namely, the Oxford University Press, publisher of most of the important books by and about Hopkins, and the volume's editor, Professor John Pick of Marquette University, author of *Gerard Manley Hopkins, Priest and Poet* . . . The body of Hopkins' work is such as to give validity to a reader of this kind. His writings are neither so extensive as to make a selection unwarrantedly arbitrary nor so limited as to make it pointless. It is in discharging his duty with taste, insight, and proportion that Professor Pick has done the cultivated reader a high service.

TODAY

All the important poems are there, along with passages from diaries and journals, essays, sermons, and letters, literary and personal, to his closest friends. There is even a sampling of Hopkins' delicate line drawings and a facsimile of one of his songs. The lucid arrangement of this material, the careful dating of each item, the brief introduction, and the excellent notes make the book as useful for the reader already familiar with Hopkins as for the newcomer to his work. Both must be grateful to Prof. Pick for presenting the poet full length.

BOSTON HERALD

About the author

Professor JOHN PICK is probably the world's leading Hopkins scholar. His biography of Father Hopkins, *Gerard Manley Hopkins: Priest and Poet,* published in 1942 drew high critical acclaim and established Dr. Pick as a leading authority in interpreting Hopkins' thought. At present Dr. Pick is Professor of English at Marquette University where he has taught for more than thirty years.

A HOPKINS READER

Sonnet

The world is charged with the grandeur of God.
  It will flame out, like shining from shook foil;
   It gathers to a greatness, like an oozing oil
Pressed. Why do men then now not reck His rod? —
Generations have trod, have trod, have trod;
  And all is seared with trade; bleared, smeared with toil;
   And wears man's smudge and shares man's smell. The soil
Is barren; nor can foot feel, being shod.

And, for all this, nature is never spent,
  There lives the dearest freshness deep down things;
And though the last lights from the black West went
  O morning, on the brown brink eastwards, springs —
Because the Holy Ghost over the bent
  World broods with warm breast and with ah! bright wings.

The Starlight Night

Look at the stars! look, look up at the skies!
  O look at all the fire-folk sitting in the air!
   The bright boroughs, the glimmering citadels there!
Look, the elf-rings! look at the out-round earnest eyes!
The grey lawns cold where quaking gold-dew lies!
  Wind-beat white-beam, airy abeles all on flare!
   Flake-doves sent floating out at a farmyard scare!
Ah well! it is a purchase and a prize.

Buy then! Bid then! — what? — Prayer, patience, alms, vows.
  Look, look — a May-mess, like on orchard-boughs,
   Look — march-bloom, like on mealed-with-yellow sallows!
These are the barn, indeed: within doors house
The shocks. This pale and parcel-close hides the spouse
  Christ and the mother of Christ and all His Hallows,

Two Sonnets by Hopkins in his own handwriting.
See page 49 and page 50

A HOPKINS READER

REVISED AND ENLARGED EDITION

SELECTIONS FROM THE WRITINGS OF

GERARD MANLEY HOPKINS

EDITED WITH AN INTRODUCTION

BY JOHN PICK

IMAGE BOOKS
A DIVISION OF DOUBLEDAY & COMPANY, INC.
GARDEN CITY, NEW YORK

Image Books Edition 1966
by special arrangement with Oxford University Press
Image Books Edition published February 1966

ISBN: 0-385-09051-x

CONTENTS

LIST OF ILLUSTRATIONS

INTRODUCTION

Fifty years ago Hopkins was unknown. Today he is in every anthology.

The publication of the poetry of Hopkins in 1918, almost thirty years after his death, was one of the major literary events of our time.

Though by the dates of his birth and death (1844–89) he falls within the Victorian period, Hopkins has been acclaimed by our own generation as even more modern than the moderns. There seems to be no end to the ever-growing stream of articles and books about him.

'Hopkins was one of the most remarkable technical inventors who ever wrote,' F. R. Leavis remarks, and 'He is likely to prove, for our time and the future, the only influential poet of the Victorian age.' W. H. Gardner concludes a two-volume study of Hopkins with the claim, 'After an intensive study of Hopkins, most other English poetry seems outwardly facile and in varying degrees inadequate.'

Contemporary interest in Hopkins brings not only edition after edition of his poetry but also the publication of every surviving letter, diary, and draft. Five stout volumes are now devoted to *Letters to Robert Bridges, Correspondence with R. W. Dixon, Further Letters, Sermons and Devotional Writings,* and *Journals and Papers*—a total of more than two thousand pages.

A Hopkins Reader selects and reprints the most important materials from these volumes as well as from the *Poems*—every completed mature poem is included—and presents them in easily accessible form. Letters are printed in their entirety. In all other cases the units are as complete as possible. Because Hopkins seldom confined himself to a single problem in any one letter, the headings under which they are arranged —Observation of Nature: Inscape, Poetic Theory, Practical Criticism, The Other Arts, and Religion—are necessarily indicative rather than definitive.

However, Hopkins's poetry stands as his own greatest monument, and the real importance of his letters, notebooks, and papers—significant as they are in their own right—is that they illuminate his poetry and help toward a deeper understanding of him as a poet.

Many things have hindered a balanced evaluation of Hopkins. So startlingly different did his early readers find him that they failed to see how deep were his roots. He was both a revolutionary and a traditionalist: for his prosody he revived and reinvigorated a tradition far older than that which had been current in English poetry since Elizabethan times; for his matter, instead of mirroring the Victorian *mélange* or inventing a new myth, he recaptured and then continued with new vitality the main tradition of Western Christendom. In manner and in matter he was both old and new, at the same time more traditional and revolutionary than either the Victorians or the moderns.

In such matters his letters and notebooks are especially helpful. On the one hand he writes, 'The effect of studying masterpieces is to make me admire and do otherwise' or 'Every true poet . . . must be original and originality a condition of poetic genius; so that each poet is like a species in nature . . . and can never recur'; and yet on the other hand, 'The examples of the great masters are the soul of education.'

When, for instance, the reader first looks at the sonnets—and Hopkins called most of his poems sonnets—he is not a little aghast at how strangely different they seem from the conventional form. But Hopkins explains in his correspondence that he was trying to approximate in English the length and weight of the original Petrarchan sonnet. In attempting to do so he introduces into English poetry what is almost a new genre.

His notebooks and correspondence also tell the story of his short life and the joys and the sorrows which are echoed in his poetry. They give a sketch of Hopkins from his days as a schoolboy until the night of his death. His brief forty-five years were not outwardly spectacular, but inwardly they were filled with a great measure of heroic dedication—'the war within', as he expressed it in one of his poems. The outlines of his life are simple, and there is really only one date of great significance: the year 1868 when he entered the Jesuit Order. This marks the turning-point of his life and divides his youth from his maturity, his adolescence from his manhood. It also marks the division between his early verse and his great poetry.

Born into a moderately High Church family, he early distinguished himself at Highgate School as a poet and a scholar. He won at least one prize for his verse which even at that time showed that delight in the sensuous world which reminds one of the young Keats and indicated a life-long bent of his artistically gifted temperament.

At Oxford, which he entered in 1863, he was in the midst of the intellectual, religious, and artistic currents of the time. Pater was one of his tutors, and the growing aesthetic movement attracted him. So did the liberalism of Jowett, who called him 'The Star of Balliol'. But after intense struggle the High Churchmen, such as Pusey and Liddon, won the allegiance of the youthful Hopkins, eager to bring under control all his faculties. Sternly he rejected his other self:

For lent. No pudding on Sunday. No tea except if to keep me awake and then without sugar. Meat only once a day. No verses in Passion Week or on Fridays. Not to sit in armchair except can work no other way. Ash Wednesday and Good Friday bread and water.

The poetry of his Oxford days shows the immediate impact of this new religious asceticism; no longer does he revel in the senses but instead he asserts pure intellect—so much so that his verse sheds most of its imagery and becomes overloaded with philosophical assertion. 'Be shèlled eyes with double dark', he wrote in one of these poems, 'And find the uncreated light.'

But Hopkins was not to stop here, here at what he called 'the half-way house'. His letters reveal a long and careful study of the position of Newman who had left the Oxford Movement for Rome back in 1845 and who was now established at Edgbaston Oratory at Birmingham. During his last year at Oxford, Hopkins finally applied to Newman for acceptance as a Roman Catholic. His Oxford career came to a close with high honours in 1867.

He had long thought of taking Orders, and after a term

as a lay master at Newman's Oratory School he eventually
decided to become a Jesuit and in 1868 entered the novitiate
at Roehampton, just outside of London. To him Newman said
at this time: 'Don't call "the Jesuit discipline hard": it will
bring you to heaven.' Hopkins entered without illusions. To
make his detachment from the past more complete, he made
a voluntary holocaust of his poetry, prepared to sacrifice it
forever.

It was during his years as a novice and seminarian that he
kept the Journal that reflects his renewed interest in the world
of nature—but with an important difference. Under the per-
vasive influence of the *Spiritual Exercises*, the great religious
handbook of St. Ignatius, he gradually discovered what was
for him a new relationship between a delight in nature and
his newly found vocation. The inspiration of all his mature
poetry will be found in such a passage as the following, which
is his précis of the opening section of the *Exercises* known as
'The Principle and Foundation':

God's utterance of Himself in Himself is God the Word, outside
Himself is this world. This world then is word, expression, news of
God. Therefore its end, its purpose, its purport, its meaning, is God,
and its life or work to name and praise Him.

For seven years after he entered the Jesuit Order, Hopkins
kept poetic silence. But in a letter to his friend Dixon he tells
how after his rector suggested in 1875 that he compose 'The
Wreck of the Deutschland', 'I held myself free to compose,
but cannot find it in my conscience to spend time upon it; so
I have done little and shall do less.' In one so scrupulous, the
word 'conscience' is here the key, and all the rest of his life
Hopkins was to debate whether he should go on writing
poetry. He found it easy enough to settle this problem on a
theoretical level but in practice it was full of difficulties.

He was keenly aware of the spiritual danger of pride and
of desire for fame, and he had not joined the Jesuits to become their poet laureate—even if he was to become precisely
that with the publication of his poetry thirty years after his
death. He submitted 'The Wreck of the Deutschland' and
later 'The Loss of the Eurydice' to their magazine *The Month*
which eventually rejected them—as indeed any Victorian

periodical would have done. He never blamed his fellow Jesuits for not appreciating his poetry. What is far stranger is that he was given so little real encouragement by those friends who did know his poetry intimately, the three poets who formed his real public: Bridges, Dixon, and Patmore. It would seem that under any circumstances, whether within the Jesuits or in the larger world of letters, he was doomed to the painful life of the unrecognized pioneer.

Numerous letters as well as poems are a detailed and heart-touching record of his struggle. Sometimes he confesses, 'Even the impulse to write is wanting, for I have no thought of publishing' or 'There is a point with me in matters of any size when I must absolutely have encouragement as much as crops rain.' As his life progressed other complications entered: he often found his immediate duties as priest or teacher so demanding as to leave little leisure or inclination for poetry; he considered city life uncongenial; he was a very English Englishman in the midst of a Dublin demanding Home Rule; he was almost obsessed by the idea that he must undertake scholarly research in the field of his teaching; and his health became more and more precarious as he neared his early grave. All these things interacted to make his life harassed and difficult.

But perhaps it is too seldom recognized that his life—especially in Dublin—was made especially painful by a state of spiritual aridity and desolation, a state which is well known in the lives of many dedicated people. His desolation made him write:

Feeling, love in particular, is the great moving power and spring of verse and the only person I am in love with seldom, especially now, stirs my heart sensibly and when he does I cannot always 'make capital' of it, it would be a sacrilege to do so.

Yet out of his anguish came almost 'unbidden and against my will' some of his most haunting and terrifying poems, the 'terrible sonnets' as they have been called. As a counterpart of his cry 'All impulse fails me: I can give myself no sufficient reason for going on. Nothing comes: I am a eunuch—but it is for the kingdom of heaven's sake'—out of this cry comes one of his last and most astringent sonnets:

> . . . birds build—but not I build; no, but strain,
> Time's eunuch, and not breed one work that wakes.
> Mine, O thou lord of life, send my roots rain.

It is futile to regret that he did not write poetry in greater quantity, and it is well to remember that his inward struggle intensified its quality and indeed gave to that poetry the very qualities which all critics recognize as its greatness.

All this story of his interior life is told in his letters and in his poetry. But there was his external life as well. After his ordination to the priesthood in 1877 he was assigned to a variety of posts as preacher and minor administrator in London, Oxford, Liverpool, and Glasgow. His sermons are closely associated with his poems, and the connexion between the two is suggested in a letter to Bridges: 'I am going to preach tomorrow . . . what I am putting not at all so plainly to the rest of the world, or rather to you and Canon Dixon, in a sonnet.' In none of these posts was he eminently successful in a worldly sense though his conscientiousness and dedication were often heroic.

Later he taught classics at Stonyhurst, the Jesuit preparatory school. Then in 1884 he who had been called by Jowett 'The Star of Balliol' was sent to Ireland as Professor of Greek at University College, Dublin, where he spent his last five years. Again, the history of his Dublin years may be read in his letters and poems. He faced his new duties weak in health, and indeed he had never been robust. Even back in 1868 just after he left Oxford he wrote to his friend Baillie: 'I have become very weak in health and do not seem to recover myself . . . I have . . . almost no energy—for I am always tired —to do anything on my own account.' Twenty years later in Dublin his burden was much the same. Some measure of the effect of ill health upon a nervous system so delicately organized may be judged from an entry in his Journal in 1873, a time when his life was as yet uncomplicated by additional trials which were to be heaped upon him; after a detailed and enthusiastic description of a walk and a sunset he adds:

> But we hurried too fast and it knocked me up. . . . In fact being unwell I was quite downcast: nature in all her parcels and faculties gaped and fell apart, *fatiscebat*, like a clod cleaving and holding only by strings of root. But this must often be.

In Dublin not only did his previous difficulties converge upon him and become intensified, but new and additional problems put him on the rack. The responsibilities of his new position he found congenial but onerous; his scrupulous attention to them—'It is killing work to examine a nation', he remarked—made them a constant anxiety, and even vacations in Wales ('always to me the mother of Muses') were little relief; more than ever he felt it his duty to produce research articles, and his letters are filled with numerous projects, almost all unfinished and uncompleted. At the same time he turned more and more to music in which he tried to make headway.

But his last years also brought their moments of exultation, and such a poem as 'That Nature is a Heraclitean Fire' is a prelude to his deathbed cry, thrice repeated, 'I am so happy', as he saw immediately before him 'the heaven-haven of the Reward'.

Such, then, is the bare outline of his life, an outline which one may fill in with the important nuances by examining his letters and correspondence. It is, however, especially in the Journal which he kept during his years of poetic silence that one will find the raw material of his mature poetry. The spirit of the Journal is indicated in a letter to Baillie:

I think I have told you that I have particular periods of admiration for particular things in Nature; for a certain time I am astonished at the beauty of a tree, shape, effect, etc then when the passion, so to speak, has subsided, it is consigned to my treasury of explored beauty, and acknowledged with admiration and interest ever after, while something new takes its place in my enthusiasm.

He bears witness to his 'admiration for particular things' throughout his Journal. When he jots down 'All the world is full of inscape' he introduces a term so frequently used in his Journal and his criticism and one so central to his poetry that once it is grasped much of the difficulty of Hopkins disappears.

Instead of viewing the world as a scientist who classifies and categorizes or as a philosopher who seeks universals, Hopkins sees each thing as highly individualized and different from all other things, so much so that each object is to

him almost a separate species and the world becomes an endless catalogue of sharply individuated selves. In his Journal he
sets down the particularity of each unique thing he observes—
and to him all things are unique. He remarks, 'I thought how
sadly beauty of inscape was unknown and buried away from
simple people and yet how near at hand it was if they had
eyes to see it', or he expresses his sorrow at the felling of a
favourite ash-tree: 'I wished to die and not see the inscapes of
the world destroyed any more.'

Eventually he applied the term to works of art as well.
Inscape is 'the very soul of art'. He examines the work of one
poet and finds it 'full of feeling, high thoughts, flow of verse,
point, often fine imagery and other virtues, but the essential
and only lasting thing left out—what I call inscape'. The most
famous passage is one in which he says of his own poetry:

As air, melody, is what strikes me most of all in music and design
in painting, so design, pattern or what I am in the habit of calling
'inscape' is what I above all aim at in poetry. Now it is the virtue of
design, pattern, or inscape to be distinctive.

With these introductory remarks in mind one may examine
his Journal and see there his attempts to inscape the world of
nature and of art. It became his preliminary sketch-pad, his
field-book, in which the rudimentary and embryonic images
of his later poetry are to be found. Often the very same
images in the Journal recur in poems written six, eight, or
even twenty years later. Even more significant is the way in
which the raw material is finally transmuted into poetry. For
example, his numerous references to the brindled and brinded
clouds, his delight in fishing, his joy over 'chestnuts as bright
as coals or spots of vermilion' become in 'Pied Beauty':

> Glory be to God for dappled things—
> For skies of couple-colour as a brinded cow;
> For rose-moles all in stipple upon trout that swim;
> Fresh-firecoal chestnut falls.

A study of the two sets of images is an important approach
to understanding the creative process, no matter how many
mysteries of that alchemy may remain unsolved.

But for Hopkins a mere catalogue of images does not make

a poem, and there is a difference between prose and poetry. The latter requires a further inscape of sound pattern; and in such an essay as 'Poetry and Verse' he insists on the necessity of 'an inscape of speech'.

Poetry for Hopkins was still more than this, for he held that: 'Works of art of course like words utter the idea.' The rudimentary images themselves are to be found in the Journal, and so also are the centralizing ideas which fuse the images into organic and living poems.

It is obvious, for instance, that the controlling idea, giving direction and significance to the scattered images of 'Hurrahing in Harvest' is parallel to such an entry as 'I do not think I have ever seen anything more beautiful than the bluebell I have been looking at. I know the beauty of our Lord by it.' So, too, 'Pied Beauty' with its opening 'Glory be to God for dappled things' is paralleled by the prose note in the Journal, 'Laus Deo—the river today and yesterday.' Such passages take their orientation from the *Spiritual Exercises* of St. Ignatius. This becomes clear if one compares the opening lines of 'God's Grandeur':

> The world is charged with the grandeur of God.
> It will flame out, like shining from shook foil;

and his prose commentary on *The Exercises:* 'All things therefore are charged with God, and if we know how to touch them give off sparks and take fire, yield drops and flow, ring and tell of Him.' It is very especially in Hopkins's 'Address on the "Principle or Foundation"' that one can see how inscapes became for him a theophany and a *laudate Dominum*.

Hopkins also held that it is in activity, in characteristic action, that the individual reveals his inscape, and he delights in dynamism:

> As kingfishers catch fire, dragonflies dráw fláme;
> As tumbled over rim in roundy wells
> Stones ring; like each tucked string tells, each hung bell's
> Bow swung finds tongue to fling out broad its name;
> Each mortal thing does one thing and the same:
> Deals out that being indoors each one dwells;
> Selves—goes itself; *myself* it speaks and spells;
> Crying *Whát I dó is me: for that I came.*

He was further confirmed in his delight in inscapes by a medieval philosopher who also saw in them a revelation of the hand of their Creator, and therefore he found Duns Scotus, 'of realty the rarest-veinèd unraveller', so congenial that he entered into his Journal:

At this time I had first begun to get hold of the copy of Scotus . . . and was flush with a new stroke of enthusiasm. It may come to nothing or it may be a mercy from God. But just then when I took in any inscape of the sky or sea I thought of Scotus.

The kinds of inscapes in which he was interested determined in large part the development of his poetry. From nature sacramentally inscaped he turns to the contrast between nature and man—man the most distinctively inscaped of all, 'nature's clearest-selvèd spark Man'—and finally in his last poems, the most personal of his work, he writes of that taste of his own self to which he refers in his commentary on the *Exercises* as 'my selfbeing . . . that taste of myself, of *I* and *me* . . . which is more distinctive than the taste of ale or alum, more distinctive than the smell of walnut-leaf or camphor . . . this selfbeing of my own'.

If inscape means that each thing is uniquely different from all other things, then an attempt to capture inscape in poetry will mean unique precision and distinctiveness in language, imagery, and metre. Each noun, each adjective, each adverb and verb must be selected to individualize. Once one understands this, many of the apparent difficulties or 'oddities' of Hopkins's vocabulary disappear. Often what is needed is merely a good dictionary.

His careful search for the exact word will be seen in all his poetry, and many of his letters reflect this same demand. Thus he writes to Bridges about the opening line of 'The Leaden Echo and the Golden Echo':

You must know that words like *charm* and *enchantment* will not do: the thought is of beauty as of something that can be physically kept and lost and by physical things only, like keys; then the things must come from the *mundus muliebris;* and thirdly they must not be markedly oldfashioned. You will see that this limits the choice of words very much indeed.

Even when he used familiar words he desired to specify;

this is illustrated in a letter about one of the lines of 'Duns Scotus's Oxford': 'You misquote . . . in writing "airy between towers": what is not so? it should be "branchy between towers"' because he felt that this particularized Oxford.

There are numerous passages which are witness to his interest in precise words. This from his Journal is representative:

Robert says the first grass from the scythe is the *swathe,* then comes the *strow* (tedding), then *rowing,* then the footcocks, then *breaking,* then the *hubrows,* which are gathered into *hubs,* then sometimes another break and *turning,* then *rickles,* the biggest of all the cocks, which are run together into *placks,* the shapeless heaps from which the hay is carted.

Many entries in both the Journal and the letters are devoted to etymologies and especially to native Anglo-Saxon words.

He tries to employ not only the exact word, but often the resources of unfamiliar meanings of familiar words. Beyond that he utilizes words themselves unfamiliar, and still beyond that he is not averse to introducing dialect words.

In a further effort to inscape he finds it necessary to forge new words and new compounds. 'I have invented a number of new words', he confesses, 'I cannot do without them.' But his coinages need cause no great difficulty because they are invariably formed by analogy with already existing words and compounds.

Just as characteristic as the precise word and image is his deployment of vocabulary and phrasing. He tends to pile up long lists of qualifying—rather than merely descriptive—adjectives in order to inscape; the opening lines of 'The Windhover' or 'Spelt from Sibyl's Leaves' are examples. What may at first glance look like mere repetition is an effort to specify the distinctive nature; the above-mentioned offer good illustrations of this, as does 'Duns Scotus's Oxford' in which his inscaping of Oxford results in such a line as 'Cuckoo-echoing, bell-swarmèd, lark-charmèd, rook-racked, river-rounded'.

Often it is remarkable what he can do toward individualizing with a single word. By shifting a single accent in the opening of 'Spring and Fall',

Márgarét, are you gríeving

he shifts the meaning from the general to the particular.

By such methods Hopkins's language takes on a new vigour and vitality. He makes constant warfare on poetic diction, and by inversion he gives freshness to the stereotyped: 'to my own heart' becomes 'to own my heart' and 'lays him low' is transformed into 'low lays him'. By a slight change he makes out of an old cliché something new as when he writes 'world without event'. Throughout, he moulds language to match his inscapes and carries out his dictum: 'Poetry must have, down to its least separable part, an individualizing touch.'

The same principle applies to his metrical theory. To match his theory of inscape he introduces into English prosody—or, rather, reintroduces—the sprung rhythm for which he is now famous. That it is just another aspect of inscape becomes apparent when one realizes that if Hopkins holds that poetry must try to inscape reality, then the metrical system itself must be very flexible and capable of distinctive individuation. The rhythm and prosody of each poem will then be unique. This is exactly what Hopkins accomplishes by sprung rhythm.

The fundamentals of sprung rhythm are simple, but they are also revolutionary in terms of the accepted convention of metrics during the three or four hundred years preceding Hopkins. It is perhaps well to emphasize that he was perfectly capable of writing 'conventional' verse forms and that his early poetry shows mastery of them. His sprung rhythm is basically traditional in that it reinstates once more in English verse a still older tradition—that of Anglo-Saxon poetry. Hopkins seemingly arrived at it independently, and only later did he read such poems as *Piers Ploughman* to confirm his theory.

Hopkins devoted half a dozen letters to explaining sprung rhythm to Bridges and Dixon, and he further clarified it in the 'Author's Preface' which he wrote as an introduction to a manuscript book of his poems which Bridges kept. Basically, he tells us, sprung rhythm consists in scanning by accents or stresses alone, without any count of the number of unaccented syllables. The term sprung rhythm he used because in this system it is possible for one stress to follow immediately upon another without any syllable intervening so that the effect is 'abrupt' or 'sprung'.

One of his most important letters on sprung rhythm tells

why he uses it. To Bridges, eventually deeply influenced by Hopkins's new prosody, he wrote:

Why do I employ sprung rhythm at all? Because it is the nearest to the rhythm of prose, that is the native and natural rhythm of speech, the least forced, the most rhetorical and emphatic of all possible rhythms, combining, as it seems to me, opposite and, one wd. have thought, incompatible excellences, markedness of rhythm —that is rhythm's self—and naturalness of expression.

He added an illustration from the second stanza of 'The Wreck of the Deutschland': 'for why, if it is forceful in prose to say "lashed: rod", am I obliged to weaken this in verse, which ought to be stronger, not weaker, into "láshed birch-ród"?'

In his letters Hopkins is insistent that sprung rhythm imposes rules of its own and that it is not to be confused with loose poetic prose. In comparing his prosody with that of Whitman, for instance, he affirms that his own is 'very highly wrought. The long lines are not rhythm run to seed: everything is weighed and timed in them.' Indeed, he goes so far as to state:

I may say my apparent licences are counterbalanced, and more, by my strictness. In fact all English verse, except Milton's, almost, offends me as 'licentious'. Remember this.

With sprung rhythm he joined many other devices to give distinctive pattern. Sometimes he combined it with counterpoint—'this is the most delicate and difficult business of all', he said—and he frequently uses, as did the Anglo-Saxons, alliteration. This he employs not ornamentally but functionally to indicate where the stresses come. His ideal was not unlike that of Dryden whose 'style and his rhythm lay the strongest stress of all our literature on the natural thew and sinew of the English language'. He also enlists assonance, end rhyme, internal rhyme, and half-rhyme, and a kind of consonantal rhyme or chime—*cynghanedd*—which he had found in Welsh poetry. He used none of these devices to 'prettify' but all to inscape more exactly and more precisely.

Hopkins found sprung rhythm eminently suited to the directness and urgency which he wished to communicate; its rise and fall 'lends itself to expressing passion'. The wrenched syntax, the inversions and omissions, the placing of words in the order of their emotional, intellectual, and psychological emphasis—all of these methods of inscaping became part of his highly wrought sprung rhythm.

The uninitiated readers of Hopkins's letters can easily become lost in his discussion of the intricacies and complexities of his prosody. Fortunately these need not detain anyone unduly, because there is a simple key which Hopkins constantly points out: the poetry is designed to be read aloud. Of his poetry he said that it 'is altogether for recital, not for perusal . . . my poetry is less to be read than to be heard . . . declaimed, the strange constructions would be dramatic and effective'. He was trying in still another way to restore the tradition in English verse of the scop and the bard. Concerning 'Spelt from Sibyl's Leaves' he urges:

Of this long sonnet above all remember what applies to all my verse, that it is, as living art should be, made for performance and that its performance is not reading with the eye but loud, leisurely, poetical (not rhetorical) recitation, with long rests, long dwells on the rhyme and other marked syllables, and so on. This sonnet should be sung: it is most carefully timed in *tempo rubato*.

His frequent references to his poetry in terms of music reinforce this advice: 'take breath and read it with the ears, as I always wish to be read, and my verse comes all right'.

He did not contend that his poetry is always easy. True, all through his correspondence one finds him objecting to obscurities and ambiguities in the work of Bridges, Dixon, and Patmore. But he also held: 'Obscurity I do and will try to avoid so far as is consistent with excellences higher than clearness at first reading.' For instance, 'The merit of a work may lie for one thing in its terseness.' His own poetry—with all of its compactness, ellipsis, and omissions of weak or unmeaning words—has a compression which at first may offer difficulties but which finally renders it rich and full-bodied and makes much other poetry seem thin and flaccid. Also:

Plainly if it is possible to express a subtle and recondite thought on a subtle and recondite subject in a subtle and recondite way and with great felicity and perfection, in the end, something must be sacrificed . . . and this may be the being at once . . . intelligible.

Even in the case of such seeming unintelligibility upon a first perusal, his sprung rhythm is designed as an aid to make the meaning finally

> Gush!—flush the man, the being with it, sour or sweet,
> Brim, in a flash, full!

—it should, to use one of his own terms, 'explode'. Hence:

One of two kinds of clearness one shd. have—either the meaning to be felt without effort as fast as one reads or else, if dark at first reading, when once made out *to explode*.

All the foregoing efforts at inscaping make it clear why in his letters he always insists on earnestness and reality as among the most important tests of poetry: 'a want of earnestness I take to be the deepest fault a work can have'. Again he reiterates:

A kind of touchstone of the highest and most living art is seriousness; not gravity but the being in earnest with your subject—reality.

Patmore's 'Tristitia' is 'perverse and founded on an unreality'. 'Any untruth to nature, to human nature,' he held, 'is frigid.' The reader of his correspondence will note that in the evaluation of the poetry of his friends, Hopkins frequently singles out for adverse criticism even minor images because they fail to correspond to the existential order. He likewise defends his own 'The Candle Indoors' with such comments as 'it is an "autobiographical" fact that I was influenced and acted on the way there said'; and of 'The Wreck of the Deutschland' he asserts: 'What refers to myself in the poem is all strictly and literally true and did all occur; nothing is added for poetical padding.'

Again and again for precisely the same reason he demands that 'a perfect style must be of its age', and:

The poetical language of an age shd. be the current language heightened, to any degree and unlike itself, but not . . . an obsolete one.

He makes constant war in his criticism on such things as

archaism which he considered 'a blight'. He denied that he was trying to write 'a sort of modern Anglosaxon', ready as he was to 'weep to think what English might have been'. Thus he condemns Doughty, for instance. His final summary is that any artificial attempt 'destroys earnest: we do not speak that way; therefore if a man speaks that way he is not serious'. Throughout his own letters and poetry there is a kind of passionate honesty, a kind of enthusiasm for reality which characterizes him.

His letters throw still further light on his own standards and ideals of poetry. Not only does he deal with the work of his friends and fellow poets, Bridges, Dixon, and Patmore, but he devotes many pages to such writers as Shakespeare, Milton, Keats, Wordsworth, Tennyson, and even Yeats and Whitman. Early he laid down as a principle: 'The most inveterate fault of critics is the tendency to cramp and hedge in by rules the free movements of genius, so I should say . . . the first requisite for a critic is liberality, and the second is liberality, and the third, liberality.' Often he is a very severe critic; yet he says of William Barnes: 'I feel that defect or limitation . . . that offended you; he lacks fire; but who is perfect all round? If one defect is fatal what writer could we read?'

Certain single letters and groups of letters are of special interest and relevance. Important for appreciating his own work in counterpoint, often in combination with sprung rhythm, are his numerous letters on Milton's *Samson Agonistes* in which he found the choruses intermediate between counterpoint and sprung rhythm.

Of particular interest in terms of his own development are the letters on Keats. Patmore had printed an unfavourable article about him, and Hopkins sprang to his defence. His own analysis of the growth of Keats is carefully qualified, but so eagerly does he pursue the subject that he closes, 'But then if I could have said this to Keats I feel sure he wd. have seen it. In due time he wd. have seen these things himself.'

Several long letters on Wordsworth are an aid in understanding Hopkins's concept of the relation between on the one hand 'strictly poetical insight and inspiration'—in which he found Wordsworth ranking high—and on the other 'rheto-

ric'. His attempt to avoid pietism in his own sonnets is reflected in a comment on Wordsworth's: 'beautiful as those are
they have an odious goodiness and neckcloth about them
which half throttles their beauty'.

Eventually he touches on most of his contemporaries. He
half regrets that he has lost his earlier enthusiasm for Tennyson, 'though it grieves me to hear him depreciated, as of late
years has often been done'. Yet he says sharply of the *Idylls:*
'He shd. have called them *Charades of the Middle Ages* (dedicated by permission to H.R.H. etc).' And he can be amusing when he indulges in parody; Carlyle's writings are 'most
inefficacious-strenuous heaven-protestations, caterwaul and
Cassandra wailings . . . *too* dubious moonstone-grindings and
on the whole impracticable-practical unveracities'. He delights in burlesquing Swinburne, a poet lacking in inscape:

Either in fact he does not see nature at all or else he overlays the
landscape with such phantasmata, secondary images, and what not
of a delirium-tremens imagination that the result is a kind of bloody
froth

—an example of his own insistence on the objectivity of inscape.

A life-long admiration of Newman does not prevent him
from commenting on the absurdity of Newman's comparing
the first chorus of *Samson Agonistes* unfavourably with Sou-
they's *Thalaba:* 'It is as if you were to compare the Panan-
thenaic frieze and a teaboard and decide in the teaboard's
favor.'

Often instead of dealing with particular writers he devotes
entire letters to such general topics as 'the three languages of
poetry', art and morality, the use of mythology, or to various
genres, the historical play or the Victorian novel.

Even his comments on various research projects are related
to his own practice of poetry. He tells, for example, of trying
to write a book on the lyric element in Greek drama in which
he has discovered two strains of thought running together like
counterpoint, the 'overthought', that which everybody immediately receives, and the 'underthought', conveyed chiefly in
the choice of metaphors—a principle operative in Hopkins's

poetry and interestingly approximating the ideas of structure and texture in the new criticism.

Frequent references in his correspondence to music may probably best be pursued in close alliance to his poetic theories, as when he writes: 'I have invented a new style, something standing to ordinary music as sprung rhythm to common rhythm.' He tells of setting some of the poems of Bridges, Dixon, and Patmore to music as well as his own 'Spring and Fall', 'Morning Midday and Evening Sacrifice', and 'Hurrahing in Harvest'. He designs 'The Leaden Echo and the Golden Echo' as a song for a play.

Often his letters mention with great admiration Purcell, and he devotes a sonnet to his praise. In spite of adverse criticism, Hopkins was as confident of his own music as of his poetry. He bluntly remarked of one of his compositions: 'If the whole world agreed to condemn it or see nothing in it I should only tell them to take a generation and come to me again.'

Numerous letters evince his deep interest in social and political conditions which are also reflected in his poetry. His famous 'communist' letter to Bridges should be compared with his own later poem 'Tom's Garland: upon the Unemployed'. Letters in which he says such things as 'My Liverpool and Glasgow experience laid upon my mind a conviction, a truly crushing conviction, of the misery of the poor, in general of the degradation even of the race, of the hollowness of this century's civilisation' are not unusual and have a counterpart in poems like 'The Sea and the Skylark' and 'God's Grandeur' with its

> Generations have trod, have trod, have trod;
> And all is seared with trade; bleared, smeared with toil.

Those letters devoted to personal friendship reveal still other facets. We watch Hopkins trying to create a public for his three fellow poets. His very first letter to Dixon is a good example of his warm appreciation of the poetry of a man who, he felt, was too little regarded; in the letter immediately following he urges Dixon to read Bridges's *Growth of Love*. This is characteristic, and we discover him introducing his friends to one another and distributing their books. In Dublin he even persuades one of the professors at Trinity College to assign to his students the poems of Bridges. Constantly he spurs on Bridges and Dixon and Patmore to write their poetry, and he gives them a measure of the encouragement which he often felt lacking in his own life. One has the impression that he gives far more than he receives—and this is an index to the love he bore his friends.

We see his letters to Bridges grow in depth of friendship, and after a time he signs himself simply 'Gerard'. At times of sickness and dejection Bridges is addressed as 'My dear heart'. There is a remarkable letter in which Hopkins replies to the future poet laureate who had been so discouraged that he almost decided to give up writing poetry.

He devoted to his friends endless letters—indeed these make up the bulk of his correspondence—giving minute and painstaking suggestions for the revision of their poetry. Said Patmore: 'Your careful and subtle fault-finding is the greatest praise my poetry has ever received. It makes me almost inclined to begin to sing again.' The full impact of his criticism on the work of the three men still remains to be studied and evaluated.

While it may sometimes sound as if his praise of their work was biased by friendship, there are many passages with a sharp 'This will never do', and he combines stricture with encouragement, gentleness with severity.

All through his letters there is an earnestness which is the mark of the man as well as of the poet, and yet this earnestness is not incompatible with humour and even whimsicality. There is manifest fun in his letters to his sister in Irish brogue; he obviously enjoys replying to Bridges's announcement of his engagement with a letter opening, 'I too am engaged'—then continuing on the next sheet, 'on examination papers.'

One of Hopkins's great sadnesses was the religious barrier which separated him from his closest friend, Bridges, and perhaps the overall impression of his letters as well as of his poetry is the earnestness, the sincerity, the reality of his religious dedication.

In all things he took as a model Christ whose life 'was doomed to succeed by failure'. At no place does he state so simply and so clearly his ideal as when he wrote:

This is that chastity of mind which seems to lie at the very heart and be the parent of all other good, the seeing at once what is best, the holding to that, and the not allowing anything else whatever to be even heard pleading to the contrary.

All of his life and all that he wrote may best be appreciated in terms of his valiant struggle to achieve final unity with that ideal.

JOHN PICK

Marquette University
Revised 1965

I

POEMS

---

*Poetry must have, down to its least separable part,
an individualising touch.*

HEAVEN-HAVEN

A nun takes the veil

I have desired to go
   Where springs not fail,
To fields where flies no sharp and sided hail
   And a few lilies blow.

And I have asked to be
   Where no storms come,
Where the green swell is in the havens dumb,
   And out of the swing of the sea.

[1864]

THE HABIT OF PERFECTION

Elected Silence, sing to me
And beat upon my whorlèd ear,
Pipe me to pastures still and be
The music that I care to hear.

Shape nothing, lips; be lovely-dumb:
It is the shut, the curfew sent
From there where all surrenders come
Which only makes you eloquent.

Be shellèd, eyes, with double dark
And find the uncreated light:
This ruck and reel which you remark
Coils, keeps, and teases simple sight.

Palate, the hutch of tasty lust,
Desire not to be rinsed with wine:
The can must be so sweet, the crust
So fresh that come in fasts divine!

Nostrils, your careless breath that spend
Upon the stir and keep of pride,
What relish shall the censers send
Along the sanctuary side!

O feel-of-primrose hands, O feet
That want the yield of plushy sward,
But you shall walk the golden street
And you unhouse and house the Lord.

And, Poverty, be thou the bride
And now the marriage feast begun,
And lily-coloured clothes provide
Your spouse not laboured-at nor spun.

[1866]

THE WRECK
OF THE DEUTSCHLAND

To the
happy memory of five Franciscan Nuns
exiles by the Falk Laws
drowned between midnight and morning of
Dec. 7th, 1875

PART THE FIRST

1

Thou mastering me
God! giver of breath and bread;
World's strand, sway of the sea;
Lord of living and dead;
Thou hast bound bones and veins in me, fastened me
flesh,
And after it almost unmade, what with dread,
Thy doing: and dost thou touch me afresh?
Over again I feel thy finger and find thee.

2

I did say yes
O at lightning and lashed rod;
Thou heardst me truer than tongue confess
Thy terror, O Christ, O God;
Thou knowest the walls, altar and hour and night:
The swoon of a heart that the sweep and the hurl of thee
trod
Hard down with a horror of height:
And the midriff astrain with leaning of, laced with fire of
stress.

3

The frown of his face
Before me, the hurtle of hell
Behind, where, where was a, where was a place?

I whirled out wings that spell
And fled with a fling of the heart to the heart of the Host.
My heart, but you were dovewinged, I can tell,
    Carrier-witted, I am bold to boast,
To flash from the flame to the flame then, tower from the
    grace to the grace.

4

I am soft sift
In an hourglass — at the wall
Fast, but mined with a motion, a drift,
    And it crowds and it combs to the fall;
I steady as a water in a well, to a poise, to a pane,
    But roped with, always, all the way down from the tall
    Fells or flanks of the voel, a vein
Of the gospel proffer, a pressure, a principle, Christ's gift.

5

I kiss my hand
To the stars, lovely-asunder
Starlight, wafting him out of it; and
    Glow, glory in thunder;
Kiss my hand to the dappled-with-damson west:
    Since, tho' he is under the world's splendour and wonder,
    His mystery must be instressed, stressed;
For I greet him the days I meet him, and bless when I under-
    stand.

6

Not out of his bliss
Springs the stress felt
Nor first from heaven (and few know this)
    Swings the stroke dealt —
Stroke and a stress that stars and storms deliver,
    That guilt is hushed by, hearts are flushed by and melt —
    But it rides time like riding a river
(And here the faithful waver, the faithless fable and miss).

7

It dates from day
Of his going in Galilee;
Warm-laid grave of a womb-life grey;
Manger, maiden's knee;
The dense and the driven Passion, and frightful sweat;
Thence the discharge of it, there its swelling to be,
Though felt before, though in high flood yet —
What none would have known of it, only the heart, being
hard at bay,

8

Is out with it! Oh,
We lash with the best or worst
Word last! How a lush-kept plush-capped sloe
Will, mouthed to flesh-burst,
Gush! — flush the man, the being with it, sour or sweet,
Brim, in a flash, full! — Hither then, last or first,
To hero of Calvary, Christ's feet —
Never ask if meaning it, wanting it, warned of it — men go.

9

Be adored among men,
God, three-numberèd form;
Wring thy rebel, dogged in den,
Man's malice, with wrecking and storm.
Beyond saying sweet, past telling of tongue,
Thou art lightning and love, I found it, a winter and
warm;
Father and fondler of heart thou hast wrung:
Hast thy dark descending and most art merciful then.

10

With an anvil-ding
And with fire in him forge thy will
Or rather, rather then, stealing as Spring
Through him, melt him but master him still:
Whether at once, as once at a crash Paul,

Or as Austin, a lingering-out swéet skíll,
  Make mercy in all of us, out of us all
Mastery, but be adored, but be adored King.

11

  'Some find me a sword; some
   The flange and the rail; flame,
  Fang, or flood' goes Death on drum,
   And storms bugle his fame.
But wé dream we are rooted in earth – Dust!
Flesh falls within sight of us, we, though our flower the
    same,
  Wave with the meadow, forget that there must
The sour scythe cringe, and the blear share come.

12

  On Saturday sailed from Bremen,
   American-outward-bound,
  Take settler and seamen, tell men with women,
   Two hundred souls in the round –
O Father, not under thy feathers nor ever as guessing
The goal was a shoal, of a fourth the doom to be
    drowned;
  Yet did the dark side of the bay of thy blessing
Not vault them, the millions of rounds of thy mercy not reeve
    even them in?

13

  Into the snows she sweeps,
   Hurling the haven behind,
  The Deutschland, on Sunday; and so the sky keeps,
   For the infinite air is unkind,
And the sea flint-flake, black-backed in the regular blow,
Sitting Eastnortheast, in cursed quarter, the wind;
  Wiry and white-fiery and whirlwind-swivellèd snow
Spins to the widow-making unchilding unfathering deeps.

14

She drove in the dark to leeward,
    She struck—not a reef or a rock
But the combs of a smother of sand: night drew her
    Dead to the Kentish Knock;
And she beat the bank down with her bows and the ride
        of her keel:
The breakers rolled on her beam with ruinous shock;
    And canvas and compass, the whorl and the wheel
Idle for ever to waft her or wind her with, these she endured.

15

Hope had grown grey hairs,
    Hope had mourning on,
Trenched with tears, carved with cares,
    Hope was twelve hours gone;
And frightful a nightfall folded rueful a day
Nor rescue, only rocket and lightship, shone,
    And lives at last were washing away:
To the shrouds they took,—they shook in the hurling and
        horrible airs.

16

One stirred from the rigging to save
    The wild woman-kind below,
With a rope's end round the man, handy and
        brave—
    He was pitched to his death at a blow,
For all his dreadnought breast and braids of thew:
They could tell him for hours, dandled the to and fro
    Through the cobbled foam-fleece, what could he do
With the burl of the fountains of air, buck and the flood of the
        wave?

17

They fought with God's cold—
    And they could not and fell to the deck
(Crushed them) or water (and drowned them) or
        rolled

With the sea-romp over the wreck.
Night roared, with the heart-break hearing a heart-broke
rabble,
The woman's wailing, the crying of child without check—
Till a lioness arose breasting the babble,
A prophetess towered in the tumult, a virginal tongue told.

18

Ah, touched in your bower of bone
Are you! turned for an exquisite smart,
Have you! make words break from me here all
alone,
Do you!—mother of being in me, heart.
O unteachably after evil, but uttering truth,
Why tears! is it? tears; such a melting, a madrigal start!
Never-eldering revel and river of youth,
What can it be, this glee? the good you have there of your
own?

19

Sister, a sister calling
A master, her master and mine!—
And the inboard seas run swirling and hawling;
The rash smart sloggering brine
Blinds her; but she that weather sees one thing, one;
Has one fetch in her: she rears herself to divine
Ears, and the call of the tall nun
To the men in the tops and the tackle rode over the storm's
brawling.

20

She was first of a five and came
Of a coifèd sisterhood.
(O Deutschland, double a desperate name!
O world wide of its good!
But Gertrude, lily, and Luther, are two of a town,
Christ's lily and beast of the waste wood:
From life's dawn it is drawn down,
Abel is Cain's brother and breasts they have sucked the
same.)

21

Loathed for a love men knew in them,
Banned by the land of their birth,
Rhine refused them. Thames would ruin them;
Surf, snow, river and earth
Gnashed: but thou art above, thou Orion of light;
Thy unchancelling poising palms were weighing the worth,
Thou martyr-master: in thy sight
Storm flakes were scroll-leaved flowers, lily showers – sweet heaven was astrew in them.

22

Five! the finding and sake
And cipher of suffering Christ.
Mark, the mark is of man's make
And the word of it Sacrificed.
But he scores it in scarlet himself on his own bespoken,
Before-time-taken, dearest prizèd and priced –
Stigma, signal, cinquefoil token
For lettering of the lamb's fleece, ruddying of the rose-flake.

23

Joy fall to thee, father Francis,
Drawn to the Life that died;
With the gnarls of the nails in thee, niche of the lance, his
Lovescape crucified
And seal of his seraph-arrival! and these thy daughters
And five-livèd and leavèd favour and pride,
Are sisterly sealed in wild waters,
To bathe in his fall-gold mercies, to breathe in his all-fire glances.

24

Away in the loveable west,
On a pastoral forehead of Wales,
I was under a roof here, I was at rest,

And they the prey of the gales;
She to the black-about air, to the breaker, the thickly
Falling flakes, to the throng that catches and quails
            Was calling 'O Christ, Christ, come quickly':
The cross to her she calls Christ to her, christens her wild-
        worst Best.

25

            The majesty! what did she mean?
            Breathe, arch and original Breath.
    Is it love in her of the being as her lover had been?
            Breathe, body of lovely Death.
They were else-minded then, altogether, the men
Woke thee with a *we are perishing* in the weather of
        Gennesareth.
        Or is it that she cried for the crown then,
The keener to come at the comfort for feeling the combating
        keen?

26

            For how to the heart's cheering
            The down-dugged ground-hugged grey
    Hovers off, the jay-blue heavens appearing
            Of pied and peeled May!
Blue-beating and hoary-glow height; or night, still
        higher,
With belled fire and the moth-soft Milky Way,
        What by your measure is the heaven of desire,
The treasure never eyesight got, nor was ever guessed what
        for the hearing?

27

            No, but it was not these.
            The jading and jar of the cart,
        Time's tasking, it is fathers that asking for ease
            Of the sodden-with-its-sorrowing heart,
Not danger, electrical horror; then further it finds
The appealing of the Passion is tenderer in prayer apart:
        Other, I gather, in measure her mind's
Burden, in wind's burly and beat of endragonèd seas.

28

But how shall I . . . make me room there:
Reach me a . . . Fancy, come faster —
Strike you the sight of it? look at it loom there,
Thing that she . . . there then! the Master,
Ipse, the only one, Christ, King, Head:
He was to cure the extremity where he had cast her;
Do, deal, lord it with living and dead;
Let him ride, her pride, in his triumph, despatch and have
done with his doom there.

29

Ah! there was a heart right!
There was single eye!
Read the unshapeable shock night
And knew the who and the why;
Wording it how but by him that present and past,
Heaven and earth are word of, worded by? —
The Simon Peter of a soul! to the blast
Tarpeian-fast, but a blown beacon of light.

30

Jesu, heart's light,
Jesu, maid's son,
What was the feast followed the night
Thou hadst glory of this nun? —
Feast of the one woman without stain.
For so conceivèd, so to conceive thee is done;
But here was heart-throe, birth of a brain,
Word, that heard and kept thee and uttered thee outright.

31

Well, she has thee for the pain, for the
Patience; but pity of the rest of them!
Heart, go and bleed at a bitterer vein for the
Comfortless unconfessed of them —
No not uncomforted: lovely-felicitous Providence
Finger of a tender of, O of a feathery delicacy, the breast
of the

Maiden could obey so, be a bell to, ring of it, and
Startle the poor sheep back! is the shipwrack then a harvest,
does tempest carry the grain for thee?

32

I admire thee, master of the tides,
Of the Yore-flood, of the year's fall;
The recurb and the recovery of the gulf's sides,
The girth of it and the wharf of it and the wall;
Stanching, quenching ocean of a motionable mind;
Ground of being, and granite of it: past all
Grasp God, throned behind
Death with a sovereignty that heeds but hides, bodes but
abides;

33

With a mercy that outrides
The all of water, an ark
For the listener; for the lingerer with a love glides
Lower than death and the dark;
A vein for the visiting of the past-prayer, pent in prison,
The-last-breath penitent spirits – the uttermost mark
Our passion-plungèd giant risen,
The Christ of the Father compassionate, fetched in the storm
of his strides.

34

Now burn, new born to the world,
Doubled-naturèd name,
The heaven-flung, heart-fleshed, maiden-furled
Miracle-in-Mary-of-flame,
Mid-numbered He in three of the thunder-throne!
Not a dooms-day dazzle in his coming nor dark as he
came;
Kind, but royally reclaiming his own;
A released shower, let flash to the shire, not a lightning of fire
hard-hurled.

35

Dame, at our door
Drowned, and among our shoals,
Remember us in the roads, the heaven-haven of
the Reward:
Our King back, oh, upon English souls!
Let him easter in us, be a dayspring to the dimness of
us, be a crimson-cresseted east,
More brightening her, rare-dear Britain, as his reign
rolls,
Pride, rose, prince, hero of us, high-priest,
Our hearts' charity's hearth's fire, our thoughts' chivalry's
throng's Lord.

[1875–76]

PENMAEN POOL

For the Visitors' Book at the Inn

Who long for rest, who look for pleasure
Away from counter, court, or school
O where live well your lease of leisure
But here at, here at Penmaen Pool?

You'll dare the Alp? you'll dart the skiff?—
Each sport has here its tackle and tool:
Come, plant the staff by Cadair cliff;
Come, swing the sculls on Penmaen Pool.

What's yonder?—Grizzled Dyphwys dim:
The triple-hummocked Giant's stool,
Hoar messmate, hobs and nobs with him
To halve the bowl of Penmaen Pool.

And all the landscape under survey,
At tranquil turns, by nature's rule,
Rides repeated topsyturvy
In frank, in fairy Penmaen Pool.

And Charles's Wain, the wondrous seven,
And sheep-flock clouds like worlds of wool,
For all they shine so, high in heaven,
Shew brighter shaken in Penmaen Pool.

The Mawddach, how she trips! though throttled
If floodtide teeming thrills her full,
And mazy sands all water-wattled
Waylay her at ebb, past Penmaen Pool.

But what's to see in stormy weather,
When grey showers gather and gusts are cool?
Why, raindrop-roundels looped together
That lace the face of Penmaen Pool.

Then even in weariest wintry hour
Of New Year's month or surly Yule
Furred snows, charged tuft above tuft, tower
From darksome darksome Penmaen Pool.

And ever, if bound here hardest home,
You've parlour-pastime left and (who'll
Not honour it?) ale like goldy foam
That frocks an oar in Penmaen Pool.

Then come who pine for peace or pleasure
Away from counter, court, or school,
Spend here your measure of time and treasure
And taste the treats of Penmaen Pool.

[1876]

THE SILVER JUBILEE:

*To James First Bishop of Shrewsbury on the 25th Year
of his Episcopate July 28, 1876*

1

Though no high-hung bells or din
Of braggart bugles cry it in –
    What is sound? Nature's round
Makes the Silver Jubilee.

2

Five and twenty years have run
Since sacred fountains to the sun
   Sprang, that but now were shut,
Showering Silver Jubilee.

3

Feasts, when we shall fall asleep,
Shrewsbury may see others keep;
   None but you this her true,
This her Silver Jubilee.

4

Not today we need lament
Your wealth of life is some way spent:
   Toil has shed round your head
Silver but for Jubilee.

5

Then for her whose velvet vales
Should have pealed with welcome, Wales,
   Let the chime of a rhyme
Utter Silver Jubilee.

[1876]

GOD'S GRANDEUR

The world is charged with the grandeur of God.
  It will flame out, like shining from shook foil;
  It gathers to a greatness, like the ooze of oil
Crushed. Why do men then now not reck his rod?
Generations have trod, have trod, have trod;
  And all is seared with trade; bleared, smeared with toil;
  And wears man's smudge and shares man's smell: the soil
Is bare now, nor can foot feel, being shod.

And for all this, nature is never spent;
   There lives the dearest freshness deep down things;
And though the last lights off the black West went
   Oh, morning, at the brown brink eastward, springs—
Because the Holy Ghost over the bent
   World broods with warm breast and with ah! bright wings.
                                       [1877]

THE STARLIGHT NIGHT

Look at the stars! look, look up at the skies!
   O look at all the fire-folk sitting in the air!
   The bright boroughs, the circle-citadels there!
Down in dim woods the diamond delves! the elves'-eyes!
The grey lawns cold where gold, where quickgold lies!
   Wind-beat whitebeam! airy abeles set on a flare!
   Flake-doves sent floating forth at a farmyard scare!
Ah well! it is all a purchase, all is a prize.

Buy then! bid then!—What?—Prayer, patience, alms, vows.
Look, look: a May-mess, like on orchard boughs!
   Look! March-bloom, like on mealed-with-yellow sallows!
These are indeed the barn; withindoors house
The shocks. This piece-bright paling shuts the spouse
   Christ home, Christ and his mother and all his hallows.
                                       [1877]

SPRING

Nothing is so beautiful as spring—
   When weeds, in wheels, shoot long and lovely and lush;
   Thrush's eggs look little low heavens, and thrush
Through the echoing timber does so rinse and wring
The ear, it strikes like lightnings to hear him sing;
   The glassy peartree leaves and blooms, they brush
   The descending blue; that blue is all in a rush
With richness; the racing lambs too have fair their fling.

What is all this juice and all this joy?
  A strain of the earth's sweet being in the beginning
In Eden garden.—Have, get, before it cloy,
  Before it cloud, Christ, lord, and sour with sinning,
Innocent mind and Mayday in girl and boy,
  Most, O maid's child, thy choice and worthy the winning.

                                     [*1877*]

THE LANTERN OUT OF DOORS

Sometimes a lantern moves along the night,
  That interests our eyes. And who goes there?
  I think; where from and bound, I wonder, where,
With, all down darkness wide, his wading light?

Men go by me whom either beauty bright
  In mould or mind or what not else makes rare:
  They rain against our much-thick and marsh air
Rich beams, till death or distance buys them quite.

Death or distance soon consumes them: wind
  What most I may eye after, be in at the end
I cannot, and out of sight is out of mind.

Christ minds; Christ's interest, what to avow or amend
  There, éyes them, heart wánts, care haúnts, foot fóllows
      kínd,
Their ránsom, théir rescue, ánd first, fást, last friénd.

                                     [*1877*]

THE SEA AND THE SKYLARK

On ear and ear two noises too old to end
  Trench—right, the tide that ramps against the shore;
  With a flood or a fall, low lull-off or all roar,
Frequenting there while moon shall wear and wend.

Left hand, off land, I hear the lark ascend,
  His rash-fresh re-winded new-skeinèd score
  In crisps of curl off wild winch whirl, and pour
And pelt music, till none's to spill nor spend.

How these two shame this shallow and frail town!
  How ring right out our sordid turbid time,
Being pure! We, life's pride and cared-for crown,

  Have lost that cheer and charm of earth's past prime:
Our make and making break, are breaking, down
  To man's last dust, drain fast towards man's first slime.

[1877]

THE WINDHOVER:

To Christ our Lord

I caught this morning morning's minion, king-
  dom of daylight's dauphin, dapple-dawn-drawn Falcon, in
      his riding
Of the rolling level underneath him steady air, and striding
High there, how he rung upon the rein of a wimpling wing
In his ecstasy! then off, off forth on swing,
  As a skate's heel sweeps smooth on a bow-bend: the hurl
      and gliding
  Rebuffed the big wind. My heart in hiding
Stirred for a bird, – the achieve of, the mastery of the thing!

Brute beauty and valour and act, oh, air, pride, plume here
  Buckle! AND the fire that breaks from thee then, a billion
Times told lovelier, more dangerous, O my chevalier!

  No wonder of it: shéer plód makes plough down sillion
Shine, and blue-bleak embers, ah my dear,
  Fall, gall themselves, and gash gold-vermilion.

[1877]

PIED BEAUTY

Glory be to God for dappled things –
  For skies of couple-colour as a brinded cow;
    For rose-moles all in stipple upon trout that swim;
Fresh-firecoal chestnut-falls; finches' wings;
  Landscape plotted and pieced – fold, fallow, and plough;
    And áll trádes, their gear and tackle and trim.

All things counter, original, spare, strange;
  Whatever is fickle, freckled (who knows how?)
    With swift, slow; sweet, sour; adazzle, dim;
He fathers-forth whose beauty is past change:
              Praise him.

                                          [1877]

HURRAHING IN HARVEST

Summer ends now; now, barbarous in beauty, the stooks arise
  Around; up above, what wind-walks! what lovely behav-
      iour
  Of silk-sack clouds! has wilder, wilful-wavier
Meal-drift moulded ever and melted across skies?

I walk, I lift up, I lift up heart, eyes,
  Down all that glory in the heavens to glean our Saviour;
  And, éyes, heárt, what looks, what lips yet gave you a
Rapturous love's greeting of realer, of rounder replies?

And the azurous hung hills are his world-wielding shoulder
  Majestic – as a stallion stalwart, very-violet-sweet! –
These things, these things were here and but the beholder
  Wanting; which two when they once meet,
The heart réars wíngs bold and bolder
  And hurls for him, O half hurls earth for him off under his
      feet.

                                          [1877]

THE CAGED SKYLARK

As a dare-gale skylark scanted in a dull cage
  Man's mounting spirit in his bone-house, mean house,
      dwells –
  That bird beyond the remembering his free fells;
This in drudgery, day-labouring-out life's age.

Though aloft on turf or perch or poor low stage,
  Both sing sometímes the sweetest, sweetest spells,
  Yet both droop deadly sómetimes in their cells
Or wring their barriers in bursts of fear or rage.

Not that the sweet-fowl, song-fowl, needs no rest—
Why, hear him, hear him babble and drop down to his nest,
    But his own nest, wild nest, no prison.

Man's spirit will be flesh-bound when found at best,
But uncumbered: meadow-down is not distressed
    For a rainbow footing it nor he for his bónes rísen.

[1877]

IN THE VALLEY OF THE ELWY

I remember a house where all were good
    To me, God knows, deserving no such thing:
    Comforting smell breathed at very entering,
Fetched fresh, as I suppose, off some sweet wood.
That cordial air made those kind people a hood
    All over, as a bevy of eggs the mothering wing
    Will, or mild nights the new morsels of spring:
Why, it seemed of course; seemed of right it should.

Lovely the woods, waters, meadows, combes, vales,
All the air things wear that build this world of Wales;
    Only the inmate does not correspond:
God, lover of souls, swaying considerate scales,
Complete thy creature dear O where it fails,
    Being mighty a master, being a father and fond.

[1877]

THE LOSS OF THE EURYDICE

Foundered March 24, 1878

The Eurydice—it concerned thee, O Lord:
Three hundred souls, O alas! on board,
    Some asleep unawakened, all un-
warned, eleven fathoms fallen   4

Where she foundered! One stroke
Felled and furled them, the hearts of oak!
    And flockbells off the aerial
Downs' forefalls beat to the burial.   8

For did she pride her, freighted fully, on
Bounden bales or a hoard of bullion?—
    Precious passing measure,
Lads and men her lade and treasure.   12

She had come from a cruise, training seamen—
Men, boldboys soon to be men:
    Must it, worst weather,
Blast bole and bloom together?   16

No Atlantic squall overwrought her
Or rearing billow of the Biscay water:
    Home was hard at hand
And the blow bore from land.   20

And you were a liar, O blue March day.
Bright sun lanced fire in the heavenly bay;
    But what black Boreas wrecked her? he
Came equipped, deadly-electric,   24

A beetling baldbright cloud thorough England
Riding: there did storms not mingle? and
    Hailropes hustle and grind their
Heavengravel? wolfsnow, worlds of it, wind there? 28

Now Carisbrook keep goes under in gloom;
Now it overvaults Appledurcombe;
    Now near by Ventnor town
It hurls, hurls off Boniface Down.   32

Too proud, too proud, what a press she bore!
Royal, and all her royals wore.
    Sharp with her, shorten sail!
Too late; lost; gone with the gale.   36

This was that fell capsize,
As half she had righted and hoped to rise
    Death teeming in by her portholes
Raced down decks, round messes of mortals.   40

Then a lurch forward, frigate and men;
'All hands for themselves' the cry ran then;
    But she who had housed them thither
Was around them, bound them or wound them with her. 44

Marcus Hare, high her captain,
Kept to her — care-drowned and wrapped in
    Cheer's death, would follow
His charge through the champ-white water-in-a-wallow, 48

All under Channel to bury in a beach her
Cheeks: Right, rude of feature,
    He thought he heard say
'Her commander! and thou too, and thou this way.'   52

It is even seen, time's something server,
In mankind's medley a duty-swerver,
    At downright 'No or yes?'
Doffs all, drives full for righteousness.   56

Sydney Fletcher, Bristol-bred,
(Low lie his mates now on watery bed)
    Takes to the seas and snows
As sheer down the ship goes.   60

Now her afterdraught gullies him too down;
Now he wrings for breath with the deathgush brown;
    Till a lifebelt and God's will
Lend him a lift from the sea-swill.   64

Now he shoots short up to the round air;
Now he gasps, now he gazes everywhere;
    But his eye no cliff, no coast or
Mark makes in the rivelling snowstorm.   68

Him, after an hour of wintry waves,
A schooner sights, with another, and saves,
    And he boards her in Oh! such joy
He has lost count what came next, poor boy. —   72

They say who saw one sea-corpse cold
He was all of lovely manly mould,
    Every inch a tar,
Of the best we boast our sailors are.   76

Look, foot to forelock, how all things suit! he
Is strung by duty, is strained to beauty,
    And brown-as-dawning-skinned
With brine and shine and whirling wind.   80

O his nimble finger, his gnarled grip!
Leagues, leagues of seamanship
    Slumber in these forsaken
Bones, this sinew, and will not waken. 84

He was but one like thousands more,
Day and night I deplore
    My people and born own nation,
Fast foundering own generation. 88

I might let bygones be – our curse
Of ruinous shrine no hand or, worse,
    Robbery's hand is busy to
Dress, hoar-hallowèd shrines unvisited; 92

Only the breathing temple and fleet
Life, this wildworth blown so sweet,
    These daredeaths, ay this crew, in
Unchrist, all rolled in ruin – 96

Deeply surely I need to deplore it,
Wondering why my master bore it,
    The riving off that race
So at home, time was, to his truth and grace 100

That a starlight-wender of ours would say
The marvellous Milk was Walsingham Way
    And one – but let be, let be:
More, more than was will yet be. – 104

O well wept, mother have lost son;
Wept, wife; wept, sweetheart would be one:
    Though grief yield them no good
Yet shed what tears sad truelove should. 108

But to Christ lord of thunder
Crouch; lay knee by earth low under:
    'Holiest, loveliest, bravest,
Save my hero, O Hero savest. 112

And the prayer thou hearst me making
Have, at the awful overtaking,
    Heard; have heard and granted
Grace that day grace was wanted.' 116

Not that hell knows redeeming,
But for souls sunk in seeming
    Fresh, till doomfire burn all,
Prayer shall fetch pity eternal.

                         120
                        [1878]

THE MAY MAGNIFICAT

May is Mary's month, and I
Muse at that and wonder why:
    Her feasts follow reason,
    Dated due to season—

Candlemas, Lady Day;
But the Lady Month, May,
    Why fasten that upon her,
    With a feasting in her honour?

Is it only its being brighter
Than the most are must delight her?
    Is it opportunest
    And flowers finds soonest?

Ask of her, the mighty mother:
Her reply puts this other
    Question: What is Spring?—
    Growth in every thing—

Flesh and fleece, fur and feather,
Grass and greenworld all together;
    Star-eyed strawberry-breasted
    Throstle above her nested

Cluster of bugle blue eggs thin
Forms and warms the life within;
    And bird and blossom swell
    In sod or sheath or shell.

All things rising, all things sizing
Mary sees, sympathising
    With that world of good,
    Nature's motherhood.

Their magnifying of each its kind
With delight calls to mind
    How she did in her stored
    Magnify the Lord.

Well but there was more than this:
Spring's universal bliss
    Much, had much to say
    To offering Mary May.

When drop-of-blood-and-foam-dapple
Bloom lights the orchard-apple
    And thicket and thorp are merry
    With silver-surfèd cherry

And azuring-over greybell makes
Wood banks and brakes wash wet like lakes
    And magic cuckoocall
    Caps, clears, and clinches all—

This ecstasy all through mothering earth
Tells Mary her mirth till Christ's birth
    To remember and exultation
    In God who was her salvation.

[1878]

BINSEY POPLARS

felled 1879

My aspens dear, whose airy cages quelled,
Quelled or quenched in leaves the leaping sun,
All felled, felled, are all felled;
    Of a fresh and following folded rank
        Not spared, not one
        That dandled a sandalled
    Shadow that swam or sank
On meadow and river and wind-wandering weed-winding
    bank.

    O if we but knew what we do
        When we delve or hew—

Hack and rack the growing green!
   Since country is so tender
To touch, her being só slender,
That, like this sleek and seeing ball
But a prick will make no eye at all,
Where we, even where we mean
      To mend her we end her,
   When we hew or delve:
After-comers cannot guess the beauty been.
  Ten or twelve, only ten or twelve
    Strokes of havoc únselve
     The sweet especial scene,
    Rural scene, a rural scene,
    Sweet especial rural scene.

                     [1879]

DUNS SCOTUS'S OXFORD

Towery city and branchy between towers;
Cuckoo-echoing, bell-swarmèd, lark-charmèd, rook-racked,
   river-rounded;
The dapple-eared lily below thee; that country and town did
Once encounter in, here coped and poisèd powers;

Thou hast a base and brickish skirt there, sours
That neighbour-nature thy grey beauty is grounded
Best in; graceless growth, thou hast confounded
Rural rural keeping – folk, flocks, and flowers.

Yet ah! this air I gather and I release
He lived on; these weeds and waters, these walls are what
He haunted who of all men most sways my spirits to peace;

Of realty the rarest-veinèd unraveller; a not
Rivalled insight, be rival Italy or Greece;
Who fired France for Mary without spot.

                     [1879]

HENRY PURCELL

The poet wishes well to the divine genius of Purcell and praises him that, whereas other musicians have given utterance to the moods of man's mind, he has, beyond that, uttered in notes the very make and species of man as created both in him and in all men generally.

Have fair fallen, O fair, fair have fallen, so dear
To me, so arch-especial a spirit as heaves in Henry Purcell,
An age is now since passed, since parted; with the reversal
Of the outward sentence low lays him, listed to a heresy,
    here.

Not mood in him nor meaning, proud fire or sacred fear,
Or love, or pity, or all that sweet notes not his might nursle:
It is the forgèd feature finds me; it is the rehearsal
Of own, of abrúpt sélf there so thrusts on, so throngs the ear.

Let him oh! with his air of angels then lift me, lay me! only I'll
Have an eye to the sakes of him, quaint moonmarks, to his
    pelted plumage under
Wings: so some great stormfowl, whenever he has walked his
    while

The thunder-purple seabeach, plumèd purple-of-thunder,
If a wuthering of his palmy snow-pinions scatter a colossal
    smile
Off him, but meaning motion fans fresh our wits with wonder.
                                          [*1879*]

PEACE

When will you ever, Peace, wild wooddove, shy wings shut,
Your round me roaming end, and under be my boughs?
When, when, Peace, will you, Peace? I'll not play hypocrite
To own my heart: I yield you do come sometimes; but
That piecemeal peace is poor peace. What pure peace allows
Alarms of wars, the daunting wars, the death of it?

O surely, reaving Peace, my Lord should leave in lieu
Some good! And so he does leave Patience exquisite,
That plumes to Peace thereafter. And when Peace here does
    house
He comes with work to do, he does not come to coo,
       He comes to brood and sit.

                [1879]

THE BUGLER'S FIRST COMMUNION

A bugler boy from barrack (it is over the hill
There) — boy bugler, born, he tells me, of Irish
    Mother to an English sire (he
Shares their best gifts surely, fall how things will),

This very very day came down to us after a boon he on
My late being there begged of me, overflowing
    Boon in my bestowing,
Came, I say, this day to it — to a First Communion.

Here he knelt then ín regimental red.
Forth Christ from cupboard fetched, how fain I of feet
    To his youngster take his treat!
Low-latched in leaf-light housel his too huge godhead.

There! and your sweetest sendings, ah divine,
By it, heavens, befall him! as a heart Christ's darling, daunt-
    less;
    Tongue true, vaunt- and tauntless;
Breathing bloom of a chastity in mansex fine.

Frowning and forefending angel-warder
Squander the hell-rook ranks sally to molest him;
    March, kind comrade, abreast him;
Dress his days to a dexterous and starlight order.

How it dóes my heart good, visiting at that bleak hill,
When limber liquid youth, that to all I teach
    Yields tender as a pushed peach,
Hies headstrong to its wellbeing of a self-wise self-will!

Then though I should tread tufts of consolation
Dáys áfter, só I in a sort deserve to
    And do serve God to serve to
Just such slips of soldiery Christ's royal ration.

Nothing élse is like it, no, not all so strains
Us: fresh youth fretted in a bloomfall all portending
    That sweet's sweeter ending;
Realm both Christ is heir to and thére réigns.

O now well work that sealing sacred ointment!
O for now charms, arms, what bans off bad
    And locks love ever in a lad!
Let mé though see no more of him, and not disappointment

Those sweet hopes quell whose least me quickenings lift,
In scarlet or somewhere of some day seeing
    That brow and bead of being,
An our day's God's own Galahad. Though this child's drift

Seems by a divíne doom chánnelled, nor do I cry
Disaster there; but may he not rankle and roam
    In backwheels though bound home? –
That left to the Lord of the Eucharist, I here lie by;

Recorded only, I have put my lips on pleas
Would brandle adamantine heaven with ride and jar, did
    Prayer go disregarded:
Forward-like, but however, and like favourable heaven heard
    these.

                        [*1879*]

MORNING MIDDAY AND EVENING
SACRIFICE

    The dappled die-away
    Cheek and wimpled lip,
    The gold-wisp, the airy-grey
    Eye, all in fellowship –
    This, all this beauty blooming,
    This, all this freshness fuming,
    Give God while worth consuming.

Both thought and thew now bolder
And told by Nature: Tower;
Head, heart, hand, heel, and shoulder
That beat and breathe in power –
This pride of prime's enjoyment
Take as for tool, not toy meant
And hold at Christ's employment.

The vault and scope and schooling
And mastery in the mind,
In silk-ash kept from cooling,
And ripest under rind –
What life half lifts the latch of,
What hell stalks towards the snatch of,
Your offering, with despatch, of!

[1879]

ANDROMEDA

Now Time's Andromeda on this rock rude,
With not her either beauty's equal or
Her injury's, looks off by both horns of shore,
Her flower, her piece of being, doomed dragon's food.
    Time past she has been attempted and pursued
By many blows and banes; but now hears roar
A wilder beast from West than all were, more
Rife in her wrongs, more lawless, and more lewd.

    Her Perseus linger and leave her tó her extremes? –
Pillowy air he treads a time and hangs
His thoughts on her, forsaken that she seems,
    All while her patience, morselled into pangs,
Mounts; then to alight disarming, no one dreams,
With Gorgon's gear and barebill, thongs and fangs.

[1879]

THE CANDLE INDOORS

Some candle clear burns somewhere I come by.
I muse at how its being puts blissful back
With yellowy moisture mild night's blear-all black,
Or to-fro tender trambeams truckle at the eye.
By that window what task what fingers ply,
I plod wondering, a-wanting, just for lack
Of answer the eagerer a-wanting Jessy or Jack
There/God to aggrándise, God to glorify. –

Come you indoors, come home; your fading fire
Mend first and vital candle in close heart's vault:
You there are master, do your own desire;
What hinders? Are you beam-blind, yet to a fault
In a neighbour deft-handed? are you that liar
And, cast by conscience out, spendsavour salt?

[1879]

THE HANDSOME HEART:

at a Gracious Answer

'But tell me, child, your choice; what shall I buy
You?' – 'Father, what you buy me I like best.'
With the sweetest air that said, still plied and pressed,
He swung to his first poised purport of reply.

What the heart is! which, like carriers let fly –
Doff darkness, homing nature knows the rest –
To its own fine function, wild and self-instressed,
Falls light as ten years long taught how to and why.

Mannerly-hearted! more than handsome face –
Beauty's bearing or muse of mounting vein,
All, in this case, bathed in high hallowing grace . . .

Of heaven what boon to buy you, boy, or gain
Not granted! – Only . . . O on that path you pace
Run all your race, O brace sterner that strain!

[1879]

AT THE WEDDING MARCH

God with honour hang your head,
Groom, and grace you, bride, your bed
With lissome scions, sweet scions,
Out of hallowed bodies bred.

Each be other's comfort kind:
Déep, déeper than divined,
Divine charity, dear charity,
Fast you ever, fast bind.

Then let the march tread our ears:
I to him turn with tears
Who to wedlock, his wonder wedlock,
Déals tríumph and immortal years.

[1879]

FELIX RANDAL

Felix Randal the farrier, O he is dead then? my duty all
    ended,
Who have watched his mould of man, big-boned and hardy-
    handsome
Pining, pining, till time when reason rambled in it and some
Fatal four disorders, fleshed there, all contended?

Sickness broke him. Impatient he cursed at first, but mended
Being anointed and all; though a heavenlier heart began
    some
Months earlier, since I had our sweet reprieve and ransom
Tendered to him. Ah well, God rest him all road ever he
    offended!

This seeing the sick endears them to us, us too it endears.
My tongue had taught thee comfort, touch had quenched thy
    tears,
Thy tears that touched my heart, child, Felix, poor Felix
    Randal;

How far from then forethought of, all thy more boisterous
    years,
When thou at the random grim forge, powerful amidst peers,
Didst fettle for the great grey drayhorse his bright and bat-
    tering sandal!

[1880]

BROTHERS

How lovely the elder brother's
Life all laced in the other's,
Lóve-laced! – what once I well
Witnessed; so fortune fell.
When Shrovetide, two years gone,   5
Our boys' plays brought on
Part was picked for John,
Young Jóhn; then fear, then joy
Ran revel in the elder boy.
Their night was come now; all   10
Our company thronged the hall;
Henry, by the wall,
Beckoned me beside him:
I came where called, and eyed him
By meanwhiles; making mý play   15
Turn most on tender byplay.
For, wrung all on love's rack,
My lad, and lost in Jack,
Smiled, blushed, and bit his lip;
Or drove, with a diver's dip,   20
Clutched hands down through clasped knees –
Truth's tokens tricks like these,
Old telltales, with what stress
He hung on the imp's success.
Now the other was bráss-bóld: 25
Hé had no work to hold
His heart up at the strain;
Nay, roguish ran the vein.
Two tedious acts were past;
Jack's call and cue at last;   30

When Henry, heart-forsook,
Dropped eyes and dared not look.
Eh, how áll rúng!
Young dog, he did give tongue!
But Harry – in his hands he has flung   35
His tear-tricked cheeks of flame
For fond love and for shame.
    Ah Nature, framed in fault,
There's comfort then, there's salt;
Nature, bad, base, and blind,   40
Dearly thou canst be kind;
There dearly thén, deárly,
I'll cry thou canst be kind.

                                        [1880]

SPRING AND FALL:

to a young child

Márgarét, are you gríeving
Over Goldengrove unleaving?
Leáves, líke the things of man, you
With your fresh thoughts care for, can you?
Áh! ás the heart grows older
It will come to such sights colder
By and by, nor spare a sigh
Though worlds of wanwood leafmeal lie;
And yet you wíll weep and know why.
Now no matter, child, the name:
Sórrow's spríngs áre the same.
Nor mouth had, no nor mind, expressed
What heart heard of, ghost guessed:
It ís the blight man was born for,
It is Margaret you mourn for.

                                        [1880]

INVERSNAID

This darksome burn, horseback brown,
His rollrock highroad roaring down,
In coop and in comb the fleece of his foam
Flutes and low to the lake falls home.

A windpuff-bonnet of fáwn-fróth
Turns and twindles over the broth
Of a pool so pitchblack, féll-frówning,
It rounds and rounds Despair to drowning.

Degged with dew, dappled with dew
Are the groins of the braes that the brook treads through,
Wiry heathpacks, flitches of fern,
And the beadbonny ash that sits over the burn.

What would the world be, once bereft
Of wet and of wildness? Let them be left,
O let them be left, wildness and wet;
Long live the weeds and the wilderness yet.

[1881]

As kingfishers catch fire, dragonflies dráw fláme;
As tumbled over rim in roundy wells
Stones ring; like each tucked string tells, each hung bell's
Bow swung finds tongue to fling out broad its name;
Each mortal thing does one thing and the same:
Deals out that being indoors each one dwells;
Selves — goes itself; *myself* it speaks and spells,
Crying *Whát I dó is me: for that I came.*

Í say móre: the just man justices;
Kéeps gráce: thát keeps all his goings graces;
Acts in God's eye what in God's eye he is —
Chríst — for Christ plays in ten thousand places,
Lovely in limbs, and lovely in eyes not his
To the Father through the features of men's faces.

[1882]

RIBBLESDALE

Earth, sweet Earth, sweet landscape, with leavès throng
And louchèd low grass, heaven that dost appeal
To, with no tongue to plead, no heart to feel;
That canst but only be, but dost that long –

Thou canst but be, but that thou well dost; strong
Thy plea with him who dealt, nay does now deal,
Thy lovely dale down thus and thus bids reel
Thy river, and o'er gives all to rack or wrong.

And what is Earth's eye, tongue, or heart else, where
Else, but in dear and dogged man? – Ah, the heir
To his own selfbent so bound, so tied to his turn,
To thriftless reave both our rich round world bare
And none reck of world after, this bids wear
Earth brows of such care, care and dear concern.

[1882]

THE LEADEN ECHO AND THE GOLDEN ECHO

(Maidens' song from St. Winefred's Well)

THE LEADEN ECHO

How to kéep – is there ány any, is there none such, nowhere
    known some, bow or brooch or braid or brace, láce,
    latch or catch or key to keep
Back beauty, keep it, beauty, beauty, beauty, . . . from van-
    ishing away?
Ó is there no frowning of these wrinkles, rankèd wrinkles
    deep,
Dówn? no waving off of these most mournful messengers, still
    messengers, sad and stealing messengers of grey?
No there's none, there's none, O no there's none,
Nor can you long be, what you now are, called fair,
Do what you may do, what, do what you may,
And wisdom is early to despair:

Be beginning; since, no, nothing can be done
To keep at bay
Age and age's evils, hoar hair,
Ruck and wrinkle, drooping, dying, death's worst, winding
    sheets, tombs and worms and tumbling to decay;
So be beginning, be beginning to despair.
O there's none; no no no there's none:
Be beginning to despair, to despair,
Despair, despair, despair, despair.

THE GOLDEN ECHO

   Spare!
There ís one, yes I have one (Hush there!);
Only not within seeing of the sun,
Not within the singeing of the strong sun,
Tall sun's tingeing, or treacherous the tainting of the earth's
    air,
Somewhere elsewhere there is ah well where! one,
Óne. Yes I cán tell such a key, I dó know such a place,
Where whatever's prized and passes of us, everything that's
    fresh and fast flying of us, seems to us sweet of us and
    swiftly away with, done away with, undone,
Úndone, done with, soon done with, and yet dearly and dan-
    gerously sweet
Of us, the wimpled-water-dimpled, not-by-morning-matchèd
    face,
The flower of beauty, fleece of beauty, too too apt to, ah! to
    fleet,
Never fleets móre, fastened with the tenderest truth
To its own best being and its loveliness of youth: it ís an
    ever-lastingness of, O it is an all youth!
Come then, your ways and airs and looks, locks, maiden gear,
    gallantry and gaiety and grace,
Winning ways, airs innocent, maiden manners, sweet looks,
    loose locks, long locks, lovelocks, gaygear, going gallant,
    girlgrace –
Resign them, sign them, seal them, send them, motion them
    with breath,
And with sighs soaring, soaring síghs deliver

Them; beauty-in-the-ghost, deliver it, early now, long before
    death
Give beauty back, beauty, beauty, beauty, back to God,
    beauty's self and beauty's giver.
See; not a hair is, not an eyelash, not the least lash lost; every
    hair
Is, hair of the head, numbered.
Nay, what we had lighthanded left in surly the mere mould
Will have waked and have waxed and have walked with the
    wind what while we slept,
This side, that side hurling a heavyheaded hundredfold
What while we, while we slumbered.
O then, weary then whý should we tread? O why are we so
    haggard at the heart, so care-coiled, care-killed, so
    fagged, so fashed, so cogged, so cumbered,
When the thing we freely fórfeit is kept with fonder a care,
Fonder a care kept than we could have kept it, kept
Far with fonder a care (and we, we should have lost it) finer,
    fonder
A care kept. – Where kept? Do but tell us where kept,
    where. –
Yonder. – What high as that! We follow, now we follow. –
    Yonder, yes yonder, yonder,
Yonder.

[1882]

THE BLESSED VIRGIN COMPARED
TO THE AIR WE BREATHE

Wild air, world-mothering air,
Nestling me everywhere,
That each eyelash or hair
Girdles; goes home betwixt
The fleeciest, frailest-flixed
Snowflake; that's fairly mixed
With, riddles, and is rife
In every least thing's life;
This needful, never spent,
And nursing element;   10

My more than meat and drink,
My meal at every wink;
This air, which, by life's law,
My lung must draw and draw
Now but to breathe its praise,
Minds me in many ways
Of her who not only
Gave God's infinity
Dwindled to infancy
Welcome in womb and breast,   20
Birth, milk, and all the rest
But mothers each new grace
That does now reach our race—
Mary Immaculate,
Merely a woman, yet
Whose presence, power is
Great as no goddess's
Was deemèd, dreamèd; who
This one work has to do—
Let all God's glory through,   30
God's glory which would go
Through her and from her flow
Off, and no way but so.

    I say that we are wound
With mercy round and round
As if with air: the same
Is Mary, more by name.
She, wild web, wondrous robe,
Mantles the guilty globe,
Since God has let dispense   40
Her prayers his providence:
Nay, more than almoner,
The sweet alms' self is her
And men are meant to share
Her life as life does air.
    If I have understood,
She holds high motherhood
Towards all our ghostly good

And plays in grace her part
About man's beating heart,   50
Laying, like air's fine flood,
The deathdance in his blood;
Yet no part but what will
Be Christ our Saviour still.
Of her flesh he took flesh:
He does take fresh and fresh,
Though much the mystery how,
Not flesh but spirit now
And makes, O marvellous!
New Nazareths in us,   60
Where she shall yet conceive
Him, morning, noon, and eve;
New Bethlems, and he born
There, evening, noon, and morn—
Bethlem or Nazareth,
Men here may draw like breath
More Christ and baffle death;
Who, born so, comes to be
New self and nobler me
In each one and each one   70
More makes, when all is done,
Both God's and Mary's Son.
      Again, look overhead
How air is azurèd;
O how! nay do but stand
Where you can lift your hand
Skywards: rich, rich it laps
Round the four fingergaps.
Yet such a sapphire-shot,
Charged, steepèd sky will not   80
Stain light. Yea, mark you this:
It does no prejudice.
The glass-blue days are those
When every colour glows,
Each shape and shadow shows.
Blue be it: this blue heaven
The seven or seven times seven
Hued sunbeam will transmit

Perfect, not alter it.
Or if there does some soft,   90
On things aloof, aloft,
Bloom breathe, that one breath more
Earth is the fairer for.
Whereas did air not make
This bath of blue and slake
His fire, the sun would shake,
A blear and blinding ball
With blackness bound, and all
The thick stars round him roll
Flashing like flecks of coal,   100
Quartz-fret, or sparks of salt,
In grimy vasty vault.

 So God was god of old:
A mother came to mould
Those limbs like ours which are
What must make our daystar
Much dearer to mankind;
Whose glory bare would blind
Or less would win man's mind.
Through her we may see him   110
Made sweeter, not made dim,
And her hand leaves his light
Sifted to suit our sight.

 Be thou then, O thou dear
Mother, my atmosphere;
My happier world, wherein
To wend and meet no sin;
Above me, round me lie
Fronting my froward eye
With sweet and scarless sky;   120
Stir in my ears, speak there
Of God's love, O live air,
Of patience, penance, prayer:
World-mothering air, air wild,
Wound with thee, in thee isled,
Fold home, fast fold thy child.

[1883]

TO WHAT SERVES MORTAL BEAUTY?

To what serves mortal beauty ' – dangerous; does set danc-
ing blood – the O-seal-that-so ' feature, flung prouder form
Than Purcell tune lets tread to? ' See: it does this: keeps warm
Men's wits to the things that are; ' what good means – where a
glance
Master more may than gaze, ' gaze out of countenance.
Those lovely lads once, wet-fresh ' windfalls of war's storm,
How then should Gregory, a father, ' have gleanèd else from
swarm-
ed Rome? But God to a nation ' dealt that day's dear chance.
To man, that needs would worship ' block or barren stone,
Our law says: Love what are ' love's worthiest, were all
known;
World's loveliest – men's selves. Self ' flashes off frame and
face.
What do then? how meet beauty? ' Merely meet it; own,
Home at heart, heaven's sweet gift; ' then leave, let that
alone.
Yea, wish that though, wish all, ' God's better beauty, grace.
[1885]

SPELT FROM SIBYL'S LEAVES

Earnest, earthless, equal, attuneable, ' vaulty, voluminous, . .
stupendous
Evening strains to be tíme's vást, ' womb-of-all, home-of-all,
hearse-of-all night.
Her fond yellow hornlight wound to the west, ' her wild
hollow hoarlight hung to the height
Waste; her earliest stars, earl-stars, ' stárs principal, overbend
us,
Fíre-féaturing heaven. For earth ' her being has unbound,
her dapple is at an end, as-
tray or aswarm, all throughther, in throngs; ' self ín self
steepèd and páshed – qúite

Disremembering, dísmémbering ' áll now. Heart, you round
  me right
With: Óur évening is over us; óur night ' whélms, whélms,
  ánd will end us.
Only the beak-leaved boughs dragonish ' damask the tool-
  smooth bleak light; black,
Ever so black on it. Óur tale, O óur oracle! ' Lét life, wáned,
  ah lét life wind
Off hér once skéined stained véined varíety ' upon, áll on twó
  spools; párt, pen, páck
Now her áll in twó flocks, twó folds – black, white; ' right,
  wrong; reckon but, reck but, mind
But thése two; wáre of a wórld where bút these ' twó tell,
  each off the óther; of a rack
Where, selfwrung, selfstrung, sheathe- and shelterless, '
  thóughts agaínst thoughts ín groans grínd.

[c. 1885]

(THE SOLDIER)

Yes. Whý do we áll, seeing of a soldier, bless him? bless
Our redcoats, our tars? Both these being, the greater part,
But frail clay, nay but foul clay. Here it is: the heart,
Since, proud, it calls the calling manly, gives a guess
That, hopes that, makesbelieve, the men must be no less;
It fancies, feigns, deems, dears the artist after his art;
And fain will find as sterling all as all is smart,
And scarlet wear the spirit of wár thére express.

Mark Christ our King. He knows war, served this soldiering
  through;
He of all can reeve a rope best. There he bides in bliss
Now, and séeing somewhére some mán do all that man can
  do,
For love he leans forth, needs his neck must fall on, kiss,
And cry 'O Christ-done deed! So God-made-flesh does too:
Were I come o'er again' cries Christ 'it should be this'.

[1885]

(CARRION COMFORT)

Not, I'll not, carrion comfort, Despair, not feast on thee;
Not untwist — slack they may be — these last strands of man
In me ór, most weary, cry *I can no more*. I can;
Can something, hope, wish day come, not choose not to be.
But ah, but O thou terrible, why wouldst thou rude on me
Thy wring-world right foot rock? lay a lionlimb against me?
     scan
With darksome devouring eyes my bruisèd bones? and fan,
O in turns of tempest, me heaped there; me frantic to avoid
     thee and flee?

  Why? That my chaff might fly; my grain lie, sheer and
     clear.
Nay in all that toil, that coil, since (seems) I kissed the rod,
Hand rather, my heart lo! lapped strength, stole joy, would
     laugh, chéer.
Cheer whom though? the hero whose heaven-handling flung
     me, fóot tród
Me? or me that fought him? O which one? is it each one?
     That night, that year
Of now done darkness I wretch lay wrestling with (my
     God!) my God.

                                     [*1885*]

No worst, there is none. Pitched past pitch of grief,
More pangs will, schooled at forepangs, wilder wring.
Comforter, where, where is your comforting?
Mary, mother of us, where is your relief?
My cries heave, herds-long; huddle in a main, a chief
Woe, wórld-sorrow; on an áge-old anvil wince and sing —
Then lull, then leave off. Fury had shrieked 'No ling-
ering! Let me be fell: force I must be brief'.

  O the mind, mind has mountains; cliffs of fall
Frightful, sheer, no-man-fathomed. Hold them cheap
May who ne'er hung there. Nor does long our small

Durance deal with that steep or deep. Here! creep,
Wretch, under a comfort serves in a whirlwind: all
Life death does end and each day dies with sleep.

[1885]

To seem the stranger lies my lot, my life
Among strangers. Father and mother dear,
Brothers and sisters are in Christ not near
And he my peace my parting, sword and strife.

   England, whose honour O all my heart woos, wife
To my creating thought, would neither hear
Me, were I pleading, plead nor do I: I wear-
y of idle a being but by where wars are rife.

   I am in Ireland now; now I am at a thírd
Remove. Not but in all removes I can
Kind love both give and get. Only what word
Wisest my heart breeds dark heaven's baffling ban
Bars or hell's spell thwarts. This to hoard unheard,
Heard unheeded, leaves me a lonely began.

[1885]

I wake and feel the fell of dark, not day.
What hours, O what black hoürs we have spent
This night! what sights you, heart, saw; ways you went!
And more must, in yet longer light's delay.

   With witness I speak this. But where I say
Hours I mean years, mean life. And my lament
Is cries countless, cries like dead letters sent
To dearest him that lives alas! away.

   I am gall, I am heartburn. God's most deep decree
Bitter would have me taste: my taste was me;
Bones built in me, flesh filled, blood brimmed the curse.
   Selfyeast of spirit a dull dough sours. I see
The lost are like this, and their scourge to be
As I am mine, their sweating selves; but worse.

[1885]

Patience, hard thing! the hard thing but to pray,
But bid for, Patience is! Patience who asks
Wants war, wants wounds; weary his times, his tasks;
To do without, take tosses, and obey.
   Rare patience roots in these, and, these away,
Nowhere. Natural heart's ivy, Patience masks
Our ruins of wrecked past purpose. There she basks
Purple eyes and seas of liquid leaves all day.

We hear our hearts grate on themselves: it kills
To bruise them dearer. Yet the rebellious wills
Of us we do bid God bend to him even so.
   And where is he who more and more distils
Delicious kindness? – He is patient. Patience fills
His crisp combs, and that comes those ways we know.
                       [1885]

My own heart let me more have pity on; let
Me live to my sad self hereafter kind,
Charitable; not live this tormented mind
With this tormented mind tormenting yet.
   I cast for comfort I can no more get
By groping round my comfortless, than blind
Eyes in their dark can day or thirst can find
Thirst's all-in-all in all a world of wet.

Soul, self; come, poor Jackself, I do advise
You, jaded, let be; call off thoughts awhile
Elsewhere; leave comfort root-room; let joy size
At God knows when to God knows what; whose smile
's not wrung, see you; unforeseen times rather – as skies
Betweenpie mountains – lights a lovely mile.
                       [1885]

TOM'S GARLAND:

upon the Unemployed

Tom – garlanded with squat and surly steel
Tom; then Tom's fallowbootfellow piles pick
By him and rips out rockfire homeforth – sturdy Dick;
Tom Heart-at-ease, Tom Navvy: he is all for his meal
Sure, 's bed now. Low be it: lustily he his low lot (feel
That ne'er need hunger, Tom; Tom seldom sick,
Seldomer heartsore; that treads through, prickproof, thick
Thousands of thorns, thoughts) swings though. Commonweal
Little I reck ho! lacklevel in, if all had bread:
What! Country is honour enough in all us – lordly head,
With heaven's lights high hung round, or, mother-ground
That mammocks, mighty foot. But no way sped,
Nor mind nor mainstrength; gold go garlanded
With, perilous, O nó; nor yet plod safe shod sound;
                    Undenizened, beyond bound
Of earth's glory, earth's ease, all; no one, nowhere,
In wide the world's weal; rare gold, bold steel, bare
                In both; care, but share care –
This, by Despair, bred Hangdog dull; by Rage,
Manwolf, worse; and their packs infest the age.

                                          [*1887*]

HARRY PLOUGHMAN

Hard as hurdle arms, with a broth of goldish flue
Breathed round; the rack of ribs; the scooped flank; lank
Rope-over thigh; knee-nave; and barrelled shank –
                Head and foot, shoulder and shank –
By a grey eye's heed steered well, one crew, fall to;
Stand at stress. Each limb's barrowy brawn, his thew
That onewhere curded, onewhere sucked or sank –
                Soared or sank –,
Though as a beechbole firm, finds his, as at a roll-call, rank
And features, in flesh, what deed he each must do –
                His sinew-service where do.

He leans to it, Harry bends, look. Back, elbow, and liquid
    waist
In him, all quail to the wallowing o' the plough: 's cheek crim-
    sons; curls
Wag or crossbridle, in a wind lifted, windlaced –
            See his wind- lilylocks -laced;
Churlsgrace, too, child of Amansstrength, how it hangs or
    hurls
Them – broad in bluff hide his frowning feet lashed! raced
With, along them, cragiron under and cold furls –
            With-a-fountain's shining-shot furls.

                        [1887]

THAT NATURE IS A HERACLITEAN FIRE
AND OF THE
COMFORT OF THE RESURRECTION

Cloud-puffball, torn tufts, tossed pillows ' flaunt forth, then
    chevy on an air-
built thoroughfare: heaven-roysterers, in gay-gangs ' they
    throng; they glitter in marches.
Down roughcast, down dazzling whitewash, ' wherever an
    elm arches,
Shivelights and shadowtackle in long ' lashes lace, lance, and
    pair.
Delightfully the bright wind boisterous ' ropes, wrestles, beats
    earth bare
Of yestertempest's creases; ' in pool and rut peel parches
Squandering ooze to squeezed ' dough, crust, dust; stanches,
    starches
Squadroned masks and manmarks ' treadmire toil there
Footfretted in it. Million-fuelèd, ' nature's bonfire burns on.
But quench her bonniest, dearest ' to her, her clearest-selvèd
    spark
Man, how fast his firedint, ' his mark on mind, is gone!
Both are in an unfathomable, all is in an enormous dark
Drowned. O pity and indig ' nation! Manshape, that shone
Sheer off, disseveral, a star, ' death blots black out; nor mark
       Is any of him at all so stark

But vastness blurs and time ' beats level. Enough! the
    Resurrection,
A heart's-clarion! Away grief's gasping, ' joyless days, de-
    jection.
                Across my foundering deck shone
A beacon, an eternal beam. ' Flesh fade, and mortal trash
Fall to the residuary worm; ' world's wildfire, leave but ash:
            In a flash, at a trumpet crash,
I am all at once what Christ is, ' since he was what I am, and
This Jack, joke, poor potsherd, ' patch, matchwood, immortal
    diamond,
            Is immortal diamond.

                            [*1888*]

In honour of
ST. ALPHONSUS RODRIGUEZ
Laybrother of the Society of Jesus

Honour is flashed off exploit, so we say;
And those strokes once that gashed flesh or galled shield
Should tongue that time now, trumpet now that field,
And, on the fighter, forge his glorious day.
On Christ they do and on the martyr may;
But be the war within, the brand we wield
Unseen, the heroic breast not outward-steeled,
Earth hears no hurtle then from fiercest fray.

Yet God (that hews mountain and continent,
Earth, all, out; who, with trickling increment,
Veins violets and tall trees makes more and more)
Could crowd career with conquest while there went
Those years and years by of world without event
That in Majorca Alfonso watched the door.

                            [*1888*]

Justus quidem tu es, Domine, si disputem tecum: verumtamen
justa loquar ad te: Quare via impiorum prosperatur? &c.

Thou art indeed just, Lord, if I contend
With thee; but, sir, so what I plead is just.
Why do sinners' ways prosper? and why must
Disappointment all I endeavour end?
    Wert thou my enemy, O thou my friend,
How wouldst thou worse, I wonder, than thou dost
Defeat, thwart me? Oh, the sots and thralls of lust
Do in spare hours more thrive than I that spend,
Sir, life upon thy cause. See, banks and brakes
Now, leavèd how thick! lacèd they are again
With fretty chervil, look, and fresh wind shakes
Them; birds build – but not I build; no, but strain,
Time's eunuch, and not breed one work that wakes.
Mine, O thou lord of life, send my roots rain.

[*1889*]

The shepherd's brow, fronting forked lightning, owns
The horror and the havoc and the glory
Of it. Angels fall, they are towers, from heaven – a story
Of just, majestical, and giant groans.
But man – we, scaffold of score brittle bones;
Who breathe, from groundlong babyhood to hoary
Age gasp; whose breath is our *memento mori* –
What bass is *our* viol for tragic tones?
He! Hand to mouth he lives, and voids with shame;
And, blazoned in however bold the name,
Man Jack the man is, just; his mate a hussy.
And I that die these deaths, that feed this flame,
That . . . in smooth spoons spy life's masque mirrored: tame
My tempests there, my fire and fever fussy.

[1889]

TO R. B.

The fine delight that fathers thought; the strong
Spur, live and lancing like the blowpipe flame,
Breathes once and, quenchèd faster than it came,
Leaves yet the mind a mother of immortal song.
Nine months she then, nay years, nine years she long
Within her wears, bears, cares and combs the same:
The widow of an insight lost she lives, with aim
Now known and hand at work now never wrong.

   Sweet fire the sire of muse, my soul needs this;
I want the one rapture of an inspiration.
O then if in my lagging lines you miss
The roll, the rise, the carol, the creation,
My winter world, that scarcely breathes that bliss
Now, yields you, with some sighs, our explanation.

[1889]

II

OBSERVATION OF NATURE: INSCAPE

I think I have told you that I have particular periods of admiration for particular things in Nature; for a certain time I am astonished at the beauty of a tree, shape, effect etc, then when the passion, so to speak, has subsided, it is consigned to my treasury of explored beauty, and acknowledged with admiration and interest ever after, while something new takes its place in my enthusiasm.

EXTRACTS FROM EARLY DIARIES

[*1863*]

Note on water coming through a lock.

There are openings near the bottom of the gates (which allow the water to pass through at all times, I suppose.) Suppose three, as there often are. The water strikes through these with great force and extends itself into three fans. The direction of the water is a little oblique from the horizontal, but the great force with which it runs keeps it almost uncurved except at the edges. The end of these fans is not seen for they strike them under a mass of yellowish boiling foam which runs down between the fans, and meeting covers the whole space of the lock-entrance. Being heaped up in globes and bosses and round masses the fans disappear under it. This turpid mass smooths itself as the distance increases from the lock. But the current is strong and if the basin into which it runs has curving banks it strikes them and the confusion of the already folded and doubled lines of foam is worse confounded.

Note on green wheat. The difference between this green and that of long grass is that first suggests silver, latter azure. Former more opacity, body, smoothness. It is the exact complement of carnation. Nearest to emerald of any green I know, the real emerald *stone*. It is lucent. Perhaps it has a chrysoprase bloom. Both blue greens.

∗

[1864]

Moonlight hanging or dropping on treetops like blue cobweb.

∗

Also the upper sides of little grotted waves turned to the sky have soft pale-coloured cobwebs on them, the under sides green.

∗

Note that the beaded oar, dripping, powders or sows the smooth with dry silver drops.

∗

Poetry at Oxford.
It is a happy thing that there is no royal road to poetry. The world should know by this time that one cannot reach Parnassus except by flying thither. Yet from time to time more men go up and either perish in its gullies fluttering *excelsior* flags or else come down again with full folios and blank countenances. Yet the old fallacy keeps its ground. Every age has its false alarms.

∗

Sept. 14. Grey clouds in knops. A curious fan of this kind of cloud radiating from a crown, and covering half the sky.

The sky minted into golden sequins.
Stars like gold tufts.
— — golden bees.
— — golden rowels.
Sky peak'd with tiny flames.
Stars like tiny-spoked wheels of fire.
Lantern of night pierced in eyelets, (or eye lets, which avoids ambiguity.)
Altogether peak is a good word. For sunlight through shutter, locks of hair, rays in brass knobs etc. Meadows peaked with flowers.

> His gilded rowels
> Now stars of blood.

Saw a curious thing on, I think, Oct 1.—A cloud hid the sun and its edges were so brilliant that the lustre prevented one seeing outlines which swam in the light. Happening to look in a pond, I saw the cloud reflected and therefore with much diminution of light, of course, and the outlines of the lightest part of the cloud were distinct and touched here and there with spots of colours.

Tuncks is a good name.
Gerard Manley Tuncks. Poor Tuncks.

[1865]

Shapes of frozen snow-drifts. Parallel ribs. Delightful curves. Saddles, lips, leaves.

*

Whorlèd wave, whelkèd wave,—and drift.

*

Crocus candles yellow and white.

Notes for poetry. Feathery rows of young corn. Ruddy, furred and branchy tops of the elms backed by rolling cloud.

Frieze of sculpture, long-membered vines tugged at by reaching pursuant fauns, and lilies.

March 12. A day of the great mercy of God.

Addis says my arguments are coloured and lose their value by personal feeling. This ought to be repressed.

Palms dotted with silver.
The sun just risen
Flares his wet brilliance in the dintless heaven.
His shaking eye.
The moon glassy.

*

Mems. The opposite sunset. The barrow clouds. The valves. The rail. Mallowy. Peace. Valved eyes. Bats' wings and images. Lobes of leaf. Theory of trees. Temper in art.

*

Sunrise at Chagford. There was a remarkable fan of clouds traced in fine horizontals, which afterwards lost their levels, some becoming oblique. Below appearing bright streaks which crowded up one after another. A white mist in the churchyard, trees ghostly in it.

Sunset here also. Over the nearest ridge of Dartmoor. Sky orange, trail of Bronze-lit clouds, stars and streaks of brilliant electrum underneath, but not for this, but effect of dark intensified foreground. Long rounded ridge of Dartmoor deep purple then trees on the descending hill, and a field with an angle so that the upper level was lighter green the lower darker, then a purplish great brown field, then the manufactory with grey white timbers (it is built of wood) and grey shingle(?) roofs. Grey sky at Hampstead lately. Clouds showing beautiful and rare curves like curds, comparable to barrows, arranged of course in parallels.

Rain railing off something.

The butterfly perching in a cindery dusty road and pinching his scarlet valves. Or wagging, one might say. And also valved eyes.

Mallowy red of sunset and sunrise clouds.

Brush and comb (how vastly absurd it is!) both apply to . . . of water ribs.

Ash clusters like grapes.

Water rushing over a sunken stone and hollowing itself to rise again seems to be devoured by the wave before which it forces up,

Reverted, with thrown back and tossing cape.

Bossy water, bosses.

Oak roots are silvery, smooth, solid and muscular.

Glazed water vaulted o'er a drowsy stone.

[1866]

For Lent. No pudding on Sundays. No tea except if to keep me awake and then without sugar. Meat only once a day. No verses in Passion Week or on Fridays. Not to sit in armchair except can work in no other way. Ash Wednesday and Good Friday bread and water.

Drops of rain hanging on rails etc seen with only the lower rim lighted like nails (of fingers). Screws of brooks and twines. Soft chalky look with more shadowy middles of the globes of cloud on a night with a moon faint or concealed. Mealy clouds with a not brilliant moon. Blunt buds of the ash. Pencil buds of the beech. Lobes of the trees. Cups of the eyes, Gathering back the lightly hinged eyelids. Bows of the eyelids. Pencil of eyelashes. Juices of the eyeball. Eyelids like leaves, petals, caps, tufted hats, handkerchiefs, sleeves, gloves. Also of the bones sleeved in flesh. Juices of the sunrise. Joints and veins of the same. Vermilion look of the hand held against a candle with the darker parts as the middles of the fingers and especially the knuckles covered with ash.

∗

EXTRACTS FROM JOURNAL

[1868]

Sept. 17. Fine.—Chestnuts as bright as coals or spots of vermilion.

Sept. 18. Thunderstorm and rain but not all day.

Henceforth I keep no regular weather-journal but only notes.

Sept. 27. The (clouded) sky at dawn was, I noticed, quite purple. There followed a thunderstorm: I saw one flash of lightning rose-colour. Afterwards wind, rain, and graceful changing clouds.

Very early on some of these days the morning mist looked like water quite still and clouded by milk or soda.

Oct. 21. From a height in Richmond Park saw trees in the river flat below inscaped in distinctly projected, crisp, and almost hard, rows of loaves, their edges, especially at the top, being a little fixed and shaped with shadow.

A fine Autumn. A Spanish chestnut and two elms in the grounds seem to fill the air up with an equable clear ochre.

Nov. 4. Some brownish paste in the library formed in big crystals.

Dec. 6. At night the most violent gale I ever heard. One of our elms snapped in half. Since then (Feb. 2, '70) a grievous gap has come in that place with falling and felling.

There were in November some days of frost but since then the autumn has been very mild, with warm wet winds.

Dec. 9—Honeysuckle out and catkins hanging in the thickets.

[1869]

Jan. 4, '69. We have had wind and rain, so that floods are out, but in temperature the weather mild to an unusual degree.—The other evening after a very bright day, the air rinsed quite clear, there was a slash of glowing yolk-coloured sunset—On the 1st frost all day (which otherwise I do not remember for a long time), the air shining, but with vapour, the dead leaves frilled, the Park grass white with hoarfrost mixed with purple shadow.—Today—another clear afternoon with tender clouding after rain—one notices the crisp flat darkness of the woods against the sun and the smoky bloom they have opposite it. The trees budded and their sprays curled as if dressed for spring.

Jan. 24. One day at the end of the year some heavy rain changed into snow which melted as it touched the ground. Else there has been no snow this winter. It was mild—sun and rain—till the 20th or 21st I think, when there were for sunrises webs of rosy cloud and afterwards ranks of sharply edged crops or slices and all day delicate clouding: this red did not mean rain, but frost followed till the 25th, on which day it was giving; the next it was gone. Since then mild weather, more and more remarkably mild, with sun, gales, and much rain. Feb. 5 and 6 were almost hot. Daffodils have been in bloom for some days. A weeping-willow here is all green. The elms have long been in red bloom and yesterday (the 11th) I saw small leaves on the brushwood at their roots. Some primroses out. But a penance which I was doing from Jan. 25 to July 25 prevented my seeing much that half-year.

Feb. 22. The first snow of the year, but not lying. Hitherto the weather has been as before.

Br. Coupe calls a basket a *whisket*.—One day when we were gathering stones and potsherds from the meadow Br. Wells said we were not to do it at random but 'in braids'.

∗

Br. Wells calls a grindstone a *grindlestone*.

To *lead* north-country for to *carry* (a field of hay etc). *Geet* north-country preterite of *get*: 'he geet agate agoing'.

Trees sold 'top and lop': Br. Rickaby told me and suggests *top* is the higher, outer, and lighter wood good for firing only, *lop* the stem and bigger boughs when the rest has been lopped off used for timber.

Br. Wells calls white bryony Dead Creepers, because it kills what it entwines.

∗

The sunset June 20 was wine-coloured, with pencillings of purple, and next day there was rain.

June 27. The weather turned warm again two or three days ago and today is warmer still. Before that there had been cold, rain, and gloom.

Br. Sidgreaves has heard the high ridges of a field called *folds* and the hollow between the *drip*.

June 28. The cuckoo *has* changed his tune: the two notes can scarcely be told apart, that is their pitch is almost the same.

✳

A few days before Sept. 25 a fine sunrise seen from no. 1, the upstairs bedroom—: long skeins of meshy grey cloud a little ruddled underneath, not quite level but aslant, rising from left to right, and down on the left one more solid balk or bolt than the rest with a high-blown crest of flix or fleece above it.

About the same time a fine sunset, which, looked at also from the upstairs windows, cut out the yews all down the approach to the house in bright flat pieces like wings in a theatre (as once before I noticed at sunrise from Magdalen tower), each shaped by its own sharp-cut shadow falling on the yew-tree next behind it, since they run E. and W. Westward under the sun the heights and groves in Richmond Park looked like dusty velvet being all flushed into a piece by the thickhoary golden light which slanted towards me over them.

Also that autumn my eye was suddenly caught by the scaping of the leaves that grow in allies and avenues: I noticed it first in an elm and then in limes. They fall from the two sides of the branch or spray in two marked planes which meet at a right angle or more. This comes from the endeavour to catch the light on either side, which falls left and right but not all round. Thus each branch is thatched with a double blade or eave of leaves which run up to a coping like the roofcrest all along its stem, and seen from some places these lie across one another all in chequers and X's.

I was at Kew Gardens somewhere about that time. I have these notes:—the leaves of the *Victoria regia* are on the under side deeply groined by red bladed ribs and these again fretted across;—in the same house the *numphœa scutifolia* lying on the water like a Maltese cross and the Egyptian sacred bean, the leaves dimpled in the middle and beautifully wimpled at the edge, the flower a water lily with the petals flagging and falling apart, edged with purplish red, the seed-vessels truncated urns;—several kinds of *hibiscus*, one with a most vivid scarlet-carnation flower.

Crossing the Common Oct. 13 a fine sunset—great gold field; along the earth-line a train of dark clouds of knopped or clustery make pitching over at the top the way they were going; higher a slanting race of tapered or else coiling fishlike flakes such as are often seen; the gold etched with brighter gold and shaped in sandy pieces and looped and waved all in waterings: what more I have forgotten.

Nov. 17 there was a very damp fog, and the trees being drenched with wet a sharp frost which followed in the night candied them with ice. Before the sun, which melted the ice and dried the trees altogether, had struck it I looked at the cedar on the left of the portico and found every needle edged with a blade of ice made of fine horizontal bars or spars all pointing one way, N. and S. (if I am not mistaken, all on the S. side of the needles). There was also an edging of frost on the clematis up the railings and, what is very striking, the little bars of which the blades or pieces of frost were made up though they lay all along the hairy  threads with which the seed-vessels of the clematis are set did not turn with their turnings but lay all in parallels N. and S.

Nov. 20—Two large planets, the one an evening star, the other distant today from it as in the diagram, both nearly of an altitude and of one size—such counterparts that each seems the reflection of the other in opposite bays of the sky and not two distinct things.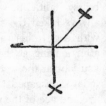

[1870]

I have no other word yet for that which takes the eye or mind in a bold hand or effective sketching or in marked features or again in graphic writing, which not being beauty nor true inscape yet gives interest and makes ugliness even better than meaninglessness.—On the Common the snow was channelled all in parallels by the sharp driving wind and upon the tufts of grass (where by the dark colour shewing through it looked greyish) it came to turret-like clusters or like broken shafts of basalt.—In the Park in the afternoon the wind was driving little clouds of snow-dust which caught the sun as they rose and delightfully took the eyes: flying up the slopes they looked like breaks of sunlight fallen through ravelled cloud upon the hills and again like deep flossy velvet blown to the root by breath which passed all along. Nearer at hand along the road it was gliding over the ground in white wisps that between trailing and flying shifted and wimpled like so many silvery worms to and from one another.

The squirrel was about in our trees all the winter. For instance about Jan. 2 I often saw it.

∗

March 12—A fine sunset: the higher sky dead clear blue bridged by a broad slant causeway rising from right to left of wisped or grass cloud, the wisps lying across; the sundown yellow, moist with light but ending at the top in a foam of delicate white pearling and spotted with big tufts of cloud in colour russet between brown and purple but edged with brassy light. But what I note it all for is this: before I had always taken the sunset and the sun as quite out of gauge with each other, as indeed physically they are for the eye after looking at the sun is blunted to everything else and if you look at the rest of the sunset you must cover the sun, but today I inscaped them together and made the sun the true eye and ace of the whole, as it is. It was all active and tossing out light and started as strongly forward from the field as a long stone or a boss in the knop of the chalice-stem: it is indeed by stalling it so that it falls into scape with the sky.

∗

May 12 Wych-elms not out till today.—The chestnuts down by St. Joseph's were a beautiful sight: each spike had its own pitch, yet each followed in its place in the sweep with a deeper and deeper stoop. When the wind tossed them they plunged and crossed one another without losing their inscape. (Observe that motion multiplies inscape only when inscape is discovered, otherwise it disfigures)[1]

∗

One day when the bluebells were in bloom I wrote the following. I do not think I have ever seen anything more beautiful than the bluebell I have been looking at. I know the beauty of our Lord by it. It[s inscape][2] is [mixed of] strength and grace, like an ash [tree]. The head is strongly drawn over [backwards] and arched down like a cutwater [drawing itself back from the line of the keel]. The lines of the bells strike and overlie this, rayed but not symmetrically, some lie parallel. They look steely against [the] paper, the shades lying between the bells and behind the cockled petal-ends and nursing up the precision of their distinctness, the petal-ends themselves being delicately lit. Then there is the straightness of the trumpets in the bells softened by the slight entasis and [by] the square splay of the mouth. One bell, the lowest, some way detached and carried on a longer foot-stalk, touched out with the tips of the petals an oval / not like the rest in a plane perpendicular to the axis of the bell but a little atilt, and so with [the] square-in-rounding turns of the petals. . . . There is a little drawing of this detached bell.—It looks square-cut in the original

∗

This skeleton inscape of a spray-end of ash I broke at Wimbledon that summer is worth noticing for the suggested

globe: it is the leaf on the left and keys on the right

Sept. 8—I took my vows

Sept. 9—To Stonyhurst to the seminary

Sept. 24—First saw the Northern Lights. My eye was caught by beams of light and dark very like the crown of horny rays the sun makes behind a cloud. At first I thought of silvery cloud until I saw that these were more luminous and did not dim the clearness of the stars in the Bear. They rose slightly radiating thrown out from the earth-line. Then I saw soft pulses of light one after another rise and pass upwards arched in shape but waveringly and with the arch broken. They seemed to float, not following the warp of the sphere as falling stars look to do but free though concentrical with it. This busy working of nature wholly independent of the earth and seeming to go on in a strain of time not reckoned by our reckoning of days and years but simpler and as if correcting the preoccupation of the world by being preoccupied with and appealing to and dated to the day of judgment was like a new witness to God and filled me with delightful fear

Oct. 20—Laus Deo—the river today and yesterday. Yesterday it was a sallow glassy gold at Hodder Roughs and by watching hard the banks began to sail upstream, the scaping unfolded, the river was all in tumult but not running, only the lateral motions were perceived, and the curls of froth where the waves overlap shaped and turned easily and idly. —I meant to have written more.—Today the river was wild, very full, glossy brown with mud, furrowed in permanent billows through which from head to head the water swung with a great down and up again. These heads were scalped with rags of jumping foam. But at the Roughs the sigh was the burly water-backs which heave after heave kept tumbling up from the broken foam and their plump heap turning open in ropes of velvet

Oct. 25—A little before 7 in the evening a wonderful Aurora, the same that was seen at Rome (shortly after its seizure by the Italian government) and taken as a sign of God's anger. It gathered a little below the zenith, to the S.E. I think —a knot or crown, not a true circle, of dull blood-coloured horns and dropped long red beams down the sky on every side, each impaling its lot of stars. An hour or so later its colour was gone but there was still a pale crown in the same place: the skies were then clear and ashy and fresh with stars and there were flashes of or like sheet-lightning. The day had been very bright and clear, distances smart, herds of towering pillow clouds, one great stack in particular over Pendle was knoppled all over in fine snowy tufts and pencilled with bloom-shadow of the greatest delicacy. In the sunset all was big and there was a world of swollen cloud holding the yellow-rose light like a lamp while a few sad milky blue slips passed below it. At night violent hailstorms and hail again next day, and a solar halo. Worth noticing too perhaps the water-runs were then mulled and less beautiful than usual

Dec. 19 or thereabouts a very fine sunrise: the higher cloud was like seams of red candle-wax

On April 29 or thereabouts *at sunset* in the same quarter of the sky I saw, as far as I could remember it, almost the very same scape, the same colour and so on, down to a wavy wisp or rather seam above the rest—and this made by the sun shining from the West instead of the East. It was not so brilliant though

The winter was long and hard. I made many observations on freezing. For instance the crystals in mud.—Hailstones are shaped like the cut of diamonds called brilliants.—I found one morning the ground in one corner of the garden full of small pieces of potsherd from which there rose up (and not dropped off) long icicles carried on in some way each like a forepitch of the shape of the piece of potsherd it grew on, like a tooth to its root for instance, and most of them bended over and curled like so many tusks or horns or/ best of all and what they looked likest when they first caught my eye/ the first soft root-spurs thrown out from a sprouting chestnut. This bending of the icicle seemed so far as I could see not merely a resultant, where the smaller spars of which it was made were still straight, but to have flushed them too.—The same day and others the garden mould very crisp and meshed over with a lace-work of needles leaving (they seemed) three-cornered openings: it looked greyish and like a coat of gum on wood. Also the smaller crumbs and clods were lifted fairly up from the ground on upright ice-pillars, whether they had dropped these from themselves or drawn them from the soil: it was like a little Stonehenge—Looking down into the thick ice of our pond I found the imprisoned air-bubbles nothing at random but starting from centres and in particular one most beautifully regular white brush of them, each spur of it a curving string of beaded and diminishing bubbles—The pond, I suppose from over pressure when it was less firm, was mapped with a puzzle of very slight clefts branched with little springs: the pieces were odd-shaped and sized—though a square angular scaping could be just made out in the outline but the cracks ran deep down through the ice markedly in planes and always the planes of the cleft on the surface. They remained and in the end the ice broke up in just these pieces

*

[1871]

I have been watching clouds this spring and evaporation, for instance over our Lenten chocolate. It seems as if the heat by *aestus*, throes/ one after another threw films of vapour off as boiling water throws off steam under films of water, that is bubbles. One query then is whether these films contain gas or no. The film seems to be set with tiny bubbles which gives it a grey and grained look. By throes perhaps which represent the moments at which the evener stress of the heat has overcome the resistance of the surface or of the whole liquid. It would be reasonable then to consider the films as the shell of gas-bubbles and the grain on them as a network of bubbles condensed by the air as the gas rises.— Candle smoke goes by just the same laws, the visible film being here of unconsumed substance, not hollow bubbles The throes can be perceived/ like the thrills of a candle in the socket: this is precisely to *reech*, whence *reek*. They may by a breath of air be laid again and then shew like grey wisps on the surface—which shews their part-solidity. They seem to be drawn off the chocolate as you might take up a napkin between your fingers that covered something, not so much from here or there as from the whole surface at one reach, so that the film is perceived at the edges and makes in fact a collar or ring just within the walls all round the cup; it then draws together in a cowl like a candleflame but not regularly or without a break: the question is why. Perhaps in perfect stillness it would not but the air breathing it aside entangles it with itself. The film seems to rise not quite simultaneously but to peel off as if you were tearing cloth; then giving an end forward like the corner of a handkerchief and beginning to coil it makes a long wavy hose you may sometimes look down, as a ribbon or a carpenter's shaving may be made to do. Higher running into frets and silvering in the sun with the endless coiling, the soft bound of the general motion and yet the side lurches sliding into some particular pitch it makes a baffling and charming sight.—Clouds however solid they may look far off are I think wholly made of film in the sheet or in the tuft. The bright woolpacks that pelt before a gale in a clear sky are in the tuft and you can see the wind unravelling and rending them finer than any sponge till within one easy reach overhead they are morselled to nothing and consumed —it depends of course on their size. Possibly each tuft in fore-pitch or in origin is quained and a crystal. Rarer and wilder packs have sometimes film in the sheet, which may be caught as it turns on the edge of the cloud like an outlying eyebrow. The  one in which I saw this was a north-east wind, solid but not crisp, white like the white of egg, and bloated-looking

What you look hard at seems to look hard at you, hence the true and the false instress of nature. One day early in March when long streamers were rising from over Kemble End one large flake loop-shaped, not a streamer but belonging to the string, moving too slowly to be seen, seemed to cap and fill the zenith with a white shire of cloud. I looked long up at it till the tall height and the beauty of the scaping —regularly curled knots springing if I remember from fine stems, like foliation in wood or stone—had strongly grown on me. It changed beautiful changes, growing more into ribs and one stretch of running into branching like coral. Unless you refresh the mind from time to time you cannot always remember or believe how deep the inscape in things is

March 17—In the morning clouds chalky and milk-coloured, with remarkably oyster-shell moulding. (From a rough pencil sketch) Between eleven and twelve at night a shock of earthquake

End of March and beginning of April—This is the time to study inscape in the spraying of trees, for the swelling buds carry them to a pitch which the eye could not else gather—for out of much much more, out of little not much, out of nothing nothing: in these sprays at all events there is a new world of inscape. The male ashes are very boldly jotted with the heads of the bloom which tuft the outer ends of the branches. The staff of each of these branches is closely knotted with the places where buds are or have been, so that it is something like a finger which has been tied up with string and keeps the marks. They are in knops of a pair, one on each side, and the knops are set alternately, at crosses with the knops above and the knops below, the bud of course is a short smoke-black pointed nail-head or beak pieced of four lids or nippers. Below it, like the hollow below the eye or the piece between the knuckle and the root of the nail, is a half-moon-shaped sill as if once chipped from the wood and this gives the twig its quaining in the outline. When the bud breaks at first it shews a heap of fruity purplish anthers looking something like unripe elderberries but these push open into richly-branched tree-pieces coloured buff and brown shaking out loads of pollen, and drawing the tuft as a whole into peaked quains—mainly four, I think, two bigger and two smaller

The bushes in the woods and hedgerows are spanned over and twisted upon by the woody cords of the honeysuckle: the cloves of leaf these bear are some purple, some grave green. But the young green of the briars is gay and neat and smooth as if cut in ivory.—One bay or hollow of Hodder Wood is curled all over with bright green garlic

The sycamores[3] are quite the earliest trees out: some have been fully out some days (April 15). The behaviour of the opening clusters is very beautiful and when fully opened not the single leaves but the whole tuft is strongly templed like the belly of a drum or bell

The half-opened wood-sorrel leaves, the centre or spring of the leaflets rising foremost and the leaflets dropping back like ears leaving straight-chipped clefts between them, look like some green lettering and cut as sharp as dice

The white violets are broader and smell; the blue, scentless and finer made, have a sharper whelking and a more winged recoil in the leaves

Take a *few* primroses in a glass and the instress of—brilliancy, sort of starriness: I have not the right word—so simple a flower gives is remarkable. It is, I think, due to the strong swell given by the deeper yellow middle

'The young lambs bound As to the tabour's sound'.

They toss and toss: it is as if it were the earth that flung them, not themselves. It is the pitch of graceful agility when we think that.—April 16—Sometimes they rest a little space on the hind legs and the forefeet drop curling in on the breast, not so liquidly as we see it in the limbs of foals though

May 6—First summer-feeling day—not to last long

The banks are 'versed' with primroses, partly scattered, partly in plots and squats, and at a little distance shewing milk-white or silver—little spilt till-fulls of silver. I have seen them reflected in green standing farmyard water

May 9—A simple behaviour of the cloudscape I have not realized before. Before a N.E. wind great bars or rafters of cloud all the morning and in a manner all the day marching across the sky in regular rank and with equal spaces between. They seem prism-shaped, flat-bottomed and banked up to a ridge: their make is like tufty snow in coats

This day and May 11 the bluebells in the little wood between the College and the highroad and in one of the Hurst Green cloughs. In the little wood/ opposite the light/ they stood in blackish spreads or sheddings like the spots on a snake. The heads are then like thongs and solemn in grain and grape-colour. But in the clough/ through the light/ they came in falls of sky-colour washing the brows and slacks of the ground with vein-blue, thickening at the double, vertical themselves and the young grass and brake fern combed vertical, but the brake struck the upright of all this with light winged transomes. It was a lovely sight.—The bluebells in your hand baffle you with their inscape, made to every sense: if you draw your fingers through them they are lodged and struggle/ with a shock of wet heads; the long stalks rub and click and flatten to a fan on one another like your fingers themselves would when you passed the palms hard across one another, making a brittle rub and jostle like the noise of a hurdle strained by leaning against; then there is the faint honey smell and in the mouth the sweet gum when you bite them. But this is easy, it is the eye they baffle. They give one a fancy of panpipes and of some wind instrument with stops—a trombone perhaps. The overhung necks—for growing they are little more than a staff with a simple crook but in water, where they stiffen, they take stronger turns, in the head like sheephooks or, when more waved throughout, like the waves riding through a whip that is being smacked—what with these overhung necks and what with the crisped ruffled bells dropping mostly on one side and the gloss these have at their footstalks they have an air of the knights at chess. Then the knot or 'knoop' of buds some shut, some just gaping, which makes the pencil of the whole spike, should be noticed: the inscape of the flower most finely carried out in the siding of the axes, each striking a greater and greater slant, is finished in these clustered buds, which for the most part are not straightened but rise to the end like a tongue and this and their tapering and a little flattening they have make them look like the heads of snakes

∗

. . . The ashes begin to open their knots: they make strong yellow crowns against the slaty blue sky

This spring I have a good deal noticed the warp of the leaves, single or in the cluster, for instance in lime and sycomore

May 24—At sunset and later a strongly marked moulded rack. I made out the make of it, thus—cross-hatching in fact—see April 21 and what is said there. Those may have been scarves of cloud bellying upwards but often I believe it is, as it looks in the perspective, downwards, and then they may be curds or globes and solid, geometrical solids/ that is, for all clouds are more or less cellular and hollow. Since that day and since this (May 24) I have noticed this kind of cloud: its brindled and hatched scaping though difficult to catch is remarkable when seen. I do not think it marks the direction of the flight.—Today (July 7) there has been much of this cloud and its make easily read. The solid seems given by little more than the lap or bay of a sheet.

It was a glowing yellow sunset. Pendle and all the hills rinsed clear, their heights drawn with a brimming light, in which windows or anything that could catch fluttered and laughed with the blaze—all bounded by the taught [*sic*] outline of a mealy blue shadow covering the valley, which was moist and giving up mist. Now where a strong shadow lay in a slack between two brows of Pendle appeared above the hill the same phenomenon I had seen twice before (once near Brussels), a wedge of light faintly edged, green on the right side, red on the left, as a rainbow would be, leaning to the right and skirting the brow of the hill with a glowing edge. It lasted as long as I looked without change—I do not know how long but between five minutes and quarter of an hour

perhaps. It had clouds it seemed to me *behind* it. Later when
it was growing dark and the glow of the sunset was quite
gone I noticed to the right of the spot a little—over Whalley
—a rack of red cloud floating away, the red being I am persuaded a native colour, in fact it could not have been borrowed, the sun having long set and the higher clouds behind
it not having it

*

Lancashire—'of all the wind instruments big droom fots me
best',—Old Wells directing someone how to set a wedge in a
tree told him that if he would put it so and so he would 'fot
it agate a riving'.—The omission of *the* is I think an extension
of the way in which we say 'Father', 'government' etc: they
use it when there is a relative in order to define.—They say
frae and *aboon*

June 13—A beautiful instance of inscape sided on the slide,
that is/ successive sidings of one inscape, is seen in the behaviour of the flag flower from the shut bud to the full blowing: each term you can distinguish is beautiful in itself and
of course if the whole 'behaviour' were gathered up and so
stalled it would have a beauty of all the higher degree

*

Later—The Horned Violet is a pretty thing, gracefully
lashed. Even in withering the flower ran through beautiful
inscapes by the screwing up of the petals into straight little
barrels or tubes. It is not that inscape does not govern the
behaviour of things in slack and decay as one can see even
in the pining of the skin in the old and even in a skeleton but
that horror prepossesses the mind, but in this case there was
nothing in itself to show even whether the flower were shutting or opening

The 'pinion' of the blossom in the comfrey is remarkable
for the beauty of the coil and its regular lessening to its centre. Perhaps the duller-coloured sorts shew it best

July 8—After much rain, some thunder, and no summer as
yet, the river swollen and golden and, where charged with

air, like ropes and hills of melting candy, there was this day a thunderstorm on a greater scale—huge rocky clouds lit with livid light, hail and rain that flooded the garden, and thunder ringing and echoing round like brass, so that there is in a manner earwitness to the χάλκεον οὐρανόν. The lightning seemed to me white like a flash from a lookingglass but Mr. Lentaigne in the afternoon noticed it rose-coloured and lilac. I noticed two kinds of flash but I am not sure that sometimes there were not the two together from different points of the same cloud or starting from the same point different ways —one a straight stroke, broad like a stroke with chalk and liquid, as if the blade of an oar just stripped open a ribbon scar in smooth water and it caught the light; the other narrow and wire-like, like the splitting of a rock and danced down-along in a thousand jags. I noticed this too, that there was a perceptible interval between the blaze and first inset of the flash and its score in the sky and that that seemed to be first of all laid in a bright confusion and then uttered by a tongue of brightness (what is strange) running up from the ground to the cloud, not the other way.

July 24—Robert says the first grass from the scythe is the *swathe*, then comes the *strow* (tedding), then *rowing*, then the footcocks, then *breaking*, then the *hubrows*, which are gathered into *hubs*, then sometimes another break and *turning*, then *rickles*, the biggest of all the cocks, which are run together into *placks*, the shapeless heaps from which the hay is carted

Aug. 6—Unusually bright. From Jeffrey Hill on the Longridge fell in the ridge opposite with Parlock Pike the folds and gullies with shadow in them were as sharp as the pleats in the new napkin and we made out in the sea, appearing as clearly outlined flakes of blue, the Welsh coast, Anglesea, and Man, and between these two the sea was as bright as brass.

Sept. 14—By boat down the river to Hamble, near where it enters Southampton Water, and a walk home. On this walk I

came to a cross road I had been at in the morning carrying it in another 'running instress'. I was surprised to recognise it and the moment I did it lost its present instress, breaking off from what had immediately gone before, and fell into the morning's. It is so true what Ruskin says talking of the carriage in Turner's Pass of Faido that what he could not forget was that 'he had come by the road'. And what is this running instress, so independent of at least the immediate scape of the thing, which unmistakeably distinguishes and individualises things? Not imposed outwards from the mind as for instance by melancholy or strong feeling: I easily distinguish that instress. I think it is this same running instress by which we identify or, better, test and refuse to identify with our various suggestions/ a thought which has just slipped from the mind at an interruption

Sept. 15—Among other clever things the parrot here says when wasps come near her 'Get along', ruffling her feathers with excitement. When I pull out a handkerchief she makes a noise of blowing the nose

[1872]

Feb. 23—A lunar halo: I looked at it from the upstairs library window. It was a grave grained sky, the strands rising a little from left to right. The halo was not quite round, for in the first place it was a little pulled and drawn below, by the refraction of the lower air perhaps, but what is more it fell in on the nether left hand side to rhyme the moon itself, which was not quite at full. I could not but strongly feel in my fancy the odd instress of this, the moon leaning on her side, as if fallen back, in the cheerful light floor within the ring, after with magical rightness and success tracing round her the ring the steady copy of her own outline. But this sober grey darkness and pale light was happily broken through by the orange of the pealing of Mitton bells

Another night from the gallery window I saw a brindled heaven, the moon just marked by a blue spot pushing its way through the darker cloud, underneath and on the skirts of the rack bold long flakes whitened and swaled like feather, below/ the garden with the heads of the trees and shrubs furry grey. I read a broad careless inscape flowing throughout

At the beginning of March they were felling some of the ashes in our grove

March 5—A letter from Challis saying he had left the Church

March 13—After a time of trial and especially a morning in which I did not know which way to turn as the account of De Rancé's final conversion was being read at dinner the verse *Qui confidunt in Domino sicut mons Sion* which satisfied him and resolved him to enter his abbey of La Trappe by the mercy of God came strongly home to me too, so that I was choked for a little while and could not keep in my tears

Stickles/ Devonshire for the foamy tongues of water below falls

March 23—They say here *th'hee road* for *the high road* and *steel* for *stile.*—Saw a lad burning big bundles of dry honeysuckle: the flame (though it is no longer freshly in my mind) was brown and gold, brighter and glossier than glass or silk or water and ran reeling up to the right in one long handkerchief and curling like a cartwhip

March 26—Snow fallen upon the leaves had in the night coined or morselled itself into pyramids like hail. Blade leaves of some bulbous plant, perhaps a small iris, were like delicate little saws, so hagged with frost. It is clear that things are spiked with the frost mainly on one side but why this is and how far different things on the same side at the same time I have not yet found

March 30, Holy Saturday—warm, with thunder, odd tufts of thin-textured very plump round clouds something like the eggs in an opened ant-hill

April 16—For a good many days now we have had pied skies or big flying clouds and cold west winds.

*

After the examinations we went for our holiday out to Douglas in the Isle of Man Aug. 3. At this time I had first begun to get hold of the copy of Scotus on the Sentences in the Baddely library and was flush with a new stroke of enthusiasm. It may come to nothing or it may be a mercy from God. But just then when I took in any inscape of the sky or sea I thought of Scotus

Aug. 5—Walking to Laxey, which is the next considerable bay north of Douglas—A little place Groudle or Growdale lies between—we heard a little girl sing a Manx song, though indeed it was but four lines, a rhyming couplet and the third line repeated, and she recited it only. It sounded just like English words done into nonsense verses: thus the third and fourth lines or burden seemed 'The brow shall loose, The brow shall loose'. Manx can be understood by a speaker of Irish. The people are the most goodnatured I think I have ever met

Aug. 6—The rocks are grey sandstone, in very regular slabs, cleaving like slate, and decayed between the slabs or flakes so as to look like wood rotted with water. I noticed from the cliff how the sea foots or toes the shore and the inlets, now with a push and flow, now slacking, returning to stress and pulling back

Aug. 7—Cormorants, called here Black Divers, flew by screaming

As we were bathing at a cove near a big hawk flew down chasing a little shrieking bird close beside us

We went mackerel fishing. Letting down a line baited with a piece of mackerel skin—tin or any glimmering thing will do —we drew up nine. A few feet down they look blue-silver as they rise. We fell away with the tide so as not to be able to get into the bay again and had to put in under shore south of Douglas and row/ hard under the cliffs to the Head. Looking up I saw a sheep hanging in one of the softly fluted green channels running down between the rocks of the cliff. The brow was crowned with that burning *clear* of silver light which surrounds the sun, then the sun itself leapt out with long bright spits of beams

Aug. 19—Again to Port Soderick. This time it was a beautiful day. I looked down from the cliffs at the sea breaking on the rocks at highwater of a spring tide—first, say, it is an install of green marble knotted with ragged white, then fields of white lather, the comb of the wave richly clustered and crisped in breaking, then it is broken small and so unfolding till it runs in threads and thrums twitching down the backdraught to the sea again

*

Aug. 22—To see Grace Wells' loom at Dutton Lee. She says *wark* for *warp* and *weft*, I think, for *woof* (there is perhaps some difference of meaning). There are what are called *by-ends* but I do not exactly know what: I think they are certain surplus warp-threads, at all events they come from the warp, are drawn together to a neap and taken backwards over the near end of the loom where they hang in one ball of 'clue', if I remember

*

There is a brook draining the bogs on the breadth of the ridge which has parted and moulded the whole in time and saws as it runs a deeper and deeper gully till at last it becomes a great cleave or valley. They had cut the grass and made a little hay on one slope of this and looking from the other side in swaths, which ran down towards the bottom of the cleft and had been washed by strong out, I caught an inscape as flowing and well marked almost as the frosting on glass and slabs; but I could not reproduce it afterwards with the pencil. I noticed damasking also in dry parched pieces of root of grass which strew the place and have perhaps fallen from the sheeps' mouths in browsing. Also I saw the same clustered-shaft make in softy miry peat (all bearing one way) as I have remarked on in snow

*

Oct. 5—A goldencrested wren had got into my room at night and circled round dazzled by the gaslight on the white cieling;[4] when caught even and put out it would come in again. Ruffling the crest, which is mounted over the crown and eyes like beetlebrows, I smoothed and fingered the little orange and yellow feathers which are hidden in it. Next morning I found many of these about the room and enclosed them in a letter to Cyril on his wedding day

✳

Ground sheeted with taut tattered streaks of crisp gritty snow. Greenwhite tufts of long bleached grass like heads of hair or the crowns of heads of hair, each a whorl of slender curves, one tuft taking up another—however these I might have noticed any day. I saw the inscape though freshly, as if my eye were still growing, though with a companion the eye and the ear are for the most part shut and instress cannot come. We started pheasants and a grouse with flickering wings. On the slope of the far side under the trees the fern looked ginger-coloured over the snow. When there was no snow and dark greens about, as I saw it just over the stile at the top of the Forty-Acre the other day, It made bats and splinters of smooth caky road-rut-colour

Dec. 19—Under a dark sky walking by the river at Brockennook. There all was sad-coloured and the colour caught the eye, red and blue stones in the river beaches brought out by patches of white-blue snow, that is/ snow quite white and dead but yet it seems as if some blue or lilac screen masked it somewhere between it and the eye: I have often noticed it. The swells and hillocks of the river sands and the fields were

sketched and gilded out by frill upon frill of snow—they must be seen: this is only to shew which way the curve lies. Where the snow lies as in a field the damasking of white light and silvery shade may be watched indeed till brightness and glare is all lost in a perplexity of shadow and in the whitest of things the sense of white is lost, but at a shorter gaze I see two degrees in it—the darker, facing the sky, and the lighter in the tiny cliffs or scarps where the snow is broken or raised into ridges, these catching the sun perhaps or at all events more directly hitting the eye and gilded with an arch brightness, like the sweat in the moist hollow between the eyebrows and the eyelids on a hot day or in the way the light of a taper Tommy was screening with his hand the other morning in the dark refectory struck out the same shells of the eyes and the cleft of the nostril and flat of the chin and tufts on the cheeks in gay leaves of gold

[1873]

Feb. 24—In the snow flat-topped hillocks and shoulders outlined with wavy edges, ridge below ridge, very like the grain of wood in line and in projection like relief maps. These the wind makes I think and of course drifts, which are in fact snow waves. The sharp nape of a drift is sometimes broken by slant flutes or channels. I think this must be when the wind after shaping the drift first has changed and cast waves in the body of the wave itself. All the world is full of inscape and chance left free to act falls into an order as well as purpose: looking out of my window I caught it in the random clods and broken heaps of snow made by the cast of a broom. The same of the path trenched by footsteps in ankledeep snow across the fields leading to Hodder wood through which we went to see the river. The sun was bright, the broken brambles and all boughs and banks limed and cloyed with white, the brook down the clough pulling its way by drops and by bubbles in turn under a shell of ice

In March there was much snow

April 8—The ashtree growing in the corner of the garden was felled. It was lopped first: I heard the sound and looking out and seeing it maimed there came at that moment a great pang and I wished to die and not to see the inscapes of the world destroyed any more

May 11—Bluebells in Hodder wood, all hanging their heads one way. I caught as well as I could while my companions talked the Greek rightness of their beauty, the

lovely/ what people call/ 'gracious' bidding one to another or
all one way, the level or stage or shire of colour they make
hanging in the air a foot above the grass, and a notable glare
the eye may abstract and sever from the blue colour/ of light
beating up from so many glassy heads, which like water is
good to float their deeper instress in upon the mind

June 16—Still brighter and warmer, southern-like. Shadows sharp in the quarry and on the shoulders of our two
young white pigeons. There is some charm about a thing such
as these pigeons or trees when they dapple their boles in
wearing its own shadow. I was on the fells with Mr. Strappini.
They were all melled and painted with colour and full of
roaming scents, and winged silver slips of young brake rising
against the light trim and symmetrical and gloried from
within reminded me of I do not remember what detail of
coats of arms, perhaps the lilies of Eton College. Meadows
smeared yellow with buttercups and bright squares of rape-
field in the landscape. Fine-weather bales of cloud. Napkin
folds brought out on the Parlick ridge and capfulls of shadow
in them. A cuckoo flew by with a little bird after it as we lay
by the quarry at Kemble End

As I passed the stables later and stayed to look at the peacocks John Myerscough came out to shew me a brood of little
peafowl (though it could not be found at that time) and the
kindness touched my heart

I looked at the pigeons down in the kitchen yard and so
on. They look like little gay juds by shape when they walk,
strutting and jod-jodding with their heads. The two young
ones are all white and the pins of the folded wings, quill
pleated over quill, are like crisp and shapely cuttleshells
found on the shore. The others are dull thundercolour or
black-grape-colour except in the white pieings, the quills and
tail, and in the shot of the neck. I saw one up on the eaves of
the roof: as it moved its head a crush of satin green came and
went, a wet or soft flaming of the light

Sometimes I hear the cuckoo with wonderful clear and
plump and fluty notes: it is when the hollow of a rising
ground conceives them and palms them up and throws them

out, like blowing into a big humming ewer—for instance under Saddle Hill one beautiful day and another time from Hodder wood when we walked on the other side of the river

July 22—Very hot, though the wind, which was south, dappled very sweetly on one's face and when I came out I seemed to put it on like a gown as a man puts on the shadow he walks into and hoods or hats himself with the shelter of a roof, a penthouse, or a copse of trees, I mean it rippled and fluttered like light linen, one could feel the folds and braids of it—and indeed a floating flag is like wind visible and what weeds are in a current; it gives it thew and fires it and bloods it in.—Thunderstorm in the evening, first booming in gong-sounds, as at Aosta, as if high up and so not reechoed from the hills; the lightning very slender and nimble and as if playing very near but after supper it was so bright and terrible some people said they had never seen its like. People were killed, but in other parts of the country it was more violent than with us. Flashes lacing two clouds above or the cloud and the earth started upon the eyes in live veins of rincing or riddling liquid white, inched and jagged as if it were the shivering of a bright riband string which had once been kept bound found a blade and danced back into its pleatings. Several strong thrills of light followed the flash but a grey smother of darkness blotted the eyes if they had seen the fork, also dull furry thickened scapes of it were left in them

July 24—A Blandyke.[5] Mr. Colley and I crossed the river at Hacking boat, went up the fell opposite near the Nab, walked some way, and coming down at Billington recrossed at the Troughs and so home. But the view was dim. A farmer on the other side at the Troughs talked of the driver of the mower (he had one) 'a-peerkin' on the seat', being perched on the seat, and said the hay was to be 'shaked'. The ferryman told us how in the hot days working in the hay he had 'Su̇pped beer till' he 'could su̇p no more'

Aug. 1—To Derby Castle at Douglas as last year
Aug. 5—Up Snae Fell with Mr. Shapter. You can see from

it the three kingdoms. The day was bright; pied skies. On the way back we saw eight or perhaps ten hawks together

Aug. 7—Baron von Hügel came to say goodbye to us

Aug. 8—Wan white sea with a darker edge on the skyline, very calm. At sunset from above it looked milky blue with blue cording of waves. Sunset fine—spokes of dusty gold; long wing of brownish cloud warping/ in the perspective. I marked well how the sea fell over from the other side of the bay, Fort Hillion and the lighthouse, to the cliff's foot, quite like the rounding of waterfall

Aug. 9—Mackerel fishing but not much sport. Besides I was in pain and could not look at things much. When the fresh-caught fish flounced in the bottom of the boat they made scapes of motion, quite as strings do, nodes and all, silver bellies upwards—something thus. Their key markings do not correspond on the two sides of the backbone. They changed colour as they lay. There was sun and wind. I saw the waves to seaward frosted with light silver surf but did not find out much, afterwards from the cliffs I saw the sea paved with wind—clothed and purpled all over with ribbons of wind

Some yellow spoons came up with the tumblers after dinner. Somebody said they were brass and I tasted them to find out and it seemed so. Some time afterwards as I came in from a stroll with Mr. Purbrick he told me Hügel had said the scarlet or rose-colour of flaminggos [sic] was found to be due to a fine copper powder on the feathers. As he said this I tasted the brass in my mouth. It is what they call unconscious cerebration, a bad phrase

Aug. 12—We made an expedition to North Barrule or rather to the inn at its foot and then dispersed. Mr. Gillett and I went down to the sea and bathed in a little shingly bay, where above the beach there stretches a small plain of grass flooded by the springtides, through which the brook runs to the sea. We passed the beautiful little mill-hamlet of Balaglas in the glen and started a shining flight of doves to settle on the roof. There is a green rich thickleaved alder by the bridge and ashes and rocks maroon-red below water up the glen. When we were back there we turned aside to follow the

brook up under groves of beech and Spanish chestnut. The
rock is limestone, smooth and pale white, not rough and
gritty, and without moss, stained red where the water runs
and smoothly and vertically hewed by the force of the brook
into highwalled channels with deep pools. The water is so
clear in the still pools it is like shadowy air and in the falls
the white is not foamed and chalky, as at Stonyhurst, but like
the white of ice or glass. Round holes are scooped in the
rocks smooth and true like turning: they look like the hollow
of a vault or bowl. I saw and sketched as well as in the rain
I could one of them that was in the making: a blade of water
played on it and shaping to it spun off making a bold big
white bow coiling its edge over and splaying into ribs. But
from the position it is not easy to see how the water could in
this way have scooped all of them. I jumped into one of the
pools above knee deep and it was raining besides; so to keep
warm, when we reached the high road I turned towards
Douglas and let them overtake me. We got home in heavy
wet and Mr. Sidgreaves covered me under his plaid

Aug. 16—We rose at four, when it was stormy and I saw
dun-coloured waves leaving trailing hoods of white breaking
on the beach. Before going I took a last look at the breakers,
wanting to make out how the comb is morselled so fine into
string and tassel, as I have lately noticed it to be. I saw big
smooth flinty waves, carved and scuppled in shallow grooves,
much swelling when the wind freshened, burst on the rocky
spurs of the cliff at the little cove and break into bushes of
foam. In an enclosure of rocks the peaks of the water romped
and wandered and a light crown of tufty scum standing high
on the surface kept slowly turning round: chips of it blew
off and gadded about without weight in the air. At eight we
sailed for Liverpool in wind and rain. I think it is the salt that
makes rain at sea sting so much. There was a good-looking
young man on board that got drunk and sung 'I want to go
home to Mamma'. I did not look much at the sea: the crests
I saw ravelled up by the wind into the air in arching whips
and straps of glassy spray and higher broken into clouds of
white and blown away. Under the curl shone a bright juice

of beautiful green. The foam exploding and smouldering under water makes a chrysoprase green. From Blackburn I walked: infinite stiles and sloppy fields, for there has been much rain. A few big shining drops hit us aslant as if they were blown off from eaves or leaves. Bright sunset: all the sky hung with tall tossed clouds, in the west with strong printing glass edges, westward lamping with tipsy buff-light, the colour of yellow roses. Parlick ridge like a pale goldish skin without body. The plain about Clitheroe was sponged out by a tall white storm of rain. The sun itself and the spot of 'session' dappled with big laps and flowers-in-damask of cloud. But we hurried too fast and it knocked me up. We went to the College, the seminary being wanted for the secular priests' retreat: almost no gas, for the retorts are being mended; therefore candles in bottles, things not ready, darkness and despair. In fact being unwell I was quite downcast: nature in all her parcels and faculties gaped and fell apart, *fatiscebat,* like a clod cleaving and holding only by strings of root. But this must often be

We found the German Divines from Ditton Hall with their rector and professors spending their villa at the college.—Fr. George Porter is new master of novices

Aug. 17—The Germans gave us a concert and again on the 19th, I think, and we a return with jokes of various kinds on the 21st

Aug. 22—We went back to the Seminary

Aug. 27—Farewell concert from the Germans, who went back to Ditton next day. They were kind, amiable, and edifying people. Some of us went down to Whalley with them and afterwards I walked with Herbert Lucas by the river and talked Scotism with him for the last time. In the evening I received orders to go to Roehampton to teach rhetoric and started next morning early, by Preston, travelling to town with Vaughan and Considine, who were bound for Beaumont. At Manresa I caught the Provincial who spoke most kindly and encouragingly

Aug. 30—Sept. 8—Retreat, of which there are notes in my meditation papers. I received as I think a great mercy about Dolben

Sept. 8—Mr. Macloughlen was here on his way from Laval.

I talked to Mr. Duffy ploughing: he told me the names of the cross, side-plate, muzzle, regulator, and short chain. He talked of something *spraying* out, meaning *splaying* out and of combing the ground

I counted in a bright rainbow two, perhaps three/ complete octaves, that is/ three, perhaps four/ strikings of the keynote or nethermost red, counting from the outermost red rim: this of course is quite independent of a double rainbow, which this also happened to be

Oct. 17—Woodpigeons come in flock into our field and on our trees: they flock at this time of year

A doe comes to our sunken fence to be fed: she eats acorns and chestnuts and stands on the bank, a pretty triped, forefeet together and hind set apart. The bucks grunt all night at this season and fight often: it is their season

At the end of the month hard frosts. Wonderful downpour of leaf: when the morning sun began to melt the frost they fell at one touch and in a few minutes a whole tree was flung of them; they lay masking and papering the ground at the foot. Then the tree seems to be looking down on its cast self as blue sky on snow after a long fall, its losing, its doing

White poplar leaves at this season silver behind, olive black in front. Birch leaves on a fading tree give three colours, green, white, and yellow

[1874]

April 6—Sham fight on the Common, 7000 men, chiefly volunteers. Went up in the morning to get an impression but it was too soon, however got this—caught that inscape in the horse that you see in the pediment especially and other basreliefs of the Parthenon and even which Sophocles had felt and expresses in two choruses of the *Oedipus Coloneus*, running on the likeness of a horse to a breaker, a wave of the sea curling over. I looked at the groin or the flank and saw how the set of the hair symmetrically flowed outwards from it to all parts of the body, so that, following that one may inscape the whole beast very simply.—They kept firing the furze—brown-ambery flames, waving in grasslines and leaping off in laces and tatters, landscape sweating through gadroons and turbulent liquid vapour as through bullseye glass, burnt twigs flying. Would have gone again in the afternoon, only Mr. Hunnybun and a friend called: however we did stand outside our gate and saw the march past and an unsheathing of swords by some cavalry, which is a stirring naked-steel lightning bit of business, I think

I made the following notes on gems—Beryl/ watery green; carnelian/ strong flesh red, Indian red; almandine/ purplish red; chalcedony/ some/ milky blue, some/ opalescent blue-green, some/ blue-green with sparkles, some/ dull yellow green, dull olive, lilac, white; jacinth/ brownish red, dull tawny scarlet; chrysoprase/ beautiful half-transparent green, some/ dull with dark cloudings; sardonyx/ milky blue flake in brown; topaz/ white, madder, sherry-colour, yellow, pale blue, wallflower red; 'dard sard' seemed purplish black; jasper (or chalcedony)/ dull flesh brown; chrysolith/ bluish with yellow gleam or *vice versa*, also pale yellow-green, also yellow—transparent; cymophane/ beautiful stone and name

April 20—Young elmleaves lash and lip the sprays. This has been a very beautiful day—fields about us deep green lighted underneath with white daisies, yellower fresh green of leaves above which bathes the skirts of the elms, and their tops are touched and worded with leaf too. Looked at the big limb of that elm that hangs over into the Park at the swinggate/ further out than where the leaves were open and saw beautiful inscape, home-coiling wiry bushes of spray, touched with bud to point them. Blue shadows fell all up the meadow at sunset and then standing at the far Park corner my eye was struck by such a sense of green in the tufts and pashes of grass, with purple shadow thrown back on the dry black mould behind them, as I do not remember ever to have been exceeded in

looking at green grass. I marked this down on a slip of paper at the time, because the eye for colour, rather the zest in the mind, seems to weaken with years, but now the paper is mislaid

July 9. To the Oratory. Addis was away but Fr. Law was kind and hospitable. I met Mr. David Lewis, a great Scotist, and at the same time old Mr. Brande Morris was making a retreat with us: I got to know him, so that oddly I made the acquaintance of two and I suppose the only two Scotists in England in one week.

Heat has come on now. The air is full of the sweet acid of the limes. The trees themselves are starrily tasselled with the blossom. I remark that our cedars, which had a warp upward in the flats of leaf, in getting their new green turn and take a soft and beautiful warp downwards: whether it is the lushness or the weight of the young needles or both I cannot tell. They are now very beautiful in shape and colour

July 12. I noticed the smell of the big cedar, not just in passing it but always at a patch of sunlight on the walk a little way off. I found the bark smelt in the sun and not in the shade and I fancied too this held even of the smell it shed in the air

July 13—The comet—I have seen it at bedtime in the west, with head to the ground, white, a soft well-shaped tail, not big: I felt a certain awe and instress, a feeling of strangeness, flight (it hangs like a shuttlecock at the height, before it falls), and of threatening

✳

In the evening I went by myself up the hills towards Bishopsteignton, by a place a little girl called Ke-am or Ku-am, perhaps she meant Coomb. Before reaching that, just out of Teignmouth, I looked over a hedge down to a row of seven slender rich elms at a bottom between two steep fields: the run of the trees and their rich and handsome leafage charmed and held me. It is a little nearer the sea in the same coomb the little girl spoke of indeed. Then near Bishopsteignton from a hilltop I looked into a lovely comb that gave

me the instress of *Weeping Winifred,* which all the west
country seems to me to have: soft maroon or rosy cocoa-dust-
coloured handkerchiefs or ploughfields, sometimes delicately
combed with rows of green, their hedges bending in flowing
outlines and now misted a little by the beginning of twilight
ran down into it upon the shoulders of the hills; in the bottom
crooked rows of rich tall elms, foreshortened by position,
wound through it: some cornfields were still being carried

The next day I was walking with Considine on the hills
from near this same spot towards Dawlish. It rained (as it
keeps doing) and this blotted out the views. However I
looked into this same and other coombs. I saw how delicately
beautiful the orchards look—from far above: the wrought-
over boughs of the appletrees made an embroidery and whole
head and wood a soft tufting and discolouring which were
melted by the distance and the rain.—: A steep sloping field
in which the sheaves were scattered and left in the rain, not
made into stooks (which by the by the Devonshire people
call shocks): at a distance they looked like straw-wisps

Aug. 17—We went over to Ugbrooke at Lord Clifford's invitation. He took us over the park, to Chudleigh Rocks, which
are a cliff over a deep and beautiful cleave quite closed with
ash-trees into which we looked down; to the Danish Camp (it
seems to be Roman but was used in Alfred's war with the
Danes—the steep *vallum* is now grown with trees, mainly
sycomore; later to a spot where Dryden wrote the *Hind and
Panther;* and to a great oak, now in its decay and shrinking
in size by the fall of its branches from time to time, which
serves as a landmark for two parishes and goes by the name
of Great Rawber (or Rowber, I think, like *how*), probably
a corruption of Magnum Robur in Latin deeds.—: Beeches
rich in leaf, rather brown in colour, one much spread—: Tall
larches on slope of a hill near the lake and mill, also a wychelm, also a beech, both of these with ivory-white bark pied
with green moss: there was an instress about this spot—:
Beautiful glittering planes—: Two great spreading laurels, one
upheld by props—: A little olivetree: leaves like privet (it is
akin to privet and ash, Mr. Sircom said) but stiffer, pricked

at the end, sober green lined with grey, the sprays free and graceful; bark smooth and grey; habit of tree trim. The day was fine, the park is beautiful, especially from the falls of ground—great brows falling over to the lakes and clothed with fern and clumps of trees and woods. In the house we were shewn a wonderful piece of embroidery—bedhangings, now taken down and displayed on great folding screens: they are of a Lady Clifford's work (they say 21 people worked 21 yrs. at them: now though there is a great deal of work of them I should have thought that number of people could have done them in that number of days) and are praised in a letter to Mrs. Delany—flowers and festoons and scarves and other half-architectural details; the designs of the flowers graceful and the execution delicate.—I liked the family: all the children spoke in a very frank and simple way which shewed innocence as well as good breeding. As we drove home the stars came out thick: I leant back to look at them and my heart opening more than usual praised our Lord to and in whom all that beauty comes home

Aug. 30—Walked with Mr. Bacan to Cŵm churchyard

Aug. 31—Walking with Henry Kerr. We talked to the old lodgekeeper at Bryn Bella: She will be 89 next month. She had been servant there to Mrs. Piozzi, Mrs. Thrale that was. Also she told us she was a Tremeirchion Cow: there are the Cŵm Calves, the Caerwys Crows, the Denbigh Cats

A silvery-brown blindworm was gliding over the road.— Hardhead, crosswort, agrimony

Sept. 6—With Wm. Kerr, who took me up a hill behind ours (ours is Mynefyr), a furze-grown and heathy hill, from which I could look round the whole country, up the valley towards Ruthin and down to the sea. The cleave in which Bodfari and Caerwys lie was close below. It was a leaden sky, braided or roped with cloud, and the earth in dead colours, grave but distinct. The heights by Snowdon were hidden by the clouds but not from distance or dimness. The nearer hills, the other side of the valley, shewed a hard and

beautifully detached and glimmering brim against the light, which was lifting there. All the length of the valley the sky-line of hills was flowingly written all along upon the sky. A blue bloom, a sort of meal, seemed to have spread upon the distant south, enclosed by a basin of hills. Looking all round but most in looking far up the valley I felt an instress and charm of Wales. Indeed in coming here I began to feel a desire to do something for the conversion of Wales. I began to learn Welsh too but not with very pure intentions perhaps. However on consulting the Rector on this, the first day of the retreat, he discouraged it unless it were purely for the sake of labouring among the Welsh. Now it was not and so I saw I must give it up. At the same time my music seemed to come to an end. Yet, rather strangely, I had no sooner given up these two things (which disappointed me and took an interest away—and at that time I was very bitterly feeling the weariness of life and shed many tears, perhaps not wholly into the breast of God but with some unmanliness in them too, and sighed and panted to Him), I had no sooner given up the Welsh than my desire seemed to be for the conversion of Wales and I had it in mind to give up everything else for that; nevertheless weighing this by St. Ignatius' rules of election I decided not to do so

✳

Sept. 24—Very bright and clear. I was with Mr. Rickaby on the hill above the house. All the landscape had a beautiful liquid cast of blue. Many-coloured smokes in the valley, grey from the Denbigh lime-kiln, yellow and lurid from two kilns perhaps on the shoulders of a hill, blue from a bonfire, and so on

Afterwards a lovely sunset of rosy juices and creams and combs; the combs I mean scattered floating bats or rafts or racks above, the creams/ the strew and bed of the sunset, passing north and south or rather north only into grey mares-tail and brush along the horizon to the hills. Afterwards the rosy field of the sundown turned gold and the slips and creamings in it stood out like brands, with jots of purple. A sodden twilight over the valley and foreground all below, holding the corner-hung maroon-grey diamonds of ploughfields to one keeping but allowing a certain glare in the green of the near tufts of grass

Sept. 27—At rising I saw a long slender straight river of dull white cloud rolling down all the bed of the Clwyd from as far as I could look up the valley to the sea, in height perhaps twice as high as the Cathedral tower. Its outline rose and fell regularly in low or shallow waves or swellings like smooth knots in a bamboo and these swellings seemed not to be upwards only but also to bulge every way, encroaching on the fields as well. I could also see that it had a flaky or vertebrated make, the flakes leaning forward and curling and falling over a little. St. Asaph with the tower and trees and other spots appeared in grey washes at thinnings or openings of the mist.—At that time it was dull but cleared to a lovely day—we have been having indeed a second summer—, but in the evening a fog came suddenly on and then cleared again

Oct. 2—There is a splendid thick-stemmed carnation-coloured lily called valotta. I saw one in the greenhouse next to an agapanthus on the same shelf: the chord of colour and even the bidding of shape in the two heads struck me very much

Oct. 8—Bright and beautiful day. Crests of snow could be seen on the mountains. Barraud and I walked over to Holywell and bathed at the well and returned very joyously. The sight of the water in the well as clear as glass, greenish like beryl or aquamarine, trembling at the surface with the force of the springs, and shaping out the five foils of the well quite drew and held my eyes to it. Within a month or six weeks from this (I think Fr. di Pietro said) a young man from Liverpool, Arthur Kent (?), was cured of rupture/ in the water. The strong unfailing flow of the water and the chain of cures from year to year all these centuries took hold of my mind with wonder at the bounty of God in one of His saints, the sensible thing so naturally and gracefully uttering the spiritual reason of its being (which is all in true keeping with the story of St. Winefred's death and recovery) and the spring in place leading back the thoughts by its spring in

time to its spring in eternity: even now the stress and buoyancy and abundance of the water is before my eyes

Nov. 8—Walking with Wm. Splaine we saw a vast multitude of starlings making an unspeakable jangle. They would
settle in a row of trees; then, one tree after another, rising
at a signal they looked like a cloud of specks of black snuff
or powder struck up from a brush or broom or shaken from
a wig; then they would sweep round in whirlwinds—you
could see the nearer and farther bow of the rings by the size
and blackness; many would be in one phase at once, all narrow black flakes hurling round, then in another; then they
would fall upon a field and so on. Splaine wanted a gun:
then 'there it would rain meat' he said. I thought they must
be full of enthusiasm and delight hearing their cries and stirring and cheering one another

III

POETIC THEORY

We should explain things, plainly state them, clear
them up, explain them; explanation—except per-
sonal—is always pure good; without explanation
people go on misunderstanding; being once ex-
plained they thenceforward understand things;
therefore always explain: but I have the passion
for explanation.

TO ALEXANDER BAILLIE[1]

Sept. 6. 1863.

DEAR BAILLIE,—And I hope I may never hold my own
in argument more, if I do not succeed in putting you out of
conceit with your canon of criticism. I cannot but think it a
little weak of you, you must pardon me for saying it, in this
and other cases, so entirely to be engrossed with one side of a
question that you cannot even see that another side exists: I
should fancy that you would aspire to a reputation for judgment, but if so, you ought to know that nothing so impairs
that reputation as the strong assertion of half-truths. And this
is what you are continually doing. If your canon is pro-
pounded as a paradox (though you hate paradoxes, I believe) it has no brilliancy, if as a deliberate belief I call it
remarkably weak. Surely it is a shallow thing, because there
are bad, narrow-minded, irritating and feeble critics, to forbid

the possibility of fine critics arising. Why not, on your grounds, disbelieve in the poets, because Nahum and Tate, Pye, Dr. Watts, Dr. Johnson, Eliza Cook and Close, the king of Bonny's laureate, have supposed themselves so? Is there no majesty in judgment? You have not far to look for a man whose whole powers have been devoted to criticism, powers which in their line are perhaps equal to those of the men whose works he criticises. Now Ruskin is a critic whom you admire. Criticism I own is a rare gift, poetical criticism at all events, but it does exist. You speak with horror of Shaksperian criticism, but it appears to me that among Shakspere's critics have been seen instances of genius, of deep insight, of great delicacy, of power, of poetry, of ingenuity, of everything a critic should have. I will instance Schlegel, Coleridge, Charles Lamb, Mrs. Jameson. While I attack your canon, remember that no one is more disgusted than I am at bad criticism. How I have hated *The Quarterly, The Edinburgh* and *Blackwood!* How I have longed for their utter extinction! And how exasperated I have felt with Dr. Johnson, or in our times with the snarls of *The Athenaeum!* But what offends me even more than wicked criticism is feebleness, such as *you* find in Forbiger, and I have seen a conspicuous instance of lately in George Brimley's essays, in the critique on Tennyson. This Brimley was a well-meaning, well-educated man, with much good sense, judgment and even in some cases discernment and taste, at whose death his friends published the essays which bear his name. You could only understand by reading him, how all the good qualities I have given him are ruined by what Ruskin would call 'gentlemanly feebleness'.

A perfect critic is very rare, I know. Ruskin often goes astray; Servius, the commentator on Virgil, whom I admire, is often too observant and subtle for his author, but nevertheless their excellences utterly outweigh their defects. The most inveterate fault of critics is the tendency to cramp and hedge in by rules the free movements of genius, so that I should say, according to the Demosthenic and Catonic expression, the first requisite for a critic is liberality, and the second liberality, and the third, liberality. But more than enough about criticism and criticism on criticism. I agree with you, you know, about general rules, but you are not nearly the first to object to them. You are only uttering your version of the often repeated warning against the dangers of generalizations.

We have had really Scotch weather here, rain in torrents day after day, for a week past. By the bye, a lady assures me she never passed through Edinburgh but what it was raining, except once when no rain was falling but there was a damp mist over all. Indeed the same is said on all hands. But perhaps the severest thing said of Edinburgh you may remember occurs in the conversation below—'But does it always rain here?' says the friend who has been staying at Edinburgh for a month of broad Bible-loving Scottish wet: 'Oh dear no', says the acclimatized Edinburgher, 'it sometimes snows'.

I am sorry also to have to differ from you *in toto* on another point. You say 'prejudices are *ipso facto weak* and foolish'. You say this *apropos* of my Anti-Scottish prejudice. Now whether that is '*weak* and foolish' is not the question; disabuse me of it if you reasonably can; but you are quite wrong about prejudices themselves. I cannot now enter into the discussion of the subject. I will only mention that my opinions on it, expressed some time ago in a school essay, were confirmed by a late article in *The Saturday*, which of course I was glad to see, on Prejudice or Prejudices. Read it if you can, but at all events ask yourselves in a thorough and unconventional manner whether Prejudices are what you say —or whether they are not, on the contrary, often a passive, and sometimes almost an active wisdom. I dare assert virtue has few greater supports than what you think so necessarily bad, prejudices. But we will have a passage of arms at Owsenford on Themmes, in the moneth of Octobre, next after ensuing, on this subject.

I am sorry to say I cannot send you a sketch. All my pencil sketches are in a book, coloured sketches I have none, and I have not the time to copy one in ink. However though I have not the opportunity of sending you anything now, I will try and keep something for you. I do not promise, but will try.

If you should write again—I should like a letter, of course but you may not think it worth while so late in the Long—

address Oak Hill, Hampstead, N.W. We leave Shanklin on Friday.

I am afraid you object to being critic of MS poetry; on one occasion I remember when I shewed you some, only a translation of a chorus in the *Prometheus Bound,* you would give no opinion on it. Indeed, I believe you were right, it is the only safe course. I hate being asked to criticize what I cannot praise. However it is absurd to speak of a critic who does not open his lips. The upshot of this is that I come under the list of those whom you anathematize so much, the writers of the new unnecessary poetry, and need a critic often, and often am dispirited. I will not however ask you to be my critic, for I should put you, I suppose, in an uncomfortable office, if you accepted it, if not, and you were silent, what good would you be to me? Now that I have said so much it appears to me that I might just as well have left it unsaid.

I must now conclude a dull and, I am afraid you will think, rather impertinent letter. Believe me, dear Baillie,

Yours affectionately,

GERARD M. HOPKINS.

TO ALEXANDER BAILLIE

Sept. 10. 1864.

DEAR BAILLIE,—Your letter has been sent to me from Hampstead. It has just come, and I do a rare thing with me, begin at once on an answer. I have just finished *The Philippics* of Cicero and an hour remains before bedtime; no one except Wharton would begin a new book at that time of night, so I was reading *Henry IV,* when your letter was brought in—a great enjoyment.

The letter-writer on principle does not make his letter only an *answer;* it is a work embodying perhaps answers to questions put by his correspondent but that is not its main motive. Therefore it is as a rule not well to write with a received letter fresh on you. I suppose the right way is to let it sink into you, and reply after a day or two. I do not know why I have said all this.

Do you know, a horrible thing has happened to me. I have

begun to *doubt* Tennyson. (Baillejus ap. Hopk.) It is a great *argumentum*, a great clue, that our minds jump together even if it be a leap into the dark. I cannot tell you how amused and I must say pleased and comforted by this coincidence I am. A little explanation first. You know I do not mistrust my judgment so soon as you do; I say it to the praise of your modesty. Therefore I do not think myself 'getting into my dotage' for that, and I will shew why. I think (I am assuming a great deal in saying this I fear) I may shew, judging from my own mind, how far we are both of us right in this, and on what, if I may use the word, more enlightened ground we may set our admiration of Tennyson. I have been thinking about this on and off since I read *Enoch Arden* and the other new poems, so that my judgment is more digested than if the ideas had only struck me while answering you. I was shaken too you know by Addis, which makes a good deal of difference.

I am meditating an essay, perhaps for the *Hexameron*, on some points of poetical criticism, and it is with reference to this a little that I have composed my thoughts on Tennyson. I think then the language of verse may be divided into three kinds. The first and highest is poetry proper, the language of inspiration. The word inspiration need cause no difficulty. I mean by it a mood of great, abnormal in fact, mental acuteness, either energetic or receptive, according as the thoughts which arise in it seem generated by a stress and action of the brain, or to strike into it unasked. This mood arises from various causes, physical generally, as good health or state of the air or, prosaic as it is, length of time after a meal. But I need not go into this; all that it is needful to mark is, that the poetry of inspiration can only be written in this mood of mind, even if it only last a minute, by poets themselves. Everybody of course has like moods, but not being poets what they then produce is not poetry. The second kind I call *Parnassian*. It can only be spoken by poets, but is not in the highest sense poetry. It does not require the mood of mind in which the poetry of inspiration is written. It is spoken *on and from the level* of a poet's mind, not, as in the other case, when the inspiration which is the gift of genius raises him above himself. For I think it is the case with genius that it is not when quiescent so very much above mediocrity as the difference between the two might lead us to think, but that it has the power and privilege of rising from that level to a height utterly far from mediocrity: in other words that its greatness is *that it can be* so great. You will understand. *Parnassian* then is that language which genius speaks as fitted to its exaltation, and place among other genius, but does not sing (I have been betrayed into the whole hog of a metaphor) in its flights. Great men, poets I mean, have each their own dialect as it were of Parnassian, formed generally as they go on writing, and at last,—this is the point to be marked,— they can see things in this Parnassian way and describe them in this Parnassian tongue, without further effort of inspiration. In a poet's particular kind of Parnassian lies most of his style, of his manner, of his mannerism if you like. But I must not go farther without giving you instances of Parnassian. I shall take one from Tennyson, and from *Enoch Arden,* from a passage much quoted already and which will be no doubt often quoted, the description of Enoch's tropical island.

> The mountain wooded to the peak, the lawns
> And winding glades high up like ways to Heaven,
> The slender coco's drooping crown of plumes,
> The lightning flash of insect and of bird,
> The lustre of the long convolvuluses
> That coil'd around the stately stems, and ran
> Ev'n to the limit of the land, the glows
> And glories of the broad belt of the world,
> All these he saw.

Now it is a mark of Parnassian that one could conceive oneself writing it if one were the poet. Do not say that *if* you were Shakespear you can imagine yourself writing Hamlet, because that is just what I think you can*not* conceive. In a fine piece of inspiration every beauty takes you as it were by surprise, not of course that you did not think the writer could be so great, for that is not it,—indeed I think it is a mistake to speak of people admiring Shakespear more and more as they live, for when the judgment is ripe and you have read a good deal of any writer including his best things, and carefully, then, I think, however high the place you give him, that you must have rated him equally with his merits however great they be; so that all after admiration cannot increase but keep alive this estimate, make his greatness stare into your eyes and din it into your ears, as it were, but not make it greater,—but to go on with the broken sentence, every fresh beauty could not in any way be predicted or accounted for by what one has already read. But in Parnassian pieces you feel that if you were the poet you could have gone on as he has done, you see yourself doing it, only with the difference that if you actually try you find you cannot write his Parnassian. Well now to turn to the piece above. The glades being 'like ways to Heaven' is, I think a new thought, it is an inspiration. Not so the next line, that is pure Parnassian. If you examine it the words are choice and the description is beautiful and unexceptionable, but it does not *touch* you. The next is more Parnassian still. In the next lines I think the picture of the convolvuluses does touch; but only the picture: the words are Parnassian. It is a very good instance, for the lines are undoubtedly beautiful, but yet I could scarcely point anywhere to anything more idiomatically Parnassian, to anything which I more clearly see myself writing *qua* Tennyson, than the words

> The glows
> And glories of the broad belt of the world.

What Parnassian is you will now understand, but I must make some more remarks on it. I believe that when a poet palls on us it is because of his Parnassian. We seem to have found out his secret. Now in fact we have not found out more than this, that when he is not inspired and in his flights, his poetry does run in an intelligibly laid down path. Well, it is notorious that Shakespear does not pall, and this is because he uses, I believe, so little Parnassian. He does use some, but little. Now judging from my own experience I should say no author palls so much as Wordsworth; this is because he writes such an 'intolerable deal of' Parnassian.

If with a critical eye and in a critical appreciative mood you read a poem by an unknown author or an anonymous poem by a known, but not at once recognizable, author, and he is a real poet, then you will pronounce him so at once, and the poem will seem truly inspired, though afterwards, when you know the author, you will be able to distinguish his inspiration from his Parnassian, and will perhaps think the very piece which struck you so much at first mere Parnassian. You know well how deadened, as it were, the critical faculties become at times, when all good alike loses its clear ring and its charm; while in other moods they are so enlivened that things that have long lost their freshness strike you with their original definiteness and piquant beauty.

I think one had got into the way of thinking, or had not got out of the way of thinking, that Tennyson was always new, *touching*, beyond other poets, not pressed with human ailments, never using Parnassian. So at least I used to think. Now one sees he uses Parnassian; he is, one must see it, what we used to call Tennysonian. But the discovery of this must not make too much difference. When puzzled by one's doubts it is well to turn to a passage like this. Surely your maturest judgment will never be fooled out of saying that this is divine, terribly beautiful—the stanza of *In Memoriam* beginning with the quatrain

> O Hesper o'er the buried sun,
>   And ready thou to die with him,
>   Thou watchest all things ever dim
> And dimmer, and a glory done.

I quote from memory. Inconsequent conclusion: Shakespear is and must be utterly the greatest of poets.

Just to end what I was saying about poetry. There is a higher sort of Parnassian which I call *Castalian*, or it may be thought the lowest kind of inspiration. Beautiful poems may be written wholly in it. Its peculiarity is that though you can hardly conceive yourself having written in it, if in the poet's place, yet it is too characteristic of the poet, too so-and-so-all-over-ish, to be quite inspiration. E.g.

> Yet despair
> Touches me not, though pensive as a bird
> Whose vernal coverts winter hath laid bare.

This is from Wordsworth, beautiful, but rather too essentially Wordsworthian, too persistently his way of looking at things. The third kind is merely the language of verse as distinct from that of prose, Delphic, the tongue of the Sacred *Plain*, I may call it, used in common by poet and poetaster. Poetry when spoken is spoken in it, but to speak it is not necessarily to speak poetry. I may add there is also *Olympian*. This is the language of strange masculine genius which suddenly, as it were, forces its way into the domain of poetry, without naturally having a right there. Milman's poetry is of this kind I think, and Rossetti's *Blessed Damozel*. But unusual poetry has a tendency to seem so at first.

There is much in what you say about moderate men. With regard to Stanley I have always been sorry for the cry, almost the scream, against him from Catholics. He is a man who *means well* or he is nothing, emphatically he means well. It is however I think easy to see why the kind of moderation visible in him is unsuccessful and distasteful. As to Macaulay it is not because he is a moderate man and an enemy that Addis etc dislike him more than an extreme enemy like Carlyle, but from individual qualities of his; an irritating assumption e.g. that Catholicism or Christianity or whatever it may be is now at last agreed on by thinking men to be an old woman's fable, which is far worse than to be bellowed at in the fiercest way. Now I hate one sort of extreme men as much to the full as you do. I assure you it fills me with humiliation, almost with despair, to see the excesses of such men as are represented by *The Church Times,* for unfortunately the letters in that paper shew that its conductors have their likes and peers. I say to you what I would not say to all heterodox, its pettiness, irreverence, vulgarity, injustice, ignorance, cant, may well make one suspect one's party. And when I think this, more and more I reverence the balance, the heartiness, the sincerity, the *greatness,* of Addis and men like him wherever they are. I assure you Dr. Newman, the extremest of the extreme, so extreme that he went beyond the extremes of that standard and took a large faction of his side with him, is a MODERATE MAN. So is Dr. Pusey, nay, you think he is, I am sure, yourself.

Read if you can a paper on *The ethics of friendship* in the September *Cornhill.* It is good and worth reading. Do you read *The Mutual Friend?* The reviews will most likely be unkindly severe on it. Dickens' literary history is melancholy to me, yet to take that view of him which is taken or will be by some people is not just or balanced. You must also read, if you have not done so, Matthew Arnold on *The literary influence of Academies* in the August *Cornhill*. Much that he says is worth attention, but, as is so often the case, in censuring bad taste he falls into two flagrant pieces of bad taste himself. I am coming to think much of taste myself, good taste and moderation, I who have sinned against them so much. But there is a prestige about them which is indescribable.

What do you think? It occurred to me that the story of *Floris in Italy* is dramatic, and all of a sudden I began to turn it into a play. It is a great experiment. I shall alter the plot to suit requirements a little. I fancy there is a fascination about the dramatic form. Beside this I have done very little since I wrote last, except three verses, a fragment, being a description of Io (transformed into a heifer.) It sounds odd.

I have been reading the twelve first (which is it? The first twelve then) books of the *Odyssey*, and have begun to receive Homer in earnest. How great his dramatic power is! Do you know, I am going, not at once of course, to reach Petronius Arbiter. I am though.

You must be tired of Parnassian by this time. I must however add a few words left out. A great deal of Parnassian lowers a poet's average, and more than anything else lowers his fame I fear. This is in the main what is meant by artificial poetry; it is all Parnassian. When one reads Pope's Homer with a critical eye one sees, artificial as it is, in every couplet that he was a great man, but no doubt to an uncritical humour and an uncritical flippant modernist it does offer a great handle.

I am ashamed to say I cannot make out the meaning of *The Voyage* in the new volume of Tennyson, though I have tried hard. Can you? After all, by the bye, perhaps his *Flower* is the best defence of him that could be written. *The Grandmother* and *Northern Farmer* are to my mind the best things in the book. They shew a knowledge of human nature which is less common in him than I could wish. *Boadicea* improves as one knows it; it is a grand thing, but I have (perhaps your cautions in criticism are here useful) doubts about the metre.

Do you notice that the first syllable is always accented, which is not the case in the Latin? I like *The Sailor Boy* much.

You know, I did not say you were 'not such a pleasant critic to keep as Bond'. On the contrary Bond would be, was in fact, much more severe; but he has not your great reticence, and blames and praises boldly, so that one knows what he means.

The vasty length this has oozed to forbids my telling you about the swells at Gurney's.

Why, you goose, did you say at the end of your first letter, that you thought there was nothing in it I could possibly misunderstand? Of course *that* was very possible to misunderstand, and also made it more easy to find something to misunderstand in the rest of the letter.

In a week or so I shall be at Hampstead I suppose, but now I am at Blunt House, Croydon—my grandfather's.

And now at last goodbye. Believe me, my dear friend, yours affectionately,

GERARD MANLEY HOPKINS.

Sept. 11. Blunt House, Croydon, S.

P.S. Here is a piece of antiquarianism for you. I believe New Inn Hall to be a blunder, a solecism. It should be Newing Hall. I argue this from the consideration of Stoke Newington, that is, *(the) wood (at the) new town,* and the *Newingate* of some town I read of, I forget what. This is called indifferently the New Gate and Newingate. *Newing* is an old participle meaning *new,* from a verb to *new* (we have *renew,* unless that is from *renovare*), and = Medieval Latin *novans,* Troynovant, the legendary name for London. Besides New *Inn* Hall is improbable in itself. What do you think?

POETIC DICTION

[An essay written for the Master of Balliol 1865 (?)]

WORDSWORTH'S view was that poetic diction scarcely differed or ought to differ from that of prose: he said 'The most interesting parts of the best poems will be found to be strictly the language of prose when prose is well written.' The protest which his criticisms and to some degree his

poetry made against the wide separation existing and believed to exist between the two things was, acting as a cor-
rective, truer for the time than anything which could be said
on the other side. His view could not however be received
as decisive without more modification than is given in his
essay.

If the best prose and the best poetry use the same language—(Coleridge defined poetry as the best thoughts in the
best words)—why not use unfettered prose of the two? Because, it would be answered, of the beauty of verse. This is
quite insufficient: then bald prose and simple statement
would be made better by verse, whereas everyone feels that
they are made worse. No, it is plain that metre, rhythm,
rhyme, and all the structure which is called verse both necessitate and engender a difference in diction and in thought.
The effect of verse is one on expression and on thought, viz.
concentration and all which is implied by this. This does not
mean terseness nor rejection of what is collateral nor emphasis nor even definiteness though these may be very well, or
best, attained by verse, but mainly, though the words are
not quite adequate, vividness of idea or, as they would especially have said in the last century, liveliness.

But what the character of poetry is will be found best by
looking at the structure of verse. The artificial part of poetry,
perhaps we shall be right to say all artifice, reduces itself to
the principle of parallelism. The structure of poetry is that of
continuous parallelism, ranging from the technical so-called
Parallelism of Hebrew poetry and the antiphons of Church
music up to the intricacy of Greek or Italian or English verse.
But parallelism is of two kinds necessarily—where the opposition is clearly marked, and where it is transitional rather or
chromatic. Only the first kind, that of marked parallelism, is
concerned with the structure of verse—in rhythm, the recurrence of a certain sequence of rhythm, in alliteration, in assonance and in rhyme. Now the force of this recurrence is to
beget a recurrence or parallelism answering to it in the words
or thought and, speaking roughly and rather for the tendency
than the invariable result, the more marked parallelism in
structure whether of elaboration or of emphasis begets more
marked parallelism in the words and sense. And moreover

parallelism in expression tends to beget or passes into parallelism in thought. This point reached we shall be able to see and account for the peculiarities of poetic diction. To the marked or abrupt kind of parallelism belong metaphor, simile, parable, and so on, where the effect is sought in likeness of things, and antithesis, contrast, and so on, where it is sought in unlikeness. To the chromatic parallelism belong gradation, intensity, climax, tone, expression (as the word is used in music), *chiaroscuro*, perhaps emphasis: while the faculties of Fancy and Imagination might range widely over both kinds, Fancy belonging more especially to the abrupt than to the transitional class.

Accordingly we may modify what Wordsworth says. An emphasis of structure stronger than the common construction of sentences gives asks for an emphasis of expression stronger than that of common speech or writing, and that for an emphasis of thought stronger than that of common thought. And it is commonly supposed that poetry has tasked the highest powers of man's mind: this is because, as it asked for greater emphasis of thought and on a greater scale, at each stage it threw out the minds unequal to further ascent. The diction of poetry could not then be the same with that of prose, and again of prose we can see from the other side that its diction ought not to be that of poetry, and that the great abundance of metaphor or antithesis is displeasing because it is not called for by, and interferes with, the continuousness of its flow. For the necessities or conditions of every art are as Lessing shews the rules by which to try it. And to come to particulars, why for instance, on Wordsworth's principle strictly interpreted, should the accentuation of the last syllable of participles, which so common as it is seems perpetually able to add fresh beauty where it is applied, be used in verse and never in prose? Or in poetry why should it give more pleasure than as being a complement of the mere structural apparatus of verse? as it does in lines like

> So I am as the rich whose blessed key
> Can bring him to his sweet up-lockèd treasure,

It is because where the structure forces us to appreciate each syllable it is natural and in the order of things for us to dwell on all modifications affecting the general result or type which the ear preserves and accordingly with such as are in themselves harmonious we are pleased, but in prose where syllables have none or little determinate value to emphasise them is unmeaning.

'ALL WORDS MEAN EITHER THINGS OR RELATIONS OF THINGS'

[Feb. 9, 1868]

ALL words mean either things or relations of things: you may also say then substances or attributes or again wholes or parts. Eg. *man* and *quarter*.

To every word meaning a thing and not a relation belongs a passion or prepossession or enthusiasm which it has the power of suggesting or producing but not always or in every one. This *not always* refers to its evolution in the man and secondly in man historically.

The latter element may be called for convenience the prepossession of a word. It is in fact the form, but there are reasons for being cautious in using form here, and it bears a valuable analogy to the soul, one however which is not complete, because all names but proper names are general while the soul is individual.

Since every definition is the definition of a word and every word may be considered as the contraction or coinciding-point of its definitions we may for convenience use word and definition with a certain freedom of interchange.

A word then has three terms belonging to it, ὅροι or moments—its prepossession of feeling; its definition, abstraction, vocal expression or other utterance; and its application, 'extension', the concrete things coming under it.

It is plain that of these only one in propriety is the word; the third is not a word but a thing meant by it, the first is not a word but something connotatively meant by it, the nature of which is further to be explored.

But not even the whole field of the middle term is covered by the word. For the word is the expression, *uttering* of the idea in the mind. That idea itself has its two terms, the image (of sight or sound or *scapes* of the other senses), which is in fact physical and a refined energy* accenting the nerves, a word to oneself, an inchoate word, and secondly the conception.

The mind has two kinds of energy, a transitional kind, when one thought or sensation follows another, which is to reason, whether actively as in deliberation, criticism, or passively, so to call it, as in reading etc; (ii) an abiding kind for which I remember no name, in which the mind is absorbed (as far as that may be), taken up by, dwells upon, enjoys, a single thought; we may call it contemplation, but it includes pleasures, supposing they, however turbid, do not require a transition to another term *of another kind*, for contemplation in its absoluteness is impossible unless in a trance and it is enough for the mind to repeat the same energy on the same matter.

Art exacts this energy of contemplation but also the other one, and in fact they are not incompatible, for even in the successive arts as music, for full enjoyment, the synthesis of the succession should give, unlock, the contemplative enjoyment of the unity of the whole. It is however true that in the successive arts with their greater complexity and length the whole's unity retires, is less important, serves rather for the framework of that of the parts.

The more intellectual, less physical, the spell of contemplation the more complex must be the object, the more close and elaborate must be the comparison the mind has to keep making between the whole and the parts, the parts and the whole. For this reference or comparison is what the sense of unity means; mere sense that such a thing is one and not two has no interest or value except accidentally.

Works of art of course like words utter the idea and in representing real things convey the prepossession with more or less success.

The further in anything, as a work of art, the organization

---

* That is when deliberately formed or when a thought is recalled, for when produced by sensation from without or when as in dreams etc it presents itself unbidden it comes from the involuntary working of nature.

is carried out, the deeper the form penetrates, the prepossession flushes the matter, the more effort will be required in apprehension, the more power of comparison, the more capacity for receiving that synthesis of (either successive or spatially distinct) impressions which gives us the unity with the prepossession conveyed by it.

The saner moreover is the act of contemplation as contemplating that which really is expressed in the object.

But some minds prefer that the prepossession they are to receive should be conveyed by the least organic, expressive, by the most suggestive, way. By this means the prepossession and the definition, uttering, are distinguished and unwound, which is the less sane attitude.

Along with this preference for the disengaged and unconditioned prepossession in these minds is often found an intellectual attraction for very sharp and pure dialectic or, in other matter, hard and telling art-forms; in fact we have in them the two axes on which rhetoric turns.

POETRY AND VERSE

[c. 1873–4]

Is all verse poetry or all poetry verse?—Depends on definitions of both. Poetry is speech framed for contemplation of the mind by the way of hearing or speech framed to be heard for its own sake and interest even over and above its interest of meaning. Some matter and meaning is essential to it but only as an element necessary to support and employ the shape which is contemplated for its own sake. (Poetry is in fact speech only employed to carry the inscape of speech for the inscape's sake—and therefore the inscape must be dwelt on. Now if this can be done without repeating it *once* of the inscape will be enough for art and beauty and poetry but then at least the inscape must be understood as so standing by itself that it could be copied and repeated. If not/ repetition, *oftening, over-and-overing, aftering* of the inscape must take place in order to detach it to the mind and in this light poetry is speech which afters and oftens its inscape, speech couched in a repeating figure and verse is spoken sound having a repeating figure.) Verse is (inscape of spoken sound, not spoken words, or speech employed to carry the inscape of spoken sound—or in the usual words) speech wholly or partially repeating the same figure of sound. Now there is speech which wholly or partially repeats the same figure of grammar and this may be framed to be heard for its own sake and interest over and above its interest of meaning. Poetry then may be couched in this, and therefore all poetry is not verse but all poetry is either verse or falls under this or some still further development of what verse is, speech wholly or partially repeating some kind of figure which is over and above meaning, at least the grammatical, historical, and logical meaning

But is all verse poetry?—Verse may be applied for use, e.g. to help the memory, and then is useful art, not μουσική ('Thirty days hath September' and 'Propria quae maribus' or Livy's *horrendum carmen*) and so is not poetry. Or it might be composed without meaning (as nonsense verse and choruses—'Hey nonny nonny' or 'Wille wau wau wau' etc) and then *alone* it would not be poetry but might be part of a poem. But if it has a meaning and is meant to be heard for its own sake it will be poetry if you take poetry to be a kind of composition and not the virtue or success or excellence of that kind, as eloquence is the virtue of oratory and not oratory only and beauty the virtue of inscape and not inscape only. In this way poetry may be high or low, good or bad, and doggrel will be poor or low poetry but not merely verse, for it aims at interest or amusement. But if poetry is the virtue of its own kind of composition then all verse even composed for its own interest's sake is not poetry

Kinds of Verse—

Verse then is speech wholly or partially repeating the same figure of sound. Partially as 'Jam satis terris nivis atque dirae' —that is/- ˘ -- | - ˘ ˘ - | ˘ --, for the common measure ˘ (= ½ -) is repeated throughout, wholly when you add 'Grandinis misit Pater et rubente'; or partially, taking the whole stanza, for it repeats the same figure for three lines but gives up in the fourth, but wholly if you take two stanzas. More clearly such an iambic as this— ˘ ˘ ⊿ | ˘ ⊿ | - ˘ ˘ | ˘ ˘ ˘ |

— ∠ | ◡ ◡ – is a partial repetition only, for this is verse though you did not add another line, and this is a whole repetition—
◡ ∠ | ◡ ∠ | ◡ ∠ | ◡ ∠ | ◡ ∠ | ◡ ∠

It is speech because we must distinguish it from music which is not verse. Music is composition which wholly or partially repeats the same figure of pitched sound (it is the aftering of pitched sound). Verse must be spoken or capable of being spoken

The figure may be repeated runningly, continuously, as in rhythm (ABABAB) or intermittently, as in alliteration and rhyme (ABCDABEFABGH). The former gives more tone, *candorem*, style, chasteness; the latter more brilliancy, starriness, quain, margaretting

[There are three artistic tones—*candor*, chasteness, 'clear', which is diffused beauty; humour, which is diffused wit; and pathos, which is diffused   .][2]

TO ROBERT BRIDGES

St. Beuno's, St. Asaph. Aug. 21 1877.

DEAREST BRIDGES,—Your letter cannot amuse Father Provincial, for he is on the unfathering deeps outward bound to Jamaica: I shd. not think of telling you anything about his reverence's goings and comings if it were it not that I know this fact has been chronicled in the Catholic papers.

Enough that it amuses me, especially the story about Wooldridge and the Wagnerite, wh. is very good.

Your parody reassures me about your understanding the metre. Only remark, as you say that there is no conceivable licence I shd. not be able to justify, that with all my licences, or rather laws, I am stricter than you and I might say than anybody I know. With the exception of the *Bremen* stanza,[3] which was, I think, the first written after 10 years' interval of silence, and before I had fixed my principles, my rhymes are rigidly good—to the ear—and such rhymes as *love* and *prove* I scout utterly. And my quantity is not like 'Fíftўtwō Bĕdfŏrd Squāre', where *fiftў* might pass but *Bĕdfŏrd* I should never admit. Not only so but Swinburne's dactyls and anapaests are halting to my ear: I never allow e.g. *I* or *my* (that is diphthongs, for *I* = a+i and *my* = ma+i) in the short or weak syllables of those feet, excepting before vowels, semi-vowels, or *r*, and rarely then, or when the measure becomes (what is the word?) molossic—thus: $\smile - \smile \mid \smile - \smile \mid \smile - \smile$, for then the first short is almost long. If you look again you will see. So that I may say my apparent licences are counter-balanced, and more, by my strictness. In fact all English verse, except Milton's, almost, offends me as 'licentious'. Remember this.

I do not of course claim to have invented *sprung rhythms* but only *sprung rhythm;* I mean that single lines and single instances of it are not uncommon in English and I have pointed them out in lecturing—e.g. 'why should this : desert be?'—which the editors have variously amended; 'There to meet : with Macbeth' or 'There to meet with Mac : beth'; Campbell has some throughout the *Battle of the Baltic*—'and their fleet along the deep proudly shone'—and *Ye Mariners* —'as ye sweep through the deep' etc; Moore has some which I cannot recall; there is one in *Grongar Hill;* and, not to speak of *Pom pom,* in Nursery Rhymes, Weather Saws, and Refrains they are very common—but what I do in the *Deutschland* etc is to enfranchise them as a regular and permanent principle of scansion.

There are no outriding feet in the *Deutschland*. An outriding foot is, by a sort of contradiction, a recognized extra-metrical effect; it is and it is not part of the metre; not part of it, not being counted, but part of it by producing a calculated effect which tells in the general success. But the long, e.g. seven-syllabled, feet of the *Deutschland,* are strictly metrical. Outriding feet belong to counterpointed verse, which supposes a well-known and unmistakeable or unforget-able standard rhythm: the *Deutschland* is not counter-pointed; counterpoint is excluded by sprung rhythm. But in some of my sonnets I have mingled the two systems: this is the most delicate and difficult business of all.

The choruses in *Samson Agonistes* are intermediate be-tween counterpointed and sprung rhythm. In reality they are sprung, but Milton keeps up a fiction of counterpointing the heard rhythm (which is the same as the mounted rhythm) upon a standard rhythm which is never heard but only counted and therefore really does not exist. The want of a metrical notation and the fear of being thought to write mere rhythmic or (who knows what the critics might not have said?) even unrhythmic prose drove him to this. Such rhythm as French and Welsh poetry has is sprung, counterpointed upon a counted rhythm, but it differs from Milton's in being calculated, not more perhaps than prose consciously written rhythmically, like orations for instance; it is in fact the *native rhythm* of the words used bodily imported into verse; whereas Milton's mounted rhythm is a real poetical rhythm, having its own laws and recurrence, but further embarrassed [*sic*] by having to count.

Why do I employ sprung rhythm at all? Because it is the nearest to the rhythm of prose, that is the native and natural rhythm of speech, the least forced, the most rhetorical and emphatic of all possible rhythms, combining, as it seems to me, opposite and, one wd. have thought, incompatible excellences, markedness of rhythm—that is rhythm's self—and naturalness of expression—for why, if it is forcible in prose to say 'lashed : rod',[4] am I obliged to weaken this in verse, which ought to be stronger, not weaker, into 'láshed birch-ród' or something?

My verse is less to be read than heard, as I have told you before; it is oratorical, that is the rhythm is so. I think if you will study what I have here said you will be much more pleased with it and may I say? converted to it.

You ask may you call it 'presumptious jugglery'. No, but only for this reason, that *presumptious* is not English.

I cannot think of altering anything. Why shd. I? I do not write for the public. You are my public and I hope to convert you.

You say you wd. not for any money read my poem again. Nevertheless I beg you will. Besides money, you know, there is love. If it is obscure do not bother yourself with the meaning but pay attention to the best and most intelligible stanzas, as the two last of each part and the narrative of the wreck. If you had done this you wd. have liked it better and sent me some serviceable criticisms, but now your criticism is of no use, being only a protest memorialising me against my whole policy and proceedings.

I may add for your greater interest and edification that

what refers to myself in the poem is all strictly and literally true and did all occur; nothing is added for poetical padding.

Believe me your affectionate friend

GERARD M. HOPKINS, S.J.

TO R. W. DIXON[5]

111 Mount Street, Grosvenor Square, W., Oct. 5 1878.

VERY REVEREND AND DEAR SIR,—A visit to Great Yarmouth and pressure of work have kept me from answering before yr. very kind letter, and my reply will now not be written at once but as I shall find leisure.

I hope, to begin with, you have quite recovered from the effects of your accident. I escaped from such a one with very little hurt not long ago in Wales, but I witnessed a terrible and fatal coach-accident years ago in the Vale of Maentwrog.

I have forgotten not only what I said about 'Fr. Prout' but even that I ever read him. I always understood that he was a very amusing writer. I do remember that I was a very conceited boy.

I have lost sight of Mr. Lobb; I do not even know whether he is alive or dead. The truth is I had no love for my school-days and wished to banish the remembrance of them, even, I am ashamed to say, to the degree of neglecting some people who had been very kind to me. Of Oxford on the other hand I was very fond. I became a Catholic there. But I have not visited it, except once for three quarters of an hour, since I took my degree. We have a church and a house there now.

Oct. 6—The other day Dr. Bridges told me he had in vain tried to get yr. volumes of poems, for want of knowing the publisher. I promised I wd. enquire of you. Was it not Smith and Elder?

I quite agree with what you write about Milton. His verse as one reads it seems something necessary and eternal (so to me does Purcell's music). As for 'proper hue', *now* it wd. be priggish, but I suppose Milton means *own hue* and they talk of *proper colours* in heraldry; not but what there is a Puritan touch about the line even so. However the word must once have had a different feeling. The Welsh have borrowed it for *pretty;* they talk of birds singing 'properly' and a little Welsh

boy to whom I shewed the flowers in a green house ex-
claimed 'They *are* proper!'—Milton seems now coming to be
studied better, and Masson is writing or has written his life
at prodigious length. There was an interesting review by Matthew Arnold in one of the Quarterlies of 'a French critic on
Milton'—Scherer I think. The same M. Arnold says Milton
and Campbell are our two greatest masters of *style*. Milton's
art is incomparable, not only in English literature but, I shd.
think, almost in any; equal, if not more than equal, to the
finest of Greek or Roman. And considering that this is shewn
especially in his verse, his rhythm and metrical system, it is
amazing that so great a writer as Newman should have fallen
into the blunder of comparing the first chorus of the *Agonistes*
with the opening of *Thalaba* as instancing the gain in smoothness and correctness of versification made since Milton's time
—Milton having been not only ahead of his own time as well
as all aftertimes in verse-structure but these particular choruses being his own highwater mark. It is as if you were to
compare the Panathenaic frieze and a teaboard and decide
in the teaboard's favour.

I have paid a good deal of attention to Milton's versification and collected his later rhythms: I did it when I had to
lecture on rhetoric some years since. I found his most advanced effects in the *Paradise Regained* and, lyrically, in the
Agonistes. I have often thought of writing on them, indeed
on rhythm in general; I think the subject is little understood.

You ask, do I write verse myself. What I had written I
burnt before I became a Jesuit and resolved to write no more,
as not belonging to my profession, unless it were by the wish
of my superiors; so for seven years I wrote nothing but two
or three little presentation pieces which occasion called for.
But when in the winter of '75 the Deutschland was wrecked
in the mouth of the Thames and five Franciscan nuns, exiles
from Germany by the Falck Laws, aboard of her were
drowned I was affected by the account and happening to
say so to my rector he said that he wished someone would
write a poem on the subject. On this hint I set to work and,
though my hand was out at first, produced one. I had long
had haunting my ear the echo of a new rhythm which now
I realised on paper. To speak shortly, it consists in scanning

by accents or stresses alone, without any account of the number of syllables, so that a foot may be one strong syllable or it may be many light and one strong. I do not say the idea is altogether new; there are hints of it in music, in nursery rhymes and popular jingles, in the poets themselves, and, since then, I have seen it talked about as a thing possible in critics. Here are instances—'*Díng, dóng, béll; Pússy's ín the wéll; Whó pút her ín? Líttle Jóhnny Thín. Whó púlled her óut? Líttle Jóhnny Stóut.*' For if each line has three stresses or three feet it follows that some of the feet are of one syllable only. So too '*Óne twó, Búckle my shóe' passim.* In Campbell you have '*Ánd their fléet alóng the déep próudly* shóne'—'Ít was tén of Ápril *mórn bý* the chíme' etc; in Shakspere 'Whý shd. *thís* désert bé?' corrected wrongly by the editors; in Moore a little melody I cannot quote; etc. But no one has professedly used it and made it the principle throughout, that I know of. Nevertheless to me it appears, I own, to be a better and more natural principle than the ordinary system, much more flexible, and capable of much greater effects. However I had to mark the stresses in blue chalk, and this and my rhymes carried on from one line into another and certain chimes suggested by the Welsh poetry I had been reading (what they call *cynghanedd*) and a great many more oddnesses could not but dismay an editor's eye, so that when I offered it to our magazine the *Month,* though at first they accepted it, after a time they withdrew and dared not print it. After writing this I held myself free to compose, but cannot find it in my conscience to spend time upon it; so I have done little and shall do less. But I wrote a shorter piece on the Eurydice, also in 'sprung rhythm', as I call it, but simpler, shorter, and without marks, and offered the *Month* that too, but they did not like it either. Also I have written some sonnets and a few other little things; some in sprung rhythm, with various other experiments—as 'outriding feet', that is parts of which do not count in the scanning (such as you find in Shakspere's later plays, but as a licence, whereas mine are rather calculated effects); others in the ordinary scanning *counterpointed* (this is counterpoint: '*Hóme to* his móther's hóuse *prívate* retúrned' and '*Bút to vánquish* by wísdom héllish wíles' etc);[6] others, one or two, in common uncounterpointed rhythm. But even the impulse to write is wanting, for I have no thought of publishing.

I should add that Milton is the great standard in the use of counterpoint. In *Paradise Lost* and *Regained*, in the last more freely, it being an advance in his art, he employs counterpoint more or less everywhere, markedly now and then; but the choruses of *Samson Agonistes* are in my judgment counterpointed throughout; that is, each line (or nearly so) has two different coexisting scansions. But when you reach that point the secondary or 'mounted rhythm', which is necessarily a sprung rhythm, overpowers the original or conventional one and then this becomes superfluous and may be got rid of; by taking that last step you reach simple sprung rhythm. Milton must have known this but had reasons for not taking it.

I read Arnold's *Essays in Criticism* at Oxford and got Maurice de Guerin's Journal in consequence, admired it, but for some reason or other never got far in it. I should be glad to read it now if I had time. But I have no time for more pressing interests. I hear confessions, preach, and so forth; when these are done I have still a good deal of time to myself, but I find I can do very little with it.

There is a certain Dr. Gordon Hake whose poems are praised by W. Rossetti and other critics. I have seen them in nothing but reviews, but two in particular, *the Young Palmist* and *the Old Snake-charmer*, were very striking. They are more like yours than anything else (for instance the *Wizard's Funeral* or the 'Dying Dawning'). You may perhaps know them.

Believe me, dear Sir, very sincerely yours

GERARD HOPKINS.

Oct. 10

TO ROBERT BRIDGES

St. Giles, Oxford, Feb. 15 '79.

DEAREST BRIDGES,—I should have added in my last that the *Silver Jubilee* has been published. It was printed at the end of a sermon, bearing the same title and due to the same occasion, of Fr. John Morris's of our Society. I have found it since I wrote and the copy I sent you from memory is not quite right. The third stanza should stand fourth and run—

> Not today we need lament
> Your lot of life is some way spent:
> Toil has shed round your head
> Silver, but for Jubilee.

The thought is more pointed. Please correct it if you put it into your album.

No, do not ask Gosse anything of the sort. (1) If I were going to publish, and that soon, such a mention would be 'the puff premilinary' [sic], which it wd. be dishonourable of me to allow of. (2) If I did, a mention in one article of one review would do very little indeed, especially as publishing now is out of the question. (3) When I say that I do not mean to publish I speak the truth. I have taken and mean to take no step to do so beyond the attempt I made to print my two wrecks in the *Month*. If some one in authority knew of my having some poems printable and suggested my doing it I shd. not refuse, I should be partly, though not altogether, glad. But that is very unlikely. All therefore that I think of doing is to keep my verses together in one place—at present I have not even correct copies—, that, if anyone shd. like, they might be published after my death. And that again is unlikely, as well as remote. I could add other considerations, as that if I meant to publish at all it ought to be more or ought at least to be followed up, and how can that be? I cannot in conscience spend time on poetry, neither have I the inducements and inspirations that make others compose. Feeling, love in particular, is the great moving power and spring of verse and the only person that I am in love with seldom, especially now, stirs my heart sensibly and when he does I cannot always 'make capital' of it, it would be a sacrilege to do so. Then again I have of myself made verse so laborious.

No doubt my poetry errs on the side of oddness. I hope in time to have a more balanced and Miltonic style. But as air, melody is what strikes me most of all in music and design in painting, so design, pattern or what I am in the habit of calling 'inscape' is what I above all aim at in poetry. Now it is the virtue of design, pattern, or inscape to be distinctive and it is the vice of distinctiveness to become queer. This vice I cannot have escaped. However 'winding the eyes'[7] is queer only if looked at from the wrong point of view: looked at as a motion in and of the eyeballs it is what you say, but I mean that the eye winds / only in the sense that its focus or point of sight winds and that coincides with a point of the object and winds with that. For the object, a lantern passing further and further away and bearing now east, now west of one right line, is truly and properly described as winding. That is how it should be taken then.[8]

TO R. W. DIXON

St. Aloysius' Presbytery, St. Giles's, Oxford.
Feb. 27 1879.

VERY REVEREND AND DEAR SIR,—You will see that I have again changed my abode and am returned to my Alma Mater and need not go far to have before my eyes 'the little-headed willows two and two' and that landscape the charm of Oxford, green shouldering grey, which is already abridged and soured and perhaps will soon be put out altogether, the Wytham and Godstow landscape (as I take it to be) of 'Love's Consolation' and 'Waiting'.[9] We have passed here a bitter winter, which indeed still holds out, and Oxford is but its own skeleton in wintertime. March 4. I have parish work to do, am called one way and another, and can find little time to write.

I am glad to hear that Dr. Bridges has sent you his *Growth of Love* (his last copy) and the new book and that you were pleased with them.

In the new book three poems, the 'Passer By', the 'Downs', and a sonnet beginning 'So hot the noon was' are written in a mitigated sprung rhythm. But to understand a new thing, such as this rhythm is, it is best to see it in an extreme example: you will then rather appreciate their peculiarities from it than that from them. March 7. I cannot just now get

at Coleridge's preface to *Christabel.* So far as I can gather
from what you say and I seem to have seen elsewhere, he
was drawing a distinction between two systems of scanning
the one of which is quite opposed to sprung rhythm, the
other *is not, but might be developed into,* that. For though
it is only a step from many popular and many literary cadences now in being to sprung rhythm and nature even without that help seems to prompt it of itself, yet the step has
never, that I know of, been taken. The distinction Coleridge,
as I suppose, was drawing (though it is a great abuse of
terms and usage to make it by the words Accent and Quantity) is between strictly *counted rhythm,* in which, if iambic
e.g., each foot has two syllables only and is an iamb; if anapaestic, each foot has three syllables and is an anapaest—
this on the one hand, and, on the other, mixed rhythm, in
which feet of the same kind may be used interchangeably,
as iambs with anapaests, because both belong to *rising
rhythm,* or trochees with dactyls, because both belong to *falling rhythm.* And this mixture may be of two sorts—*equal-
timed,* as in the hexameter, where the spondee is used as
the alternative of the dactyl, because it is of equal length; or
logaoedic, as when in classical and therefore strictly timed
metres dactyls are mixed with trochees, which feet are of
unequal length. (I leave out here all consideration of the still
freer mixed lyric rhythms of antiquity.) However this last
division is of little importance or meaning in English verse.
It is enough that we can interchange two-syllabled with
three-syllabled feet. This is freely done in ballad-measures
and Coleridge does it in *Christabel.* In the more stately metres the poets of the last century as well as others before and
since employ only the stricter counted rhythm,[*] but even in
the fivefoot iambic Tennyson and other modern poets often
make two light syllables count for one.

This practice is founded upon an easily felt principle of
equal strengths, as in the classic hexameter the substitution
of spondees for dactyls is founded on the principle of equal
lengths (or times). To go a little deeper, it supposes not only

---

[*] Even to the absurdities of 'fond mem'ry's voice' and 'th'
umbrageous grove'.

that, speaking in the abstract, any accent is equal to any other (by accent I mean *the* accent of a word) but further that each accent may be considered to be accompanied by an equal quantity of slack or unaccented utterance, one, two, or more such unaccented syllables; so that wherever there is an accent or stress, there is also so much unaccentuation, so to speak, or slack, and this will give a foot or rhythmic unit, viz. a stress with its belonging slack. But now if this is so, since there are plenty of accented monosyllables, and those too immediately preceded and followed by the accents of other words, it will come about that a foot may consist of one syllable only, and that one syllable has not only the stress of its accent but also the slack which another word wd. throw on one or more additional syllables, though here that may perhaps be latent, as though the slack syllables had been absorbed. What I mean is clearest in an antithesis or parallelism, for there the contrast gives the counterparts equal stress; e.g. 'sanguinary consequences, terrible butchery, frightful slaughter, fell swoop': if these are taken as alternative expressions, then the total strength of *sanguinary* is no more than that of *terrible* or of *frightful* or of *fell* and so on of the substantives too.

Now granting this, if the common ballad measure allows of our having (say) in a fourfoot line 'Terrible butchery, frightful slaughter' why, on principle, shd. we not say 'Terrible butchery, fell swoop' and that be four feet? or further why not 'Sanguinary consequences, terrible butchery'?—except indeed, what of course in practice and actual versewriting is important, that *consequences* is a clumsy halting word which makes the line lag. This then is the essence of sprung rhythm: *one stress makes one foot*, no matter how many or few the syllables. But all that I have said is of course shewing you the skeleton or flayed anatomy, you will understand more simply and pleasantly by verses in the flesh.

March 10—You are kind enough to ask to see my poems. You shall do so when I have got the two shipwreck-pieces back, which are not at hand, and have copied the sonnets out fair. But though the number is small I find this no easy matter.

Reading over what I have written above I find it very hurried and confused: I hope you may gather some meaning out of it. I shd. add that the word Sprung which I use for this rhythm means something like *abrupt* and applies by rights only where one stress follows another running, without syllable between. Besides the bare principle which I have been explaining I employ various artifices which you will see in reading.

To turn to your letter—I am not surprised at what Arnold says of Campbell. Cold and dull as the *Pleasures of Hope* is and much more that he wrote, there is always the 'free-hand' of a master in his work beyond almost all our poets, and when one turns from his frigidities to what are held his masterpieces and will always keep his name green, the *Battle of the Baltic* and so forth, one finds a kind of inspired felicity seen no where else that he himself could not have analysed or justified. An inversion and a phrase like 'On the deck of fame that died' or the lines 'But the might of England flushed To anticipate the scene' seem to me as if the words had fallen into their places at a magic signal and not by any strain and continuance of thought.

Marvel, of whom I have only read extracts, is a most rich and nervous poet. Thomas[10] Vaughan's poems were reprinted not so long ago. He was a follower of Herbert both in life and style: he was in fact converted from worldly courses by reading Herbert's poems on a sickbed and even his muse underwent a conversion (for he had written before). He has more glow and freedom than Herbert but less fragrant sweetness. Somewhere he speaks of some spot 'primrosed and hung with shade' and one piece ends

> And here in dust and dirt, O here
> The lilies of his love appear

(I am assuming that you have not got the book.) Still I do not think him Herbert's equal.

You call Tennyson 'a great outsider'; you mean, I think, to the soul of poetry. I feel what you mean, though it grieves me to hear him depreciated, as of late years has often been done. Come what may he will be one of our greatest poets. To me his poetry appears 'chryselephantine'; always of precious mental material and each verse a work of art, no botchy places, not only so but no half wrought or low-toned ones, no drab, no brown-holland; but the form, though fine, not the perfect artist's form, not equal to the material. When the inspiration is genuine, arising from personal feeling, as in *In Memoriam*, a divine work, he is at his best, or when he is rhyming pure and simple imagination, without afterthought, as in the *Lady of Shalott*, *Sir Galahad*, the *Dream of Fair Women*, or *Palace of Art*. But the want of perfect form in the imagination comes damagingly out when he undertakes longer works of fancy, as his Idylls: they are unreal in motive and incorrect, uncanonical so to say, in detail and keepings. He shd. have called them *Charades from the Middle Ages* (dedicated by permission to H.R.H. etc). The Galahad of one of the later ones is quite a fantastic charade-playing trumpery Galahad, merely playing the fool over Christian heroism. Each scene is a triumph of language and of bright picturesque, but just like a charade—where real lace and good silks and real jewelry are used, because the actors are private persons and wealthy, but it is acting all the same and not only so but the make-up has less pretence of correct keeping than at Drury Lane. His opinions too are not original, often not independent even, and they sink into vulgarity: not only *Locksley Hall* but *Maud* is an ungentlemanly row and *Aylmer's Field* is an ungentlemanly row and the *Princess* is an ungentlemanly row. To be sure this gives him vogue, popularity, but not that sort of ascendency Goethe had or even Burns, scoundrel as the first was, not to say the second; but then they spoke out the real human rakishness of their hearts and everybody recognised the really beating, though rascal, vein. And in his rhetorical pieces he is at his worst, as the *Lord of Burleigh* and *Lady Clare Vere de Vere* (downright haberdasher). But for all this he is a glorious poet and all he does is chryselephantine. Though by the by I owe him a grudge for *Queen Mary*, written to please the mob, and for that other drama where a portent of a man in flaxen locks and ring-mail mouths rationalism 'to torment us before the time'.

I remember what I said about Latin elegiacs but I think

I was wrong. Ovid carried the elegiac couplet to a perfection beyond which it could not go and his work remains the
standard of excellence. He fixed the system of counterpoint
for the elegiac couplet, as Horace for the Sapphic and Alcaic
stanzas. This is a long intricate matter, to which I have paid
some attention but I can write little about it now. It shd. however be said that in the *Fasti* Ovid does now and then employ
the three-syllable ending. To shew the advance made in
counterpointing of the elegiac couplet take the following
small point. Words with *-que, -ne, -ve* attached were always
accented on the syllable before, whereas when the *-que* etc
was part of the word itself (as in *utique, itaque* it may be)
it followed the usual accentuation. In such a dactyl then as
armaque the accent of the word would not in elegiac verse
agree with the accent of the verse, the stress; which shd. fall
on the first syllable. Here at once is counterpoint. Now in the
sensitive places of the couplet, the fifth foot of the hexameter
and the second half of the pentameter, Propertius never ventures on this counterpointing except once in all his works.
Ovid employs and parades it: the first pentameter of the *Fasti*
is

Lapsáque sub térras ortáque sígna cánam—

in which the word-accent only once (in *signa*) agrees with
the stress of the rhythm. The accentuation is the same as in
English would be

The rísings and séttings of stárs I méan to síng of—

which is nothing like a pentameter.

I have just got back my two wreck-pieces, which with the
sonnets I hope to send you in a few days. This letter is longer
than I had any business to write.

Believe me your sincere friend

GERARD M. HOPKINS S.J.

March 12 1879.

March 13—I have been up to Godstow this afternoon. I am
sorry to say that the aspens that lined the river are everyone
felled.

TO R. W. DIXON

8 Salisbury Street, Liverpool. Dec. 22 1880.

MY DEAR FRIEND,—A letter was already owing from me to you and I had long been meaning to write and had your name on a list before me, when your last, now five weeks old, overtook me in the midst of my lingerings and my hinderings. I began to answer it, but that answer was never finished: perhaps this happened more than once. My parish work has been very wearisome; of late especially; it appeared to me at last that I should never be able to get my letters written. Now I am flattering myself that this big paper helps me on.

I thank you very much for your comforting phrases. I cannot see what should make me overrate your poems: I had plenty of poetry old and new to compare with them and to guide my taste, I read them of my own choice years before I ever thought of communicating with you. I did not, it is true, care very much for some of them, such as the Romance beginning 'Rightly be swift', and there are passages in most of them, even in those I value most, which I could not and can not understand, obscurities of expression which are, I think, of themselves and not through the reader's want of apprehension faulty; but against these I set their extreme beauties—imagery inheriting Keats's mantle, the other-world of imagination (constructive imagination is rare even among poets), the 'instress' of feeling, and a pathos the deepest, I think, that I have anywhere found. (By the by there is one thing that Keats's authority can never excuse, and that is rhyming open vowels to silent *rs*, as *higher* to *Thalia*: as long as the *r* is pronounced by anybody, and it is by a good many yet, the feeling that it is there makes this rhyme most offensive, not indeed to the ear, but to the mind). Your second volume I never knew so well as the first nor did the historic odes themselves interest me so much as the pieces of Christ's Company, not that they do not mark an advance in power, but for just the reason that their subjects or motives had less interest and also perhaps because they were transitional and

you had not altogether made your own some new ground
you seemed moving on to. But pieces like the Ode to Summer in that volume are in point of art and execution more
perfect than any in the older one.

Bridges of course told me about his visit to you when I
saw him in town in the summer. He spoke of your epic on
some legend of the northern mythology, and praised its
beauties, but said he had pointed out to you that it too much
resembled *Hyperion*. I had thought of asking you to let me
see it but held back for want of time. Now however I shall
be only too happy to see the pieces you offer to send and
will, if you wish, make what remarks may occur to me as
opportunity shall serve. I read some beautiful pieces of yours
in his book—the Murder in the Dark, some sonnets on Man,
a reflective Ode on the pleasures of learning and the sorrows
of sympathy (I forget its name), perhaps some other things
I cannot now recall. This Ode expresses something of what
your letter speaks of in the case of Tennyson, the loss of
taste, of relish for what once charmed us. I understand that
state of mind well enough; it used at one time to dismay and
dishearten me deeply, it made the best of things seem empty.
I think that many things contribute to it and play a part. One
is real disenchantment, the correction of the earlier untrained
judgment or taste by the maturer one—as, suppose a child
thought Macaulay's Lays the finest poetry that ever was
penned: I daresay many do. Another is the shortcoming of
faculty in us, because the enchanting power in the work is
finite or because the mind after a certain number of shocks
or stimuli as the physiologists would say, is spent and flags;
and this is plainly the case with jokes, however witty and
whimsical: you know that they *are* good, you laughed and
were right to laugh heartily when you first heard them, but
now they are stale to you and you could laugh no more. Another is that insight is more sensitive, in fact is more perfect,
earlier in life than later and especially towards elementary
impressions: I remember that crimson and pure blues seemed
to me spiritual and heavenly sights fit to draw tears once;
now I can just see what I once saw, but can hardly dwell
on it and should not care to do so. Another is—or it comes to
one of the above—the greater demand for perfection in the

work, the greater impatience with technical faults. In the particular case of Tennyson's Ode to Memory I find in my own case all these: it has a mysterious stress of feeling, especially in the refrain—I am to my loss less sensitive to that; it has no great meaning of any importance nor power of thought—I am to my advantage more alive to that; from great familiarity with the style I am deadened to its individuality and beauty, which is again my loss; and I perceive the shortcomings of the execution, which is my own advance in critical power. Absolutely speaking, I believe that if I were now reading Tennyson for the first time I should form the same judgment of him that I form as things are, but I should not feel, I should lose, I should never have gone through, that boyish stress of enchantment that this Ode and the *Lady of Shalott* and many other of his pieces once laid me under. Rose Hall, Lydiate (a country house where I sometimes spend a night as occasion requires and take the opportunity to write my letters). Jan. 11, 1880. And here I must stop for tonight.

Jan. 14 8 Salisbury Street, Liverpool—The new prosody, Sprung Rhythm, is really quite a simple matter and as strict as the other rhythm. Bridges treats it in theory and practice as something informal and variable without any limit but ear and taste, but this is not how I look at it. We must however distinguish its εἶναι and its εὖ εἶναι the writing it somehow and the writing it as it should be written; for written anyhow it is a shambling business and a corruption, not an improvement. In strictness then and simple εἶναι it is a matter of accent only, like common rhythm, and not of quantity at all. Its principle is that all rhythm and all verse consists of feet and each foot must contain one stress or verse-accent: so far is common to it and Common Rhythm; to this it adds that the stress alone is essential to a foot and that therefore even one stressed syllable may make a foot and consequently two or more stresses may come running, which in common rhythm can, regularly speaking, never happen. But there may and mostly there does belong to a foot an unaccented portion of 'slack': now in common rhythm, in which less is made of stress, in which less stress is laid, the slack must be always one or else two syllables, never less than one and never more than two, and in most measures fixedly one or fixedly two, but in sprung rhythm, the stress being more *of* a stress, being more important, allows of greater variation in the slack and this latter may range from three syllables to none at all—*regularly,* so that paeons (three short syllables and one long or three slack and one stressy) are regular in sprung rhythm, but in common rhythm can occur only by licence; moreover may in the same measure have this range. Regularly then the feet in sprung rhythm consist of one, two, three, or four syllables and no more, and if for simplicity's sake we call feet by Greek names, taking accent for quantity, and also scan always as for rising rhythm (I call *rising rhythm* that in which the slack comes first, as in iambs and anapaests, *falling* that in which the stress comes first, as in trochees and dactyls), scanning thus, the feet in sprung rhythm will be monosyllables, iambs, anapaests, and fourth paeons, and no others. But for particular rhythmic effects it is allowed, and more freely than in common rhythm, to use any number of slack syllables, limited only by ear. And though it is the virtue of sprung rhythm that it allows of 'dochmiac' or 'antipastic' effects or cadences, when the verse suddenly changes from a rising to a falling movement, and this too is strongly felt by the ear, yet no account of it is taken in scanning and no irregularity caused, but the scansion always treated, conventionally and for simplicity, as rising. Thus the line 'She had cóme from a crúise, tráining séamen' has a plain reversed rhythm, but the scanning is simply 'She had cóme | from a crúise | tráin | ing séa | men'—that is/ rising throughout, having one monosyllabic foot and an overlapping syllable which is counted to the first foot of the next line. Bridges in the preface to his last issue says something to the effect that all sorts of feet may follow one another, an anapaest a dactyl for instance (which would make four slack syllables running): so they may, if we look at the real nature of the verse; but for simplicity it is much better to recognize, in scanning this new rhythm, only one movement, either the rising (which I choose as being commonest in English verse) or the falling (which is perhaps better in itself), and always keep to that.

In lyric verse I like sprung rhythm also to be *over-rove,* that is the scanning to run on from line to line to the end of the stanza. But for dramatic verse, which is looser in form,

I should have the lines 'free-ended' and each scanned by itself.

Sprung rhythm does not properly require or allow of counterpoint. It does not require it, because its great variety amounts to a counterpointing, and it scarcely allows of it, because you have scarcely got in it that conventionally fixed form which you can mentally supply at the time when you are actually reading another one—I mean as when in reading 'Bý the wáters of life where'er they sat' you mentally supply 'By thé watérs', which is the normal rhythm. Nevertheless in dramatic verse I should sparingly allow it at the beginning of a line and after a strong caesura, and I see that Bridges does this freely in *London Snow* for instance. However by means of the 'outrides' or looped half-feet you will find in some of my sonnets and elsewhere I secure a strong effect of double rhythm, of a second movement in the verse besides the primary and essential one, and this comes to the same thing or serves the same purpose as counterpointing by reversed accents as in Milton.

But for the εὖ εἶναι of the new rhythm great attention to quantity is necessary. And since English quantity is very different from Greek or Latin a sort of prosody ought to be drawn up for it, which would be indeed of wider service than for sprung rhythm only. We must distinguish strength (or gravity) and length. About length there is little difficulty: plainly *bidst* is longer than *bids* and *bids* than *bid*. But it is not recognized by everybody that *bid*, with a flat dental, is graver or stronger than *bit*, with a sharp. The strongest and, other things being alike, the longest syllables are those with the circumflex, like *fire*. Any syllable ending in *ng*, though *ng* is only a single sound, may be made as long as you like by prolonging the nasal. So too *n* may be prolonged after a long vowel or before a consonant, as in *soon* or *and*. In this way a great number of observations might be made: I have put these down at random as samples. You will find that Milton pays much attention to consonant-quality or gravity of sound in his line endings. Indeed every good ear does it naturally more or less/ in composing. The French too say that their feminine ending is graver than the masculine and that pathetic or majestic lines are made in preference to end with it.

One may even by a consideration of what the music of the
verse requires restore sometimes the pronunciation of Shakspere's time where it has changed and shew for instance that
cherry must have been *cher-ry* (like *her, stir, spur*) or that
heavy was *heave-y* in the lines 'Now the heavy ploughman
snores All with weary task foredone'. You speak of the word
over. The *o* is long no doubt, but long *o* is the shortest of the
long vowels and may easily be used in a weak place; I do not
however find that Tennyson uses it so in the Ode to Memory:
in the line 'Over the dewy dark [or 'dark dewy'] earth forlorn' it seems to be in a strong place.

I will inclose a little piece I composed last September in
walking from Lydiate.[11] It is to have some plainsong music
to it. I found myself quite unable to redeem my promise of
copying you out the pieces you have not seen: time would
not allow it. However I think you have seen them since in
Bridges' book. Liverpool is of all places the most museless.
It is indeed a most unhappy and miserable spot. There is
moreover no time for writing anything serious—I should say
for composing it, for if it were made it might be written.

I do not despair of our coming to meet, for business might
perhaps bring you here. Meanwhile believe me your affectionate friend

GERARD M. HOPKINS S.J.

Jan. 14. 1881

You will then send the poems, I hope, as soon as possible. Jan.
16—I have added another piece, the *Brothers*.

TO R. W. DIXON

Manresa House, Roehampton, London, S.W.

(By the by have you read Lothair? because this house is the
divine Theodora's: some of the scenes are laid here.)

Oct. 12 1881.

MY DEAR FRIEND,—Some of the sonnets are very, I
must say unpardonably, licentious in form. I recognise stricter
and looser forms and the Shakespearian sonnet, though it is
a sonnet only *in genere* and not one if by sonnet you mean

the Italian sonnet, which is the sonnet proper—but this is a question of names only—the Shakespearian sonnet is a very beautiful and effective species of composition in the kind. But then, though simpler, it is as strict, regular, and specific as the sonnet proper. Moreover it has the division into the parts 8+6, at all events 4+4+4+2. Now it seems to me that this division is the real characteristic of the sonnet and that what is not so marked off and moreover has not the octet again divided into quatrains is not to be called a sonnet at all. For in the cipher 14 is no mystery and if one does not know nor avail oneself of the opportunities which it affords it is a pedantic encumbrance and not an advantage. The equation of the best sonnet is

$$(4+4)+(3+3) = 2.4+2.3 = 2(4+3) = 2.7 = 14.$$

This means several things—(A) that the sonnet is one of the works of art of which the equation or construction is unsymmetrical in the shape $x+y = a$, where x and y are unequal in some simple ratio, as $2:1$, $3:2$, $4:3$: perhaps it would be better to say $mx = nx = a$. Samples of this are the Hexameter and Ionic Trimeter, divided by their caesura, as St. Austin *De Musica* suggests, so as to give the equation $3^2+4^2 = 5^2$ (it is not very clear how he makes it out, but at all events they give the equation $2\frac{1}{2}+3\frac{1}{2} = 6$ or $5+7 = 12$). The major and minor scales again consist of a pentachord + a tetrachord and in Plainsong music all the 'Authentic' Modes have this order and all the 'Plagal' the reverse, the tetrachord first. And I could shew, if there were time, that it would be impracticable to have a ratio of the sort required with numbers higher than 4 and 3. Neither would $4:2$ do, for it wd. return to $2:1$, which is too simple. (B) It is divided symmetrically too in multiples of two, as in all effects taking place in time tend to be, and all very regular musical composition is: this raises the 7 to 14. (C) It pairs off even symmetrical members with symmetrical (the quatrains) and uneven or unsymmetrical with uneven (the tercets). And even the rhymes, did time allow, I could shew are founded on a principle of nature and cannot be altered without loss of effect. But when one goes so far as to run the rhymes of the octet into the sestet a downright prolapsus or hernia takes place and the sonnet is crippled for life.

I have been longer and perhaps more dogmatic than I shd. have been over this point. Of the sonnets themselves those on the World, except for happy touches, do not interest me very much and that to Corneille has a certain stiffness, as the majority of Wordsworth's have, great sonneteer as he was, but he wrote in 'Parnassian', that is the language and style of poetry mastered and at command but employed without any fresh inspiration: and this I feel of your sonnet here. The rest, that to George Sand and those on Shakespeare and Milton, are rich in thought, feeling, and diction.

On a Young Bird etc.—This is a truly touching and finished little piece, the tale told with great flow and simplicity: the pathos of a little tale like this is unique as a well-told jest and has its own point as that has. There are however two flaws worth noticing. It seems strange and, I think, unlawful to call a 'naked floor' a bower: a bower is a *camera,* an arched shelter whether of boughs or of cieling [*sic*]. Also stanza 4. begins with the same rhyme as 3. ends with, which is an awkwardness.

Ode on the Death of Dickens is fine and stirring; the Aryan image of the cloud cows and the dog particularly striking; but the anapaests are heavily loaded. For myself I have been accustomed to think, as many critics do, that Dickens had no true command of pathos, that in his there is something mawkish; but perhaps I have not read the best passages. Just such a gale as this poem paints is blowing today (Oct. 14) and two of my fellow Tertians have been injured by the fall of almost half a tall cedar near my room, which wrecked the woodshed where they happened to be and battered and bruised them with a rain of tiles.

The Fall of the Leaf—I have spoken of this beautiful poem before.

I cannot remember if I spoke of *Nature and Man,* the one beginning 'Blue in the mists all day'. At all events it is one of the most perfect of all, both in thought and expression. The thing had to be said. I suppose 'pod' means some pod-like bud, for I think, scientifically speaking, the pod is only a seed vessel.

There only remain the two tales; of which I will write another day, though it must be less fully than they deserve. I
will finish with remarks called out by your most welcome
letter of yesterday.

In speaking of 'frigid fancy' I referred to the particular passage only. But Browning has, I think, many frigidities. Any
untruth to nature, to human nature, is frigid. Now he has
got a great deal of what came in with Kingsley and the Broad
Church school, a way of talking (and making his people talk)
with the air and spirit of a man bouncing up from table with
his mouth full of bread and cheese and saying that he meant
to stand no blasted nonsense. There is a whole volume of
Kingsley's essays which is all a kind of munch and a not standing of any blasted nonsense from cover to cover. Do you
know what I mean? The *Flight of the Duchess,* with the repetition of 'My friend', is in this vein. Now this is *one* mood or
vein of human nature, but they would have it all and look
at all human nature through it. And Tennyson in his later
works has been 'carried away with their dissimulation'. The
effect of this style is a frigid bluster. A true humanity of
spirit, neither mawkish on the one hand nor blustering on
the other, is the most precious of all qualities in style, and
this I prize in your poems, as I do in Bridges'. After all it is
the breadth of his human nature that we admire in Shakespeare.

I read some, not much, of the *Ring and the Book,* but as
the tale was not edifying and one of our people, who had
been reviewing it, said that further on it was coarser, I did
not see, without a particular object, sufficient reason for going
on with it. So far as I read I was greatly struck with the skill
in which he displayed the facts from different points of view:
this is masterly, and to do it through three volumes more
shews a great body of genius. I remember a good case of
'the impotent collection of particulars' of which you speak in
the description of the market place at Florence where he
found the book of the trial: it is a pointless photograph of
still life, such as I remember in Balzac, minute upholstery
description; only that in Balzac, who besides is writing prose,
all tells and is given with a reserve and simplicity of style
which Browning has not got. Indeed I hold with the old-

fashioned criticism that Browning is not really a poet, that
he has all the gifts but the one needful and the pearls without the string; rather one should say raw nuggets and rough
diamonds. I suppose him to resemble Ben Jonson, only that
Ben Jonson has more real poetry.

As for Carlyle; I have a letter by me never sent, in answer
to a pupil of mine, who had written about him, and I find I
there say just what you do about his incapacity of general
truths. And I always thought him morally an imposter, worst
of all imposters a false prophet. And his style has imposture
or pretence in it. But I find it difficult to think there is imposture in his genius itself. However I must write no more
criticism.

I see you do not understand my position in the Society.
This Tertianship or Third Year of Probation or second Noviceship, for it is variously called in the Institute, is not really a
noviceship at all in the sense of a time during which a candi-
date or probationer makes trial of our life and is free to withdraw. At the end of the noviceship proper we take vows
which are perpetually binding and renew them every six
months (not *for* every six months but for life) till we are professed or take the final degree we are to hold, of which in the
Society there are several. It is in preparation for these last
vows that we make the tertianship; which is called a *schola
affectus* and is meant to enable us to recover that fervour
which may have cooled through application to study and contact with the world. Its exercises are however nearly the same
as those of the first noviceship. As for myself, I have not only
made my vows publicly some two and twenty times but I
make them to myself every day, so that I should be black with
perjury if I drew back now. And beyond that I can say with
St. Peter: To whom shall I go? *Tu verba vitae asternae habes.*
Besides all which, my mind is here more at peace than it has
ever been and I would gladly live all my life, if it were so to
be, in as great or a greater seclusion from the world and be
busied only with God. But in the midst of outward occupa-
tions not only the mind is drawn away from God, which may
be at the call of duty and be God's will, but unhappily the will
too is entangled, worldly interests freshen, and worldly ambi-
tions revive. The man who in the world is as dead to the world

as if he were buried in the cloister is already a saint. But this is our ideal.

Our Rector Fr. Morris shd. be known to you as a historian in your own field and epoch of history.

Believe me your affectionate friend
GERARD M. HOPKINS S.J.

Oct. 17 1881.

TO R. W. DIXON

Manresa House, Roehampton, S.W. Oct. 29 1881.

MY DEAR FRIEND,—First I will bring to an end my criticisms on your poems; for I hear that our month's retreat is to begin on Wednesday evening. *Too Much Friendship*, though written with a flowing and powerful pen, I find less pleasure in than in *Love's Casuistry*. The story has something of the primness of *Elegant Extracts* about it and this has infected the diction even. The motive is good, the strain and its reaction, but between these two extremes the intermediate action has in it something, as Horace calls it, 'odiously incredible'. One feels, you must have felt, that Hypatia (whom Septimius could never have trusted: she would play the same trick after marriage) told her husband that Alcander was a *muff*, she had always felt it and his behaviour in the matter of the surrender made her certain; and that they were not grateful, on the contrary they could not forgive him the obligation he laid them under, looked sheepish when he turned up, and after his death without shame said that that was happiest for all concerned. The language is a quaint medley of Middle-Ages and 'QueenAnnery', a combination quite of our age and almost even of our decade, as we see in Morris and that school (to which you, I suppose, belong), and having a charm of its own that I relish and admire, but as a thing alien to me. Here is a pleasing instance:

> Rattled her keys, unfavourable sign,
> And on her turning wheel gan to decline.

The first line is like the *Rape of the Lock*:

> Spadillio first, unconquerable lord—

the second is like Spencer.[12] It is the opening, I think, that suffers most from Popery: one thinks it should have more epigram or less of it. This spirit you throw off first at the fine passage about the beasts in Spring.

The other passages that strike me as finest are Septimius' passionate cries and confession, especially at 'I cannot name her'; Alcander's return from seeing the couple off in stormy weather; 'With him he long conferred . . . next he made'; 'There as he sat alone . . . car was seen', especially the stroke about the clouds; and Alcander's mad soliloquy. The couplet about the bat and dove is of canonical beauty and the phrase about 'the perfect pattern wretch', besides of course many scattered touches like 'walked when Hesper bid'.

Alas! a fat lot of comfort the poor creature got from seeing those two worldlings from St. John's Wood kneel over him, in mortal dread that he would come to again.

The passage about Rome 'Beside the Virgin's Fount . . . itself hath built' seems to me like taskwork and written in Castalian (which is a better name than Parnassian).

I have now then nothing to do but to fold up your precious packet and return it, begging your pardon much for having kept it so long and expressing the pleasure the reading it has given me. The poems have grown on me while they have been in my keeping and would, I dare say, grow on me more if I read them longer, so that I feel that perhaps the objections I have made would fade away with a better appreciation and as my mind took from familiarity the right perspective of each thought as it came. On the beauties which characterise the whole I have spoken on different occasions in the course of criticising particulars and I do not like to repeat myself now. Their Muse still keeps the hold on my mind and affections it established many years ago. My mind indeed is older, its tastes undergo change, but then of course so is yours, and if I could not now be moved with such a fresh enthusiasm (I am not sure at least how it would be) as my almost boyhood was with the appletrees in *Mother and Daughter*, the nine lovers and their names and drapery in *Love's Consolation*, the march-past in *St. John*, the garland of images about the Church or the Beloved in the same, and many things in your first volume more, perhaps then I shd.

not so well have appreciated the wind and wetness of your MS landscape pieces now by me. However this may be, richness of imagery belongs especially to youth, broader effects to the maturer; what therefore I now want to see is that great work, the epic or romance of which Bridges seemed to say great things, but the very subject of which I never learnt— And also those other pieces of which you spoke. But this cannot be just now, not until my time of tertianship is over. Of course they will not lose by keeping, if God spares your life. You shall therefore have the MS packet in a day or two after I send this.

As for my music, there are four tunes—(1) to 'the Feathers of the Willow' made years ago and only now extant in my memory; (2) to *Sky that rollest ever:* my sister is harmonising this; she says she is doing her very best and as she likes it best of all the airs of mine she has seen it is likely she will make a good thing of it; and she is to send it straight to you, so that you may get it any day; (3) to the *Rainbow:* this is so very peculiar, that I cannot trust anyone to harmonise it and must, if the opportunity should offer and my knowledge ever be sufficient, do it myself; (4) to *Does the South Wind:* this is not quite finished and only written in sol-fa score; it will wait too.

On the Sonnet and its history a learned book or two learned books have been published of late and all is known about it— but not by me. The reason why the sonnet has never been so effective or successful in England as in Italy I believe to be this: it is not so long as the Italian sonnet; it is not long enough, I will presently say how. Now in the form of any work of art the intrinsic measurements, the proportions, that is, of the parts to one another and to the whole, are no doubt the principal point, but still the extrinsic measurements, the absolute quantity or size goes for something. Thus supposing in the Doric Order the Parthenon to be the standard of perfection, then if the columns of the Parthenon have so many semidiameters or modules to their height, the architrave so many, and so on these will be the typical proportions. But if a building is raised on a notably greater scale it will be found that these proportions for the columns and the rest are no longer satisfactory, so that one of two things—either the proportions must be changed or the Order abandoned. Now if the Italian sonnet is one of the most successful forms of composition known, as it is reckoned to be, its proportions, inward and outward, must be pretty near perfection. The English sonnet has the same inward proportions, 14 lines, 5 feet to the line, and the rhymes and so on may be made as in the strictest Italian type. Nevertheless it is notably shorter and would therefore appear likely to be unsuccessful, from want not of comparative but of absolute length. For take any lines from an Italian sonnet, as

> Non ha l'ottimo⌒artista⌒alcun concetto
> Che⌒un marmor solo⌒in se non circonscriva.

Each line has two elisions and a heavy ending or 13 syllables, though only 10 or, if you like, 11 count in the scanning. An Italian heroic line then and consequently a sonnet will be longer than an English in the proportion 13 : 10, which is considerable. But this is not all: the syllables themselves are longer. We have seldom such a delay in the voice as is given to the syllable by double letters (as *ottimo* and *concetto*) or even by two or more consonants (as *artista* and *circonscriva*) of any sort, read as Italians read. Perhaps then the proportions are near 4 : 3 or 3 : 2. The English sonnet is then in comparison with the Italian short, light, tripping, and trifling.

This has been instinctively felt and the best sonnets shew various devices successfully employed to make up for the shortcoming. It may be done by the mere gravity of the thought, which compels a longer dwelling on words, as in Wordsworth (who otherwise is somewhat light in his versification), e.g.

> Earth has not anything to shew more fair—etc;

or by inversion and a periodic construction, which has something of the same effect: there is a good deal of this in Bridges' sonnets; or by breaks and pauses, as

> Captain or colonel or knight-at-arms;

or by many monosyllables, as

> Both them I serve and of their train am I:

this is common with τοὺς περὶ[13] Swinburne; by the weight of the syllables themselves, strong or circumflexed and so on, as may be marked in Gray's sonnet, an exquisite piece of art, whatever Wordsworth may say,

> In vain to me the smiling mornings shine—

(this sonnet is remarkable for its falling or trochaic rhythm—

> In | vain to | me the | smiling | mornings | shine—

and not

> In vain | to me | the smil | ing morn | ings shine),

and it seems to me that for a mechanical difficulty the most mechanical remedy is the best: none, I think, meet it so well as these 'outriding' feet I sometimes myself employ, for they more than equal the Italian elisions and make the whole sonnet rather longer, if anything, than the Italian is. Alexandrine lines (used throughout) have the same effect: this is of course a departure from the Italian, but French sonnets are usually in Alexandrines.

The above reasoning wd. shew that any metre (in the same rhythm) will be longer in Italian than in English and this is in fact, I believe, the case and is the reason perhaps why the *ottava rima* has never had the success in England it has had in Italy and why Spencer[14] found it necessary to lengthen it in the ration from 20 to 23 (= 80 to 92).

Surrey's sonnets are fine, but so far as I remember them they are strict in form. I look upon Surrey as a great writer and of the purest style. But he was an experimentalist, as you say, and all his experiments are not successful. I feel ashamed however to talk of English or any literature, of which I was always very ignorant and which I have ceased to read.

The alteration 'seek a part' will meet the difficulty of the mixed metaphor. 'Love's mast' will then be the post. But I had imagined that you were speaking of that mast itself as a place of danger, subject to the storms of speculation, panics, failures, inflations, depressions, 'bears', 'bulls', and swindles.

This must be my last letter on literary matters while I stay here, for they are quite out of keeping with my present duties. I am very glad my criticisms should be of any service to you: they have involved a labour of love.

Nov. 2—My sister is unwilling to send you the music, with which she is not satisfied, till I have seen it. It must therefore wait awhile.

I am ashamed at the expressions of high regard which your last letter and others have contained, kind and touching as they are, and do not know whether I ought to reply to them or not. This I say: my vocation puts before me a standard so high that a higher can be found nowhere else. The question then for me is not whether I am willing (if I may guess what is in your mind) to make a sacrifice of hopes of fame (let us suppose), but whether I am not to undergo a severe judgment from God for the lothness I have shewn in making it, for the reserves I may have in my heart made, for the backward glances I have given with my hand upon the plough, for the waste of time the very compositions you admire may have caused and their preoccupation of the mind which belonged to more sacred or more binding duties, for the disquiet and the thoughts of vainglory they have given rise to. A purpose may look smooth and perfect from without but be frayed and faltering from within. I have never wavered in my vocation, but I have not lived up to it. I destroyed the verse I had written when I entered the Society and meant to write no more; the *Deutschland* I began after a long interval at the chance suggestion of my superior, but that being done it is a question whether I did well to write anything else. However I shall, in my present mind, continue to compose, as occasion shall fairly allow, which I am afraid will be seldom and indeed for some years past has been scarcely ever, and let what I produce wait and take its chance; for a very spiritual man once told me that with things like composition the best sacrifice was not to destroy one's work but to leave it entirely to be disposed of by obedience. But I can scarcely fancy myself asking a superior to publish a volume of my verses and I own that humanly there is very little likelihood of that ever coming to pass. And to be sure if I chose to look at things on one side and not the other I could of course regret this bitterly. But there is more peace and it is the holier lot to be unknown than to be known.—In no case am I willing to write anything while in my present condition: the time is precious and will not return again and I know I shall not regret my forbearance. If I do get hereafter any opportunity of writing poetry I could find it in my heart to finish a tragedy of which I have a few dozen lines written and the leading thoughts for the rest in my head on the subject of St. Winefred's martyrdom: as it happens, tomorrow is her feastday.

I hope you may have all happiness in your marriage. You have, I think, no children of your own, but Bridges told me he met your two step daughters at Hayton.

I am afraid our retreat will not begin tonight after all.

Believe me always your affectionate friend

GERARD M. HOPKINS S.J.

I should tell you that my letters now are opened.

TO ROBERT BRIDGES

Stonyhurst College, Blackburn. Oct. 18 1882.

DEAREST BRIDGES,—I have read of Whitman's (1) 'Pete' in the library at Bedford Square (and perhaps something else; if so I forget), which you pointed out; (2) two pieces in the *Athenaeum* or *Academy*, one on the Man-of-War Bird, the other beginning 'Spirit that formed this scene'; (3) short extracts in a review by Saintsbury in the *Academy*: this is all I remember. I cannot have read more than a half a dozen pieces at most.

This, though very little, is quite enough to give a strong impression of his marked and original manner and way of thought and in particular of his rhythm. It might be even enough, I shall not deny, to originate or, much more, influence another's style: they say the French trace their whole modern school of landscape to a single piece of Constable's exhibited at the Salon early this century.

The question then is only about the fact. But first I may as well say what I should not otherwise have said, that I always knew in my heart Walt Whitman's mind to be more like my own than any other man's living. As he is a very great scoundrel this is not a pleasant confession. And this also makes

me the more desirous to read him and the more determined
that I will not.

Nevertheless I believe that you are quite mistaken about
this piece and that on second thoughts you will find the fancied resemblance diminish and the imitation disappear.[15]

And first of the rhythm. Of course I saw that there was to
the eye something in my long lines like this, that the one
would remind people of the other. And both are in irregular
rhythms. There the likeness ends. The pieces of his I read
were mostly in an irregular rhythmic prose: that is what they
are thought to be meant for and what they seemed to me
to be. Here is a fragment of a line I remember: 'or a handkerchief designedly dropped'. This is in a dactylic rhythm—or
let us say anapaestic; for it is a great convenience in English
to assume that the stress is always at the end of the foot;
the consequence of which assumption is that in ordinary verse
there are only two English feet possible, the iamb and the
anapaest, and even in my regular sprung rhythm only one
additional, the fourth paeon: for convenience' sake assuming
this, then the above fragment is anapaestic—'or a hánd | ker-
chief . . . | . desígn | edly drópped'—and there is a break
down, a designed break of rhythm, after 'handkerchief', done
no doubt that the line may not become downright verse, as it
would be if he had said 'or a handkerchief purposely
dropped'. Now you can of course say that he meant pure
verse and that the foot is a paeon—'or a hánd | kerchief desígn
| edly drópped'; or that he means, without fuss, what I should
achieve by looping the syllable *de* and calling that foot an
outriding foot—for the result might be attained either way.
Here then I must make the answer which will apply here
and to all like cases and to the examples which may be found
up and down the poets of the use of sprung rhythm—*if they
could have done it they would*: sprung rhythm, once you hear
it, is so eminently natural a thing and so effective a thing
that if they had known of it they would have used it. Many
people, as we say, have been 'burning', but they all missed
it; they took it up and mislaid it again. So far as I know—I am

enquiring and presently I shall be able to speak more de-
cidedly—it existed in full force in Anglo saxon verse and in
great beauty; in a degraded and doggrel shape in *Piers
Ploughman* (I am reading that famous poem and am coming
to the conclusion that it is not worth reading); Greene was
the last who employed it at all consciously and he never continuously; then it disappeared—for one cadence in it here and
there is not sprung rhythm and one swallow does not make
a spring. (I put aside Milton's case, for it is altogether singular.) In a matter like this a thing does not exist, is not *done*
unless it is wittingly and willingly done; to recognise the form
you are employing and to mean it is everything. To apply
this: there is (I suppose, but you will know) no sign that
Whitman means to use paeons or outriding feet where these
breaks in rhythm occur; it seems to me a mere extravagance
to think he means people to understand of themselves what
they are slow to understand even when marked or pointed
out. If he does not mean it then he does not do it; or in short
what he means to write—and writes—is rhythmic prose and
that only. And after all, you probably grant this.

Good. Now prose rhythm in English is always one of two
things (allowing my convention about scanning upwards or
from slack to stress and not from stress to slack)—either
iambic or anapaestic. You may make a third measure (let us
call it) by intermixing them. One of these three simple measures then, all iambic or all anapaestic or mingled iambic and
anapaestic, is what he in every case means to write. He
dreams of no other and he *means* a rugged or, as he calls it
in that very piece 'Spirit that formed this scene' (which is
very instructive and should be read on this very subject),
a 'savage' art and rhythm.

Extremes meet, and (I must for truth's sake say what
sounds pride) this savagery of his art, this rhythm in its last
ruggedness and decomposition into common prose, comes
near the last elaboration of mine. For that piece of mine is
very highly wrought. The long lines are not rhythm run to
seed: everything is weighed and timed in them. Wait till they
have taken hold of your ear and you will find it so. No, but
what it *is* like is the rhythm of Greek tragic choruses or of
Pindar: which is pure sprung rhythm. And that has the same

changes of cadence from point to point as this piece. If you want to try it, read one till you have settled the true places of the stress, mark these, then read it aloud, and you will see. Without this these choruses are prose bewitched; with it they are sprung rhythm like that piece of mine.

Besides, why did you not say *Binsey Poplars* was like Whitman? The present piece is in the same kind and vein, but developed, an advance. The lines and the stanzas (of which there are two in each poem and having much the same relation to one another) are both longer, but the two pieces are greatly alike: just look. If so how is this a being untrue to myself? I am sure it is no such thing.

The above remarks are not meant to run down Whitman. His 'savage' style has advantages, and he has chosen it; he says so. But you cannot eat your cake and keep it: he eats his offhand, I keep mine. It makes a very great difference. Neither do I deny all resemblance. In particular I noticed in 'Spirit that formed this scene' a preference for the alexandrine. I have the same preference: I came to it by degrees, I did not take it from him.

About diction the matter does not allow me so clearly to point out my independence as about rhythm. I cannot think that the present piece owes anything to him. I hope not, here especially, for it is not even spoken in my own person but in that of St. Winefred's maidens. It ought to sound like the thoughts of a good but lively girl and not at all like—not at all like Walt Whitman. But perhaps your mind may have changed by this.

I wish I had not spent so much time in defending the piece. Believe me your affectionate friend

GERARD.

Oct. 19 1882. I am not sure I shall not ask C. D. to let me see at least one packet of Mano. He should, every one should now, use one of these reproductive processes: it is next to printing and at least it secures one against irretrievable loss by the post. All our masters here use the gelatine process for flying sheets etc.

TO ALEXANDER BAILLIE

Stonyhurst College, Blackburn. Jan. 14 1883.

DEAREST BAILLIE,—I believe I am writing chiefly to withdraw something I said at our last meeting, though if there had been nothing to withdraw still I ought to write; but blackguardry stamps my whole behaviour to you from first to last.

Strong words are seldom much good and the more of heat the less of reason. The strong word I repent of using was that if ever there was a humbug it was Swedenborg. What I might reasonably have said (and what I really meant) was that Swedenborgianism (what a word!) is humbug. But I ought not to have seemed to imply that Swedenborg himself was an imposter or anything of the nature of Cagliostro, for so far as I know there is no ground for saying this. He had some very strange experiences: how he came by them no matter, but he may have related them faithfully. It is however a great folly of his followers to build on them. His first dealing with the other world took place at an eating-house in London, where after a very heavy dinner (so he is quoted as saying in his journal) he saw the cieling [sic] (or the floor) covered with hideous reptiles. Then he was aware of a light in a corner of the room and of a luminous figure which sternly said to him 'Do not eat so much'. After that he began to receive communications. The circumstances suggest delirium tremens, as everyone must feel. Whatever the explanation, no sensible man would feel happy in a religion which began to be revealed in that way.

I am here to coach classics for the London University Intermediate (say Moderations) and B.A. (say Greats) examinations. I like my pupils and do not wholly dislike the work, but I fall into or continue in a heavy weary state of body and mind in which my go is gone (the elegance of that phrase! as Thackeray says, it makes one think what vast sums must have been spent on my education!) I make no way with what I read, and seem but half a man. It is a sad thing to say. I try, and am even meant to try, in my spare time (and if I were fresher or if it were anyone but myself there would be a good deal of spare time taking short and long together) to write some books; but I find myself so tired or so harassed I fear they will never be written. The one that would interest you most is on the Greek Lyric Art or on, more narrowly, the art of the choric and lyric parts of the Gk. plays. I want it to be in two parts, one the metre, the other the style. It is, I am afraid, too ambitious of me, so little of a scholar as I am; only I think what I should say would throw a new light and that if I did not perhaps no one else would. But it is a laborious business and why shd. I undertake it? There are, I believe, learned books lately written in Germany on the choric metres and music, which if I could see and read them would either serve me or quench me; but on the other head I do not anticipate being anticipated—so to say. My thought is that in any lyric passage of the tragic poets (perhaps not so much in Euripides as the other) there are—usually; I will not say always, it is not likely—two strains of thought running together and like counterpointed; the overthought that which everybody, editors, see (when one does see anything—which in the great corruption of the text and original obscurity of the diction is not everywhere) and which might for instance be abridged or paraphrased in square marginal blocks as in some books carefully written; the other, the underthought, conveyed chiefly in the choice of metaphors etc used and often only half realised by the poet himself, not necessarily having any connection with the subject in hand but usually having a connection and suggested by some circumstance of the scene or of the story. I cannot prove that this is really so except by a large induction of examples and perhaps not irrefragably even then nor without examples can I even make my meaning plain. I will give only one, the chorus with which Aeschylus' *Suppliants* begins. The underthought which plays through this is that the Danaids flying from their cousins are like their own ancestress Io teazed by the gadfly and caressed by Zeus and the rest of that foolery. E.g. δῖαν δὲ λιποῦσαι | χθόνα σύγχορτον Συρίᾳ φεύγομεν: the suggestion is of a herd of cows feeding next a herd of bulls. Shortly follows a mention of Io and her story. Then comes δεξαισθ' ἱκετην | τὸν θηλυγενῆ στόλου αἰδοίῳ | πνεύματι χώρας this alludes to the ἐπίπνοια by which Epaphus was conceived—ἀρσενοπληθῆ δ᾽ ἑσμοῦ ὑβριστὴν Αἰγυπτογενῆ etc:[16] this suggests the gadfly. Perhaps what I ought to say is that the underthought is commonly an echo or shadow of the overthought, something like canons and repetitions in music, treated in a different manner, but that sometimes it may be independent of it. I find this same principle of composition in St. James' and St. Peter's and St. Jude's Epistles, an undercurrent of thought governing the choice of images used. Perhaps I spoke of this to you before.

I could write more, but have written enough now. Tell me about the Rossetti exhibition; but you need not enlarge on Dante's Dream or on Mr. Rae's pictures, for these I have seen. In an old letter of yours, many years old (I have been reading them again), you speak of Pindar, taking exception to some things and giving examples. I do not on the whole agree with your objections and should defend the *examples. This sort of thing I should explain in that book if it were written. I shd. also give some fancy music to some choruses and odes, plainchant, not an attempted reproduction of Gk. music but as a means of bringing out the rhythm.

Be very interesting and entertaining: what else could a letter of yours be? Meanwhile and ever after believe me your affectionate and grateful friend

GERARD HOPKINS S.J.

---

* It turns on their explanation. If the explanation suits them it defends them.

TO COVENTRY PATMORE

Stonyhurst. Nov. 7 1883.

MY DEAR MR. PATMORE,—It would be a calamity in literature if *Tamerton Church Tower* were suppressed and a consummation devoutly to be wished against, but being to find fault I found the songs faulty, though I knew they could not now be altered. It is an early piece and so immature, but so is *Love's Labour's Lost* and others of Shakspere's plays, which are faulty though they teem with genius and could never be spared. It is recognized by sound critics that poets

ripen and that faults of youth and immaturity can be found
in works which are even masterpieces in other ways. I say
the same, in proportion, of the *Kiss* excepting that the objection I made there was made on another ground. We must
also acknowledge that if we criticise in the rigour of justice
no human work except short pieces of music and small examples in the arts of design could stand.

I now make some remarks on the *Study on English Metrical Law*. There are some things in this essay I do not find
myself altogether in agreement with, but on these I do not
touch; I only point out what seem to be overstatements or
understatements and so forth upon the ground there taken.

P. 20 'With us, the places . . . coincide', p. 22 'Let me now
ask', with all that follows—The treatment of English spoken
accent here is unsatisfactory: you nowhere say what it is.
Now if, as you say, the learned are pretty well agreed what
the old Greek accent was, which no living ear ever heard,
we must surely be able to know and say with certainty what
the English is, which we cannot even dispute about without
exhibiting as fast as we open our mouths. If some books say
it is long quantity, that is so grossly stupid as to need no
refutation; it is enough to quote words—'thŏrough pācéd
blăckgūard, ăgŏnīsīng hĕadache, mĕssĕngērs, căttle mărket, ĭl-
lūstrating, Bĭllīngsgate, Lĭvērpoōl' and so on. But I do not remember ever hearing any sensible man say that. It is plain
and, so far as I know, it is commonly agreed that it is stress.
The Greek accent was a *tonic accent*, was tone, pitch of note:
it may have included a stress, but essentially it was pitch. In
like manner the English accent is *emphatic accent*, is stress:
it commonly includes clear pitch, but essentially it is stress.
Pitch totally disappears in whispering, but our accent is perfectly given when we whisper. But perhaps one ought further
to explain what stress is. Stress appears so elementary an idea
as does not need and scarcely allows of definition; still this
may be said of it, that it is the making a thing more, or making it markedly, what it already is: it is the bringing out its
nature. Accordingly stress on a syllable (which is English accent proper) is the making much of that syllable, more than
of others; stress on a word or sentence (which is emphasis) is
the making much of that word or sentence, more than of

others. Commonly and naturally what we emphasise we say louder, and the accented syllables, words, and so on are in fact what we catch first and lose last in a distant speaker; but this is not essential. Also what we emphasise we say clearer, more distinctly, and in fact to this is due the slurring in English of unaccented syllables; which is a beauty of the language, so that only misguided people say Dev-*il*, six-*pence* distinctly; still even this is not essential. The accented syllable then is the one of which the nature is well brought out, whatever may become of the others. When the others are as well brought out then, but this is seldom, happens that which you so acutely point out, that the mind, as it does to the tick tock of a clock, supplies for a while that difference which has ceased to be marked outwardly. And this is clearly seen in singing; for, however smoothly and equally the notes are sung, if the accent of the syllable does not fall on the accent, primary or secondary, of the bar—though in fact neither the note nor the syllable sung to it were any louder than the rest —the effect is intolerable; if for instance instead of

Full fa-thom five thy *etc.*

we made it

Now full fa - thom five —

I put aside of course syncopations and other calculated effects, as in all art.

It only remains to say that the stress, the *ictus,* of our verse is founded on and in the beginning the very same as the stress which is our accent. In fact in smooth and simple and especially in strongly marked lyric measures, as, say, Poe's *Raven,* one may read on a long while together without a single discrepancy, and when discrepancies do arise they begin so naturally that people may well not notice them: as suppose a man said in prose 'a penniless adventurer is often in extremities'—this can be seen to run into alternate strong and weak beats, say iambs or trochees, according to where you begin scanning; and perhaps people wd. not notice that every other strong beat, every fourth syllable, that is, is really scarcely marked at all, so inevitably does the mind supply it. This indeed falls into double-iambic or double-trochaic feet, or in music bars of four time, in which the first accent is stronger than the second, but from the same kind of sentences may also arise the *blank stresses*, as I am accustomed to call them, of the ten-syllable line and other lines; for in fact in Milton few lines have five real stresses, one or two being blank, though in idea there are always five.—However you hold that the ten-syllable line has three bars, I remember; but you will agree with what I have been saying.

I have written a great deal on this head, but all comes to this, that you ought, in my opinion, to say once clearly what English accent is and not, after quoting different views, leave the truth unexpressed as if there could be or in fact were any doubt about the matter.

(By the by, though I have done it above and it is a momentary convenience, it is a radically bad principle to call English feet iambs and trochees. In music it is still worse; it is a complete overturning of the meaning of words. A Greek would say that the bar I have given of 'Full fathom five' contained a spondee followed by a syncopated trochee—in Greek notation | ∠ – | | ∠ ⌣ | —or was a syncopated fourth epitrite — | ∠ – ∠ ⌣ |; whereas modern musical writers would, I suppose, say it contained two trochees. Names ought to be invented for rhythmic feet. In modern verse much harm does not arise from this confusion—though what you are saying at pp. 66 and 79 would not have needed so much explanation but for it—, but music is just the very place where the difference of time-feet and rhythm-feet recognised in Greek poetry is still in force and where therefore the established meaning of words ought rigidly to be kept to.)

P. 22, the paragraph on tonic accent—The best thing I have read on Greek accent is an essay by the late American Professor Hadley (in his collected Essays). It seems to me that, looking at such facts as you here cite, we shall be justified in saying the acute tonic accent was the best marked pitch in each word; which pitch was commonly a rise (say of a fifth, to the dominant—the most natural interval) from the keynote or readingnote; but sometimes a fall of, say, a fourth, to the same dominant, I mean of course the octave of the other, below. In like manner the grave accent, which Hadley reasonably says means not a lower note, that is, one lower than the keynote or readingnote, but only one not so high as the acute above it, will commonly be a rise of, say, a major third, to the mediant, but sometimes a fall of, say, a minor third, to the submediant. The circumflex is no doubt a sort of turn or shake, two notes to a syllable instead of one or a rise and fall instead of a rise only. It is to be remarked that men seem to have found it hard to reach the simple notion of a note. In the passage you quote at p. 15 Cicero says there are only three sounds in music, the turn, the rise, and the fall— for so I interpret him; and it is believed that our present musical notation arose from a complicated system of accents, rising, falling, and so on (a great variety of marks, now unnecessary, may be seen in books on the history of plain chant, e.g. Helmore's Primer in Novello's Music Primer series); as though men first were struck by the change or passage of sound and later seized the points of departure and arrival. It is true this does not agree with what I have said above about the grave accent, but modern critics, as Roby and Munro, strongly suspect Cicero, Quintilian, and the Latin writers of bungling on the subject and misapplying Greek theory to Latin, and if it is true (but I have not verified it) what a friend told me of Lucretius, that he says *distant objects do not appear smaller but only less distinct,* I could believe anything of a Roman writer.

As then the English accent is stress and yet we can make the stress on the unaccented syllables of an emphatic word more marked than on the accented of an unemphatic one, the general or rhetorical emphasis overriding the particular and syllabic, so in Greek no doubt it was possible for the accent to be ordinarily a high tone and yet for the lowest note of one word to be higher than the highest of another or even for the note usually raised on occasion to be lowered as markedly the general and rhetorical intonation here too controlling and modifying the syllabic and particular. More shortly, emphasis does not destroy our accent of stress nor need intonation have destroyed their accent of tone, and I should have liked something of the sort to be expressed here.

P. 30 'In song, we have gradually' etc—Here I would say 'Art advised of that?' for so far as I know it is not the fact. Grétry should not be trusted about the short compass of old songs, for French popular music is remarkable, it is said, for just this monotony and short compass, while British is not. The Welsh air of the *Camp*, better known as 'Of a noble race was Shenkin', to my mind the most majestic pure melody that was ever composed, is of great range, from G above the treble down to B below the ledger line. 'And how should I your true-love know?' has one note less (as I used to know it). *Maggie Lauder* a fine air has the same, twelve notes. 'Full fathom five' has the same; and twelve notes, that is an octave and the dominant above, is so natural a range that many airs must have it. Other things being alike, the greater the range the greater the room for fine effects. The rise or fall of an octave is a most vigorous effect and it is inconvenient not to be able to set this on, say, any but the keynote. The Welsh air I have quoted, besides several splendid octave falls, rises its whole range at once in one place and ten notes in another. You may of course have had real cases in your mind, but it is possible you were thinking of very low or very high notes in airs not of great range but set low or high for display's sake. For my part I am rather struck with the tameness of modern songs. It is true I seldom hear them.

P. 52 I should like you to reconsider the matter of alliteration in vowels. To my ear no alliteration is more marked or more beautiful, and I used to take it for granted as an obvious fact that every initial vowel lettered to every other before ever I knew that anything of the sort was practised in Anglo Saxon verse. I cannot agree that this alliteration is destroyed by using the same vowel. No doubt the effect is more beautiful, more artistic, with a change of vowels; still with the same one it is heard. How this alliteration arises is, I know, very hard to say, but to my ear there is no doubt about the fact.

But about Pope's line 'And apt alliteration's artful aid' (if that is the line in full) there is more to be said. Pope was the great master of metre of his day, as we know, but (like Tennyson in our day, who on his own ground is so strong but has made a sad mess of his classical experiments) he was nothing *ultra crepidam* and here he seems to have gone *ultra crepidam*. He meant the line as a sample of the effect of alliteration, but in doing so he made two blunders. For first no doubt he thought, because every word began with *a*, therefore every word began with the same vowel. But in fact there are four initial vowels or three at the least in that line. The *a* in *apt* is the common English short *a*. The *a artful* is the English broad *a*, a very different thing. The *ai* in *aid* is called long *a* in English, but is really one of the continental *es*, and is still more different. Then the initials of *and* and *alliteration*, if you bring them distinctly out, are the same as that of *apt* no doubt, but slurred, as we commonly pronounce them, they are another vowel still. And secondly if the vowel was really the same throughout then it was not the better but rather the worse for that. Still it seems to me that the line does alliterate and that Pope's ear heard that, though his reason was astray on the subject.

P. 56 'This metre . . outlived the Anglo-Saxon language several centuries'—You know the attack made of late on the name Anglo-Saxon. I think and I see that others think it is pedantic, but it seems to me that if ever an objection could be made to the use of the term 'Anglo-Saxon language' without reserve or explanation it might be in this sentence. For 'several centuries' cannot mean less than three; which would carry us back from Piers Ploughman to the Conquest. Now anyone can see by glancing at a few lines that the language of England before and after the Conquest for some time differed only by almost imperceptible differences.

P. 63 note on Welsh verse—I shd. like to lay what I know of the facts shortly before you, but will do it, if I can, in another letter.

P. 79 'Six real anapaests counting "wrastling" as one'—You must mean that 'wrastling' is of three syllables and the last two of these enter into one of the anapaests, not that it is an anapaest as it stands: of itself it is rather a dactyl.

I forgot to say that in *L'Allegro* p. 101 the line 'Between such friends as thou and I' is strange and, I rather think, indefensible grammar. You must mean *are* to be understood, but can it be understood when there is no verb in the other limb of the parallel? The odd use of *I* after prepositions in Shakspere is a colloquialism I should think inadmissible in such verse as this.

I will not write of *Mano* yet awhile.

Believe me, dear Mr. Patmore, yours very sincerely

GERARD M. HOPKINS S.J.

I will try and let you have my remarks on the *Eros* volume soon, if it is not too late. This being your ripest work I feel more distrust of my judgment upon it.

Nov. 10 1883.

Perhaps you do not know that the Latin writers exchanged and misapplied the Greek words *arsis* and *thesis*. *Arsis* is properly the rise of the foot in dancing or of the conductor's arm in beating time, *thesis* the fall of the same. *Arsis* therefore is the light part of the foot, I call it the 'slack'; *thesis* is the heavy or strong, the stress. For this reason some writers now refuse to say *arsis* and *thesis* and use *ictus* only. It is clear the Latin writers thought of *arsis* as effort, *thesis* as the fall to rest after effort.

AUTHOR'S PREFACE[17]

[c. 1883]

THE poems in this book are written some in Running Rhythm, the common rhythm in English use, some in Sprung Rhythm, and some in a mixture of the two. And those in the common rhythm are some counterpointed, some not.

Common English rhythm, called Running Rhythm above, is measured by feet of either two or three syllables and (putting aside the imperfect feet at the beginning and end of lines and also some unusual measures, in which feet seem to be paired together and double or composite feet to arise) never more or less.

Every foot has one principal stress or accent, and this or the syllable it falls on may be called the Stress of the foot and the other part, the one or two unaccented syllables, the Slack. Feet (and the rhythms made out of them) in which the stress comes first are called Falling Feet and Falling Rhythms, feet and rhythm in which the slack comes first are

called Rising Feet and Rhythms, and if the stress is between
two slacks there will be Rocking Feet and Rhythms. These
distinctions are real and true to nature; but for purposes of
scanning it is a great convenience to follow the example of
music and take the stress always first, as the accent or the
chief accent always comes first in a musical bar. If this is
done there will be in common English verse only two possible
feet—the so-called accentual Trochee and Dactyl, and cor-
respondingly only two possible uniform rhythms, the so-called
Trochaic and Dactylic. But they may be mixed and then
what the Greeks called a Logaoedic Rhythm arises. These
are the facts and according to these the scanning of ordinary
regularly-written English verse is very simple indeed and to
bring in other principles is here unnecessary.

But because verse written strictly in these feet and by
these principles will become same and tame the poets have
brought in licences and departures from rule to give variety,
and especially when the natural rhythm is rising, as in the
common ten-syllable or five-foot verse, rhymed or blank.
These irregularities are chiefly Reversed Feet and Reversed
or Counterpoint Rhythm, which two things are two steps or
degrees of licence in the same kind. By a reversed foot I
mean the putting the stress where, to judge by the rest of the
measure, the slack should be and the slack where the stress,
and this is done freely at the beginning of a line and, in the
course of a line, after a pause; only scarcely ever in the second foot or place and never in the last, unless when the poet
designs some extraordinary effect; for these places are characteristic and sensitive and cannot well be touched. But the
reversal of the first foot and of some middle foot after a strong
pause is a thing so natural that our poets have generally done
it, from Chaucer down, without remark and it commonly
passes unnoticed and cannot be said to amount to a formal
change of rhythm, but rather is that irregularity which all
natural growth and motion shews. If however the reversal is
repeated in two feet running, especially so as to include the
sensitive second foot, it must be due either to great want of
ear or else is a calculated effect, the super-inducing or *mounting* of a new rhythm upon the old; and since the new or
mounted rhythm is actually heard and at the same time the

mind naturally supplies the natural standard foregoing rhythm, for we do not forget what the rhythm is that by rights we should be hearing, two rhythms are in some manner running at once and we have something answerable to counterpoint in music, which is two or more strains of tune going on together, and this is Counterpoint Rhythm. Of this kind of verse Milton is the great master and the choruses of *Samson Agonistes* are written throughout in it—but with the disadvantage that he does not let the reader clearly know what the ground-rhythm is meant to be and so they have struck most readers as merely irregular. And in fact if you counterpoint throughout, since only one of the counter rhythms is actually heard, the other is really destroyed or cannot come to exist, and what is written is one rhythm only and probably Sprung Rhythm, of which I now speak.

Sprung Rhythm, as used in this book, is measured by feet of from one to four syllables, regularly, and for particular effects any number of weak or slack syllables may be used. It has one stress, which falls on the only syllable, if there is only one, or, if there are more, then scanning as above, on the first, and so gives rise to four sorts of feet, a monosyllable and the so-called accentual Trochee, Dactyl, and the First Paeon. And there will be four corresponding natural rhythms; but nominally the feet are mixed and any one may follow any other. And hence Sprung Rhythm differs from Running Rhythm in having or being only one nominal rhythm, a mixed or 'logaoedic' one, instead of three, but on the other hand in having twice the flexibility of foot, so that any two stresses may either follow one another running or be divided by one, two, or three slack syllables. But strict Sprung Rhythm cannot be counterpointed. In Sprung Rhythm, as in logaoedic rhythm generally, the feet are assumed to be equally long or strong and their seeming inequality is made up by pause or stressing.

Remark also that it is natural in Sprung Rhythm for the lines to be *rove over*, that is for the scanning of each line immediately to take up that of the one before, so that if the first has one or more syllables at its end the other must have so many less at its beginning; and in fact the scanning runs on without a break from the beginning, say, of a stanza to the end and all the stanza is one long strain, though written in lines asunder.

Two licences are natural to Sprung Rhythm. The one is rests, as in music; but of this an example is scarcely to be found in this book, unless in the *Echos,* second line. The other is *hangers* or *outrides,* that is one, two, or three slack syllables added to a foot and not counting in the nominal scanning. They are so called because they seem to hang below the line or ride forward or backward from it in another dimension than the line itself, according to a principle needless to explain here. These outriding half feet or hangers are marked by a loop underneath them, and plenty of them will be found.

The other marks are easily understood, namely accents, where the reader might be in doubt which syllable should have the stress; slurs, that is loops *over* syllables, to tie them together into the time of one; little loops at the end of a line to shew that the rhyme goes on to the first letter of the next line; what in music are called pauses ⌒, to shew that the syllable should be dwelt on; and twirls ∼, to mark reversed or counterpointed rhythm.

Note on the nature and history of Sprung Rhythm—Sprung Rhythm is the most natural of things. For (1) it is the rhythm of common speech and of written prose, when rhythm is perceived in them. (2) It is the rhythm of all but the most monotonously regular music, so that in the words of choruses and refrains and in songs written closely to music it arises. (3) It is found in nursery rhymes, weather saws, and so on; because, however these may have been once made in running rhythm, the terminations having dropped off by the change of language, the stresses come together and so the rhythm is sprung. (4) It arises in common verse when reversed or counterpointed, for the same reason.

But nevertheless in spite of all this and though Greek and Latin lyric verse, which is well known, and the old English verse seen in 'Pierce Ploughman' are in sprung rhythm, it has in fact ceased to be used since the Elizabethan age, Greene being the last writer who can be said to have recognised it. For perhaps there was not, down to our days, a single, even short, poem in English in which sprung rhythm is employed—not for single effects or in fixed places—but as the governing principle of the scansion. I say this because the contrary has been asserted: if it is otherwise the poem should be cited.

Some of the sonnets in this book are in five-foot, some in six-foot or Alexandrine lines.

['Pied Beauty' and 'Peace'] are Curtal-Sonnets, that is they are constructed in proportions resembling those of the sonnet proper, namely, 6+4 instead of 8+6, with however a half-line tailpiece (so that the equation is rather $\frac{12}{2} + \frac{9}{2} = \frac{21}{2} = 10\frac{1}{2}$).

IV

PRACTICAL CRITICISM

The most inveterate fault of critics is the tendency to cramp and hedge in by rules the free movements of genius, so that I should say . . . the first requisite for a critic is liberality, and the second liberality, and the third liberality.

TO EDWARD BOND[1]

DEAR EDWARD,—This letter is going to be quite short, as the paper shews. I am at Douglas in the Isle of Man again, same house as last year. Next year (from September) will be spent in teaching at Stonyhurst or elsewhere. Then I am to begin my theology and the course lasts four years.

I want to ask another question. Have you read *Roots?* and who is it by? It is said to be an open secret but to me it is quite close.

I have brought Mat Arnold's poems, the Empedocles volume, down here with me and read them with more interest than rapture, as you will easily understand, for they seem to have all the ingredients of poetry without quite being it—no ease or something or other, like the plum pudding at the English ambassador's, but still they do not leave off of being, as the French say, very beautiful. Besides he seems a very earnest man and distinctly seeing the difference between jest and earnest and a master of both, and this praise will also apply to you, I hope. But then very unhappily he jokes at the wrong things, as I see by a very profane passage quoted from his new book: however that passage though profane is not blasphemous, for we are obliged to think of God by human thoughts and his account of them is substantially true. (I am obliged to go to broad guage [*sic*] paper.) This reminds me that I have been reading the *Grammar of Assent:* have you? It is perhaps heavy reading. The justice and candour and gravity and rightness of mind is what is so beautiful in all he writes but what dissatisfies me (in point of style) is a narrow circle of instance and quotation—in a man too of great learning and of general reading—quite like the papers in the *Spectator* and a want, I think a real want, of brilliancy (which foolish people think every scribbler possesses, but it is no such thing). But he remains nevertheless our greatest living master of style—unless you think otherwise—and widest mind. Now I should be writing more carefully if it were not that people all about are reading extracts of the *Manx Sun* and *Mrs. Brown* and repeating a constructive pun I found my way into at supper and so on.

Besides all this have you read De Morgan's *Budget of Paradoxes?* Now I have given you some matter to write about.

Tomorrow I am going up Snae Fell, from which the Manxman can see the three kingdoms and reflect on the happiness of living under the House of Keys, which is what they call the national parliament.

Remember me very kindly to your people and believe me yr. affectionate friend

GERARD HOPKINS S.J.

Derby Castle, Douglas, Aug. 4, '73.

Aug. 5—I had written the above when yr. letter containing your kind proposal came to hand, after slowly following me fr. Stonyhurst. I am sorry to have been thus unavoidably slow in answering. I am afraid that I must not avail myself of your kindness. On the score of time indeed there wd. be no difficulty on my side but leave for invitations to stay with friends who are not kindred without some more pressing reason than I could shew is so seldom given that I should not wish even to ask it. But it would have been a great pleasure to me if it had been possible.

TO ROBERT BRIDGES

Stonyhurst College, Blackburn (or Whalley). May 13 1878.
DEAREST BRIDGES,—Remark the above address. After July I expect to be stationed in town—111 Mount Street, Grosvenor Square.

I hope your bad cold is gone.

I am very glad to hear the Rondeliers have come to see the beauty of your poetry. I have little acquaintance with their own. I have read a rondeau or rondel by Marzials in the *Athenaeum* beginning and ending 'When I see you': it was very graceful and shewing an art and finish rare in English verse. This makes me the more astonished about *Flop flop*.[2] Is his name Spanish, Provençal, or what? Barring breach of confidence I wish I could have seen his letter and that of the habitually joyous.[3] I think that school is too artificial and exotic to take root and last, is it not?

I enclose you my Eurydice, which the *Month* refused. It is my only copy. Write no bilgewater about it: I will presently tell you what that is and till then excuse the term. I must tell you I am sorry you never read the Deutschland again.

Granted that it needs study and is obscure, for indeed I was not over-desirous that the meaning of all should be quite clear, at least unmistakeable, you might, without the effort that to make it all out would seem to have required, have nevertheless read it so that lines and stanzas should be left in the memory and superficial impressions deepened, and have liked some without exhausting all. I am sure I have read and enjoyed pages of poetry that way. Why, sometimes one enjoys and admires the very lines one cannot understand, as for instance 'If it were done when 'tis done' sqq., which is all obscure and disputed, though how fine it is everybody sees and nobody disputes. And so of many more passages in Shakspere and others. Besides you would have got more weathered to the style and its features—not really odd. Now they say that vessels sailing from the port of London will take (perhaps it should be / used once to take) Thames water for the voyage: it was foul and stunk at first as the ship worked but by degrees casting its filth was in a few days very pure and sweet and wholesomer and better than any water in the world. However that maybe, it is true to my purpose. When a new thing, such as my ventures in the Deutschland are, is presented us our first criticisms are not our truest, best, most homefelt, or most lasting but what come easiest on the instant. They are barbarous and like what the ignorant and the ruck say. This was so with you. The Deutschland on her first run worked very much and unsettled you, thickening and clouding your mind with vulgar mud-bottom and common sewage (I see that I am going it with the image) and just then unhappily you *drew off* your criticisms all stinking (a necessity now of the image) and bilgy, whereas if you had let your thoughts cast themselves they would have been clearer in themselves and more to my taste too. I did not heed them therefore, perceiving they were a first drawing-off. Same of the Eurydice—which being short and easy please read more than once.

Can you tell me who that critic in the *Athenaeum* is that writes very long reviews on English and French poets, essayists, and so forth in a style like De Quincey's, very acute in his remarks, provoking, jaunty, and (I am sorry to say) would-be humorous? He always quotes Persian stories (unless he makes them up) and talks about Rabelæsian humour.[4]

My brother's pictures, as you say, are careless and do not aim high, but I don't think it would be much different if he were a bachelor. But, strange to say—and I shd. never even have suspected it if he had not quite simply told me—he has somehow in painting his pictures, though nothing that the pictures express, a high and quite religious aim; however I cannot be more explanatory.

Your bodysnatch story is ghastly, but so are all bodysnatch stories. My grandfather was a surgeon, a fellow-student of Keats', and once conveyed a body through Plymouth at the risk of his own.

Believe me your affectionate friend

GERARD M. HOPKINS, S.J.

May 21 1878.

Please remember me very kindly to your mother.

To do the Eurydice any kind of justice you must not slovenly read it with the eyes but with your ears, as if the paper were declaiming it at you. For instance the line 'she had come from a cruise training seamen' read without stress and declaim is mere Lloyd's Shipping Intelligence; properly read it is quite a different thing. Stress is the life of it.

TO ROBERT BRIDGES

St. Giles's, Oxford. May 26 1879.

DEAREST BRIDGES,—Your answerable letterage is three deep at least, but nevertheless work is work and of late Fr. Parkinson has sprung a leak (exema) in his leg and been laid up and I in consequence laid on all the harder: indeed he will never, I believe, be very active more, though now he does go about a little.

I shall be very glad to have your brother's book when it appears, and to trace the prototype of you in it will be very interesting.

I have seen no more reviews of you.

The poem you send is fine in thought, but I am not satisfied with the execution altogether: the pictures, except in the first stanza, are somewhat wanting in distinction (I do not of course mean distinctness), and I do not think the rhythm perfect, e.g. 'woodbine with' is a heavy dactyl. Since the syllables in sprung rhythm are not counted, time or equality in strength is of more importance than in common counted rhythm, and your times or strengths do not seem to me equal enough. The line you mark does resemble something in the Deutschland, now that you point it out, but there is no resemblance in the thought and it does not matter. I do not think the line very good; it is besides ambiguous. I understand, I believe everybody would understand, 'O if it were only for thee' to mean/ If I had no guide (to nature's true meaning) but thee: the leading thought is that nature has two different, two opposite aspects, teaching opposite lessons of life—that one is between two stools with the two of them. Is it not? The whole mood and vein is remote; unknown to many temperaments; ineffective, I should think, with any;

belonging to the world of imagination, but genuinely so. I believe you might have expressed it more pointedly though.

Of course I am very much pleased that you like my period-building (or whatever we are to call it) but do not see what is the matter with Patmore's. It is his Unknown Eros you refer to, I suppose. The faults I see in him are bad rhymes; continued obscurity; and, the most serious, a certain frigidity when, as often, the feeling does not flush and fuse the language. But for insight he beats all our living poets, his insight is really profound, and he has an exquisiteness, farfetchedness, of imagery worthy of the best things of the Caroline age. However I cannot spend more time on his praises.

I agree with you that English terza rima is (so far as I have seen it) badly made and tedious and for the reason you give, but you are mistak[en] in thinking the triplet structure is unknown: Shelley's West Wind ode (if I mistake not) and some other ones are *printed* in detached 3-line stanzas. I wrote a little piece so printed when at school and published it in *Once a Week*.

The sestet of the Purcell sonnet is not so clearly worked out as I could wish. The thought is that as the seabird opening his wings with a whiff of wind in your face means the whirr of the motion, but also unaware gives you a whiff of knowledge about his plumage, the marking of which stamps his species, that he does not mean, so Purcell, seemingly intent only on the thought or feeling he is to express or call out, incidentally lets you remark the individualising marks of his own genius.

Sake is a word I find it convenient to use: I did not know when I did so first that it is common in German, in the form *sach*. It is the *sake* of 'for the sake of', *forsake, namesake, keepsake*. I mean by it the being a thing has outside itself, as a voice by its echo, a face by its reflection, a body by its shadow, a man by his name, fame, or memory, *and also* that in the thing by virtue of which especially it has this being abroad, and that is something distinctive, marked, specifically or individually speaking, as for a voice and echo clearness; for a reflected image light, brightness; for a shadow-casting body bulk; for a man genius, great achievements, amiability, and so on. In this case it is, as the sonnet says, distinctive quality in genius.

Wuthering is a Northcountry word for the noise and rush of wind: hence Emily Brontë's 'Wuthering Heights'.

By *moonmarks* I mean crescent shaped markings on the quill-feathers, either in the colouring of the feather or made by the overlapping of one on another.

My sister Kate is staying here with my aunt Mrs. Marsland Hopkins (who has now a house in Holywell).

Believe me your affectionate friend

GERARD M. HOPKINS, S.J.

May 31 1879.

TO ROBERT BRIDGES

St. Giles's, Oxford. Aug. 14 1879.

MY DEAREST BRIDGES,—I must try and tersely scribble you something.

That German word is *sache*, not *sach*, except in compounds: you should have set me right.

Your Picnic verses are very good, the rhymes capital, beyond the ingenuity I credited you with. Some lines however are faulty, as 'Anything more delicious'.

Muirhead, who called here on Sunday, was on that party. I mean Muirhead, who was on that party, called etc.

I wish you would send me all the music you have, to try. I wd. return it. I do not yet the present piece nor comment on it, as I have not had an opportunity of hearing it. I feel sure you have a genius in music—on the strength of the only piece I know 'O earlier': it is an inspiration of melody, but somewhat 'sicklied o'er', as indeed the words are.

To rejoin on some points of your criticisms. Though the analogy in the Candle sonnet may seem forced, yet it is an 'autobiographical' fact that I was influenced and acted on the way there said.

I send a recast of the Handsome Heart. Nevertheless the offence of the rhymes is repeated. I felt myself the objection you make and should only employ the device very sparingly, but you are to know that it has a particular effect, an effect of climax, and shd. so be read, with a rising inflection, after which the next line, beginning with the enclitic, gracefully falls away. And in like manner with proclitics and so on: if a strong word and its epithet or other appendage are divided so that the appendage shall end one line and the supporting word begin the next, the last becomes emphasised by position and heads a fall-away or diminuendo. These little graces help the 'overreaving' of the verse at which I so much aim, make it flow in one long strain to the end of the stanza and so forth.

I am somewhat surprised at your liking this sonnet so much. I thought it not very good. The story was that last Lent, when Fr. Parkinson was laid up in the country, two boys of our congregation gave me much help in the sacristy in Holy Week. I offered them money for their services, which the elder refused, but being pressed consented to take it laid out in a book. The younger followed suit; then when some days after I asked him what I shd. buy answered as in the sonnet. His father is Italian and therefore sells ices. I find within my professional experience now a good deal of matter to write on. I hope to enclose a little scene that touched me at Mount St. Mary's. It is something in Wordsworth's manner; which is, I know, inimitable and unapproachable, still I shall be glad to know if you think it is a success, for pathos has a point as precise as jest has and its happiness 'lies ever in the ear of him that hears, not in the mouth of him that makes'. I hope also soon to shew you a finer thing, in a metre something like the Eurydice, not quite finished yet; also a little song not unlike 'I have loved flowers that fade'. I have added some strokes to the Vale of Clwyd and have hopes of some day finishing it: it is more like your Hymn to Nature than anything else I can think of, the rhythm however widely unlike. Lastly I enclose a sonnet on which I invite minute criticism. I endeavoured in it at a more Miltonic plainness and severity than I have anywhere else. I cannot say it has turned out severe, still less plain, but it seems almost free from quaintness and in aiming at one excellence I may have hit another.

I had quite forgotten the sonnet you have found, but can now recall almost all of it; not so the other piece, birthday lines to my sister, I fancy.

Baliol is the old spelling and the one I prefer, but they have adopted Balliol and one must conform.

I was almost a great admirer of Barnes' Dorset (not Devon) poems. I agree with Gosse, not with you. A proof of their excellence is that you may translate them and they are nearly as good—I say nearly, because if the dialect plays any lawful part in the effect they ought to lose something in losing that. Now Burns loses prodigiously by translation. I have never however read them since my undergraduate days except the one quoted in Gosse's paper, the beauty of which you must allow. I think the use of dialect a sort of unfair play, giving, as you say, 'a peculiar but shortlived charm', setting off for instance a Scotch or Lancashire joke which in standard English comes to nothing. But its lawful charm and use I take to be this, that it sort of guarantees the spontaneousness of the thought and puts you in the position to appraise it on its merits as coming from nature and not books and education. It heightens one's admiration for a phrase just as in architecture it heightens one's admiration of a design to know that it is old work, not new: in itself the design is the same but as taken together with the designer and his merit this circumstance makes a world of difference. Now the use of dialect to a man like Barnes is to tie him down to the things that he or another Dorset man has said or might say, which though it narrows his field heightens his effects. His poems use to charm me also by their Westcountry 'instress', a most peculiar product of England, which I associate with airs like Weeping Winefred, Polly Oliver, or Poor Mary Ann, with Herrick and Herbert with the Worcestershire, Herefordshire, and Welsh landscape, and above all with the smell of oxeyes and applelofts: this instress is helped by particular rhythms and these Barnes employs; as, I remember, in 'Linden Ore' and a thing with a refrain like 'Alive in the Spring'.

By the by I have seen a Westcountryman—V.

                                                                                  S.

                                                                                  S.

                                                                                          Coles—

for the first time since I went down. I am truly fond of him and wish . . . except these bonds.

I should be very glad to see your prose of Michelangelo's sonnets and also your verse, for though I do not like verse-renderings of verse (according to the saying *Traduttore traditore*), yet I think you could do them if anyone can. I have seen something of them, in particular a most striking one beginning—

Non ha l'ottimo artista alcun concetto.

By the by, inversions—As you say, I do avoid them, because they weaken and because they destroy the earnestness or in-earnestness of the utterance. Nevertheless in prose I use them more than other people, because there they have great advantages of another sort. Now these advantages they should have in verse too, but they must not seem to be due to the verse: that is what is so enfeebling (for instance the finest of your sonnets to my mind has a line enfeebled by inversion plainly due to the verse, as I said once before 'Tis joy the falling of her fold to view'—but how it should be mended I do not see). As it is, I feel my way to their use. However in a nearly finished piece I have a very bold one indeed. So also I cut myself off from the use of *ere, o'er, wellnigh, what time, say not* (for *do not say*), because, though dignified, they neither belong to nor ever cd. arise from, or be the elevation of, ordinary modern speech. For it seems to me that the poetical language of an age shd. be the current language heightened, to any degree heightened and unlike itself, but not (I mean normally: passing freaks and graces are another thing) an obsolete one. This is Shakespeare's and Milton's practice and the want of it will be fatal to Tennyson's Idylls and plays, to Swinburne, and perhaps to Morris.

21 Trenchard Street, Bristol. Aug 21. I am spending a few days here. I have roughly finished the little song and enclose it.

Remember me very kindly to Mrs. Molesworth and believe me your loving friend

GERARD M. HOPKINS, S.J.

TO ROBERT BRIDGES

St. Joseph's, Bedford Leigh, Lancashire. Oct. 8 1879.

DEAREST BRIDGES,—I have left Oxford. I am appointed to Liverpool, I do not know for what work, but am in the meantime supplying at the above address. Leigh is a town smaller and with less dignity than Rochdale and in a flat; the houses red, mean, and two storied; there are a dozen mills or so, and coalpits also; the air is charged with smoke as well as damp; but the people are hearty. Now at Oxford every prospect pleases and only man is vile, I mean unsatisfactory to a Catholic missioner. I was yesterday at St. Helen's, probably the most repulsive place in Lancashire or out of the Black Country. The stench of sulphuretted hydrogen rolls in the air and films of the same gas form on railing and pavement.

I had put the letter containing your two sonnets, as I thought, in my pocket, but it is another, older one, and the sonnets are somewhere packed up. Oct. 9. I have found them. No. 39 is a beautiful work and breathes that earnestness and tenderness which you have at command. But I make the following remarks. Line 3 is commonplace in cadence; I shd. prefer something like

The leaves and careless ecstasy of May.

The next quatrain is dark. One of two kinds of clearness one shd. have—either the meaning to be felt without effort as fast as one reads or else, if dark at first reading, when once made out *to explode*. Now this quatrain is not plain at first reading nor, if I am right in my taking of it, did that meaning explode. I suppose it to mean/ If I could only get rid of the fear, which comes every morning, that that day would put a final end to my lover's hopes. And 'promise of hope' is a pleonasm.

I shd. prefer 'O then were hideous duty'
And then

'But that 'twas I who once did, 'tis, this stings',

(or

'But that 'twas I who once did, this, this stings')

   2   1
'Once dwell within the gate that angels guard
And should be yet there, had I heavenly wings'/

(or

        'And yet should dwell there').

No. 32 seems imperfect in execution, the octet. I want
something like

'I heard great Hector hurling war's alarms
Loud in the ears of listless ghosts; he strode
As though etc
He still the trust of all, Troy's king at arms.*
But over those mild meads etc
Etc
Like night's poor creeping candle in the road,
Whose cold flame cannot comfort, only charms—'

Something like that.

Something short of a commentary indeed but more of a
clue than the bare titles wd. be a gain in my opinion to the
Growth of Love, for instance some words added to the titles.

I cannot well bestow such minute criticism on the others
you promise, for time will not allow, but still let me see them.

What, more definitely, is that change that you say has
taken place in you?

What part of the country do you reckon the Bridges to
have come from?

The little hero of the Handsome Heart has gone to school at
Boulogne to be bred for a priest and he is bent on being a
Jesuit.

I enclose a poem, the Bugler. I am half inclined to hope
the Hero of it may be killed in Afghanistan.

Did you like the song 'The dappled dieaway Cheek'?[5]

I have a greater undertaking on hand than any yet, a tragedy on St. Winefred's Martyrdom and then one on Margaret
Clitheroe's. The first has made some way and, since it will
no doubt be long before it is finished, if ever, I can only send
you some sample scenes. But I hope to be able to send you

---

* Or 'He still Troy's hope, still trusted king at arms.'

the murder scene and some more not very long hence. I mean them to be short, say in 3 or even 2 acts; the characters few. I have been writing St. Winefred in alexandrines, and am, I hope, getting a certain control of them, and in sprung rhythm, which lends itself to expressing passion. I seem to find myself, after some experiment, equal to the more stirring and critical parts of the action, which are in themselves the more important, but about the filling in and minor parts I am not sure how far my powers will go. I have for one thing so little varied experience. In reading Shakespeare one feels with despair the scope and richness of his gifts, equal to everything; he had besides sufficient experience of life and, of course, practical knowledge of the theatre.

I have not been able to make out much in the hymn music. You shall have it presently.

Remember me very kindly to Mrs. Molesworth and believe me your affectionate friend

GERARD M. HOPKINS, S.J.

Oct. 16 1879.

By the by how can you speak of Patmore as you do? I read his *Unknown Eros* well before leaving Oxford. He shews a mastery of phrase, of the rhetoric of verse, which belongs to the tradition of Shakespeare and Milton and in which you could not find him a living equal nor perhaps a dead one either after them.

TO ROBERT BRIDGES

Stonyhurst College, Blackburn.

Nov. 26 1882. And 'in spite of the boasted civilisation of this so-called nineteenth century' this letter cannot even start from here for more than 24 hours nor reach you before Tuesday morning; nor could it indeed if you lived at Blackburn.

DEAREST BRIDGES,—This is to be a mere jottery. And first if you like to send *Prometheus* I will review and reply as fast as I can.

I wrote to Lang and he is going presently to write to me on the subject of Dragons. I return his letter to you. We are on terms of mother's milk.

Yes, I do wish I could have seen Yattendon.

I have written to Canon Dixon. I hardly dare to undertake anything about *Mano*, because I have somewhat rashly promised to revise for style's sake a historical work by one of ours, which cannot but take a great deal of time, I am afraid.

Of course I do and must pay attention to your criticisms on the Echos and everything else.[6] I am however somewhat dismayed about that piece and have laid it aside for a while. I cannot satisfy myself about the first line. You must know that words like *charm* and *enchantment* will not do: the thought is of beauty as of something that can be physically kept and lost and by physical things only, like keys; then the things must come from the *mundus muliebris;* and thirdly they must not be markedly oldfashioned. You will see that this limits the choice of words very much indeed. However I shall make some changes. *Back* is not pretty, but it gives that feeling of physical constraint which I want. More of this perhaps hereafter.

I never saw Hall Caine's sonnet book. I saw some review of it. He has written a memoir of Rossetti.

I always said Gosse was a good fellow and I am glad you speak of him so. I should like to meet him. So I should a little Marzials. Did you tell me or is it my fancy that Marzials looks like a Jew?

Can you really mean that *II.II.* is to appear this month?— and not this year? There are now only four days of the month. If you mean that, revision must be done by return—no, by calculation on my fingers the thing is chronologically impossible.

Talking of chronologically impossible and long words the Rev. Wm. Barnes, good soul, of Dorset-dialect poems (in which there is more true poetry than in Burns; I do not say of course vigour or passion or humour or a lot of things, but the soul of poetry, which I believe few Scotchmen have got) has published a 'Speech craft of English Speech' = English Grammar, written in an unknown tongue, a sort of modern Anglosaxon, beyond all that Furnival in his wildest Forewords ever dreamed. He does not see the utter hopelessness of the thing. It makes one weep to think what English might have been; for in spite of all that Shakspere and Milton have done with the compound I cannot doubt that no beauty in a language can make up for want of purity. In fact I am learning Anglosaxon and it is a vastly superior thing to what we have now. But the madness of an almost unknown man trying to do what the three estates of the realm together could never accomplish! He calls degrees of comparison pitches of suchness: we *ought* to call them so, but alas!

My sisters met Wooldridge at dinner at Hampstead.

I daresay you made a capital speech. Everyone shd. at least be able to speak on an occasion.

When I reproached you for treating me as if I were not in earnest I meant, and I mean now, to open up no further questions; it was only of the injustice to myself I was thinking then. But 'pain' is not the word: it was a mild rebuke to you for being so unreasonable towards me. However a man who is deeply in earnest is not very eager to assert his earnestness, as they say when a man is really certain he no longer disputes but is indifferent. And that is all I say now, that to think a man in my position is not in earnest is unreasonable and is to make difficulties. But if you have made them and can solve them by a solution which must be wrong, no matter.

The sonnet you ask about is the greatest offender in its way that you could have found.[7] It was written in my Welsh days, in my salad days, when I was fascinated with *cynghanedd* or consonant-chime, and, as in Welsh *englyns*, 'the sense', as one of themselves said, 'gets the worst of it'; in this case it exists but is far from glaring. To answer in detail:

The word is *more* and is a midline rhyme to *score*, as in the next line *round* is meant in some way to rhyme to *down*. 'Rash-fresh more' (it is dreadful to explain these things in cold blood) means a head-long and exciting new snatch of singing, resumption by the lark of his song, which by turns he gives over and takes up again all day long, and this goes on, the sonnet says, through all time, without ever losing its first freshness, being a thing both new and old. *Repair* means the same thing, *renewal, resumption*. The skein and coil are the lark's song, which from his height gives the impression (not to me only) of something falling to the earth and not vertically quite but tricklingly or wavingly, something as a skein

of silk ribbed by having been tightly wound on a narrow card
or a notched holder or as fishingtackle or twine unwinding
from a reel or winch:* the laps or folds are the notes or
short measures and bars of them. The same is called a score
in the musical sense of score and this score is 'writ upon a
liquid sky trembling to welcome it', only not horizontally. The
lark in wild glee races the reel round, paying or dealing out
and down the turns of the skein or coil right to the earthfloor,
the ground, where it lies in a heap, as it were, or rather is all
wound off on to another winch, reel, bobbin, or spool in Fancy's eye by the moment the bird touches earth and so is
ready for a fresh unwinding at the next flight. There is, you
see, plenty meant; but the saying of it smells, I fear, of the
lamp, of salad oil, and, what is nastier, in one line somewhat
of Robert Browning. I felt even at the time that in the endless
labour of recasting those lines I had lost the freshness I
wanted and which indeed the subject demands. 'As a dare-
gale skylark' is better in that respect. The peerage would be
well earned.—*Crisp* means almost *crisped*, namely with notes.

Believe me your affectionate friend

GERARD HOPKINS S.J.

---

* Or as pearls strung on a horsehair.

TO ROBERT BRIDGES

Stonyhurst, Blackburn. Dec. 1 1882.

DEAREST BRIDGES,—You shall have *II.II.* back soon. I
do not feel as if I could make any criticism of value, my mind
not being fresh.

I still do not like *domeless*. It is not archaeologically right,
though I believe the so-called Tomb or Treasury of Atreus
has a rude dome; neither does it convey much image to my
mind. And I cannot see but the fourth line is poor and halting. It must be meant to express by its rhythm the act of
alighting briskly, but most readers will miss this and will only
find it halt, as I do even with that in view.

I agree with you that English compounds do not seem real
single words or properly unified till by some change in form

or spelling or slur in pronunciation their construction is disguised. This seems in English a point craved for and insisted on, that words shall be single and specific marks for things, whether self-significant or not; and it is noticeable how unmeaning our topographical names are or soon become, while those in Celtic languages are so transparent—not that their unmeaningness is any virtue, rather a vice; still it shews the tendency. But your instances are not fair: if icebergs had been common in British seas a name would have been found for them either not compounded at all or if compound as good as *iceberg* is or better and certainly a great deal better than *icelump*, which is caricature. *Thimble* is singler than *thumbstall* (I do not believe it comes from that but from *thumb-le*), but it is a meaner word. The absurdity of 'finger hut' is not in its being a compound but in its impropriety, in the particular trope employed. *Fingerhood* or indeed *fingerstall* seems to me to be well enough. *Potato* is certainly one of the ugliest and most laughable words in the language and cannot well be used in verse, whereas *earthapple* is stately: *potato* has one virtue only, the being specific.

If one is to bandy plays upon names Burns might mean Scalds and Barnes Granaries of Plenty. I have a cousin by the by called Barne or Barnes.

The very worst compound ever I heard in English was Tyndal's word *clangtint* = *klangfarbe* in German = *timbre* in French for the quality of musical instruments.

Your affectionate friend

GERARD M. HOPKINS S.J.

TO ROBERT BRIDGES

Stonyhurst College, Blackburn. Jan. 4 1883.
DEAREST BRIDGES,—Since our holidays began I have been in a wretched state of weakness and weariness, I can't tell why, always drowsy and incapable of reading or thinking to any effect. And this must be why I was, before that, able to do so little on your *Prometheus.*

I think the sonnet a fine work, but should like the phrasing to be more exquisite in lines 2, 4, and perhaps elsewhere. Still it has to me an unspontaneous artificial air. I cannot con-

sider the goblet and 'golden foil' a success. It is out of keeping
with sons of toil and the adornment of their brides. It is obscure too: it means, I suppose, that the goblet is of gold and
that this gold sets off and is set off by the colour of the wine.
This much resemblance there is, that as the goblet draws or
swallows up and sort-of-drinks the material of the goblet so
the body absorbs sleep and sleep the body. But the images of
gold and crimson are out of keeping: brilliancy is only in the
way. You were, you say, driven to it: I protest, and with in-
dignation, at your saying I was driven to the same image.
With more truth might it be said that my sonnet might have
been written expressly for the image's sake.[8] But the image
is not the same as yours and I do not mean by foil set-off at
all; I mean foil in its sense of leaf or tinsel, and no other word
whatever will give the effect I want. Shaken goldfoil gives
off broad glares like sheet lightning and also, and this is true
of nothing else, owing to its zigzag dints and creasings and
network of small many cornered facets, a sort of fork lightning too. Moreover as it is the first rhyme, presumably it
engendered the others and not they it. This reminds me that
I hold you to be wrong about 'vulgar', that is obvious or necessary, rhymes. It follows from your principle that if a word
has only one rhyme in the language it cannot be used in self-
respecting poetry at all. The truth seems to me that a problem
is set to all, how to use that same pair (or triplet or any set)
of rhymes, which are invariable, to the finest and most natural effect. It is nothing that the reader can say / he had to
say it, there *was* no other rhyme: you answer/ shew me what
better I could have said if there had been a million. Hereby,
I may tell you, hangs a very profound question treated by
Duns Scotus, who shews that freedom is compatible with necessity. And besides, common sense tells you that though if
you say A_1 you cannot help saying A_2 yet you can help saying A_1+A_2 at all; you could have said B_1+B_2 or C_1+C_2
etc. And is not music a sort of rhyming on seven rhymes and
does that make it vulgar? The variety is more, but the principle the same. Come, you are as much cast in this matter as
Lawes was in the Belt case—though I am grievously afraid
there was a miscarriage of justice in that trial; not that I like
to side against a judge's sentence.

Jan. 5—Hall Caine's 'Disquisition' on Rossetti's picture of Dante's Dream bought by the city of Liverpool reached me this morning, I suppose from the author. Noel Paton is quoted as saying, with goodnatured gush, that it may be ranked with the Madonna di San Sisto. Now, you know, it may *not,* and I am considering whether I shall tell Hall Caine so.

To return to your sonnet, could you not find another rhyme? there is *spoil, despoil, turmoil,* not to speak of *coil, boil, parboil,* and Hoyle on whist—the very sight of which dreary jugglery brings on yawns with me.

You speak of writing the sonnet in prose first. I read the other day that Virgil wrote the Aeneid in prose. Do you often do so? Is it a good plan? If it is I will try it; it may help on my flagging and almost spent powers. Years ago one of ours, a pupil of mine, was to write some English verses for me, to be recited: he had a real vein. He said he had no thoughts, but that if I would furnish some he would versify them. I did so and the effect was very surprising to me to find my own thoughts, with no variation to speak of, expressed in good verses quite unlike mine.

The sonnet on Purcell means this: 1–4. I hope Purcell is not damned for being a Protestant, because I love his genius. 5–8. And that not so much for gifts he shares, even though it shd. be in higher measure, with other musicians as for his own individuality. 9–14. So that while he is aiming only at impressing me his hearer with the meaning in hand I am looking out meanwhile for his specific, his individual markings and mottlings, 'the sakes of him'. It is as when a bird thinking only of soaring spreads its wings: a beholder may happen then to have his attention drawn by the act to the plumage displayed.—In particular, the first lines mean: May Purcell, O may he have died a good death and that soul which I love so much and which breathes or stirs so unmistakeably in his works have parted from the body and passed away, centuries since though I frame the wish, in peace with God! so that the heavy condemnation under which he outwardly or nominally lay for being out of the true Church may in consequence of his good intentions have been reserved, 'Low lays him' is merely 'lays him low', that is/ strikes him heavily, weighs upon him. (I daresay this will strike you as more professional than you had anticipated.) It is somewhat dismaying to find I am so unintelligible though, especially in one of my very best pieces. 'Listed', by the by, is 'enlisted'. 'Sakes' is hazardous: about that point I was more bent on saying my say than on being understood in it. The 'moonmarks' belong to the image only of course, not to the application; I mean not detailedly: I was thinking of a bird's quill feathers. One thing disquiets me: I *meant* 'fair fall' to mean *fair (fortune be)-fall*; it has since struck me that perhaps 'fair' is an adjective proper and in the predicate and can only be used in cases like 'fair fall the day', that is, *may the day fall, turn out, fair*. My line will yield a sense that way indeed, but I never meant it so. Do you know any passage decisive on this?

Would that I had Purcell's music here.

Did you see Vernon Lee's paper in the December *Contemp.?* I don't like it. She professes herself a disciple of a Mr. Edmund Gurney, who by way of reaction against the gush of programmes ('sturdy old tone-poet'—'inimitable drollery of the semi demiquavers in the dominant minor' and so on) says that we enjoy music because our apish ancestors serenaded their Juliet-apes of the period in rudimentary recitatives and our emotions are the survival—that sexual business will in short be found by roking the pot. This is to swing from pap to poison. Would that I had my materials ready to talk sense.

Yours affectionately

GERARD HOPKINS S.J.

Jan. 5 1883.

Is it not too much for two lines running to have the rhythm reversed in the 4th foot? as your 13 and 14. Perhaps not. Twelfth night.

TO COVENTRY PATMORE

Stonyhurst. Sept. 24 1883

MY DEAR MR. PATMORE,—I have found since writing yesterday that the line 'Her virtue all virtue so endears' may with forethought be so read as to run smoothly, even with a stress on 'all'. I think however that how to do this will not strike everybody and that the line will mostly be a stumbling-block in reading aloud.

There is also some metrical objection to 'Disappointment'. The cadences 'found in none', 'found in one' strike one as identities, not rhymes: they are really rhymes, but there is a 'false relation' suggested. This correction would be easy.

Also I am dissatisfied with 'Beauty' p. 159 sq. The text and principle stated is noble and deeply true, the development seems to me a decline and surrender. It comes to this: beautiful evil is found, but it is nature's monstrosity. Then is *qui supplet locum idiotae,* the worldling, Philistine (or whatever he is to be called) answers: and all I have to add is that the monstrosity is very common, and so we are agreed. And so it wd. come to the same thing to say Beauty deludes or Ugliness does. This was not to be granted. It is certain that in nature outward beauty is the proof of inward beauty, outward good of inward good. Fineness, proportion, of feature comes from a moulding force which succeeds in asserting itself over the resistance of cumbersome or restraining matter; the bloom of health comes from the abundance of life, the great vitality within. The moulding force, the life, is the form in the philosophic sense, and in man this is the soul. But because its available activity is limited the matter it has to struggle with may be too much for it and the wax is either too cold and doughy (so to speak) and will not take or is too hot and boiling blots out the stamp of the seal—I speak under an old but a very apposite image not easily improved. This explains why 'ugly good' is found. But why do we find beautiful evil? Not by any freak of nature, nature is incapable of producing beautiful evil. The explanation is to be sought outside nature; it is old, simple, and the undeniable fact. It comes from wicked will, freedom of choice, abusing the beauty, the good of its nature. 'Thou wert' the Scripture says and great writers apply it to the Devil 'the seal of resemblance'. The instance is palmary and shews how far evil can be beautiful or beauty evil and what the phenomenon means when it occurs.—This at least is how the subject strikes me and I find it more interesting and pathetic so; it maybe however that you think no otherwise, only that I have missed the turn of your thought.

Whether you agree with me or not about the above points they are all trifles and altered or let stand little affect the poem. The following is the matter where I have to make a serious objection.

P. 202 'Women *should* be vain', p. 217 'The Koh-i-noor' no. 1. p. 251 'Because, although in act and word, . . . unattain'd desert'—In the midst of a poem undertaken under a kind of inspiration from God & to express what, being most excellent, most previous, most central and important and even obvious in human life, nevertheless no one has ever yet, unless passingly thought of expressing you introduce a vice, the germ of widespread evils, and make the highest relish of pure love come from the base 'smell of mortality'. Everyone has some one fault he is tender to and vice he tolerates. We do this ourselves, but when another does it towards another vice not our own favourite (of tolerance, I do not say of commission) we are disgusted. The *Saturday Review* contrasting the Catholic and Protestant ideal of a schoolboy came out with the frank truth, that it looked on chastity as a feminine virtue (= lewdness a masculine one: it was not quite so raw as I put it, but this was the meaning). Mommsen a brilliant historian I find thinks great nations should break treaties. Dr. Ward (in his younger days) said candour was anything but a saintly virtue (perhaps he did not but is misquoted: let it at least serve as an illustration). Then violence is admired and, above all, insolence and pride. But it is our baseness to admire anything evil. It seems to me we shd. in everything side with virtue, even if we do not feel its charm, because good is good.

In particular how can anyone admire or (except in charity, as the greatest of sins, but in judgment and approval) tolerate vanity in women? Is it not the beginning of their saddest and most characteristic fall? What but vanity makes them first publish, then prostitute their charms? In Leonardo's famous picture 'Modesty and Vanity' is it not almost taken for granted that the one figure is that of a virgin, the other that of a courtezan? If modesty in women means two things at once, purity and humility, must not the pair of opposites be no great way apart, vanity from impurity? Who can think of the Blessed Virgin and of vanity? Then in one's experience, in my own, it seems to me that nothing in good women is more beautiful than just the absence of vanity and an earnestness of look and character which is better than beauty. It teaches me (if I may give such an instance—I cannot easily give others) in my own sisters that when they let me see their compositions in music or painting, which I, with a brother's biassed judgment but still sincerely admire, they seem to be altogether without vanity—yet they might be with reason vainer of these than of their looks, and towards a brother not be ashamed to shew it (and I towards them can hardly conceal mine): they are glad when I admire nevertheless. It is the same in literature as in life: the vain women in Shakspere are the impure minded too, like Beatrice (I do not know that I may not call her a hideous character): those whose chastity one could have trusted, like Desdemona, are free from vanity too.

It is a lover who speaks in the 'Koh-i-noor', but that proves very little. He happens to be a good one, and therefore tolerates nothing worse than carelessness, talkativeness, and vanity, but take a bad one: he will want the smell of mortality stronger. What does the adulterer love in his neighbour's wife but her obligingness in committing adultery? Tennyson makes Guenevere say 'The low sun makes the colour': it is a happy touch and the whole passage is instructive. Those also who write of moral monsters born without a fault and 'Let other bards of angels sing [in the House or elsewhere] Bright suns without a spot; But thou are no such perfect thing: Rejoice that thou are not', these people never saw and had lost the idea of holiness/ and are no authority.

You will say that everything else, her own words and what others say of her, shew that in Honoria there was in reality no vanity and that your lines are not to be taken in such grim earnest. But the truth seems to me to be that in writing you were really in two inconsistent moods, a lower and a higher, and that the record of both is in your pages.

Naturally a lurking error appears in more places than one and a false principle gives rise to false consequences. An ideal becomes an idol and false worship sets in. So I call it at p. 251, where it is said that a wife calls her husband lord by courtesy, meaning, as I understand, only by courtesy and 'not with her least consent of will' to his being so. But he *is* her lord. If it is courtesy only and no consent then a wife's lowliness is hypocrisy and Christian marriage a comedy, a piece of pretence. How much more truly and touchingly did you make Mrs. Graham speak! But if she was right then the contrary is wrong. Perhaps I misunderstand the passage: I hope I do, but then I hope you will prevent other people misunderstanding it. And now pernicious doctrines and practice are abroad and the other day the papers said a wretched being refused in church to say the words 'and obey': if it had been a Catholic wedding and I the priest I would have let the sacrilege go no further.

Honoria's letter in the 'Love-letters' pp. 202, 203 by itself would be well enough, it contains its own correction ('I hope in jest'), though the incident always struck me as very trivial if also very natural, and I on no account want to lose the lovely turn 'But I was very dull, dear friend' and what follows; but the other two convey, it seems to me, though in small quantities, a poison. And they may be quoted in support of evil and do mischief commended by the lustre of your name (I hope it will be illustrious then) years after you are dead.

If I have written strongly I am sure it is in a zeal for the poem. Believe me yours very sincerely

GERARD MANLEY HOPKINS S.J.

TO COVENTRY PATMORE

University College, Stephen's Green, Dublin. May 14. 1885.
MY DEAR MR. PATMORE,—Thank you very much for the *Angel in the House,* which reached me the night before last: to dip into it was like opening a basket of violets. To have criticised it looks now like meddling with the altar-vessels; yet they too are burnished with washleather.

I see that this is the 6th edition, which shews a steady popularity or a steadily reading public. But it is a popularity and a public rather below the surface. This may content you, in itself it is not satisfactory. A good book is to educate the world at large. The *Angel in the House* is in the highest degree instructive, it is a book of morals and in a field not before treated and yet loudly crying to be treated. It cannot indeed ever be popular quite with the general, but I want it to be popular as a classic is, read by many, recognised by all. And I am not satisfied because it is not enough recognised. I cannot now say more, but remain your very sincere friend

GERARD M. HOPKINS S.J.

TO ROBERT BRIDGES

University College, Stephen's Green, Dublin. May 17 1885

DEAREST BRIDGES,—I must write something, though not so much as I have to say. The long delay was due to work, worry, and languishment of body and mind—which must be and will be; and indeed to diagnose my own case (for every man by forty is his own physician or a fool, they say; and yet again he who is his own physician has a fool for his patient—a form of epigram, by the bye, which, if you examine it, has a bad flaw), well then to judge of my case, I think that my fits of sadness, though they do not affect my judgment, resemble madness. Change is the only relief, and that I can seldom get.

I saw that *Ulysses* was a fine play, the action and interest well centred, the characters finally drawn and especially Penelope, the dialogue throughout good; nevertheless, perhaps from my mood of mind, I could not take to it, did not like it, beyond a dry admiration. Not however to remain in a bare Doctor Felldom on the matter, I did find one fault in it which seems indeed to me to be the worst fault a thing can have, unreality. I hope other people will think otherwise, but the introduction in earnest of Athene gave me a distaste I could not recover from. With *Prometheus* it was not the same. Three kinds of departure from truth I understand and agree to in a play—first in a History those changes and conventions without which, as in other works of art, the facts could not be presented at all; secondly a plot of fiction: though the facts never actually happened they are a picture of life and a sample of the sort of facts that do—those also subject to their own changes and conventions; lastly an allegory, where things that neither do nor could be mask and mean something that is. To this last class *Prometheus*, as I take it, belongs;

moreover it was modelled on the Greek and scarcely meant
for acting. But *Ulysses* is to act; and in earnest, not allegori-
cally, you bring in a goddess among the characters: it re-
volts me. Then, not unnaturally, as it seemed to me, her
speech is the worst in the play: being an unreality she must
talk unreal. Believe me, the Greek gods are a totally unworkable material; the merest frigidity, which must chill and
kill every living work of art they are brought into. Even if
we put aside the hideous and, taken as they stand, unspeakable stories told of them, which stories nevertheless are as
authentic as their names and personalities—both are equally
imaginary; if you do not like that, both equally symbolical—,
putting these out of sight and looking only at their respectable
side, they are poor ignoble conceptions enobled bodily only
(as if they had bodies) by the artists, but once in motion and
action worthless—not gentlemen or ladies, cowards, loungers,
without majesty, without awe, antiquity, foresight, character; old bucks, young bucks, and Biddy Buckskins. What did
Athene do after leaving Ulysses? Lounged back to Olympus
to afternoon nectar. Nothing can be made of it. May 21, 1885.
The background of distance and darkness and doom which a
tragedy should always have is shut out by an Olympian drop-
scene; the characters from men become puppets, their blood-
shed becomes a leakage of bran. (This, upon my word, is to
ply the lash and to be unpardonable.) I see the nobility of the
rest, but this one touch to my eye spoils all; it looks to me like
fine relief all daubed and creamed over with heavy whitewash.

I do not wonder at those ladies reading *Nero* through at a
sitting. It *is* very interesting and I feel quite the same. You
offered to send me a correcter copy: I shd. be glad if you
now would.

I must add there was another fault I had to find with *Ulysses* and it was to the same effect and same defect, of unreality; I mean the archaism of the language, which was to my
mind overdone. I hold that by archaism a thing is sicklied o'er
as by blight. Some little flavours, but much spoils, and always
for the same reason—it destroys earnest: we do not speak that
way; therefore if a man speaks that way he is not serious, he
is at something else than the seeming matter in hand, *non*

hoc agit, aliud agit. I believe you agree with me in principle: if so I think that your practice in that play is beyond what your principle allows. But slight changes would satisfy me. The example of Shakspere (by a 'corrupt following', for it is an absurd fallacy—like a child having to repeat the substance of something it has been told and saying *you* and *I* wherever the speaker said *you* and *I*, whereas it should say *I* where he said *you* and so on) has done ever so much harm by his very genius, for poets reproduce the diction which in him was modern and in them is obsolete. But you know all this.

How did Michael Field in the end go off?

It is too bad that I shd. so abuse *Ulysses* after your encouragement of *St. Winefred.* But how cd. you think such a thing of me as that I shd. in cold blood write 'fragments of a dramatic poem'?—I of all men in the world. To me a completed fragment, above all of a play, is the same unreality as a prepared impromptu. No, but we compose fragmentarily and what I had here and there done I finished up and sent as samples to see if I cd. be encouraged to go on—and I was encouraged; that is by your last, for before I thought you thought they wd. not do. There is a point with me in matters of any size when I must absolutely have encouragement as much as crops rain; afterwards I am independent. However I am in my ordinary circumstances unable, with whatever encouragement, to go on with *Winefred* or anything else. I have after long silence written two sonnets, which I am touching: if ever anything was written in blood one of these was.

Of two metrical criticisms you made on the fragments one I did not well understand, the other was a misunderstanding on your part.

About the music I shd. like to write at some length. But for the present I only say first, how could you think I shd. be offended at your criticism or remarks or wanted you to express yourself so modestly? May 28, 1885. Next I am much obliged for the quotations from Purcell, but could not get my household musician to play the one in open score nor have had time or opportunity of running after professionals, besides that for myself I have kept away some time now from the piano. Thirdly the bass solo you give me to shew the variety Purcell could command by the modern system—well of that beautiful passage I have to say that it illustrates the wellknown variety of the minor as we now understand it, a variety for which Purcell particularly prized it, but that that variety I did not need the illustrating of and, ahem, I can send you an illustration of my own which as it seems to me is happy in that way—made long ago. Then of course I admire and surely I could produce—it requires no more knowledge than I have already got for at least the simpler effects and in fact modulation even to remote keys and so on is not difficult to do; it may be to explain—could produce and have produced modulations, but in the two first verses of the *Battle of the Baltic* (which has some eleven) I wanted to see what could be done (and for how long I could go on) without them. — of course thought they cd. not be done without even for that length and I do not dispute the judgment; I scarcely had myself heard my second verse—for that is the great difficulty, in reality my only, and I fear my insuperable, one, that I cannot play. But nevertheless Palestrina and the old madrigal writers and others did produce masterpieces— and Hullah says actually final in their kind, that is which you cannot develope by modern science; you can only change the school and kind—without modulations, but employing the modes; without even the authentic cadence: I wish I cd. study them. Then 'do I mean to rival Purcell and Mozart?' No. Even given the genius, a musician must be that and nothing else, as music now is; at least so it has been with all the great musicians. But I did aim at two things not in themselves unattainable, if to me far easier things were not now unattainable. But of these, if ever, hereafter.

Believe me your affectionate friend

GERARD M. HOPKINS S.J.

May 29 1885.

TO R. W. DIXON

University College, Stephen's Green, Dublin. Aug. 7 '86.
MY DEAR FRIEND,—The note you speak of did not reach me and no doubt was never posted, for the post never misses

(if there is a never in human things) and every alternative should be exhausted before we come to that. (And therefore I say that the number of the *Academy* which shd. have come to hand this morning was also not posted or, what is more likely, has gone astray in the house.)

If the poem is printed it may rest, but I am going to see the Provincial tomorrow or the next day, and will ask him about it. I ought to have settled this before; but since I last wrote I have been altogether overwhelmed with examination-work, six or seven weeks of it without any break, Sundays and weekdays. Even now—but it is no use talking of it.

Mr. Rawnsley's name is quite unknown to me.

It is not possible for me to do anything, unless a sonnet, and that rarely, in poetry with a fagged mind and a continual anxiety; but there are things at which I can, so far as time serves, work, if it were only by snatches. For instance I am writing (but I am almost sure I never shall have written) a sort of popular account of Light and Ether. Popular is not quite the word; it is not meant to be easy reading, for such a difficult subject can only be made easy by a very summary and sketchy treatment; rather it is meant for the lay or unprofessional student who will read carefully so long as there are no mathematics and all technicalities are explained; and my hope is to explain things thoroughly and make the latter to such a reader, as far as I go in it, perfectly intelligible. No such account exists and scientific books, especially in English, are very unsatisfactory. The study of physical science has, unless corrected in some way, an effect the very opposite of what one would suppose. One would think it might materialise people (no doubt it does make them or, rather I shd. say, they become materialists; but that is not the same thing: they do not believe in Matter more but in God less); but in fact they seem to end in conceiving only of a world of formulas, with its being properly speaking in thought, towards which the outer world acts as a sort of feeder, supplying examples for literary purposes. And they go so far as to think the rest of mankind are in the same state of mind as themselves. I daresay I may gather together some illustrations of this: one will serve now. 'It is very remarkable' says Tait on *Light* 'how slowly the human race has reached some even of the simplest, facts of optics [he rather means laws]. We can easily understand how constant experience must have forced on men the conviction [as if they were resisting it: the force would have been to make them think the contrary] that light usually moves in straight lines—i.e. that we see an object in the direction in which it really lies. [Where else shd. one expect to see it?] But' etc.

It will in any case be a pity for S.J. to have been added to my name in the book, for the letters act like italics, asterisks, or rubric.

Some learned lady having shewn by the flora that the season of the action in *Hamlet* is from March to May, a difficulty is raised about the glowworm's ineffectual fire in the first act, since glowworms glow chiefly from May to September. Mr. Furnival having consulted an authority learns that the grub, though not so easily found, shines nearly as bright as the full-grown worm, that is beetle, and begins in March, and so all is saved. Does this not strike you as great trifling? Shakspere had the finest faculty of observation of all men that ever breathed, but it is ordinary untechnical observation, neither scientific nor even, like a farmer's professional, and he might overlook that point of season. But if he knew it he would likely enough neglect it. There are some errors you must not make, as an eclipse at the halfmoon or a lobster 'the Cardinal of the seas', but others do not matter and convention varies with regard to them. If I am not mistaken, there are notorious and insoluble inconsistencies in *Hamlet*, due to Shakespere's having recast the play expressly for Burbage, who was elderly, 'short, stout, and scant of breath' (or something of the sort), without taking the trouble to correct throughout accordingly—not even wishing I dare say; for no one can so conceive of Hamlet's person. Besides there are inconsistencies in the Iliad, Aeneid, Don Quixote, Three Musketeers, and so on; it is a frailty of literature. And indeed on reflection the defence makes the matter worse. For few of the audience could know that glowworms do shine, if you look well for them, in March. So that Shakspere would have been breaking Aristotle's rule, that in art likely seeming fiction is better than unlikely seeming fact.

By the by, why should Wordsworth-worship be 'a difficult

thing'? It is a common one now, is it not? Not *the* common, but like soldiers in a crowd, not a numerous but a notable fact. Did you see what Lord Selborne lately said? What I suppose grows on people is that Wordsworth's particular grace, his *charisma*, as the theologians say, has been granted in equal measure to so very few men since times was—to Plato and who else? I mean his spiritual insight into nature; and this they perhaps think is above all the poet's gift? It is true, if we sort things, so that art is art and philosophy philosophy, it seems rather the philosopher's than the poet's: at any rate he had it in a sovereign degree. He had a 'divine philosophy' and a lovely gift of verse; but in his work there is nevertheless *beaucoup à redire*: it is due to the universal fault of our literature, its weakness is rhetoric. The strictly poetical insight and inspiration of our poetry seems to me to be of the very finest, finer perhaps than the Greek; but its rhetoric is inadequate—seldom firstrate, mostly only just sufficient, sometimes even below par. By rhetoric I mean all the common and teachable element in literature, what grammar is to speech, what thorough-bass is to music, what theatrical experience gives to playwrights. If you leave out the embroidery (to be sure the principal thing) of for instance the *Excursion* and look only at the groundwork and stuff of the web is it not fairly true to say 'This will never do'? There does seem to be a great deal of dulness, superfluity, aimlessness, poverty of plan. I remember noticing as a boy, it was the discovery of a trade secret, how our poets treat spirit and its compounds as one syllable: it is, though founded really on a mistake, the mere change of pronunciation, a beautiful tradition of the poets. Wordsworth had told himself or been told this trifle: why did he not learn or someone tell him that sonnets have a natural *charpente* and structure never, or at least seldom, to be broken through? For want of knowing this his inspired sonnets, εὔμορφοι κολοσσοί[9] suffer from 'hernia', and combine the tiro's blunder with the master's perfection.

Believe me your affectionate friend

GERARD HOPKINS. Aug. 9.

TO COVENTRY PATMORE

University College, Stephen's Green, Dublin. Oct. 6 1886

MY DEAR MR. PATMORE,—I have just returned from a very reviving fortnight or so of North Wales, the true Arcadia of wild beauty.

I have a long letter somewhere to you, but shall never send it. I read with pleasure the account of you in the *World*, but you have not sent the papers from the *St. James's*.

You are not to think I now begin to admire Barnes: I always did so, but it was long since I read him. (Bridges is quite wrong about him and off his orthodoxy.) I scarcely understand you about reflected light: every true poet, I thought, must be original and originality a condition of poetic genius; so that each poet is like a species in nature (*not* an *individuum genericum* or *specificum*) and can never recur. That nothing shd. be old or borrowed however cannot be, and that I am sure you never meant.

Still I grant in Barnes an unusual independence and originality, due partly to his circumstances. It is his naturalness that strikes most; he is like an embodiment or incarnation or manmuse of the country, of Dorset, of rustic life and humanity. He comes, like Homer and all poets of native epic, provided with epithets, images, and so on which seem to have been tested and digested for a long age in their native air and circumstances and to have a *keeping* which nothing else could give; but in fact they are rather all of his own finding and first throwing off. This seems to me very high praise. It is true they are not far-fetched or exquisite (I mean for instance his mentions of rooks or of brooks) but they are straight from nature and quite fresh. His rhythms are charming and most characteristic: these too smack of the soil. However his employment of the Welsh *cynghanedd* or chime I do not look on as quite successful. To tell the truth, I think I could do that better, and it is an artificial thing and not much in his line. (I mean like *Paladore* and *Polly dear*, which is in my judgment more of a miss than a hit.) I have set tunes to two of them which appear to me very suitable to the words and as if drawn out of them, and one I have harmonised and got today played; but I can never succeed with piano music, for the piano cannot really execute independent parts, as I make mine; indeed my pianist said to me, Your music dates from a time before the piano was invented. However two schoolboys sang the air; which went well. But now no more of Barnes or of music, for I have overhanging me 500 examination papers and that only one batch out of three.

With the kindest remembrances to Mrs. Patmore and the Miss Patmores, I am your sincere friend

GERARD M. HOPKINS S.J.

Before I went to Wales I was much pulled down: that was why I did not sooner write. Bridges says Barnes has no fire, and this I think we must grant.

TO R. W. DIXON

University College, St. Stephen's Green, Dublin. Oct. 23 1886

MY DEAR FRIEND,—There are some points in your letter I have to reply to. First of the Greek mythology. Of course I agree with the rest of the world in admiring its beauty. Above everything else the Greeks excelled in art: now their mythology was the earliest of their arts that have in any way survived, older in the main than Homer's poems, and is I daresay as much more beautiful than other mythologies as Homer's epic is than other epics; speaking of the epic proper. It is free from that cumber of meaningless and childish rubbish which interrupts and annoys one even in the midst of fine invention in for instance the Irish legends.

This however is to speak of it as stories, as fairytales, well invented well told fairytales. But mythology is something else besides fairytale: it is religion, the historical part of religion. It must have been this side of the Greek mythology I was speaking of in that letter; and could I speak too severely of it? First it is as history untrue. What is untrue history? Nothing and worse than nothing. And that history religion? Still worse. I cannot enter on this consideration without being brought face to face with the great fact of heathenism. Now we mostly pass heathenism by as a thing utterly departed, which indeed it is not but in India rank and flourishing; but

if for once we face it what are we to say of it? For myself
literally words would fail me to express the loathing and horror with which I think of it and of man setting up the work
of his own hands, of that hand within the mind the imagination, for God Almighty who made heaven and earth. But the
Greek gods are rakes, and unnatural rakes. Put that aside
too; put yourself in the position of a man who like Homer first
believes in them, next forgets or passes over their wickedness:
even so are the Greek gods majestic, awe inspiring, as Homer
that great Greek genius represents them? They are not. The
Indian gods are imposing, the Greek are not. Indeed they are
not brave, not self controlled, they have no manners, they
are not gentlemen and ladies. They clout one another's ears
and blubber and bellow. You will say this is Homer's fun,
like the miracle-plays of Christendom. Then where is his earnest about them? At their best they remind me of some company of beaux and fashionable world at Bath in its palmy
days or Tunbridge Wells or what not. Zeus is like the Major
in *Pendennis* handsomer and better preserved sitting on
Olympus as behind a club-window and watching Danae and
other pretty seamstresses cross the street—not to go farther.
You will think this is very Philistine and vulgar and be
pained. But I am pained: this is the light in which the matter
strikes me, the only one in which it will; and I do think it is
the true light.

But I grant that the Greek mythology is very susceptible
of fine treatment for instance, allegorical treatment for instance, and so treated gives rise to the most beautiful results.
No wonder: the moral evil is got rid of and the pure art,
morally neutral and artistically so rich, remains and can be
even turned to moral uses.

The letter you saw must have been in criticism of Bridges'
Ulysses. I was set against that play by the appearance of
Athene in the prologue or opening. Bridges took her almost
seriously: so then did I, and was disgusted. But I hold it was
a false step of his: the heathen gods cannot be taken seriously
on our stage; nowadays they cannot even be taken humor-
ously; and it would tell against the play's success. I know
that was a noble play; but I had another objection besides
to it, the great severity, the aridity even and joylessness of

the lyrics. So I damped and damned and must have hurt Bridges.

I feel now that I am warm and my hand is in for my greater task, Wordsworth's ode; and here, my dear friend, I must earnestly remonstrate with you; and must have it out with you. Is it possible that—but it is in black and white: you say the ode is not, for Wordsworth, good; and much less great.

To say it was the second ode in the language was after all only a comparative remark: one might maintain, though I daresay you will not, that English is not rich in odes. The remark therefore is not of itself extravagant. But if the speaker had said that it was one of the half dozen finest odes of the world I must own that to me there would have seemed no extravagance. There have been in all history a few, a very few men, whom common repute, even where it did not trust them, has treated as having had something happen to them that does not happen to other men, as having *seen something*, whatever that really was. Plato is the most famous of these. Or to put it as it seems to me I must have written to you or to somebody, human nature in these men saw something, got a shock; wavers in opinion, looking back, whether there was anything in it or no; but is in a tremble ever since. Now what Wordsworthians mean is, what would seem to be the growing mind of the English speaking world and may perhaps come to be that of the world at large/ is that in Wordsworth when he wrote that ode human nature got another of those shocks, and the tremble from it is spreading. This opinion I do strongly share; I am, ever since I knew the ode, in that tremble. You know what happened to crazy Blake, himself a most poetically electrical subject both active and passive, at his first hearing: when the reader came to 'The pansy at my feet' he fell into a hysterical excitement. Now commonsense forbid we should take on like these unstrung hysterical creatures: still it was a proof of the power of the shock.

The ode itself seems to me better than anything else I know of Wordsworth's, so much as to equal or outweigh everything else he wrote: to me it appears so. For Wordsworth was an imperfect artist, as you say: as his matter varied in importance and as he varied in insight (for he had a profound insight of some things and little of others) so does the value of his work vary. Now the interest and importance of the matter were here of the highest, his insight was at its very deepest, and hence to my mind the extreme value of the poem.

His powers rose, I hold, with the subject: the execution is so fine. The rhymes are so musically interlaced, the rhythms so happily succeed (surely it is a magical change 'O joy that in our embers'), the diction throughout is so charged and steeped in beauty and yearning (what a stroke 'The moon doth with delight'!). It is not a bit of good my going on if, which is to me so strange in you and disconcerting, you do not feel anything of this. But I do hope you will consider it. For my part I shd. think St. George and St. Thomas of Canterbury wore roses in heaven for England's sake on the day that ode, not without their intercession, was penned: for, to better a little the good humoured old cynical proverb, 'When grace of God is gone and spent Then learning is most excellent' and goes to make the greatness of a nation—which is what I urge on Bridges and now on you, to get yourselves known and be up betimes on our Parnassus.

Now no more. I will copy you soon some odd ends, sonnets. Have you my song for my play of St. Winefred called The Leaden Echo and the Golden Echo? If not I will try and copy it as time serves: I never did anything more musical.

May the Muses bring you to a better mind. May God Almighty, and this without reserve. I am your affectionate friend

GERARD M. HOPKINS S.J.

Oct. 24. Examinations over and I begin lecturing tomorrow.

TO COVENTRY PATMORE

University College, Stephen's Green, Dublin. Nov. 7. 1886.
MY DEAR MR. PATMORE,—Your pamphlet must, I think, have miscarried: the name How I managed my Estate or to that effect is familiar but I believe from a review in the Academy. It is like a dream to me that I saw such a pamphlet lying about, but at any rate I did not recognise it as belonging

to me, much less read it. And therefore I shd. be glad if you wd. be so kind as to send another copy.

The long letter I spoke of was cancelled, as it often happens to me to cancel letters and it would be better if it happened oftener still; best of all would be never to write anything that could need cancelling.

I seem to have been among odds and ends of poets and poetesses of late. One poetess was Miss Kate Tynan, who lately published a volume of chiefly devotional poems, highly spoken of by reviews. She is a simple brightlooking Biddy with glossy very pretty red hair, a farmer's daughter in the County Dublin. She knows and deeply admires your Muse and said this, which appears in some way noteworthy—complaining that you are sometimes austere or bare or something like that: 'How is it, Fr. Hopkins, that however bare is it it is always poetry?' I am at present Bridges' Muse-broker and had to send Miss Tynan an invoice of him. I am to read Miss Tynan herself when she comes, that is, as many pages as she has walked to and fro over—to say of her what one might say of any writer. Then there is a young Mr. Yeats who has written in a Trinity College publication some striking verses and who has been perhaps unduly pushed by the late Sir Samuel Ferguson (I do not know if you have read or heard of him: he was a learned antiquary, a Protestant but once an ally of Thomas Davis and the Young Ireland Party, but he withdrew from them and even suppressed some of his best poems for fear they, or he, shd. be claimed by the Nationalists of later days; for he was a poet; the *Forging of the Anchor* is, I believe, his most famous poem; he was a poet as the Irish are —to judge by the little of his I have seen—full of feeling, high thoughts, flow of verse, point, often fine imagery and other virtues, but the essential and only lasting thing left out—what I call *inscape*, that is species or individually-distinctive beauty of style: on this point I believe we quite agree, as on most: but this is a serious parenthesis). I called on his, young Yeats's, father by desire lately; he is a painter; and with some emphasis of manner he presented me with *Mosada: a Dramatic Poem* by W. B. Yeats, with a portrait of the author by J. B. Yeats, himself; the young man having finely cut intellectual features and his father being a fine draughtsman.

For a young man's pamphlet this was something too much: but you will understand a father's feeling. Now this *Mosada* I cannot think highly of, but I was happily not required then to praise what presumably I had not then read, and I had read and could praise another piece. It was a strained and unworkable allegory about a young man and a sphinx on a rock on the sea (how did they get there? what did they eat? and so on: people think such criticisms very prosaic; but commonsense is never out of place anywhere, neither on Parnassus nor on Tabor nor on the Mount where our Lord preached; and, not to quote Christ's parables all taken from real life but in the frankly impossible, as in the *Tempest*, with what consummate and penetrating imagination is Ariel's 'spiriting' put before us! all that led up and that must follow the scenes in the play is realised and suggested and you cannot lay your finger on the point where it breaks down), but still containing fine lines and vivid imagery.

I find that Miss Tynan has a great admirer in Lord Lytton who writes to her at length and has invited her to visit him.

By the bye I saw a letter of yours to the *Times* written as a rally against Mr. Gladstone, not however proposing any alternative policy.

This is a foolish letter of gossip, I must bring it to an end. Since I returned from Wales I have been in better health than usual, fitter for work; and very much better spirits. And I am hoping to write (if not this year a book, yet) this year a paper for the *Society of Hellenic Studies*, to which I belong, (or some other quarter) on the Dorian Measure, the true scansion of perhaps half or more than half of the Greek and Latin lyric verse: I do believe it is a great and it is an unsuspected discovery. Give my kind regards to your circle and believe me your sincere friend

GERARD HOPKINS S.J.

TO COVENTRY PATMORE

University College, St. Stephen's Green, Dublin. Oct. 20 1887

MY DEAR MR. PATMORE,—I find I began writing to you a fortnight since. I was then examining: I am still, but am nearly at an end. I enclose the Paper you sent, suppos-

ing that you could not wait for it longer. I had meant to write
some remarks on it, but I cannot delay the Paper for them. I
may send them afterwards.

But I make one now which will amaze you and, except
that you are very patient of my criticisms, may incense you.
It is that when I read yr. prose and when I read Newman's
and some other modern writers' the same impression is borne
in on me: no matter how beautiful the thought, nor, taken
singly, with what happiness expressed, you do not know what
writing prose is. At bottom what you do and what Cardinal
Newman does is to think aloud, to think with pen to paper.
In this process there are certain advantages; they may outweigh those of a perfect technic; but at any rate they exclude
that; they exclude the belonging technic, the belonging rhetoric, the own proper eloquence of written prose. Each
thought is told off singly and there follows a pause and this
breaks the continuity, the *contentio*, the strain of address,
which writing should usually have.

The beauty, the eloquence, of good prose cannot come
wholly from the thought. With Burke it does and varies with
the thought; when therefore the thought is sublime so does
the style appear to be. But in fact Burke has no style properly
so called: his style was colourlessly to transmit his thought.
Still he was an orator in form and followed the common
oratorical tradition, so that his writing has the strain of address I speak of above.

But Newman does not follow the common tradition—of
writing. His tradition is that of cultured, the most highly educated, conversation; it is the flower of the best Oxford life.
Perhaps this gives it a charm of unaffected and personal sincerity that nothing else could. Still he shirks the technic of
written prose and shuns the tradition of written English. He
seems to be thinking 'Gibbon is the last great master of traditional English prose; he is its perfection: I do not propose to
emulate him; I begin all over again from the language of conversation, of common life'.

You too seem to me to be saying to yourself 'I am writing
prose, not poetry; it is bad taste and a confusion of kinds to
employ the style of poetry in prose: the style of prose is to
shun the style of poetry and to express one's thoughts with

point'. But the style of prose is a positive thing and not the absence of verse-forms and pointedly expressed thoughts are single hits and give no continuity of style.

After all the very Paper which leads me to make these remarks is entitled 'Thoughts on Knowledge' etc, so that I am blaming you for not doing what you do not attempt to do. Perhaps then I ought to blame you for not attempting and doing. However I have said my say and feel inclined to burn it.

In the Paper itself there are some things I feel hard but do not speak of now. The parable of the carcase is in the highest degree illustrative and ghastly-vivid: it ought to be everywhere known.

During the summer examinations one of my colleagues brought in one day a *St. James's Gazette* with a piece of criticism he said it was a rare pleasure to read. It proved to be a review by you of Colvin's book on Keats. Still, enlightening as the review was, I did not think it really just. You classed Keats with the feminine geniuses among men and you would have it that he was not the likest but rather the unlikest of our poets to Shakspere. His poems, I know, are very sensuous and indeed they are sensual. This sensuality is their fault, but I do not see that it makes them feminine. But at any rate (and the second point includes the first) in this fault he resembles, not differs from Shakspere. For Keats died very young and we have only the work of his first youth. Now if we compare that with Shakspere's early work, written at an age considerably more than Keats's, was it not? such as *Venus and Adonis* and *Lucrece*, it is, as far as the work of two very original minds ever can be, greatly like in its virtues and its vices; more like, I do think, than that of any writer you could quote after the Elizabethan age; which is what the common opinion asserts. It may be that Keats was no dramatist (his *Otho* I have not seen): but it is not for that, I think, that people have made the comparison. The *Cap and Bells* is an unhappy performance, so bad that I could not get through it; senselessly planned to have no plan and doomed to fail: but Keats would have found out that. He was young; his genius intense in its quality; his feeling for beauty, for perfection intense; he had found his way right in his Odes; he would find his way right at last to the true functions of his mind. And he was at a great disadvantage in point of education compared with Shakspere. Their classical attainments may have been much of a muchness, but Shakespere had the school of his age. It was the Renaissance; the ancient Classics were deeply and enthusiastically studied and influenced directly or indirectly all, and the new learning had entered into a fleeting but brilliant combination with the medieval tradition. All then used the same forms and keepings. But in Keats's time, and worst in England, there was no one school; but experiment, division, and uncertainty. He was one of the beginners of the Romantic movement, with the extravagance and ignorance of his youth. After all is there anything in *Endymion* worse than the passage in *Romeo and Juliet* about the County Paris as a book of love that must be bound and I can't tell what? It has some kind of fantastic beauty, like an arabesque; but in the main it is nonsense. And about the true masculine fibre in Keats's mind Matthew Arnold has written something good lately.

My brother also sent me a paper of yours on Women's Rights, very, perhaps cruelly, plainspoken.

The night, I think, before I began this letter I had a dream touching you which raises a point of interest. I thought I was at a station where cheap trips were advertised. I went to the booking-office and pulling out what I had in my purse, about three and sixpence, said 'I don't care where I go: put me down as near the sea as you can'. The clerk gave me a ticket for Lewes. I rejoiced and said to myself that I should now be able to get over to you at Hastings for a night. I think I have never been near Lewes these twenty years but in passing it to and from Hastings on my visit to you. So then, though I felt surprised at the Lewes ticket, it would seem that in my dream it was really Hastings suggested Lewes, not Lewes Hastings, and that I was really constructing the plot which should bring Hastings about, unknown to myself, all the time.

Believe me very sincerely yours

GERARD M. HOPKINS.

Oct. 24, 1887.

In reality I was in August in England at Haslesmere, where my family now live, and had thoughts of trying to get over to see you, but time (principally) did not serve. Remember me kindly to all.

After rereading your letter—I can by no means remember, when I was enjoying your hospitality, that it was give on my part and take on yours; and if it was, it seems to me I must have babbled greatly.

TO ROBERT BRIDGES

University College, St. Stephen's Green, Dublin. Nov. 6 1887

DEAREST BRIDGES,—I must write at once, to save you the trouble of copying that music: I reproduced it by a jelly-process at Stonyhurst on purpose and only wanted the copy back in case you had one already. I do not remember anything about the harmony: it is the tune I think so good, and this I revived my memory of before I sent it you. I cannot at all make out the meaning of 'If your sister has learnt harmony I can't understand what the moderns mean'. Grace did learn harmony, but girls are apt not to study things thoroughly and perhaps she has not kept it up as she should. I remember years ago that the organist at Liverpool found fault with a hymn of hers, in four parts, very regular, for hidden fifths in the inner parts But he was an ignoramus: I did not know then but I know now that hidden fifths must be and are freely used in the inner parts and are only faintly kept out of the outer ones. And see what became of him: he got drunk at the organ (I have now twice had this experience: it is distressing, alarming, agitating, but above all delicately comic; it brings together the bestial and the angelic elements in such a quaint entanglement as nothing else can; for musicians never play such clever descants as under those circumstances and in an instant everybody is thrilled with the insight of the situation) and was dismissed. He was a clever young fellow and thoroughly understood the properties of narrow-necked tubes.

I am thankful to you for the account of the Coda, over which you gave yourself even unnecessary trouble. You say the subject is treated in many books. That was just it. I had not got those books and the readiest source of information was you. It seems they are formed on an invariable plan and that Milton's sonnet gives an example. Of course one example was enough if there is but one type; but you should have said so.

I want Harry Ploughman to be a vivid figure before the mind's eye; if he is not that the sonnet fails. The difficulties are of syntax no doubt. Dividing a compound word by a clause sandwiched into it was a desperate deed, I feel, and I do not feel that it was an unquestionable success. But which is the line you do not understand? I do myself think, I may say, that it would be an immense advance in notation (so to call it) in writing as the record of speech, to distinguish the subject, verb, object, and in general to express the construction to the eye; as is done already partly in punctuation by everybody, partly in capitals by the Germans, more fully in accentuation by the Hebrews. And I daresay it will come. But it would, I think, not do for me: it seems a confession of unintelligibility. And yet I don't know. At all events there is a difference. My meaning surely *ought* to appear of itself; but in a language like English, and in an age of it like the present, written words are really matter open and indifferent to the receiving of different and alternative verse-forms, some of which the reader cannot possibly be sure are meant unless they are marked for him. Besides metrical marks are for the performer and such marks are proper in every art. Though indeed one might say syntactical marks are for the performer too. But however that reminds me that one thing I am now resolved on, it is to prefix short prose *arguments* to some of my pieces. These too will expose me to carping, but I do not mind. Epic and drama and ballad and many, most, things should be at once intelligible; but everything need not and cannot be. Plainly if it is possible to express a sub[t]le and recondite thought on a subtle and recondite subject in a subtle and recondite way and with great felicity and perfection, in the end, something must be sacrificed, with so trying a task, in the process, and this may be the being at once, nay perhaps even the being without explanation at all, intelligible. Neither, in the same light, does it seem to be to me a real objection (though this one I hope not to lay myself open to) that the argument should be even longer than the piece; for the merit of the work may lie for one thing in its terseness.

It is like a mate which may be given, one way only, in three moves; otherwise, various ways, in many.

There is some kind of instinct in these things. I wanted the coda for a sonnet which is in some sort 'nello stilo satirico o bernesco'. It has a kind of rollic at all events. The coda is an immense resource to have. This sonnet, I hope, very shortly.

In glancing over the Paper[10] I am much pleased with the additions and final treatment. (I remark various faults of punctuation.) I shall nudge the professors of English about this book and paper. Just now something catches my eye, p. viii.—'a pronunciation *eale*'. Better write *eel:* that is a word. Now *eale* is not strictly 'a pronunciation' but is the actual printed word of the passage in Shakspere about the 'dram of eale', to which if you use this form you should certainly refer. Otherwise why this fantastic spelling? I am afraid it is however too late.

Mr. Tyrrell (a devout convert) sets you to Trinity men to turn 'into the original Greek'.* More, more by token! The wreck of me that remains to study anything is studying Aeschylus, chiefly the lyrics, for a book (or set of Papers in the *Classical Review* perhaps) thereon. He has made a number of happy conjectures, though I say it that know him too well, and yesterday a very happy one, *Seven against Thebes* 424–434, which redispose thus: ΕΤ. θεοὺς ἀτίζων . . Ζηνὶ κυμαίνοντ' ἔπη (428–430). | Ζεὺς δ' οὐκ ἀπειλεῖ (for Καπανεὺς δ' ἀπειλεῖ), δρᾶν παρεσκευασμένος (427.). | καί τῷδε κέρδει (viz. the having heaven on our side) κέρδος ἄλλο τίκτεται (viz. that his boastful words will prove to the enemy an omen of his defeat). | τῶν τοι ματαίων . . κατήγορος (424–426.) | ἀνὴρ δ' ἐπ' αὐτῷ (contrasted with Ζεὺς above), κεἰ στόμαργός ἐστ' ἄγαν etc (434 sqq.). The source of all the confusion was reading ZEYC | NEYC, and then supplying ΚΑΠΑ and of course striking out οὐκ. But see how Aeschylus has borrowed your 'And him Zeus stayed not to deride'. Misplacing of lines in Aeschylus is almost certain.

Your affectionate friend

GERARD M. HOPKINS S.J.

---

* I do not mean literally that he says that.

No, I do not ask 'enthusiastic praise'. But is it not the case that the day when you could give enthusiastic praise to anything is passing or past? As for modern novels I will only say one thing now. It is in modern novels that wordpainting most abounds and now the fashion is to be so very subtle and advanced as to despise wordpainting and to say that old masters were not wordpainters. Just so. Wordpainting is, in the verbal arts, the great success of our day. Every age in art has its secret and its success, where even second rate men are masters. Second rate, third rate men are fine designers in Japan; second rate men were masters of painting in Raphael's time; second rate men were masters of sculpture in Phidias' time; second rate men of oratory in Cicero's; and so of many things. These successes are due to steady practice, to the continued action of a school: one man cannot compass them. And wordpainting is in our age a real mastery and the second rate men of this age often beat at it the first rate of past ages. And this I shall not be bullied out of.

For my case I shd. also remark that we turned up a difference of taste and judgment, if you remember, about Dryden. I can scarcely think of you not admiring Dryden without, I may say, exasperation. And my style tends always more towards Dryden. What is there in Dryden? Much, but above all this: he is the most masculine of our poets; his style and his rhythms lay the strongest stress of all our literature on the naked thew and sinew of the English language, the praise that with certain qualifications one would give in Greek to Demosthenes, to be the greatest master of bare Greek. I am driven to the blackguard device of a palimpsest envelope.

TO ROBERT BRIDGES

University College, St. Stephen's Green, Dublin. Feb. 10 1888
DEAREST BRIDGES,—Know that the copy of your Paper never came, so that I have none at all, and you said I might have several: I am content with one and please send one; if two, I can do better still.

I laughed outright and often, but very sardonically, to think you and the Canon could not construe my last sonnet;[11] that he had to write to you for a crib. It is plain I must go no farther on this road: if you and he cannot understand me who will? Yet, declaimed, the strange constructions would be dramatic and effective. Must I interpret it? It means then that, as St. Paul and Plato and Hobbes and everybody says, the commonwealth or well ordered human society is like one man; a body with many members and each its function; some higher, some lower, but all honourable, from the honour which belongs to the whole. The head is the sovereign, who has no superior but God and from heaven receives his or her authority: we must then imagine this head as bare (see St. Paul much on this) and covered, so to say, only with the sun and stars, of which the crown is a symbol, which is an ornament but not a covering; it has an enormous hat or skull cap, the vault of heaven. The foot is the daylabourer, and this is armed with hobnail boots, because it has to wear and be worn by the ground; which again is symbolical; for it is navvies or daylabourers who, on the great scale or in gangs and millions, mainly trench, tunnel, blast, and in others ways disfigure, 'mammock' the earth and, on a small scale, singly, and superficially stamp it with their footprints. And the 'garlands' of nails they wear are therefore the visible badge of the place they fill, the lowest in the commonwealth. But this place still shares the common honour, and if it wants one advantage, glory or public fame, makes up for it by another, ease of mind, absence of care; and these things are symbolized by the gold and the iron garlands. (O, once explained, how clear it all is!) Therefore the scene of the poem is laid at evening, when they are giving over work and one after another pile their picks, with which they earn their living, and swing off home, knocking sparks out of mother earth not now by labour and of choice but by the mere footing, being strongshod and making no hardship of hardness, taking all easy. And so to supper and bed. Here comes a violent but effective hyperbaton or suspension, in which the action of the mind mimics that of the labourer—surveys his lot, low but free from care; then by a sudden strong act throws it over the shoulder or tosses it away as a light matter. The witnessing of which lightheartedness makes me indignant with the fools of Radical Levellers. But presently I remember that this is all very well for those who are in, however low in, the

Commonwealth and share in any way the Common weal; but that the curse of our times is that many do not share it, that they are outcasts from it and have neither security nor splendour; that they share care with the high and obscurity with the low, but wealth or comfort with neither. And this state of things, I say, is the origin of Loafers, Tramps, Cornerboys, Roughs, Socialists and other pests of society. And I think that it is a very pregnant sonnet and in point of execution very highly wrought. Too much so, I am afraid.

I have more, not so hard and done before, but I am not prepared . . .[12]

On referring to yr. letter I see you speak of modern music, not music of this century. It is, I suppose, as you say. I hope your rheumatism is abated, is gone: why not gone? But I have a poor, very charming friend on his back with spinal disease: when he complains of rheumatic pains his doctor rubs his hands with joy and says nothing cd. be better.

TO COVENTRY PATMORE

Milltown Park, Milltown, Dublin May 6 1888

MY DEAR MR. PATMORE,—I have greatly to beg your pardon for leaving you so long unanswered. This however is the second letter begun, and the other ran some length, but is cancelled.

Your news was that you had burnt the book called *Sponsa Dei*, and that on reflexion upon remarks of mine. I wish I had been more guarded in making them. When we take a step like this we are forced to condemn ourselves: either our work shd. never have been done or never undone, and either way our time and toil are wasted—a sad thought; though the intention may at both times have been good. My objections were not final, they were but considerations (I forget now, with one exception, what they were); even if they were valid, still if you had kept to yr. custom of consulting your director, as you said you should, the book might have appeared with no change or with slight ones. But now regret is useless.

Since I last wrote I have reread Keats a little and the force of your criticism on him has struck me more than it did. It is impossible not to feel with weariness how his verse is at every turn abandoning itself to an unmanly and enervating luxury. It appears too that he said something like 'O for a life of impressions instead of thoughts.' It was, I suppose, the life he tried to lead. The impressions are not likely to have been all innocent and they soon ceased in death. His contemporaries, as Wordsworth, Byron, Shelley, and even Leigh Hunt, right or wrong, still concerned themselves with great causes, as liberty and religion; but he lived in mythology and fairyland the life of a dreamer. Nevertheless I feel and see in him the beginnings of something opposite to this, of an interest in higher things and of powerful and active thought. On this point you shd. if possible read what Matthew Arnold wrote. His mind had, as it seems to me, the distinctively masculine powers in abundance, his character the manly virtues, but while he gave himself up to dreaming and self indulgence of course they were in abeyance. Nor do I mean that he wd. have turned to a life of virtue—only God can know that—, but that his genius wd. have taken to an austerer utterance in art. Reason, thought, what he did not want to live by, would have asserted itself presently and perhaps have been as much more powerful than that of his contemporaries as his sensibility or impressionableness, by which he did want to live, was keener and richer than theirs. His defects were due to youth—the self indulgence of his youth, its ill-education; and also, as it seems to me, to its breadth and pregnancy, which, by virtue of a fine judgment already able to restrain but unable to direct, kept him from flinging himself blindly on the specious Liberal stuff that crazed Shelley and indeed, in their youth, Wordsworth and Coleridge. His mind played over life as a whole, so far as he a boy, without (seemingly) a dramatic but still with a deeply observant turn and also without any noble motive, felt at first hand, impelling him to look below its surface, cd. at that time see it. He was, in my opinion, made to be a thinker, a critic, as much as a singer or artist of words. This can be seen in certain reflective passages, as the opening to *Endymion* and others in his poems. These passages are the thoughts of a mind very ill instructed and in opposition; keenly sensible of wrongness in things established but unprovided with the principles to correct that by. Both his principles of art and his practice were in many things vicious, but he was correcting them, even eagerly; for *Lamia* one of his last works shews a deliberate change in manner from the style of *Endymion* and in fact goes too far in change and sacrifices things that had better have been kept. Of construction he knew nothing to the last: in this same *Lamia* he has a long introduction about Mercury, who is only brought in to disenchant Lamia and ought not to have been employed or else ought to be employed again. The story has a moral element or interest; Keats was aware of this and touches on it at times, but could make nothing of it; in fact the situation at the end is that the sage Apollonius does more harm than the witch herself had done—kills the hero; and Keats does not see that this implies one of two things, either some lesson of the terrible malice of evil which when it is checked drags down innocence in its own ruin or else the exposure of Pharisaic pretence in the wouldbe moralist. But then if I could have said this to Keats I feel sure he wd. have seen it. In due time he wd. have seen these things himself. Even when he is misconstructing one can remark certain instinctive turns of construction in his style, shewing his latent power—for instance the way the vision is introduced in *Isabella*. Far too much now of Keats.

You sent me also a paper of yours in the *St. James's*. But I did not like the text of it, from Newman, and so I could not like the discourse founded on that. This was a paradox, that man is not a rational or reasoning animal. The use of a paradox is to awake the hearer's attention; then, when it has served that end, if, as mostly happens, it is not only unexpected but properly speaking untrue, it can be, expressly or silently, waived or dropped. But this you do not do with the paradox in question; you appear to take it in earnest. I always felt that Newman made too much of that text; it is still worse that you should build upon it. In what sense is man contemplative, or active, and not rational? In what sense may man be said not to be rational and it might not as truly be said he was not active or was not contemplative? He does not always reason; neither does he always contemplate or always act—of course human action, not merely so through animal or vegetable functions. Everyone sometimes reasons; for everyone, arrived at the age of reason, sometimes asks Why and sometimes says Because or Although. Now whenever we use one of these three words we reason. Longer trains of reasoning are rarer, because common life does not present the need or opportunity for them; but as soon as the matter requires them they are forthcoming. Nor are blunders in reasoning any proof that man is not a rational or reasoning being, rather the contrary: we are rational and reasoners by our false reasoning as we are moral agents by our sins.—I cannot follow you in your passion for paradox; more than a little of it tortures.

Now, since writing the above, I have read the paper again, but indeed I cannot like it at all. The comment makes the text worse; for you say contemplation is in this age very rare indeed: is then reasoning in this age very rare indeed or none? Other paradoxes follow; as that 'persons like General Gordon or Sir Thomas More would stare if you called anything they did or suffered by the name of sacrifice'. Did they then make no sacrifices? And if their modesty shrank from that word (I do not feel sure that it would) is the word not true? And do we not speak of Christ's sacrifice? and they were following him.

Also the 'truly sensible man never opines', though 'many things may be dubious to him'. But the definition of opinion is belief accompanied by doubt, by fear of the opposite being true; for, since many things are likely only but not certain, he who feels them to be most likely true knows also that they may possibly be untrue, and that is to opine them—though in English the word *opine* is little used except jocularly. Here no doubt you did not want to speak with philosophic precision (and in the same way say that 'to see rightly is the first of human qualities': I suppose it is the rightness or clearness or clearsightedness of the seeing that is the quality, for surely seeing is an act): but then the matter is philosophical, the title is so, the reference is to a philosophical work, and therefore philosophical precision would be in place and I in reading crave for it. But you know best what comes home to the readers you are aiming at. Yet after all there is nothing like the plain truth: paradox persisted in is not the plain truth and ought not to satisfy a reader. The conclusion, about the unpardonable sin, is on dangerous ground: but I do not understand it and few readers, I think, will. You see, dear Mr. Patmore, that I am altogether discontented with this paper and can do nothing but find fault.

I saw somewhere (I do not think you told me) that the Second Part of the *Angel* is to appear or has appeared in the same cheap form as the First and I am glad. Also having been asked to write a paper for a review I said I would write on your poems, but I am not sure I shall be able to carry this out, for work presses and I am in a languishing state of body.

And now, with kind regards to all your circle, I am, my dear Mr. Patmore, yours very sincerely

GERARD M. HOPKINS.

May 7 1888. Yesterday was the anniversary of the Phoenix Park murders. The present also is a crisis, owing to the Pope's late action. I have not time now to speak of matters political, but they must engross the mind of people living where I do and would do so even if I were in England.

I lately read Blackmore's last book *Springhaven:* perhaps you have. I am a devoted admirer of his descriptions, his wordpainting, which is really Shaksperian. Otherwise this book is disappointing. The construction is clumsy, the character drawing superficial and sometimes melodramatic, and there is a vein of stupid jocularity all about 'nose' and 'stomach' and 'breeches' and 'fine feeding' which downright disgusts me. Hardy is a finer man.

V

THE OTHER ARTS

Can you tell me what in music answers to realism in painting? The other arts seem to depend on truth (no: Truth) as well as Beauty. What then answers to, I mean what is, Truth in music?

TO ALEXANDER BAILLIE

July 10. 1863.

DEAR BAILLIE,

Yes. You are a Fool.
I can shew it syllogistically, by an Epimediculum or paradoxling. For you will allow that he who lies is a fool in the long run, and that he who lies without any object to gain thereby is immediately and directly a fool. Now you are not a fool. But you say you are a fool. Therefore you lie. Syllogistically then.

MAJOR PREMISS.
He who lies without an object to gain is a fool.

MINOR PREMISS.
You have lied without an object to gain.

CONCLUSION.
Therefore you are a fool.

Epimendicularly proved. However it contains two assumptions you might not perhaps allow me.

I do not see the precise object of your tirade; I am afraid I must call it a tirade, or—a favourite word of mine—rhodomontade. It is weak, you know; and conscious. What you say about a man whose powers are above mediocrity being a 'greater fool than a simple, decently well-formed etc.' contains thought and truth. You remember that after More's execution, one of his contemporaries doubted whether to call him a foolish wise man or a wise fool. Some one of the same age also says of some one else that he had not wit enough to play the fool. Indeed it is a subject on which I have theories, but as it may be said *latius patere*, we will dogmatize more at leizure at another time.

The Princess did not come. I might have known she would not. Whenever I wait on a contingency like that, inevitably I am disappointed. I am the victim of false alarms. I have waited to see the Queen come up to Miss Burdett Coutts's at Highgate in the same way, and on numberless other like occasions have had the same success. However, determined to see her once more I put myself in her way as she went to the station and got a good passing look, and, as I was alone at the particular spot, I think a bow. The Princess is different every time I see her, but in all her phases is beautiful.

We all got through Smalls. Hardy after the seizure of his *testamur* became light-headed, light-hearted, light-heeled. He, Brown and I proceeded to booze at the Mitre, and I forgot to pay my share, but I believe Hardy meant to feast us, in his delight.

For the first week of the Long I read the Georgics with Bond, taming him *en passant*, but he takes longer to tame than you. Now I am with all our tribe at Shanklin. In the mornings I read the Histories of Tacitus. I must say they are very hard, and the *cruces* have a hopelessness about them which I do not think I find anywhere else in the classics. I have Tacitus and Cicero's Philippics to read (enough certainly) alone, for would you believe it? I have no Greek lexicon of any kind here. Shanklin is a delightful place. If you were here you would have soon

> —forgot the clouded Forth,
> The gloom that saddens heaven and earth,
> The biting East, the misty summer
> And grey metropolis of the North.[1]

where I do not envy you. The sea is brilliantly coloured and always calm, bathing delightful, horses and boats to be obtained, walks wild and beautiful, sketches charming, walking tours and excursions, poetic downs, the lovely Chine, fine cliffs, everything (except odious Fashionables.) My brothers and cousin catch us shrimps, prawns and lobsters, and keep aquariums. Ah and I will tell you a Pöpehenic anecdote. I thought it would look strikingly graceful etc to wear sea-anemones round my forehead. (Mermaids do it, you know. Fragment from an unpublished?) So I put a large one on in the middle, and it fixed itself correctly. Now one has heard of their stinging, but I had handled them so often unharmed, and who could have imagined a creature stinging with its—base, you call it in sea-anemones? But it did, loudly, and when the pain had ceased a mark remained, which is now a large red scar.

About Millais' Eve of S. Agnes, you ought to have known me well enough to be sure I should like it. Of course I do intensely—not wholly perhaps as Keats' Madeline but as the conception of her by a genius. I think over this picture, which I could only unhappily see once, and it, or the memory of it, grows upon me. Those three pictures by Millais in this year's Academy have opened my eyes. I see that he is the greatest English painter, one of the greatest of the world. Eddis, the painter, said to me that he thought some of its best men—he instanced Millais—were leaving the school. Very unfairly, as you will see. If Millais drops his mannerisms and becomes only so far prominent from others' styles as high excellence stands out from mediocrity, then how unfair to say he is leaving his school, when that school, represented in the greatest perfection by him, passing through stage after stage, is at last arriving at Nature's self, which is of no school—inasmuch as different schools represent Nature in their own more or less truthful different ways, Nature meanwhile having only one way.

I will be humble to you on one of your tenets, I mean General Rules. Although I had had opinions resembling yours before, yet you had arrived at a definite decision on them which I could not at first fully enter into. You were in advance. I am now seeing the truth of your objection to them.

My daily experience is stumbling on them and rubs its shins cursing; if you see the force of the metaphor.

I am sketching (in pencil chiefly) a good deal. I venture to hope you will approve of some of the sketches in a Ruskinese point of view:—if you do not, who will, my sole congenial thinker on art? There are the most deliciously graceful Giottesque ashes (should one say *ashs*?) here—I do not mean Giottesque though, Peruginesque, Fra-Angelical (!), in Raphael's earlier manner. I think I have told you that I have particular periods of admiration for particular things in Nature; for a certain time I am astonished at the beauty of a tree, shape, effect etc, then when the passion, so to speak, has subsided, it is consigned to my treasury of explored beauty, and acknowledged with admiration and interest ever after, while something new takes its place in my enthusiasm. The present fury is the ash, and perhaps barley and two shapes of growth in leaves and one in tree boughs and also a conformation of fine-weather cloud. You remember the sketch that you would not criticize: I had continued it to my satisfaction, when an insane fury induced me to ravage it—

None, I think, but an idiot could,—with a sky. It is now spoilt.

I will write again, and so please do you.

Believe me, dear Baillie, yours very sincerely,

GERARD M. HOPKINS.

Manor Farm, Shanklin, Isle of Wight. July 13.

I think I could save my life by swimming on the river now.

My objection to the so-called Logical Mind rests finally on the same ground as yours to General Rules.

EXTRACTS FROM EARLY DIARIES

[1863]

NOTE. There is now going on what has no parallel that I know of in history of art. Byzantine or Romanesque Architecture started from ruins of Roman, became itself beautiful style, and died, as Ruskin says, only in giving birth to another more beautiful than itself, Gothic. The Renaissance appears now to be in the process of being succeeded by a spon-

taneous Byzantinesque style, retaining still some of bad
features (such as pilasters, rustic-work etc) of the Renaissance. These it will throw aside. Its capitals are already, as in
Romanesque art, most beautiful. Whether then modern
Gothic or this spontaneous style conquer does not so much
matter, for it is only natural for latter to lead to a modern
spontaneous Gothic, as in middle ages, only that the latter is
putting off what we might be or rather are doing now. Or
the two may coalesce.

[1864]

Walked with Gurney to Elsfield. Sketched E. window of
church, which is in transition from decorated to perpendicular, or rather decorated with traces of perpendicularity. It
had strange all its windows except the E. and two or perhaps
three others. The E. had original tracery (see sketch book).
These others were 3-lighted square-headed; as far as I remember the lights were lancet-shaped and cinquefoiled. The
mullions were carried up to the head. The parson's son kindly
let us in to see the Easter decorations. The widest and most
charming views from Elsfield. A plain lies on the opposite
side to Oxford with villages crowned with square church-
towers shining white here and there. The lines of the fields,
level over level, are striking, like threads in a loom. Splendid
trees—elms, and farther on great elliptic-curve oaks. Bloomy
green of larches. Standing on a high field on all sides over the
hedge the horizon balanced its blue rim. The cowslips'
heads, I see, tremble in wind. Noticed also frequent partings
of ash-boughs.

Walked with Addis to Stanton Harcourt. The Church is
cruciform and rather large, with a Norman door and several
windows etc, Early English E. end and other windows, windows in tower (probably) Decorated, a Decorated or more
probably Perpendicular parapet, and Perpendicular windows.
The E. E. is certainly unattractive, however the Church is
evidently in Egypt and Churchwardenship. We did not go

into it, nor into the tower (close to the church, in Perpendicular, rather shorter than that of the church,) in the top story of which Pope finished his fifth volume of Homer, or of the Iliad, nor into the Octagon-roofed kitchen which except one at Glastonbury is unparalleled in England, nor into the chapel, which with the tower and kitchen belonged to Stanton Harcourt Manorhouse, I believe.

Villari in a note to his *Life and times of Savonarola* says 'It was with this promise', viz. 'to bring the faithful into direct relation with the Almighty', 'that the Reformation first saved a large portion of the human race from scepticism and materialism; these first led Catholicism to declare war against it; and afterwards, in the struggle, to recover its strength, and in part renew its youth. This is the settled opinion of the most orthodox "Romanist" writers.'—of the most orthodox writers, we may say, Anglican and Romanist.

Notes for essay on *Some Aspects of Modern Medievalism.*
Title not such as might be wished, but represents pictorially what is meant. May be objected that the various movements of the Century which have mediaeval externals deeper than a mere return to middle age forms. Very true. But no other title conveys so much of what I mean.

Subject treated not through all its bearings but remarks on various points to be made.

Historical remarks.

German movement. Tieck etc. This I must get up. The Schlegels. Goethe, whose balanced mind must not be considered as the ideal of the century, representing the most desired union of the classical and mediaeval. [June c. 28. 1864]

Cornelius, Overbeck and some one else (Rechel?) founders of German medievalism. Cornelius used to draw his smallest figures in charcoal.

Rethel a man of real genius would have been the master of the school but died young

Düsseldorf School, a poor affair. Now split into sects. Chiefly imitates the French.

Belgian School. Has one great medievalist Henri Huys. His followers feeble.

Sort of French Preraphaelitism, but very little medievalism *in feeling* though medieval subjects. [July 24. 1864]

Dixon. The Brownings. Miss Rossettii. D. G. Rossetti

The Preraphaelite brotherhood. Consisting of D. G. Rossetti, Millais, Holman Hunt, Woolner, and three others. One of these three went out to Australia.

EXTRACTS FROM JOURNAL

[1868]

WE drove down the Rhone Valley to Visp and soon entered a Catholic canton. The churches here have those onion steeples nearly all, the onion being in some cases newly covered with bright tin or lead: they remind one of tinselled humming-tops too.—They enclose the head of the cross in a triangle as below very commonly: it looks like a beacon at sea.

*

At Orsières there is an interesting spired tower: I got into it. It is pierced with pair-lights first, higher with a triplet. The spire, which is not acute, has a coronet part-way up pierced with small lights. The arches were round. Bädeker calls it 'a remarkable and very ancient tower like that of St. Pierre', of which the date is 1010. This we had passed without noticing. So far as I understand, the prevalence of these deep round-headed triplets of windows in the church towers is due to the perpetuation of this type after its common extinction and to imitation in fact down to this time: they appear both in Switzerland and in Germany. At Sembranchier in the valley of the Dranse was a tower coronetted and other-

wise like that of Orsières but later, the tower lights well and
boldly foiled: the spire had been capped with bright metal.

In the morning to see the cathedral, which is remarkable
for the great beauty of the capitals, especially their abacuses;
the mouldings too of two arches near the door we came in
by were very beautiful and elaborate and wanted long study,
which I could not give; there was also interesting brass-work
(for iron-work) on some doors, the outer band bordering the
outlines of the door being pierced with a succession of qua-
terfoils etc perpetually varied.

With Baillie to the National Portraits. Beautiful Holbeins,
one a portrait of Lord Delaware; another a portrait of a gentleman with some beautiful conventionalised leafage behind
—palmate leaves disposed along an equally-waved stem; a
third Lord Surrey with a lady (who holds a red pear)—small.
Portraits of Keats and Shelley. But I was turned out before
I had seen all.

Walked to St. Alban's with Baillie and back by train. The
country is very green and set with good trees. The abbey is,
I suppose, the least injured in England. It stands high, with
a great massive Norman tower now empoverished in look by
brown plaster, in which the tympana of the highest window-
arches—otherwise flush and blind: the tympana I mean—are
pierced oddly with three-cornered pigeon-holes. The nave is
very long, the roof, Third-Pointed, very low, invisible in fact,
except at the end. The nave divides itself accidentally at the
points where the work of conversion of style began or ended:
thus, on the S. side all the Norman work is converted—in the
clearstory the western part to First, the eastern to Second
Pointed; the triforium I forget; the aisle windows are wide
and well traceried but small; below these are the blind
traceried arches of the inner side of the cloisters (not now
standing)—these last and some windows in the antechapel to

the east between the church and the ladychapel are beautiful and in the purest style—on the N. side the clearstory is in the western part converted to First Pointed, the rest remains Norman; the rest I forget. None of this side has any Middle pointed. The outside on the whole is plain and, where Norman, barbarous. The great number of the clearstory windows gives it character and beauty. Inside the whitewash has been cleared and the carving is fresh to a degree, the stone, which comes from not far off, being when covered from the weather durable though soft. The conversion is very perceptible inside. In the depth of the round arches has been laid bare some simple and broad diaper painting (chequers, stripes, etc) and on piers on the western side of the pillars (above altars now gone from their places) frescos of the crucifixion—the same subject differently treated in each—and, below sometimes, other subjects. Note that one of the crosses was a tree, as at Godshill, Isle of Wight. The ceiling with its old painting is complete from end to end; that of the choir was Middle Pointed and the effect of the slant stripes on the ribs of the groining, especially where they met, was noticeable. The Third-Pointed altar-screen, especially behind, and the choir screen of the same character were beautiful in design and proportion. So also are two chantries, one on the N. side of the high altar, the other Duke Humphrey's on the S. behind. The abbot's passage so called is remarkable for the curious astragalus moulding of the interlaced wall-tracery. There is a little Saxon work, like rude turning in the carpentry, merely barbarous. The building is mostly of tiles taken from the Roman walls of Verulam. It is perhaps worth noticing that the curled ends of some corbels in the nave are freakishly turned each a different way.

*

To Ely. Noticed on the way that the E. counties trees are upright in character, not squat. The country more burnt than at Hampstead.

In the cathedral the great Norman tower is fine in effect; otherwise the Norman work (transitional) is not striking but some of the foliate trailing on the capitals etc remains and has been repainted: it is in fact the loss of this correction that makes the style heavy and barbarous. The First Pointed work has not much that is very good unless the large and taper corbels in the choir, some of them ribbed with long slant stems alternately leaved wound across them. The Flowing work is the middle interest of the building. In this the lantern and three bays of the choir eastwards, of Alan of Walsingham's work (1322 sqq.), are original, imaginative, and graceful, strict beauty being almost forbidden by the excess of the climacteric. The most striking points in this are the open-traceried arches of the triforium in the choir; the scroll of open tracery between the choir and octagon arches, the flight or spirit in which it is impossible not to feel; the triplets of candleflame-shaped canopies over brackets (now dismounted of their figures) above the lower arches in cross or lesser sides of the octagon; and most of all perhaps the pierced hoods formed by a blunter arch springing from the same points as the acuter one which encloses the greater windows in these same cross sides and so cutting off the upper part of their tracery: the quasi-fleurdelys tracery in these

 hoods is very happy. The nave is not very interesting but it is skilfully and successfully designed as to concentrate and enclose the view up to the choir and not through width and scattering in the side arches let it lose or escape. The cieling of the nave painted by L'Estrange and after his death by Parry is contributively speaking effective, and quiet and good in colour, but the design is babyishly archaic. But even this suck-a-thumb is not so bad as the modern brasses and the window with the queen in her coronation robes and the bachelor and undergraduate and butler and bed-maker. The transept roof is painted and long angels with scarlet wings (original?) support the principals. The Ladychapel (1321 sqq.) has its walls bordered all round with an ogee-canopied arcade of great richness, but the E. and W. windows are strangely clumsy.—The all-powerfulness of instress in mode and the immediateness of its effect are very remarkable.

Prior Crauden's chapel (he was prior 1321–1341) is beautiful in proportion and even in detail (viz. the tracery of the

E. window: it is that window with the border of tracery enclosing a smaller arch), but I did not see it inside.

Sept. 2. Fine; at Hampstead dim.

Home. I had to start early to see the cathedral again. The
galilee is full of good detail, the door seeming beautiful especially two mouldings of the arch, looking like the bending
down of leafy rods, but scaffolding broke it up and hid it.

[1871]

In the afternoon to Netley Abbey, a spot which everything
makes beautiful—the ruins, the lie of the ground, the ivy, the
ashtrees, and that day the bright pieces of evening light. The
ashes it would not be easy to match but some are dead, others dying, and one in the chapterhouse fallen across, the roots
to the ground but higher up the stem/ resting on the wall:
others have been felled. There is one notable dead tree in
the N.W. corner of the nave, the inscape markedly holding
its most simple and beautiful oneness up from the ground
through a graceful swerve below (I think) the spring of
branches up to the tops of the timber. The finest of all stands
I think in the monks' day-room. In the building the most
beautiful and noticeable things are the east window; the triplet windows on the S. side of the nave, the middle light
trefoiled the other two lancets: outside they are flush with
the wall but inside hooded under arches which spring lower
than their sills or at least than the top of the sill; a pair of
plain three-light lancets in each clearstory of the S. transept,
which dwell on the eye with a simple direct instress of trinity; a fine piece of blind tracery in the quasi-triforium of this
transept at the S. end—two broad arcade-arches (subdivided
I think but this has gone) and containing in the head a
quaterfoiled roundel each, the two surmounted by a great
sixfoiled roundel (sharp-hung)—plate tracery and the roundel having no immediate gearing with the two arches; lastly
three beautiful windows in the chapterhouse, not quite of
equal breadth etc—a plain sixfoil, clear, not enclosed in any
roundel, at least inside, riding two plain broad lancets: the
cusps were sharp and both it and the lancets had no work

beyond the splay inwards but the jambs (?) of the head to
the whole window were moulded and stripes of red colour
could be seen in the splay of the lancets of one window radiating from the opening as so following the splay. I notice
a predominance of the series 1, 2, 4, 8 in parts, perhaps
throughout—in the east window four lights gathered into two
greater heads (the middle and greater mullion still stands)
and an eight-foil in the circle riding them, four pillars in the
jambs each carrying a moulding of four ribs, thus 16 in all,
the two middle ribs carrying a band, fillet, or whatever it is
 called; two windows of two lights in each
side of the choir, that is, I suppose, two
bays; two bays in the transepts, eight in the
nave etc. This deserves note. Division by 2
is of course the simplest of all division but
this will not explain the choice of the four
mouldings for instance here, which are so
taken for their own sake and clearly do not
arise from subdivision

[1872]

Stepped into a barn of ours, a great shadowy barn, where
the hay had been stacked on either side, and looking at the
great rudely arched timberframes—principals (?) and tie-
beams, which make them look like bold big As with the
cross-bar high up—I thought how sadly beauty of inscape was
unknown and buried away from simple people and yet how
near at hand it was if they had eyes to see it and it could be
called out everywhere again

To see Peel Castle. On the way we went into the churchyard of Kirk Braddan, as beautiful as any I ever saw: fine
and beautiful ashes and a wychelm with big glossy happy
and shapely leaves, spanish chestnuts and other trees sur-
round it and others stand in groves beyond; the ground slopes
down to the road with tier upon tier of thick black grave-
stones. There are several Danish crosses with runes engraved

and curious work containing dragons and monsters, more odd than pretty and a little Japanese in look. We also went into the little ruined chapel of Kirk Trinnian growing ashes now and half pulled down by them, about which there is a foolish legend of a tailor and a goblin called a Buggane: the legend is told in guidebooks but our driver home told it also as he had always heard it from a child, so that it lives. We passed the Tynevald (from Thingvollr) mound too, from which the Manx laws were published—now they only read the titles of the acts. It is an earthen mound of four rounds or stages one within the other like Ecbatana, each about a yard high perhaps, but a way up of lower steps is cut on the side towards the church: every part is of green turf

Peel castle is a ruin. It is built wholly or partly of red sandstone. The walls and windows of St. German's cathedral, in First Pointed, are in some degree of preservation. There is also a red chapel (with herringbone work) and round tower nearly perfect ascribed to St. Patrick (444) or if he was never in the island connected with his mission. And in other ways the Castle has historical interest. But what pleased me most were the great seas under a rather heavy swell breaking under the strong rocks below the outer side of the castle—glass-green, as loose as a great windy sheet, blown up and plunging down and bursting upwards from the rocks in spews of foam; but in a great gale, our funny meek old guide told us, it is a grander sight than we saw

[1873]

At the Kensington Museum. Bold masterly rudeness of the blue twelvemonth service of plates or platters by Luca Della Robbia—Giovanni's (1260) and Niccola (early in next century) Pisano's pulpits—Bronze gilt doors for Cathedral of Florence by　　　?—The cartoons and a full sized chalk drawing from the Transfiguration—Standard portfolios of Indian architecture—also of Michael Angelo's paintings at the Vatican: the *might*, with which I was more deeply struck than ever before, though this was in the dark side courts and I could not see well, seems to come not merely from the simplifying and then amplifying or emphasising of parts but from a masterly realism in the simplification, both these things: there is the simplifying and strong emphasising of anatomy in Rubens, the emphasising and great simplifying in Raphael for instance, and on the other hand the realism in Velasquez, but here force came together from both sides—Thought more highly of Mulready than ever before—Watts: Two sisters and a couple of Italian peasants with a yoke of oxen—instress of expression in the faces, as in other characteristic English work, Burne Jones', Mason's, Walker's etc—Musical instruments—harpsichords (English for clavecin); spinets (small portable harpsichords); virginals (square, differing from spinet, which is three-cornered like the harpsichord as cottage

piano from grand); dulcimers (this-shaped)

lutes; theorbos; (viols, I think, differ from lutes in having slacks, hollows, in the sides, so as to be the original of the violin); mandolas and mandolines (small lutes, I think); viol-de-gambois (held between the knees); citherns; panduras

Yes, the viol is the origin of the violin. It has been thought the parent of all the viol family is the Welsh crwth. The name looks against this. They are characterised by the bridge and the use of the bow. The viol has 5 strings. Another day at the Kensington I made some notes. The lute is round-bottomed and has frets—Fétis[2] says 10 and 11 strings, 9 of them double, 3 tuned in unison and 6 in octaves. The theorbo I have noted to have the neck very much put back, two sets of pegs (Fétis says it has 2 fingerboards, the smaller that of the lute, the other, much bigger, with 8 strings for the bass—but my note says it has no frets). The pandora again I have marked as round-bottomed: Fétis says it differs from the lute in being flat and having metal instead of cat-gut strings. The mandola is round-bottomed, with frets: Fétis says it has 4 strings 'tuned from 5ths to 4ths'. The mandoline he says is smaller and with a fingerboard like a guitar, played with a quill, and the strings tuned in unison with the violin. The cither is very like a guitar, flat-bottomed, with frets.

∗

[1874]

I went with Arthur to the winter exhibition of the Water Colours. Walker's *Harbour of Refuge,* smaller water-colour reproduction of the oilpainting in the Academy for '72: that sold for £ 1500, this for £ 1000. Execution rough, the daisies and may brought out by scratching and even rudely, but perhaps this is more lasting than chinese white. The sunset sky and boughs of tree against it most rude, yet true and effective enough—at a distance, though this seemed inconsistent, for the details of the faces needed to be looked at close. When I wrote these notes my memory was a little duller. The young man mowing was a great stroke, a figure quite made up of dew and grace and strong fire: the sweep of the scythe and swing and sway of the whole body even to the rising of the one foot on tiptoe while the other was flung forward was as if such a thing had never been painted before, so fresh and very strong. In contrast the young girl with the old woman on her arm with an enforced langour in her; in face the same type as Catherine Beamish in the *Village on the Cliff*,[3] very pensive and delicate and sweet; auburn hair; beautiful, rather full, hands, crossed; a pretty clever halo of a cap. The background of the long line of almshouse rather heavy and inartistic: there seems to remain in his work a clod of rawness not wrought into perfect art, which in a Frenchman would not be

There was also a pretty medieval ploughing-scene by Pinwell and some good things by Macbeth, also a masterly little thing, the Fluteplayer, Roman of course, by Alma Tadema

*

To the Soane Museum with Fr. Goldie. His uncle Mr. Bonomi is curator and we had been to call on him at Wandsworth at 'the Camels' one day but he was not this day at the museum. I was most interested by the gems—one especially in a two-coloured stone, perhaps onyx: in the midst a ramshorn completely relieved; then in white, like cameo a fourfold head, two female faces, back to back like a she-Janus, the long way of the stone, which was oval; above them along the crown, their common crown, looking up like a mask put back from the right-hand face, a man's face—these three delicately featured; below, across the neck, looking down, the snub Silenus' face, the hair in crisp peaked and shapen flamelet-texture, somewhat Alexandrine; the ground or field same colour as the horn

We also visited the National Gallery. Especial notice (to be renewed, I hope) of two new Michael Angelos not seen before: touches of hammer-realism in the Entombment (also a touch of imperfection or archaism) and masterly inscape of drapery in the other—But Mantegna's inscaping of drapery (in the grisaille Triumph of Scipio and the Madonna with saints by a scarlet canopy) is, I think, unequalled, it goes so deep

To Kensington museum with Br. Tournade the young Frenchman bound for China. Looked at a Graeco-Roman statue of Melpomene: these Greek gowns are of linen which makes crisp pleat-like folds; I marked especially how on the bosom the folds were sprayed like slips of rue or some slenderer-leaved herb, severe and beautiful.—There was a shew of beautiful Japanese work, modern, from which one gathers that their art is very flourishing: there was a capital fight between a night-hawk and a dragon on a gilded platter; ivory relief, I don't know how to call the work, but it was, I think, by cutting out certain beds or fields and in them relieving the figures (incised work?), which gives rather precision to the whole than simple relief and then further heightening, on one side only, the edges of the figures within the fields or dies or else the edges, cliffs/ of these dies with Indian ink, which gives great finish; also there were complete soldiers' accoutrements with masks for the face, which shewed the type of features and that was ugly

I went one day to the Academy and again June 12, when Fr. Johnson (Superior in the absence of Fr. Porter, who is gone to take the waters at Carlsbad in Bohemia) kindly sent me to town with Br. Bampton for change. These are the notes on the two days—

Phillis on the new-mown hay (R. W. Macbeth)—Very pretty but the Phillis a copy, a close gross copy in expression, gold red hair, circle of cap, large shapeless hands etc from the girl in Walker's *Harbour of Refuge*

Briton Rivière's Apollo (from Euripides)—Like a roughened boldened Leighton, very fine. Leopards shewing the flow and slow spraying of the streams of spots down from the backbone and making this flow word-in and inscape the whole animal and even the group of them; lion and lioness's paws outlined and threaded round by a touch of fur or what not, as one sees it in cats—very true broad realism; herd of stags between firtrees all giving one inscape in the moulding of their flanks and bodies and hollow shell of the horns

Queen of the Tournament—P. H. Calderon—*Clear:* composition in the pieces, the figures singly, not in the picture or piece in the oldfashioned sense of piece; clever frank treatment of bright armour. His name is Spanish: I think there is something Spanish about him

Millais—*Scotch Firs: 'The silence that is in the lonely woods'*—No such thing, instress absent, firtrunks ungrouped, four or so pairing but not markedly, true bold realism but quite a casual install of woodland with casual heathertufts, broom with black beanpods and so on, but the master shewn in the slouch and toss-up of the firtree-head in near background, in the tufts of firneedles, and in everything. So too *Winter Fuel: 'Bare ruined choirs'* etc—almost no sorrow of autumn; a rawness (though I felt this less the second time), unvelvety papery colouring, especially in the raw silver and purple birch-stems, crude rusty cartwheels, aimless mess or mingle-mangle of cut underwood in under-your-nose foreground; aimlessly posed truthful child on shaft of cart; but then most masterly Turner-like outline of craggy hill, silver streaked with birch-trees, which fielded in an equally masterly rust-coloured young oak, with strong curl and seizure in the dead leaves. There were two scales of colour in this picture—browns running to scarlet (in the Red-Riding-Hood girl) and greys to blue (little girl's bow or something) and purple in the smoke on the hill, heather, birch-woods, and in foreground the deep mouldy purple of the stems; then for a gobetween a soft green meadow. There was a beautiful spray-off of the dead oak-scrolls against dark trees behind with flowing blue smoke above. Toss or dance of twig and light-wood hereabouts

North-West Passage—Characteristic *ruffling*—in grandfather's coat, girl's skirts and *rouches*, in chart and the creased flag. This picture more unsatisfying than the others, want of arch-inscape even to scattering; besides old sea-captain seemed crumpled together somehow

Young *Nathaniel de Rothschild*—Must be the very life—hair (just bridled with a gilded curl or two), lips, eyes, crimson scarf, stride, embroidered bright-leather shoes carried to a knifeblade edge and a little rising; but then scapeless aimless background of tapestry, a cannon, and so on, just like him. Should be remarked how he makes his figures out into pieces—scarlet turning of the coat-collar, white waistcoat, red tie, face, hair, scarf, breeches etc. So also in the *Picture of Health* the head curls on either side, green-blue butterfly of scarf, velvet coat, muff

Daydream—a Millais-Gainsborough most striking crossbreed: colouring raw, blue handkerchief not any stuff in particular but Reynold's emphatic *drapery*, background (bushes and tank) either unfinished or mere mud. Intense expression of face, expression of character, not mood, true inscape—I think it could hardly be exceeded. Features long, keeling, and Basque. The fall away of the cheek (it is a ¾ face) masterly. Great art in the slighted details of the hat on the lap, blue of the bracelet, lace of the scarf; fingers resting on or against one another very true and original (see on Holman Hunt's *Shadow of Death* much the same thing)

Alma Tadema—*Joseph overseer of Pharaoh's granaries*—Joseph in sort of white linen toga, sceptre stained or painted like a lotus, black wig; merely antiquarian but excellent in that way

The Picture Gallery—Less antiquarian; lighting just a little studio-fashioned; two Romans with check or patterned tunics like a snake's slough, the arm of one resting on the other's shoulder very faithful drawing; little colour; happy use of openings, accidental installs, people's feet, hands etc seen through, use of square scaping

I saw also a good engraving of his *Vintage Festival*, which impressed the thought one would gather also from Rembrandt in some measure and from many great painters less than Rembrandt/ of a master of scaping rather than of inscape. For vigorous rhetorical but realistic and unaffected scaping holds everything but no arch-inscape is thought of

Leighton—*Moorish Garden: a dream of Granada*—Whimsical little girl, blown together of Andalusian afternoon air, leading a white and a coloured peacock (its train brown in the light exhibited); brown and green cypresses parcelled into flakes, which were truthfully slanted, trellised alley, rushing stream down a marble channel, blue inlaid dome in distance; no central inscape either architecturally or in the figure grouping—little girl should have transomed the trailing sweep of the peacocks' trains, as indeed their necks did but not markedly enough; however beautiful chord of blue and green browns ※ and reds

Old Damascus: Jews' Quarter seemed to me the gem of the exhibition. Marble paved striped court of house, striped pillar, delicately capitalled brace of corbel-pillars springing from the channelled half-architrave Arab capital, vault of arch as well as heads or lintels of doors covered with inlaid roundels of all sorts of designs, the nearest arch however not in roundels but in more highly wrought arabesque patterns. The child with her arms held straight out to hold up her frock to catch the lemons gave a horizontal line carried on by something in the waist of the woman with the staff to knock them down and perhaps by other things: don't know whether he saw or meant this. Woman in foreground rather aimless in pose and drapery and in fact what is she doing with the slanted pot of pinks? The lemontree foliage cleverly interfered with the braced window-lights. Clever rich shading (αἰόλον) of the brown marble in the head of the two pairs of lights. There was in the picture a luscious chord of colour (which grew on me)—glaucous (blue, with green and purple sidings) ※ browns (with reds to match). In the green scale, which was part of the glaucous or blue faction, were the lemontree, the duller-green striped and flowered sort-of-dressing gown the flowerpot woman wore, her pinks, and the bluer green flowerpot plants behind her; purple appeared in the roundels; in the blue scale, which was domi-

nant or predominant in the whole picture were the inlaid
blue-panelled door, which struck the keynote, and the panel-
ling in the shade of the arches within the   ,[4] some
of the roundels, mosaics in the vault of the arch etc, stripes
on pillars on wall, stripes on pavement, and the lemon-wom-
an's scarf and drawers, the child's skirt, which was rosier, the
flowers in the pots, some mosaic and the brown marble fram-
ing of the braced windows, in which, as I have said there
was a beautiful flush of dark. The frame of this picture was
margaretted with round arabesques in black but after much
looking I did not find much inscape in them, though richness
and grace

Clytaemnestra watching the beaconfires—very smooth and
waxen; addled cream-drapery, rhetorical, not recognised;
scaping in it; moonlight clear and white, without any exaggeration or sillybillying in blue and bottleglass, delicately
browning her arms; face fine, scornful voluptuous curl and all
that (as it was really there must say so); behind tall-up bat-
tlements, not massive

J. Brett—*Summer Noon in the Scilly Isles*—Emerald and
lazuli sea; true drawing of clouds; sooty-mossed boulders in
foreground a little scratchy and overdry—not quite satisfying
picture but scarcely to be surpassed for realism in landscape

J. S. Raven—*Let the hills be joyful together*—Like what I
have seen of his before—grace of line and colour: the colour
gathers in rosy or in purple tufts and blooms; trees, clouds,
and mountaintops 'seized' or 'shrugged', as in Turner

W. L. Wylie—*Goodwin Sands*—Fiery truthful rainbow-
end; green slimy races of piers; all clean, atmospheric, truthful, and scapish

Several Tissots—Atmosphere; green and yellow chestnut
leaves; atmospheric women in clouds of drapery with mooning-up eyes and mooning-up nostrils of oddly curved noses:
his interesting management of modern costumes (as in the
Ball on Shipboard) is very clever but he should not have
tried to paint Bluecoatboys' yellow legs

Bright Japanese pictures are the rage. The best was *Five
O'clock Tea* by Mrs. Jopling

W. Richmond's *Prometheus Bound*—Fine; academic in attitude and colouring, as dark tinsel-blue sea, big moon, brown clouds, fine anatomy

J. Parker—*Phoebe Dawson* and *Abbey Stream, Abingon*—pretty and Boyce-like

Maclaren (Uncle Edward's friend at Capri)—*Girls playing at knuckle-bones*—Much tone; colouring quite (Italian) classical—black, two siennas, green, blue (both Raphael-like), rosepink flowers, bamboo-yellow fence, grey ground, figures a little weak though and flattened

A. S. Wortley—*In Wharncliffe Chace*—Much sense of growth in bare oaks and much cast (so I have written: I hardly understand it) in the boulders

C. Green—*May it please your Majesty* (a royal entry, burghers, carpets etc)—Tone; projection; colour studio-muffled

H. Bource (?)—*Day after the Tempest*

H. Moore—*Rough weather in the Mediterranean*—Fine wave-drawing; waves glass-blue and transparent with under-lights. So also a coast-scene with wave breaking, but there the moustache of foam running before the wave or falling back to it seemed a little missed or muddled

Hughes—*Convent boat*—Piecing and parting of the ivy, poplars, and other trees attempted but not quite mastered

✳

Fr. Johnson sent me to town with Bampton, when I made some of the above notes at the Academy. After that we went to All Saints' Margaret Street. I wanted to see if my old enthusiasm was a mistake, I recognised certainly more than before Butterfield's want of rhetoric and telling, almost to dullness, and even of enthusiasm and zest in his work—thought the wall-mosaic rather tiresome for instance. Still the rich nobility of the tracery in the open arches of the sanctuary and the touching and passionate curves of the lilyings in the ironwork under the baptistry arch mark his genius to me as before. But my eye was fagged with looking at pictures

Then we went to Holman Hunt's *Shadow of Death*. First impression on entering—great glare and lightsomeness (so that, strange to say, I could not help knowing what a woman behind me meant by saying that, well, it reminded her of those pictures they hang up in national schools); true sunset effect—that is/ the sunset light lodged as the natural light and only detected by its heightening the existing reds, especially in the golden-bronze skin he has given to our Lord's figure, and by contrast in the blue shadows on white drapery and puce-purple ones on pink silk. Also thin unmuscular but most realistic anatomy of arm and leg. Also type of figure not very pleasing—seems smaller from the waist down, head overlarge, and the feet not inscaped but with a scapeless look they sometimes no doubt have (I can remember and do not put it down for reverence: see above on Millais' *Daydream*) and veined too, which further breaks their scaping. On the whole colour somewhat overglaring. The pale weathered brick (?) interior throws up the glare of our Lord's figure. Face beautiful, sweet and human but not quite pleasing. Red and white embroidery of broad flat belt giving a graceful inscape and telling in the picture. Clever addled folds of the white cloth. Shavings and all the texture too tufty and woolly—and you get the thought of this from the sea-shot blue-and-green woollen gown our Lady wears. The saws and other tools seemed over-blue. No inscape of composition whatever—not known and if it had been known it could scarcely bear up against such realism

At Marychurch we went to Mr. Brownlow's. (By the by I saw there Maderna's beautiful statue of St. Cecilia: he was a contemporary of Bernini's but the natural grace of this figure is due to its having been made after the body of the saint as it was found lying.) Then I went, with John Lynch, who had come to meet me, to Butterfield's Church at Babbicombe. It is odd and the oddness at first sight outweighed the beauty. It is long and low, only a foot or so, just to mark the break, between the nave and aisle (lean-to) roofs (I am nearly sure I remember there being once a wider interval with quaterfoil fanlights); the windows scattered; the steeple rather detached, not, I thought, very impressive, with an odd openwork diaper of freestone over marble pieces on the tower/ and on the spire scale-work, and with turrets at cor-

ners. There is a hood of the same diaper at the east-end gable
from the spring of the arch of the east window about upward.
Tracery all simple. Inside chancel-arch much as at St. Alban's, Holborn—a cross and lozenges in freestone enclosing
black-and-white patterned tiles set in chequer and the pattern, more by suggestion than outright,
passing from one to the other—some-
thing of this sort: I am not so sure of the
tiles being square-hung—they may have
been lozenges. Same sort of thing down
the nave above and in the spandrils of the
arches—diamonds and tiles but also seven-foiled blind tracery
in the spandrils meant to contain mosaic, the foils not symmetrical but somehow thus—. And in other
places were other such openings, whether
lights of windows or blind and enclosing
mosaics, as in the reredos and each side of
the choir, some six-foiled fishes, some otherwise. In two of them he makes use of the
split or spiked cusp (I call it)—⌢⌣⌢⌣⌢.
Much marble is employed—pillars, font, pulpit, choir pavement, reredos, medallions round east window etc—and everything very solid and perfect. Pulpit beautiful, like a church
or shrine and in three storeys, basement, triforium etc. Medallions by east window/ alternate inscapes—all five-spoked
wheels or roses—odd. Some of these patterns in the marble,
as on the floor and on the stage or block by the font, were
large and simple but not very striking. There was a more
quarried look about the designing than he commonly has (in
the cieling for instance). The nave roof-timbers and choir
cieling were remarkably flattened: I like this. The enrich-
ment grows towards the altar, the choir cieling having two
degrees of it. Rafters there fluted and striped, webs between
sown with bigger and smaller stars or rowels on pale sea-
green ground. Wrought brass chancel gates with a running
inscape not quite satisfying, continued by deep marble party-
wall (as at Margaret Street) pierced by quater-foils. Very
graceful gasjets from the walls

✳

To Bristol with Mr. Foley and Considine. Fr. Walter Clifford kindly shewed us the lions, taking us to St. Mary Redcliff, the Cathedral, the Puseyite St. Raphael's (where I was with Addis) etc. St. Mary Redcliff—narrow and so looks high; spire just lately completed—it has been truncated, one storey only. It is under restoration by Godwin and so the choir boxed off as at Exeter Cathedral. It is mostly good and rich early Third-Pointed but the steeple and North Porch are Middle-Pointed rich and terminal (split cusps etc), some parts are First-Pointed and the whole shell of the church I believe is so. This north porch is striking: it is a hexagon, if I remember; the windows richly foiled but the cusps not split, though the effect is much the same: buttresses run up and end in a wedge upon their mullions, with odd effect. Within, opening on the church, two beautiful First-Pointed arcades with the heartfelt grace and flush in the foliation of the capitals that belongs to that keeping. Odd windows in transepts with a band of quater-foils enclosing the rest (Third-Pointed). Third-Pointed finely proportioned tomb behind altar, in two compartments with canopy. The Geometrical windows at the west end of aisle and in basement of tower are modern. Here and at the Cathedral tombs with fine rich remarkably designed Middle Pointed canopies. Of the Cathedral we could not see much. Street is adding a nave to it: designs cold, not pleasing

To Westminster Abbey, where I went round the cloisters, examined the diaper, took in the beautiful paired triforium-arcade with cinquefoiled wheels riding the arches (there is a simplicity of instress in the cinquefoil) etc. Then to the National Gallery, where I made notes. As I hurried from picture to picture at first these words came to my mind—'Studious to eat but not to taste'.

To St. Asaph: the people call it Llan-elwy. We passed Mrs. Hemans' house and saw her monument in the Cathedral. Though it is no bigger than a large parish church it has an imposing rather Cathedral-like look. It has old choir stalls and

a massive tower but as it is restored (and under restoration) I can no longer tell what is old

Sept. 3—For the first time to the Rock. The Rock is a great resort of hawks and owls. Then with Mr. Purbrick to Trefnant, where we went into a pretty little new church built of the same limestone as St. Beuno's and the pillars of a mottled grey, I suppose local, marble. Capitals all of that sort which is common—two rows or rings of tufts of leaf or flower, one above the other, the upper the bigger, and the two rows alternate with one another. These were good work, also the corbels

With Mr. Bacon to Ffynnon-y-capel or Ffynnon-Fair (Mair?), such another well as St. Winefred's, standing in a beautiful spot in the valley of the Elwy at a ruined chapel. We said a prayer and drank the water. The shape is something as opposite: the five points are perhaps to recall the five porches of Bethesda and their symbolism. The basis of pillars (which would have supported a canopy having five openings in circuit and two at the side between the well and the trough or  bath) can be seen. The remains of the chapel are Third-Pointed. Thence we went to Cefn (the *f*, that is *v*, is very soft, almost a vowel, perhaps what the Greek *v* in diphthongs is now or has been in reaching its present sound), Cefn Rocks, from which the view of the deep valley of the Elwy, the meeting of two, which makes three, glens indeed, is most beautiful. The woods, thick and silvered by sunlight and shade, by the flat smooth banking of the tree-tops expressing the slope of the hill, came down to the green bed of the valley. Below at a little timber bridge I looked at some delicate flying shafted ashes—there was one especially of single sonnet-like inscape—between which the sun sent straight bright slenderish panes of silvery sunbeams down the slant towards the eye and standing above an unkept field stagged with patchy yellow heads of ragwort. In the evening I watched a fine sunset from the tower: the place is famous for them

[*1875*]

One day in the winter I walked to Bodlewyddan church with Henry Kerr and Wagner. This is the modern church of white limestone the spire of which in the plain towards the sea makes a bright feature in our landscape. It has no real beauty but is very rich and solid in Caen stone, Derbyshire alabaster, and Welsh, French, and Italian marble. The pillars, each four shafts clustered, are single blocks of marble

The day was bright, the sun sparkling through a frostfog which made the distance dim and the stack of Denbigh hill, as we came near, dead mealy grey against the light: the castle ruins, which crown the hill, were punched out in arches and half arches by bright breaks and eyelets of daylight. We went up to the castle but not in: standing before the gateway I had an instress which only the true old work gives from the strong and noble inscape of the pointedarch. We went to eat our lunch to a corner opening by a stone stile upon a wilderness by which you get down to the town, under the outer wall, overgrown with ivy, bramble, and some graceful herb with glossy lush green sprays, something like celery

TO ROBERT BRIDGES

8 Salisbury Street, Liverpool. June 18 1880.

DEAREST BRIDGES,—I hear you are going to be married. Is this so? who is she?

The *Academy* had a notice of *Wet Days*. It blamed its cynical spirit but praised the nobility of the thought and quoted *Courcy* in instance. You are surprised that I found no fault with this same cynicism. It is over sour, I think; but your brother's dislikes seem to be much the same as mine and I do not mind hearing someone else say what I feel more strongly than I mean myself to say it.

When you shall next call at Oak Hill I want you to hear

my music to the Spring Odes, to which Grace[5] has set accompaniments, which accompaniments I have not myself seen yet. I sorely wish I knew some harmony. And say whether you like them and they suit your meaning in the words. I have also a feeling air for 'I have loved flowers that fade', but that is not quite fixed yet, still less written out. I wish I could pursue music; for I have invented a new style, something standing to ordinary music as sprung rhythm to common rhythm: it employs quarter tones. I am trying to set an air in it to the sonnet 'Summer ends now'.[6]

Some unlucky miscarriage seems to have taken place about Mr. Rae's pictures and Mr. Bowes' Japanese ware and I am afraid I shall not see them.

I have never seen that portrait of me but once. I believe that I am in some ways like my brother Arthur.

When you see Mr. Gosse ask him what were those works on Keats which he speaks of as having lately appeared, in a notice by him of a book by some lady on the same subject.

I will enclose a sonnet and little lyric,[7] the only things I have written in nine months.

Believe me your affectionate friend

GERARD M. HOPKINS S.J.

Remember me very kindly to your mother. It is a great comfort to me when I think of your and her coming to know my people so well. I know my sisters and all of them are much attached to Mrs. Molesworth. I hope your marriage will not lessen this intimacy.

June 21—Wyatt-Edgell that was, Lord Braye that is, is staying with us. So I spoke of you and I found he did not know (that is/does not remember, for I fancy I spoke to him on the subject in London) that you wrote. And now I am considering whether—however I have done it, namely lent him yr. last book. He is going to make a selection from the 3 volumes of poetry he has published and so reduce them to one.

June 23. The line 'most men dislike slops, particularly gruel' does not scan. For we say *pă˘ ticyulă˘ ly*, shortening the 1st and 4th syllables, and the *i* is long by position. False quantities of this kind abound also in the 'O you chorus of indolent reviewers'. He might have said 'Most men dislike slops and gruel especially'. At all events I answer—

Try the common means used to manage the slop-difficulty—

You can take half a glass of gin: it adds a relish. And this does scan.

TO ROBERT BRIDGES

8 Salisbury Street, Liverpool Sept. 5 1880

DEAREST BRIDGES,—I take up a languid pen to write to you, being down with diarrhoea and vomiting, brought on by yesterday's heat and the long hours in the confessional. Yesterday was in Liverpool the hottest day of the year. To-day there is rain.

Your poems have lain long on my table almost unopened, so much has my work set in. Today however I have read all the early volume, which to be sure is only 31 short pages. But of both volumes I will write hereafter, only saying now what a delight I take in them. The present is meant as an answer to your last.

I am very happy that you (and that Woolrych, and by the by I think that is how the name is spelt and not as you write it, Wooldridge) [8] like my music and, as Pepys might say, do pray that that same may continue and increase—upon your further trying of it. But the 'I have loved flowers' is in a rude state, wanting improvements and a third verse, which will considerably differ from the two others, and unluckily Grace has not returned me the rough copy, which was left lying about. I therefore cannot tell whether there was an oversight, as Woolrych thought, in the phrase 'Proclaim the spirit's desire'; but that phrase, though I and Grace too had a great deal of trouble to get it down, is in itself, if you could hear it played or sung, very marked and unmistakeable. The rhythm, to imitate it in verse, is 'Betráying the hearts' desíre, betráying the héarts' desíre, desíre O'.*

---

* I believe it shd. be written thus, in monotone—

Pro - claim . . . . . the spi-rit's de - sire,   de - sire;   then

I have now an air for 'Thou didst delight my eyes', which some day you shall see. Your poetry is highly songful and flies into tunes.

Grace made on the first version of the first of the Spring Odes the same criticism as Woolrych, that a greater compass, a higher note was wanted; accordingly I supplied it. I do not feel that now it is too narrow in compass, but perhaps the other one, the Reply, is.

In the setting I should have been glad if Grace had been bolder. The accompaniment should have a shower of semiquavers or demisemis, with great chords at certain places. On the words 'And where the bare trunks', where a note is four times repeated, the chord should have been varied four times, rising or descending, an obvious and beautiful effect of counterpoint, and not been repeated, as she has done. If I could make my own harmonies much of the expression of the piece could be conveyed in the accompaniments of course.

The Brothers was rather suggested by Wordsworth than Patmore. It was first written in stanzas in Wordsworth's manner, but when I compared it with his inimitable simplicity and gravity I was disgusted and meant to destroy it, till the thought struck me of changing the metre, which made it do. I do not myself recognise anything Patmorial in it: what do you find? I shall enclose a corrected version. The incident took place at Mount St. Mary's in Derbyshire.

You shall also see the *Leaden Echo* when finished. The reason I suppose, why you feel it carry the reader along with it is that it is dramatic and meant to be popular. It is a song for St. Winefred's maidens to sing. I hope some time soon to send you some speeches from the play, but I should be sorry for you to have judged what it would be like from the fragments Kate sent me on a blue paper. They were the roughest first thoughts, which in me are of a too lyrical and not enough dramatic cast.

Do you not feel Patmore's pathos? To me it is harrowing. Read for instance the *Azalea* in the *Unknown Eros* and some others there.

I have not studied Wyatt, but Surrey I used to read: he, I think, is a greater man. He was an accomplished rhythmist, not that the experiments in couplets of long twelves and thirteens are pleasing, though this is better than couplets both twelves or both thirteens. He has a very fine style free from Euphuism. However, to speak of the sample you send, I must say that I think you have missed the clue. You take the rhythm for free triple time, iambs and anapaests say, and four feet to a line (except the refrain). But to get this you have to skip, in two lines out of these few, a whole foot as marked and stressy as any other foot. This is a licence unpardonable by the reader and incredible in the writer.

Before offering my own thoughts I must premise something. So far as I know triple time is in English verse a shy and late thing, I have not studied *Piers Ploughman* and so cannot pronounce how far triple time is boldly employed in it; at least it must have been suggested. But on the Romance side of our versification triple time appeared, I think, late. It may have been suggested by *Piers Ploughman's* rhythm, as I have said, but partly I conjecture it arose from a simple misunderstanding or misreading of Chaucer and the verse of that date and thereabouts. Chaucer and his contemporaries wrote for a pronunciation fast changing (everybody knows that final *e* for instance has often to be sounded in Chaucer, but everybody does not know that mostly it is *not* to be sounded and that the line which scans by its aid is really to be scanned another way). Their versification was popular and hit the mark in its time, but soon, as far as I can see, became obsolete, and they being much read and not rightly scanned thus came to suggest rhythms which they never thought of. The same sort of thing has, I think, happened often in the history of verse. And so far, Wyatt's piece might be scanned as you scan it—but for the two lines with a foot too much.

Now in particular I suppose that the verse called doggrel (in which the play of *Royster Doyster* is written and parts of *Love's Labour*, the *Shrew* etc) arose in this way: I do not know how else such a shapeless thing can have arisen. If it were a spontaneous popular growth it wd. [be] simpler and stronger. It must be the corruption or degeneration of something literary misunderstood or disfigured. Its rule is: couplets, with a pause dividing each line and on either side of this either two or three (perhaps sometimes even more) stresses, so that the line may range from four to six feet, and the rhythm variable too, iambic or anapaestic.

This wretched doggrel I think Surrey was systematising and raising in that couplet of his of which I spoke above and, to come to the point, I conjecture that Wyatt is dealing with the same thing here. The main point is the pause or caesura; on that the line turns. The notion of pause or caesura had come to English versification from two different quarters— from *Piers Ploughman* and the older native poetry on the one hand, where it is marked by a sort of Greek colon or by a stroke, and from France on the other, where it is essential both to the Alexandrine and to the old ten-syllable or five-foot line of the Chansons and is marked after the fourth syllable, I find.

The midpause then being essential and the rhyme double, not triple, which to Wyatt would have been a barbarism perhaps, he thinks himself at liberty to give each wing of the line two or three stresses at pleasure, as in doggrel, but not, as I have said, more than two syllables, a stress and a slack, to each foot. His rhythm, I have noticed myself in the little I have read of his, is very French and lightsome, lighter than Surrey's and weaker, and that appears here; for instance I think he wd. scan—'it sittéth me néar', that is, really, 'it sitteth me néar' or, as I like to write it, 'it sitteth me near', the black ball marking the real

or heard stress, the white the dumb or conventional one.

However I write under correction and you may be in a position to bowl me over. But see whether what I suggest will not apply to other of his pieces. I should add that as both parts of his line may begin with the stress or slack at option he gets an effect of sprung rhythm, which however from the weakness of his stresses is slight.

I enclose a little piece composed since I began this letter, not founded on any real incident.[9] I am not well satisfied with it and do not copy it on paper of the size you like.

I hope your Elegy will be immortal, as it deserves to be— for everything and most for the line 'As scarce she dared to be

delighted'. But I think the Lethe mythology of the last stanza
is a fall-off and unrealises the whole.

Believe me your loving friend

GERARD HOPKINS S.J.

Sept. 10 1880.

I find I have not time just now to copy out the *Brothers*,
but will send it shortly. However I have copied the shorter
piece out again, improved and on paper of the size you like.
Sept. 11.

I forgot to say that the first phrase of the second Spring
Ode should be,

not— 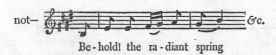 &c.

Be - hold! the ra - diant spring

but—  &c.

Be - hold! the ra - diant spring

and so on throughout except for 'Then what charm company'—

G. M. H.

Sept. 13 1880. 8 Salisbury Street, Liverpool.

TO ROBERT BRIDGES

write more would weary you.[10]

You asked me not long ago about my dramatic poem. It is
a play: I do not hold with dramatic poems. That is it will
be if ever it gets done. But since I have been here it has
made no way. At Hampstead I did some dozen lines or less.
Every impulse and spring of art seems to have died in me,
except for music, and that I pursue under almost an impos-
sibility of getting on. Nevertheless I still put down my pieces,
for the airs seem worth it; they seem to me to have something in them which other modern music has not got. I have
now also one little piece harmonised: it is only two part
counterpoint at present, but it sounds impressive and is a vast

improvement on the naked air. If I could only finish the harmony to 'Thou didst delight mine eyes' I hope you would like it.

I could say plenty more, but this has been kept far too long already. Believe me your affectionate friend

GERARD M. HOPKINS, S.J.

I expect not long hence to leave Liverpool. April 3 1881.
Hall Caine has written a review of a poem in the *Academy*.

TO ROBERT BRIDGES

Stonyhurst College, Blackburn. [Early October, 1882.]

DEAREST BRIDGES,—You are in the infinite leisure of Yattenden and you do not write.

I send with this the air to *I have loved flowers that fade.* A young Mr. Fitzpatrick is going to put me an accompaniment to it, but in the meantime I want you to see the tune. Playing it is of little use, unless it were on the violin; the snapping of a piano cannot give the extreme smoothness I mean: it must be sung. If you do not like it I think it must be a misunderstanding, for properly rendered I believe it could not fail to please you.

I want to go on with the study of harmony, but now my scholastic work is beginning and at first at all events I fear I shall not have time even for necessities, let alone luxuries or rather bywork.

I have finished the Leaden and Golden Echoes (meant for a maidens' song in *St. Winefred*) and am pleased with it: I shall send it you when I have put the last touches; it would be rash to send it today.

I want to see Prometheus out and when published for people here to see it. Remember me very kindly to Mrs. Molesworth and believe me your affectionate friend

GERARD M. HOPKINS S.J.

Better let me have it soon back, and then if you like it you cd. afterwards have an accompanied copy.

TO ROBERT BRIDGES

Stonyhurst, April 19 1883.

I am writing with a glass tube pen homemade and home-brewed ink.

DEAREST BRIDGES,—I wish you would write; it make me disconsolate punctually every morning to get no letter.

I want to know if you know any one who knows music, counterpoint, *thoroughly*, or, what comes to the same thing, if you know Stainer[11] thoroughly, enough to ask him a favour. For I shall shortly have finished an exercise in the second species in two parts on 'Pray, Goody, please to moderate', pretty elaborate, and I want to know on authority if it is correct and if not where. It has taken much time and I shall never write anything so long again by way of exercise. It is rather, not very, pretty.

I shall of course be glad to see Nero. Is there then to be a Second Part? You forgot that I had read the triolet in MS. It is witty in the last century but one sense of that word. I do not see that the anagrams in it are of any importance.

No more now.

Your affectionate friend

GERARD M. HOPKINS S.J.

TO ROBERT BRIDGES

Stonyhurst College, Blackburn. May 18 1883.

(fine day, with a solar halo; holiday; our boys to have a match)

DEAREST BRIDGES,—Fine bass! I should think so. But did you never hear *Pray Goody* before? I am glad I have introduced it to you. (I think it far better to take fine things like that to practise on than the maundering exercises in books.) And it is but one out of a host of such masculine and (what some one called) earnest melodies, little known here and abroad I suppose totally unknown. It is simple truth that no German since Mozart has been capable of anything of the sort. The Germans are great and I believe unsurpassable in expressing mood and feeling, but for the bone, frame, and *charpente* of music they cannot come up to this kind of thing.

On the contrary anything that Simcox says is important. But for rhymes like those search the scriptures, thumb the poets, and you will find they readily allow monosyllables and dissyllables like *higher* and *fire* to rhyme.* It is true it is not very consistent of me to appeal to them when I profess to follow a more excellent way; still when I am told so and so is indefensible I must shew that it is defensible. Authority justifies it and the pronunciation can be so adjusted as to satisfy the ear. What is serious, you seem to think I took the objection over-seriously. And now I think I am going out by woods and waters alone.

Yours GERARD.

---

* You will say a monosyllable cannot rhyme to a monosyllable and a dissyllable both at once, in the same stanza, that is. But if it can ever, then one of the two is accommodated to the other; and if one can be so can two or if one to one then one to two. Do you see the reasoning?

TO ROBERT BRIDGES

Stonyhurst College, Blackburn. May 29 1883.

DEAREST BRIDGES,—I am very grateful and greatly indebted to your friend ——.[12] His judgment and notes are also reassuring, for the composition is in fact my second exercise and no more, in the species my first ('tis true I took trouble over it) and the objections he makes are to things Dr. Bridge's book[13] had warned me against either not properly or not at all. Here indeed is a difficulty: I do not know if there are or where I can find examples (and the examples of the great masters are the soul of education) of existing counterpoint—if such a thing does exist; not short exercises in books (and of these I have only seen Dr. B's). Thus —— speaks of 'figures repeated two or three times': now I, bless us all, put these in for beauties, especially in a passage he marks as monotonous (and so it is if I ought to have kept changing). Clearly they are against the spirit of the kind of composition; though according to that of others, as fugue.

How then am I to advance without models? Somewhere models must be. And if he could tell me where, I should be glad. I hesitate over your offer to get him to write: it might entangle him in more than he meant and he will be in this busy world busy. Of course I should like it in itself.

I took to counterpoint not for itself but as the solid foundation of harmony. But I soon began to suspect it was only an invention of theorists and a would-be or fancy-music, for what is written in it? Not even the preludes to Bach's fugues. There are two-part preludes which seem as if they ought to be in the second or third species and are not, the rules are in smithereens: then WHAT IS in true counterpoint?

I meant to be as conservative as —— could be and my accidentals I always intended not to be chromatic but fragments of related keys, I did not always know what.

I have exhibited a poem, which I hope to send you when I can copy it, but it is longish for copying. Yours

GERARD.

TO ROBERT BRIDGES

University College, Stephen's Green, Dublin. Nov. 11 1884

DEAREST BRIDGES,—My heavy examination work is now some while over and I have begun to lecture: it is time therefore that I shd. write; indeed I have done so once, but the letter did not please and this is its recast.

I was very glad you gave me some word of your married life; I wish it had been more. I have a kind of spooniness and delight over married people, especially if they say 'my wife', 'my husband', or shew the wedding ring.

I shall read *Eros and Psyche*[14] with the greatest joy; so let civilisation execute its daily eggtrick over the book with the usual adroitness as far as the south side of Stephen's Green.

Mr. Tom Arnold (but I dreamt I told you this before) asked me to write a short notice of Canon Dixon for a new edition of his handbook of English literature. I did it, but whether it was time enough (for he was in the press) and short enough (for he was under pressure) I have not heard.

I have some musical matters to speak of. Stainer has written a capital Treatise on Harmony which has earned him the heartfelt thanks of people as ignorant as myself (I cannot say his Novello-Primer of the same earned them) and of others, I believe, not ignorant at all. For instance Sir Robert Stewart,[15] learned musican of this city, much given to Purcell, Handel, and Bach, says it is the most scientific treatment he has seen. Though his theory is not final, it is a great step forward and has quite a daylight, a *grand jour*, of sense. I am sure Stainer must be very nice to know and meet.

I have a great light on the matter of harmony itself, new, I need not say (framed on the model of Mr. Pecksniff's 'pagan, I regret to say'); true, I hope.

You saw and liked some music of mine to Mr. Patmore's *Crocus*. The harmony came in the end to be very elaborate and difficult. I sent it through my cousin to Sir Frederick Gore Ousely[16] for censure and that censure I am awaiting.

Before leaving Stonyhurst I began some music, Gregorian, in the natural scale of A, to Collins' *Ode to Evening*. Quickened by the heavenly beauty of that poem I groped in my soul's very viscera for the tune and thrummed the sweetest and most secret catgut of the mind. What came out was very strange and wild and (I thought) very good. Here I began to harmonise it, and the effect of harmony well in keeping upon that strange mode (which, though it is, as far as notes go, the same as the descending minor, has a character of which the word minor gives you little notion) was so delightful that it seems to me (and I think you would find the same) as near a new world of musical enjoyment as in this old world we could hope to be. To the novelty of effect the rhythm and a continued suspense natural to the mode and easy to carry further contribute too. It is meant for a solo and a double choir singing in unison, the organ or a string band bearing all the harmony. It is in three movements, something like a glee, the third returning to the first.

If this letter is dull the writer was so and wearifully tired. So goodnight, and goodnight to Mrs. Bridges or (what is more beautiful) to your wife:

I am your affectionate friend

GERARD M. HOPKINS S.J.

Nov. 12—You asked me some time since if I would write you a short paper on English scanning. I should like to do this if you still want it, but all that we Jesuits publish (even anonymously) must be seen by censors and this is a barrier which I do not know how anything of mine on a large scale would ever pass. In this particular case no doubt there would be no difficulty.

TO ROBERT BRIDGES

University College, Stephen's Green, Dublin. Feb. 8 1885
DEAREST BRIDGES,—I daresay I shall be able to send you your book in a day or two now. I am in the last Measure.* The first Measure is perhaps the least satisfactory and it is only at the 5th or 6th that I have begun to revise carefully.

I admire the equable beauty of the work and the quaint-ness and freshness of the pictures. The story you have not elevated but confined yourself to making it please. Eros is little more than a winged Masher, but Psyche is a success, a sweet little 'body' rather than 'soul'. The dramatic side of the poem is very good, the characters say all the right things, and so on. I should think it would be widely and lastingly ad-mired. On particular points I do not further dwell.

I am now ready to send my piece of music, the two first verses of the *Battle of the Baltic*, set of course for the piano, for what else can I do? but really meant for an orchestra—if I cd. orchestrate. But this is indeed to fly before I can walk, as a severe musician told me (but I did not care) of some-thing else. Any lights —— gives me, any remarks he makes I shall be very grateful indeed for. I hope of course he will not find the thing 'impossible', not the first verse surely, which even on the piano sounds a success; but the ground bass in the second needs a body of easily distinguishable instru-ments to bring it out. My hope is that, however complicated the harmony, the whole wd. be quite intelligible with a choir (the bigger the better) and an orchestra. My poor Crocus went to Sir Frederick Gore Ouseley and has not been heard of since. I fear it is hopelessly lost.

---

* I resumed the work this morning after a long break.

Remember me very kindly to Mrs. Bridges and believe me your affectionate friend

GERARD M. HOPKINS S.J.

The critical remarks above will strike you perhaps as faint praise, but take it for said that the beauties of the poem are extreme: the seagull under water alone is immortal and so are lots of things, pretty well everything that amounts to a feature.

Try my music yourself, at all events the first verse, and say what you think.

[Composed, as here, for the piano, for which instrument it is unfitted, because the parts and particularly the ground bass in the second verse cannot properly be distinguished; but I can do no otherwise. I am sensible that the rhythms of the second verse are very confusing and see now how bars 1, 2 might be made more intelligible, but nevertheless prefer to send it off as it is and correct afterwards. There shd. be a great body of voices and the ground bass shd. be done by bells or something of the sort. The triplets shd. be taken as made with notes of the same length as the couplets, that is the quaver is the same in both and no shorter in the triplet than in the couplet.][17]

TO ROBERT BRIDGES

University College, Stephen's Green, Dublin. April 1 1885

DEAREST BRIDGES,—*Ulysses* is safe, but I will not write of it now. I am afraid I cannot be of much service. Holidays are begun, but I am not in the frame of body or mind to avail myself of them for work, as I should wish.

I return your Alexandrines and enclose my own. Please return these, remarking what may strike you. Metrically they will save my commenting on yours. I daresay our theory is much the same. I hold that each half line is by nature a dimeter, two bars or four feet, of which commonly one foot is silent or lost at the pause. You will find it sometimes employed in full. The third sample is patchwork: I once thought well of the pieces, I do not know that I do now. But A and B please me well enough. I do not like 'recĕnt enough'.

You will see that as the feeling rises the rhythm becomes freer and more sprung: I think I have written nothing stronger than some of those lines. In the passage following Caradoc is to die impenitent, struck by the finger of God.

Your self quotation 'mortal overthrow' is from the sonnet 'In all things beautiful', last line:

> Unshaken by man's mortal overthrow.

I remember it, for the book is not here. It must be left in the sonnet and should therefore, I think, be changed in *Psyche*.

Do and *did* 'weak' present and perfect—It is a question of usage of words. The usage I follow is, I suppose, taken from the German, but now it is established, and that is enough. I object myself to calling *do come, did come* tenses at all: *do, did* are tenses (of *do*); *come* is a tense (if you like) of another mood of another verb. Two tenses and two moods and two verbs do not make a tense nor a mood nor a verb. It is the same confusion to call *of him* the genitive case: it is a preposition and an accusative case. These things are obvious, but scarcely anybody sees them.

You do not seem quite to have followed my meaning about the supper. The scene was ghastly of course. I feared that your scene was not ghastly enough. The stress was on 'quaintness', that the ghastly or the tragic was carried off in a quaint coincidence instead of being driven home. But you may be right and on the stage perhaps that treatment might be the most effective.

I am thankful to —— and did not want him hurried, as it is plain from the *Athenaeum* itself how busy he must be kept: however that is done now. His remarks are to be sure not in my circumstances encouraging, but they are instructive and if I could manage it I should attend Sir Robert Stewart's or somebody else's course, as he advises; only that I seem more in the way to compose my own requiem, like Mozart, but in plain chant, than any other musical exercise. Still there is something I do not understand. My piece puzzled you. Why? —— found it so plain, far too plain. (By the by, he does not speak of nor mark any mistake: that is the main thing, to be correct; if I am that, that is the great point gained.) As for not modulating, that was deliberate: I look on modulation as a corruption, the undoing of the diatonic style. What they call the key of the dominant, viz. one in which the fourth of the tonic is sharpened, I say is not the key of the dominant (which is in another mode than the key of the tonic and has no leading note) but the key of the tonic misplaced and transposed. I believe that —— and I would give diametrically opposite names to the same things: what he calls variety I call sameness, because modulation reduces all the rich diatonic keyboard with its six or seven authentic, not to speak of plagal, modes, to one dead level of major; where he finds tameness I find variety, specific quality (not of key, which is not specific, but) of mode. Here however, I must allow, is the hitch. For if I am right in theory, in practice I am bound to give that variety by my own methods. I find a difficulty in doing so and I am obliged to resort to devices of counterpoint (would I knew more of them!). Still I do hear plenty of variety which pleases me in that piece, and I hoped others would: it seems not; there is the mischief. To me plain chant melody has an infinite expressiveness and dramatic richness. The putting in or leaving out of a single note in an 'alphabetic' passage changes the emotional meaning: all we admirers of plain chant feel this, the rest of the world (and I expect this includes ——) do not; and it is the old story, *Fieri non potest ut idem sentiant qui aquam et qui vinum bibunt;* we are sober, they intoxicated with rich harmonies cannot taste our fine differences. When I hear one of Chopin's fragmentary airs struggling and toss on a surf of accompaniment what does it matter whether one or even half a dozen notes are left out of it? its being and meaning lies outside itself in the harmonies; *they* give the tonality, modality, feeling, and all. But I could write reams on this matter, which time does not allow my further running on about. When the *Ode to Evening* is done or well advanced I will send you that; study it yourself till you see my meaning (it is slow and easy to play); it is a test too: if you do not like it it is because there is something you have not seen and I see. That at least is my mind, and if the whole world agreed to condemn it or see nothing in it I should only tell them to take a generation and come to me again. But as it is I am well contented with —— judgment of the other thing and thankful to him for it; if I were otherwise than I am it would brisk me up and set me to work, but in that coffin of weakness and dejection in which I live, without even the hope of change, I do not know what I can make or, making, could keep up the exertion of learning better.

By the by, the mark ☐ in the verses means a sort of spondee, two long syllables equally accented or nearly so, though nominally one of the two has the stress. This is my difficulty, what marks to use and when to use them: they are so much needed and yet so objectionable. About punctuation my mind is clear: I can give a rule for everything I write myself and even for other people, though they might not always agree with me perhaps.

Believe me your affectionate friend

GERARD M. HOPKINS S.J.

Holy Thursday '85.

You once objected to the word *fleeced*, which you will find in sample B: I mean the velvetiness of roseleaves, flesh, and other things, *duvet*.

I had almost forgotten to say that Michael Field is the author of *Callirrhoe, Fair Rosamund,* and other plays one or all published very lately and much praised by the critics. He is a dramatist: nought which concerns the drama concerns not him, he thinks. It might indeed do him good to know that you had never heard of him, but I hope you will not let him make up a trio of enemies (*spretae injuria formae* you know) with Marzials and Hall Caine. The last has just written a novel said to be very good indeed. M.F. may perhaps be Irish: Field is a common, Michael a very common Irish name. Do be wise.

TO R. W. DIXON

University College, St. Stephen's Green, Dublin. June 30 '86

MY DEAR FRIEND,—I am in the midst of my heaviest work of the year, the summer examinations, and not at all fit for them. This is why I delay writing and is some excuse for not earlier answering your former letter; which was however a fault.

There are first two points of what we may call business.

The dedication: this is a great honour, which on the one hand I do not like to decline but which nevertheless I have some dread of, for I do not want my name to be before the public. It is true your poems do not command a large public, unhappily; but then the small one might contain enemies, so to call people, of mine. So do which you think best: if you dedicate I am flattered, if you do not I am reassured.

I think there could be no objection to my lines appearing in the Birthday Book,[18] especially anonymously (as I should wish), but I ought to get a formal leave and I will. However I should tell you that the poem in question is in three stanzas: did you know that? Nevertheless the first, the one you quote, might stand by itself. If so the text should be something about First-fruits: there must be several that would do, but I think of none just now. The second line had better be 'Cheek and the wimpled lip' and the count made up to six. And the stopping 'This, all this, beauty' etc is cumbrous: it is better 'This, all this beauty'. I have nothing else to send, but something new might strike me. There is a 3-stanza piece made at a wedding that possibly might do, but I rather think not: it is too personal and, I believe, too plain-spoken.

I saw the Academy. There was one thing, not a picture, which I much preferred to everything else there—Hamo Thornycroft's statue of the *Sower*, a truly noble work and to me a new light. It was like Frederick Walker's pictures put into stone and indeed was no doubt partly due to his influence. The genius of that man, poor Walker, was amazing: he was cut off by death like Keats and his promise and performance were in painting as brilliant as Keats's in poetry; in fact I doubt if a man with purer genius for painting ever lived. The sense of beauty was so exquisite; it was to other painters' work as poetry is to prose: his loss was irretrievable. Now no one admires more keenly than I do the gifts that go into Burne Jones's works, the fine genius, the spirituality, the invention; but they leave me deeply dissatisfied as well, where Walker's works more than satisfy. It is their technical imperfection I can not get over, the bad, the unmasterly drawing—as it appears to me to be. They are not masterly. Now this is the artist's most essential quality, masterly execution. It is a kind of male gift and especially marks off men from women, the begetting of one's thought on paper, on verse, on whatever the matter is; the life must be conveyed into the work and be displayed there, not suggested as having been in the artist's mind: otherwise the product is one of those hen's-eggs that are good to eat and look just like live ones but never hatch (I think they are called wind eggs: I believe most eggs for breakfast *are* wind eggs and none the worse for it).—Now it is too bad of me to have compared Burne Jones's beautiful and original works to wind-eggs: moreover on better consideration it strikes me that the mastery I speak of is not so much the male quality in the mind as a puberty in the life of that quality. The male quality is the creative gift, which he markedly has. But plainly, while artists may differ indefinitely in the degree and kind or variety of their natural gifts, all shd., as artists, have come, at all events shd., in time come, to the puberty, the manhood of those gifts: that should be common to all, above it the gifts may differ.

It may be remarked that some men exercise a deep influence on their own age in virtue of certain powers at that time original, new, and stimulating, which afterwards ceasing to stimulate their fame declines; because it was not supported by an execution, an achievement equal to the power. For nothing but fine execution survives long. This was something of Rossetti's case perhaps.

There is a Scotch painter Macbeth whom I much admire. My brother Arthur, who is a painter too, took me to Macbeth's studio when I was last in town. There happened to be little of Macbeth's own there then, but he was employed on an etching of Walker's *Fisherman's Shop* for Messrs. Agnew and the original was of course with him. It is not a work that I care for very much except so far as I revere everything that Walker did (I remember the news of his death gave me a shock as if it had been a near friend's), though artists greatly admire the technic of it; but there were other etchings by Macbeth and other reproductions of Walker's pieces and most of them new to me, the *Ferry* I think it is called (an upper-Thames riverside scene), the *Plough* (a divine work), the *Mushroom Gatherers,* and others. If you have not yet studied Walker's work you have a new world of beauty to open and go in. You shd. also study where you can *North's* things. It was my brother drew my attention to him. It seems Walker—I do not know that he studied under North but he learnt methods from him: 'North' said someone in vulgar phrase to my brother 'learnt', that is taught, 'Walker to paint'. He survived his pupil, if Walker was that. His landscapes are of a beautiful and poetical delicacy and truth at once. But I have seen very little of his.

I agree to Whistler's striking genius—feeling for what I call *inscape* (the very soul of art); but then his execution is so negligent, unpardonably so sometimes (that is, I suppose, what Ruskin particularly meant by 'throwing the pot of paint in the face of the public'): *his* genius certainly has not come to puberty.

Now something on music. A piece of mine, called, not by my wish, a madrigal on the programme, is to be performed at a school-concert in Dublin tomorrow. It is *Who is Sylvia?* set as a duet and chorus the tune made very long ago, the harmonies lately set (and very great fears about their puberty entertained). I made it for a string orchestra. And I am very slowly but very elaborately working at 'Does the South Wind' for solos, chorus, and strings. Some years ago I went from Glasgow, where I was, one day to Loch Lomond and landed at Inversnaid (famous through Wordsworth and Matthew Arnold) for some hours. There I had an inspiration of a tune. The disproportion is wonderful between the momentary conception of an air and the long long gestation of its setting. I endeavour to make the under parts each a flowing and independent melody and they cannot be independently invented, they must be felt for along a few certain necessary lines enforced by the harmony. It is astonishing to see them come; but in reality they are in nature bound up (besides many others) with the tune of the principal part and there is, I am persuaded, a world of profound mathematics in this matter of music: indeed no one can doubt that.

I have written a few sonnets: that is all I have done in poetry for some years.

I have not seen Bridges' comedy.

Swinburne has written for the *Times* an ode on the crisis,
Somebody called it a rigmarole and I cd. not say it was not:
on the contrary everything he writes is rigmarole. But I wonder how he finds it suits him to be clerical, as this ode appeals
to conscience and declaiming against assassination is. Moreover there was an earlier ode of his in honour of the 'Manchester Martyrs', as the Irish call them: so then he has
changed as much as Gladstone. As they neither of them
have any principles it is no wonder. But the passage about
Gordon and so on is to the point. With this sad thought I
must conclude and am your affectionate friend

GERARD M. HOPKINS S.J.

Some hindrance happened and the madrigal was not sung.
If it had been I could not have heard it, for I was helping to
save and damn the studious youth of Ireland.

July 3, 1886.

You speak of 'powerful drawing' in Burne Jones's picture.
I recognise it in the mermaid's face and in the treatment of
her fishments and fishmanship, the tailfin turning short and
flattening to save striking the ground—a stroke of truly artistic genius; but the drowned youth's knees and feet are very
crude and unsatisfactory in drawing, as it seemed to me.

[19] I have found your former letter, as old as December
last, and must add a little more.

The sonnet of Gray's that you ask about is the wellknown
one (the only one, I daresay) 'In vain to me': I remarked on
its rhythmical beauty, due partly to the accent being rather
trochaic than iambic. Wordsworth says somewhere of it that
it is 'evident' the only valuable part of it is (I believe) 'For
other notes' and the quatrain that follows. Such a criticism is
rude at best, since in a work of art having so strong a unity
as a sonnet one part which singly is less beautiful than
another part may be as necessary to the whole effect, like the
plain shaft in a column and so on. But besides what he calls
evident is not so, nor true.

You make a criticism on Handel. I have the very same
feeling about him and you 'tell me my own dream', that 'one
can never hear five bars of him without feeling that some-

thing great is beginning, something full of life'. A piece of his at a concert seems to flutter the dovecot of the rest of them, to be a hawk among poultry. The immediateness of the impression must be due, I suppose, to his power being conveyed into smaller sections of his work than other men's and not needing accumulation for its effect.

I was glad of an appreciative review of your third volume in the *Academy* (I think) and much interested. Would I could read the work! but I cannot under present, which are permanent, circumstances do that.

I could wish you had been elected to that Chair. But 'life is a short blanket'—profoundest of homely sayings: great gifts and great opportunities are more than life spares to one man. It is much if we get something, a spell, an innings at all. See how the great conquerors were cut short, Alexander, Caesar just seen. Above all Christ our Lord: his career was cut short and, whereas he would have wished to succeed by success—for it is insane to lay yourself out for failure, prudence is the first of the cardinal virtues, and he was the most prudent of men—nevertheless he was doomed to succeed by failure; his plans were baffled, his hopes dashed, and his work was done by being broken off undone. However much he understood all this he found it an intolerable grief to submit to it. He left the example: it is very strengthening, but except in that sense it is not consoling.

I passed a delightful day at Yattendon. Mrs. Bridges not as I had fancied her (which was but faintly), but none the worse for that.

TO ROBERT BRIDGES

University College, St. Stephen's Green, Dublin. Oct. 6 1886.
DEAREST BRIDGES,—I forgot to speak of the copies of *Prometheus* and *Odes and Eclogues* (but whose? for I do not remember that any publication of yours had that title). I could make, I think, good use of them: I should give one copy to Mr. Tyrrell of Trinity and get *Prometheus* known among Trinity men if I could.

But in general Irishmen are no poets nor critics of poetry, though much alive to what we vaguely called poetry in nature and language and very capable of expressing it in a vague, a rhetorical way. They always mistake the matter of poetry for poetry. However education goes for much in such a case.

A consignment of 331 examination papers tonight, I [am sorry] to say, and more will come.

Yours

GERARD HOPKINS.

I no[w se]e my time will be so short that it will go hard with the Feast of Bacchus.

You are quite wrong about Barnes's poems—not to admire them ever so much more. I have two good tunes to two of them. I had one played this afternoon, but as the pianist said: Your music dates from a time before the piano was. The parts are independent in form and phrasing and are lost on that instrument. Two choristers, who were at hand, sang the tune, which to its fond father sounded very flowing and a string accompaniment would have set it off, I do believe. By the bye, I will send you this thing as a sample and if it does not suit the piano you will at least see what is meant. Consider it and return it. The harmonies are *not* commonplace, with leave of Mr. —— and there is plenty of modulation. (I told you I am acting on Mr. —— advice.)

TO ROBERT BRIDGES

University College, St. Stephen's Green, Dublin. Sept. 13, 14 '88

DEAREST BRIDGES,—I am interested to hear Mr. Rockstro is staying with you. It must be through Wooldridge that you know him. I know *of* him through George Fitzpatrick, a dear young friend of mine but now not seen for 5 years.

I am very glad you like the tune and greatly honoured by Mr. Rockstro's setting an accompaniment, which nevertheless can scarcely be read and as yet we have no piano in the house to try it by. I believe, in spite of what he says, that it allows of contrapuntal treatment; indeed, with some improvements I have since yesterday made, it may be accompanied in canon at the octave two bars off. Nor does it strike me as unlike modal music, but quite the contrary; so that I am surprised at the criticism. I will transpose it to F of course: all keys are the same to me and to every one who thinks that music was before instruments and angels before tortoises and cats. I should like you to tell me what are the ordinary limits to voices, that I may act accordingly.

If there is good in Doughty no doubt I shall find it out (here there seems some kind of jingling and punning, not meant, but may serve for future use) and no doubt there is good as you say so. But come, is it not affectation to write obsolete English? You know it is.

I have nothing now the matter with me but gout in the eyes, which is unpleasant and disquieting. The feeling is like soap or lemons.

I heard a goodish concert this afternoon. A Herr Slapoff-ski (real name) played Handel's violin Sonata in A: what a genius! what a native language music was to him; such sense, such fluency, such idiom, and such beauty!

Yours ever

GERARD M. HOPKINS.

My stars! will my song be performed? But if so why not perform my madrigal in canon? a most ambitious piece and hitherto successful but suspended for want of a piano this long while. You could not help liking it if even Sir Robert Stewart unbent to praise it (the most genial of old gentlemen, but an offhand critic of music and me). I can send you the first verse to see—four parts; of course no instrumental accompaniment; the canon is exact, at the octave, 4 bars off, between treble and tenor, and runs in the first verse to 44 bars, I think.

TO ARTHUR HOPKINS

Univ. Coll., Stephen's Green, Dublin. Nov. 26 1888.

DEAR ARTHUR,—I hope your exhibition has turned out a great success and sold your pictures and led to commissions.

You have sent me nothing of yours since those *Atalanta* children, but some kind person has just this minute posted me your 'no. 18'. Not that this is my first sight of it by a great deal. The resident students hung it in their reading-room and

I have studied it and heard it discussed. It is admired, and it is a sweet and pretty face; but now I am sorry to say, that is all I can write in its favour. I have to remonstrate with you about it.

In the first place it has to me the look of a sketch enlarged. A picture of that size whether engraved from drawing or painting ought to be a picture, not a sketch. The enlargement of a sketch will not make a picture. This was Doré's weakness: he was a sketcher only: his large drawings and the engravings after his paintings (for the paintings themselves I have never seen) are the works of a sketcher sketching on a great scale; the limbs, the draperies, the buildings have the outlines, contours, folds, shading, everything of a sketch; the suggestion of things, not their representation. Or to speak more precisely, this head looks as if it had been first a picture proper, then a sketch on a small scale made from that, and then this sketch enlarged to the original size, the execution proper to a picture being in the meantime lost. This appears in the hair, but flagrantly in the drapery of the breast: there is no searchingness in the drawing of these things. Then the line of the nose, which in a sketch might be well enough, is not subtle enough for the size. There the engraver however may have injured you.

You came very near producing a very beautiful thing: the face has a Madonna-like pensiveness and sweetness; but there is also a certain foolishness in the expression and the updrawn upper lip is too much of an upper lip, it is not successful.

Fr. Mallac also makes the following criticisms. He says you are not strong in your perspective and that the off-side of the face is out of drawing and has the distortion given by some lenses to photographs. Also he says the back of the head is suppressed. I do not feel sure of this but about the side of the face I think he is right, though it is difficult to point out where the fault is. But his greatest complaint on the score of drawing is about the dwarfing of the breasts, which are altogether much too high up and probably too flat. It is generally agreed that a finely proportioned figure is divided in half exactly at the groin and into quarters at the nipples and lowest point of the kneecap respectively. These proportions will not suit your girl at all.

He complains also of the intense shadow between the lips, which makes the upper lip stand up from the paper. This also comes from carrying the method of sketching into a finished picture, for in a sketch exaggeration of shadow to indicate certain things is necessary and suppression of it for others.

In conception this is a beautiful head and grows on one, as people have said of it to me; and the beauty is regular. Now the number of really and regularly beautiful faces (on a considerable scale and not the simple repetition of a type, as in allegorical figures) is quite small in art; for ancient works, which are perfectly regular, are mostly much wanting in grace, so much so that those Venuses of Cnidus and Milo and what not can scarcely be said to be beautiful in face at all; while modern ones, which have plenty of charms, are often irregular: I think Leonardo's La Gioconda even, perhaps the greatest achievement of modern art in the ideal treatment of the human face, is not quite regular in the comformation of the cheeks. If I were you then I would keep this type by me, correct its drawing, carefully compose *in life* and then from life draw the draperies, and work at it till I had made the most perfect thing of it I could. That scrawl of folds on the breast 'must come out, Bishop', as Mrs. Proudie said; and the breasts must go down lower vertically and come up horizontally. The hair and ear and all must be thoroughly done. And for the drawing of the face, here is a diagram which will shew you what I suppose to be the matter with it. It is a bird's eye view. (Never mind *my* bad drawing: mind yours.) I believe it will carry conviction.[20]

I am afraid this ballyragging will make you gloomy; I hope not angry. For then I shall not be able to ask you, as I do, if you have such a thing by you as a portecrayon and some drawing chalk or charcoal, for there is nothing like it, and I want to be able to draw with it again; and I am obliged to husband my seldom seen pocket-money. I enclose some trifles, which please return, only to shew you how far my hand is in. Could you tell of a way of bringing out high lights in a drawing better than the watery Chinese-white I have employed on the ox in the Phoenix Park? The unintelligible Roebuck sketch was a brilliant autumn sunset effect in a lovely lane.

That drawing of the copse at Shanklin (in what year could it have been? I suppose 1866) has gone to be photographed, that it may not perish; but the photographs will be smaller. I will send you one when they come: they are a precious time doing. That drawing appears to me unique in its kind: it is a pity it is not finished, which was only a few days' more work.

With best love to the vine and olives, I am your affectionate brother

GERARD.

Nov. 30 1888.

TO ROBERT BRIDGES

Univ. Coll., Stephen's Green, Dublin. April 29 1889.

DEAREST BRIDGES,—I am ill to-day, but no matter for that as my spirits are good. And I want you too to 'buck up', as we used to say at school, about those jokes over which you write in so dudgeonous a spirit. I have it now down in my tablets that a man may joke and joke and be offensive; I have had several warnings lately leading me to make the entry, tho' goodness knows the joke that gave most offence was harmless enough and even kind. You I treated to the same sort of irony as I do myself; but it is true it makes all the world of difference whose hand administers. About Daniel I see I was mistaken: if he pays you more than and sells you as much as other publishers (which however is saddening to think of: how many copies is it? five and twenty?) my objections do not apply. Then you ought to remember that I did try to make you known in Dublin and had some little success. (Dowden I will never forgive: could you not kill Mrs. Bridges? then he might take an interest in you). Nay I had great success and placed you on the pinnacle of fame; for it is the pinnacle of fame to become educational and be set for translation into Gk. iambics, as you are at Trinity: this is to be a classic; 'this', as Lord Beaconsfield said to a friend, who told him he found his young daughter reading *Lothair,* 'O this is fame indeed'. And Horace and Juvenal say the same thing. And here I stop, for fear of it ripening into some kind of joke.

I believe I enclose a new sonnet. But we greatly differ in feeling about copying one's verses out: I find it repulsive, and let them lie months and years in rough copy untransferred to my book. Still I hope soon to send you my accumulation. This one is addressed to you.

Swinburne has a new volume out, which is reviewed in its own style: 'The rush and the rampage, the pause and the pullup of these lustrous and lumpophorous lines'. It is all now a 'self-drawing web'; a perpetual functioning of genius without truth, feeling, or any adequate matter to be at function on. There is some heavydom, in long waterlogged lines (he has no real understanding of rhythm, and though he sometimes hits brilliantly at other times he misses badly) about the *Armada,* that pitfall of the patriotic muse; and *rot* about babies, a blethery bathos into which Hugo and he from opposite coasts have long driven Channel-tunnels. I am afraid I am going too far with the poor fellow. Enough now, but his babies make a Herodian of me.

My song will be a very highly wrought work and I do hope a fine one. Do you think canon wd. spoil the tune? I hope not, but the contrary. But if the worst came to the worst, I could, since a solo voice holds its own against instruments, give the canon-following to a violin. I shall hear what Sir Robert Stewart says about it. This is how it now stands. I tried at first to make the air such that it shd. be rigidly the same in every note and rhythm (always excepting the alterations to save the tritone) in all its shifts; but I found that impracticable and that I had reached the point where art calls for loosing, not for lacing. I now make the canon strict in each verse, but allow a change, which indeed is besides called for by the change of words, from verse to verse. Indeed the air becomes a generic form which is specified newly in each verse with excellent effect. It is like a new art this. I allow no modulation: the result is that the tune is shifted into modes, viz. those of La, Mi, and Sol (this is the only way I can speak of them, and they have a character of their own

Silent Fallen Rain.
(Silent fell the rain) words by Canon Dixon

Song. 'Fallen Rain'

which is neither that of modern major and minor music nor yet of the plain chant modes, so far as I can make out). The first shift is into the mode of La: this shd. be minor, but the effect is not exactly that; rather the feeling is that Do is still the keynote, but has shifted its place in the scale. This impression is helped by the harmony, for as the Third is not flattened the chords appear major. The chord at the beginning of every bar is the common chord or first inversion; the $\frac{6}{4}$ may appear in course of the bar and discords are in passing or prepared. Perhaps the harmony may be heavy, but I work according to the only rules I know. I can only get on slowly with it and must hope to be rewarded in the end. Now I must lie down.

Who is Miss Cassidy? She is an elderly lady who by often asking me down to Monasterevan and by the change and holiday her kind hospitality provides is become one of the props and struts of my existence. St. Ernin founded the monastery: a singular story is told of him. Henry VIII confiscated it and it became the property of Lord Drogheda. The usual curse on abbey lands attends it and it never passes down in the direct line. The present Lord and Lady Drogheda have no issue. Outside Moore Abbey, which is a beautiful park, the country is flat, bogs and river and canals. The river is the Barrow, which the old Irish poets call the dumb Barrow. I call it the burling Barrow Brown. Both descriptions are true. The country has nevertheless a charm. The two beautiful young people live within an easy drive.[21]

With kind love to Mrs. Bridges and Mrs. Molesworth, I am your affectionate friend

GERARD.

VI

PERSONAL LETTERS

The letter-writer on principle does not make his
letter only an answer; it is a work embodying per-
haps answers to questions put by his correspondent
but that is not its main motive.

TO ALEXANDER BAILLIE

MY DEAR BAILLIE,—Though my unwillingness to write
letters, important or unimportant, now amounts to a specific
craze I see quite fixedly that not to do so is virtually to see
and hear no more of you. But even now that I have just begun I seem suddenly to have everything to say and an impatience to do little else than to communicate myself εἰς ἄπειρον.[1]
I am very much obliged to you for your letters for many reasons, and you must remember that I normally need the spur.
I will answer yr questions before anything else. About *Ecce*
Homo, I am ashamed to be in the position I am but the truth
is I have not read it: somehow the very kind of notoriety it
had made me not care and it was also the case that I had no
time hardly for anything but schools reading when it came
out. I see that I ought to have and I will when I can. About
Garrett I also keep saying why does he not write? I sent a
letter begging him to let me hear from him to his agents some
time ago. Fr. the nature of things one cannot lay one's finger
on him in the way that one can on other people. Is it certain
that he has not left England? By this time you must have

been in for that B.N.C. fellowship but I see papers so brokenly
and seldom here that I cannot tell whether you have it or
not. I wish, do you know, that you would get one (if you
have not). I was much disappointed about Poutiatine: I
failed to write to his address at Mr. Popove's in Welbeck
Street and I have not heard from Parish yet. I have not read
Ruskin's new book: the title is perhaps vulgar. Ruskin is full
of follies but I get more and more sympathetic with 'the true
men' as agst. the Sophistik (observe I say K—it is not the
same thing as sophistical), Philistine, Doctrinaire, Utilitarian,
Positive, and on the whole Negative (as Carlyle wd. put it)
side, and prefer to err with Plato. This reminds me to say
that I find myself in an even prostrate admiration of Aristotle
and am of the way of thinking, so far as I know him or know
about him, that he is the end-all and be-all of philosophy.
But I shd. be sorry to bore you with philosophy, of which you
no doubt have had enough what with reading for fellow-
ships: with me on the contrary an interest in philosophy is
almost the only one I can feel myself quite free to indulge in
still.

I have begun learning the violin: I am glad I have.

I must say that I am very anxious to get away from this
place. I have become very weak in health and do not seem
to recover myself here or likely to do so. Teaching is very
burdensome, especially when you have much of it: I have.
I have not much time and almost no energy—for I am always
tired—to do anything on my own account. I put aside that
one sees and hears nothing and nobody here. Very happily
Challis of Merton is now here; else the place were without
reservation 'damned, shepherd'. (This is not swearing.) I
ought to make the exception that the boys are very nice indeed. I am expecting to take orders and soon, but I wish it
to be secret till it comes about. Besides that it is the happiest
and best way it practically is the only one. You know I once
wanted to be a painter. But even if I could I wd. not I think,
now, for the fact is that the higher and more attractive parts
of the art put a strain upon the passions which I shd. think it
unsafe to encounter. I want to write still and as a priest I
very likely can do that too, not so freely as I shd. have liked,
e.g. nothing or little in the verse way, but no doubt what

wd. best serve the cause of my religion. But if I am a priest it will cause my mother, or she says it will, great grief and this preys on my mind very much and makes the near prospect quite black. The general result is that I am perfectly reckless about things that I shd. otherwise care about, uncertain as I am whether in a few months I may not be shut up in a cloister, and this state of mind, though it is painful coming to, when reached gives a great and real sense of freedom. Do you happen to know of any tutorship I cd. take for a few months after Easter? as I am anxious to leave this place then and also not to leave it without having secured something to live upon till, as seems likely, I take minor orders.

Is it at Mrs. Cunliffe's that you are staying? If so she has gone and renumbered herself again.—O that one shd. ever have been younger and more foolish! Do you know—my mother reminded me—that Mrs. Cunliffe once asked me to dinner and I refused, Puseyite that I was, because it was a Friday. I went to call there last summer but she was not in.

Wood is going or gone to America for a visit.

Now I think of it it is very unlikely that Garrett shd. have left England.

Is it true that Rogers was mobbed out of his chair or on the contrary that he is incapable of reelection?

When this letter comes to hand you must be very corresponsive: you must, please, write news, criticism, confidences, and where I can get the above-mentioned employment.

There has come out a transl. of Horace in verse by one Mathews, a Cambridge man, very good, the best I ever saw.

Have you read the *Pervigilium Veneris?* It is about equal to the Atys and, I think, as beautiful as or more beautiful than anything of the same length in Latin.

Believe me always your affectionate friend.

GERARD M. HOPKINS.

The Oratory. Feb. 12, 1868.

TO HIS MOTHER

For March 3 see end.

MY DEAREST MOTHER,—Everybody must be in spirits

with this pleasant change. I hear that before that the whole world was out of sorts.

We have here a very jolly old gentleman, Father Baron by name, under nursing. He fell on getting out of the train and broke his thigh, and after that he passed such a night that he said he never knew there was such pain in the world. However they brought him here in a spring cart with india-rubber round the wheels and got him the most wonderful and delightful bed that cd. be made: it has every convenience possible, with winches and screws to raise or lower or do what you like with. A staff of novices and others always wait on him, read to him, and write his letters, so that any-one might wish to have his thigh broken if you cd. have it broken in the present without having broken it in the past. I do not know whether it is a fable or not but one of his jokes is that he is going to make use of the 'Alexandrian step' when he can walk, that is the step wh. suddenly became the thing at court when the Princess of Wales got lame with a sore knee.

We have got a little iron church in our grounds now, on the right hand as you come in. It is not yet opened.

I have had a long letter from Edward Bond in very good spirits and with Oxford news.

Did I tell you that we have here a young Canadian who told me about Frances' dress ball? He is half French and very clever and really a most charming man and it is a greater pleasure to hear him talk than anyone I ever listened to.

As it has slowly turned March while I have been writing this I shall make it a birthday letter and wish you many very happy returns of the day after tomorrow: I think you wd. rather have it then than earlier and none then. I remember that last year we had violets out, it being so mild, and I meant to have got some to send you but something hindered me at the last: I now send a duck's feather with my love. I practise at present the evangelical poverty which I soon hope to vow, but no one is ever so poor that he is not (without prejudice to all the rest of the world) owner of the skies and stars and everything wild that is to be found on the earth, and out of this immense stock I make over to you my right to one particular.

Give my best love to all. It is very sad about Mr. Bockett.
Believe me your loving son

GERARD HOPKINS.

Roehampton, March 1, '70.

TO ALEXANDER BAILLIE

MY DEAR BAILLIE,—Your letters are always welcome
but often or always it is more pleasant to get them than easy
to see how they are to be answered. So with today's dinner
and tomorrow twelve month's butcher's bill. My time is short
both for writing and reading, so that I can seldom write and
when I do I have nothing to say. Don't you know, it is mainly
about books and so on that I shd. be writing and I read so
few. I am going through a hard course of scholastic logic (not
just at present: it is holidays) which takes all the fair part of
the day and leaves one fagged at the end for what remains.
This makes the life painful to nature. I find now too late *how*
to read—at least some books, e.g. the classics: now I see things,
now what I read tells, but I am obliged to read by snatches.
—I will not go a step further till I have explained that down
to the bottom of the last page I was writing with the worst of
steel pens and most of it with a dreadfully cold hand but
now the grey goose and I are come to terms at the point of
the knife—this to forestall your cuts and snarls at my material
worsening.

I will tell you something about this place. Perpetual winter
smiles. In the first place we have the highest rain-guage [*sic*]
in England, I believe: this our observatory shews and a local
rhyme expresses as much. Early in the year they told me
there wd. be no spring such as we understood it in the south.
When I asked about May they told me they had hail in May.
Of June they told me it had one year been so cold that the
procession could not be held on Corpus Christi. The country
is also very bare and bleak—what its enemies say of Scotland,
only that a young Campbell at Roehampton shewed me that
Argyleshire was the warmest part of Great Britain, that
greenhouse fuchsias grew in the open air, and that the pome-
granate was for ever on the bough. But nevertheless it is fine
scenery, great hills and 'fells' with noble outline often, sub-

ject to charming effects of light (though I am bound to say that total obscuration is the commonest effect of all), and three beautiful rivers. The clouds in particular are more interesting than in any other place I have seen. But they must be full of soot, for the fleeces of the sheep are quite black with it. We also see the northern lights to advantage at times. There is good fishing for those who do not see that after bad fishing the next worst thing is good fishing. At the College close by is a big library.

Let me see what books I can speak of.—I find nothing or nothing that I cd. at present say shortly and if I keep this longer I might perhaps never send it. I am glad to hear literary etc news as I am here removed from it and get much behind. I hope you find yourself happy in town: this life here though it is hard is God's will for me as I most intimately know, which is more than violets knee-deep. This spring of rhetoric brings me to a close. Believe me always your affectionate friend—

GERARD M. HOPKINS.

Stonyhurst, Whalley, Lancashire. April 10, 1871.

TO KATE HOPKINS

MY DEAR KATIE,—Many thanks for your letter, which I was delighted to get. When it first came to hand I stood balancing in my mind who it could be from, there was such a youngladyship and grownupdom about the address, until I remembered that you were older than you used to be. As for me I will say no more than this, that I have prescribed myself twenty four hourglasses a day (which I take even during sleep, such is the force of habit) and that even this does not stop the ravages of time.

What month in the year it may be at Hampstead I will not be sure; with us it is a whity-greeny January. What with east winds, cloud, and rain I think it will never be spring. If we have a bright afternoon the next morning it is winter again.

We were all vaccinated the other day. The next day a young Portug[u]ese came up to me and said 'Oh misther'

Opkins, do *you* feel the cows in *yewer* arm?' I told him I felt the horns coming through. I do I am sure. I cannot remember now whether one ought to say the calf of the arm or the calf of the leg. My shoulder is like a shoulder of beef. I dare not speak above a whisper for fear of bellowing there now, I was going to say I am obliged to speak low for fear of lowing. I dream at night that I have only two of my legs in bed. I think there is a split coming in both my slippers. Yesterday I could not think why it was that I would wander about on a wet grass-plot: I see now. I chew my pen a great deal. The long and short of it is that my left forequarter is swollen and painful (I meant to have written arm but I cowld not). Besides the doctor has given us medicine, so that I am in a miserable way just now.

From cows I will turn to lambs. Our fields are full of them. When they were a little younger and nicer and sillier they wd. come gambolling up to one as if one were their mother. One of them sucked my finger and my companion took another up in his arms. The ewes then came up and walked round us making suspicious sheep's eyes at us, as people say. Now, when they are not sucking the breast (to do which they make such terrific butts and digs at the old dam that two of them together will sometimes lift her off her hind legs) they spend their time in bounding and spinning round as if they were tumblers. The same thing is I daresay to be seen (and earlier than this) about Hampstead: still as many of these lambs are ours I cannot pass it by and must tell you of it in black and white.

One thing made me very sad the day we were vaccinated. I was coming away: I left a number of my companions in a room in the infirmary—some had come from the doctor and others were waiting for their turn—all laughing and chatting. As I came down one of the galleries from the room I saw one of our young men standing there looking at a picture. I wondered why he stayed by himself and did not join the rest and then afterwards I remembered that he had had the smallpox and was deeply marked with it and all his good looks gone which he would have had and he did not want to face the others at that time when they were having their fun taking safe precautions against catching what it was too late for him to take any precautions against.

I want to know two things by the next person who writes —first some particulars from Arthur about the American yacht Sappho which seems to have had such great successes last year and next whether it is true that the cuckoo has come unusually early this year, as I heard said. It has not come here yet and I do not know if it will.

With best love to all believe me your loving brother

GERARD M. HOPKINS.

Stonyhurst, April 25, 1871.

TO ROBERT BRIDGES

MY DEAR BRIDGES,—Our holidays have begun, so I will write again. I feel inclined to begin by asking whether you are secretary to the International as you seem to mean me to think nothing too bad for you but then I remember that you never relished 'the intelligent artisan'. I must tell you I am always thinking of the Communist future. The too intelligent artisan is master of the situation I believe. Perhaps it is what everyone believes, I do not see the papers or hear strangers often enough to know. It is what Carlyle has long threatened and foretold. But his writings are, as he might himself say, 'most inefficacious-strenuous heaven-protestations, caterwaul, and Cassandra-wailings'. He preaches obedience but I do not think he has done much except to ridicule instead of strengthening the hands of the powers that be. Some years ago when he published his *Shooting Niagara* he did make some practical suggestions but so vague that they should rather be called 'too dubious moonstone-grindings and on the whole impracticable-practical unveracities'. However I am afraid some great revolution is not far off. Horrible to say, in a manner I am a Communist. Their ideal bating some things is nobler than that professed by any secular statesman I know of (I must own I live in bat-light and shoot at a venture). Besides it is just.—I do not mean the means of getting to it are. But it is a dreadful thing for the greatest and most necessary part of a very rich nation to live a hard life without dignity, knowledge, comforts, delights, or hopes in the midst of plenty—which plenty they make. They profess that they do not care what they wreck and burn, the old civilisation and order must be destroyed. This is a dreadful look out but what has the old civilisation done for them? As it at present stands in England it is itself in great measure founded on wrecking. But they got none of the spoils, they came in for nothing but harm from it then and thereafter. England has grown hugely wealthy but this wealth has not reached the working classes; I expect it has made their condition worse. Besides this iniquitous order the old civilisation embodies another order mostly old and what is new in direct entail from the old, the old religion, learning, law, art, etc. and all the history that is preserved in standing monuments. But as the working classes have not been educated they know next to nothing of all this and cannot be expected to care if they destroy it. The more I look the more black and deservedly black the future looks, so I will write no more.

I can hardly believe that this is August and your letter dated May. True there has been here and I believe elsewhere no summer between. There seems some chance now. In a fortnight we are going, also for a fortnight, to Inellan in Argyleshire on the Clyde. After that I expect to pay my people a short visit down near Southampton, where they have taken a cottage. None of them are turned Catholics: I do not expect it.—Believe me your affectionate friend

GERARD HOPKINS, S.J.
Stonyhurst, Whalley, Lancashire. Aug. 2, 1871.

TO ROBERT BRIDGES

MY DEAR BRIDGES,—My last letter to you was from Stonyhurst. It was not answered, so that perhaps it did not reach you. If it did I supposed then and do not know what else to suppose now that you were disgusted with the *red* opinions it expressed, being a conservative. I have little reason to be red: it was the red Commune that murdered five of our Fathers lately—whether before or after I wrote I do not remember. So far as I know I said nothing that might not fairly be said. If this was your reason for not answering it seems to shew a greater keenness about politics than is common.

I heard of you lately from an Eton and Oxford man I met —So and so, he told me, breeds fowls and Bridges writes— but nothing distinct. But in last week's *Academy* I came upon an appreciative review of a Mr. Bridges' poems, Robert Bridges the title shewed. And the characteristics the writer found in the poems were true to you. Did I ever before see anything of yours? say in Coles' book? I cannot remember. But given that you write and have changed then I can fancy this yours—

> Next they that bear her, honoured on this night,
> And then the maidens in a double row.

Short extracts from six poems were given. To have seen these gave me an occasion to write again. I think, my dear Bridges, to be so much offended about that red letter was excessive.

One of my sisters, who has become musical beyond the common, urged me to find her the music you wrote for 'O earlier shall the roses blow': I hunted for it twice without finding it but I cannot have lost it. I never was quite reconciled to the freak of leaving off away from the keynote and have put imaginary endings to it several times. I myself am learning the piano now, self-taught alas! not for execution's sake but to be independent of others and learn something about music. I have very little time though. I am professor of rhetoric here since last September. Always yr. affectionate friend

GERARD M. HOPKINS, S.J.
Manresa House, Roehampton, S.W. Jan. 22, 1874.

TO HIS MOTHER

St. Beuno's. June 26 '76.

MY DEAREST MOTHER,—I am glad to say that I have again heard from Lionel.

You ask about my poem on the Deutschland. You forget that we have a magazine of our own, the *Month*. I have asked Fr. Coleridge the editor, who is besides my oldest friend in the Society, to take it, but I had to tell him that I felt sure he wd. personally dislike it very much, only that he was to consider not his tastes but those of the *Month's* readers. He replied that there was in America a new sort of poetry which did not rhyme or scan or construe; if mine rhymed and scanned and construed and did not make nonsense or bad morality he did not see why it shd. not do. So I sent it. Hitherto he has not answered; which is a sign it cannot appear in the July number but otherwise seems to shew he means to take it.

June 28—I have heard from him this morning. The poem was too late for July but will appear in the August number. He wants me however to do away with the accents which mark the scanning. I would gladly have done without them if I had thought my readers would scan right unaided but I am afraid they will not, and if the lines are not rightly scanned they are ruined. Still I am afraid I must humour an editor, but some lines at all events will have to be marked.

Whom did Ernest Coleridge marry?

You must never say that the poem is mine.

With best love to all I am your loving son

GERARD M. HOPKINS S.J.

There is a lamentable account in the *Graphic* of the sweeping away of the old civilisation in Japan.

$$\text{Aunt} \left\{ \begin{array}{c} \text{Anne} \\ \text{Kate} \end{array} \right\} \text{'s address.}$$

TO ROBERT BRIDGES

St. Beuno's (and not Bruno's) College, St. Asaph (nor yet Asaph's),
North Wales. Feb. 24, 1877.

DEAREST BRIDGES,—You have forgotten or else you never got a letter I wrote *from this place* a year or so ago: it was in answer to one of yours about Henry Heine and other things, and there too you, with the same kindness and futility as now, proposed to come and see me at Roehampton hundreds of miles away. Instead therefore of coming to see me or, as your present letter proposes, my going to see you which would indeed be the greatest pleasure but cannot however be, write that long and interesting letter. And as for your letters being opened—you made that an objection before, I remember—it is quite unreasonable and superstitious to let it make any difference. To be sure they are torn half open—and so for the most part as that one can see the letter has never been out of the envelope—but how can a superior have the time or the wish to read the flood of correspondence from people he knows nothing of which is brought in by the post? No doubt if you were offering me a wife, a legacy, or a bishopric on condition of leaving my present life, and someone were to get wind of the purpose of the correspondence, *then* our letters would be well read or indeed intercepted. So think no more of that.

And as your letter to which I am to answer has yet to be written and I am on Saturday to undergo a very serious examination I will say no more now. The pamphlets, you know, need not wait for the letter, only I shall not read them through this week: how I wonder what they are about!—Always your affectionate friend

GERARD M. HOPKINS, S.J.

Usen't you to call me by my christian name? I believe you did. Well if you did I like it better.

TO R. W. DIXON

Stonyhurst College, Blackburn. June 4 1878.
VERY REV. SIR,—I take a liberty as a stranger in addressing you, nevertheless I did once have some slight acquaintance with you. You will not remember me but you will remember taking a mastership for some months at Highgate School, the Cholmondeley School, where I then was. When you went away you gave, as I recollect, a copy of your book *Christ's Company* to one of the masters, a Mr. Law if I am not mistaken. By this means coming to know its name I was curious to read it, then pleased, at last I became so fond of it that I made it, so far as that could be, a part of my own mind. I got your other volume and your little Prize Essay too. I introduced your poems to my friends and, if they did not share my own enthusiasm, made them at all events admire. And to shew you how greatly I prized them, when I entered my present state of life, in which I knew I could have

no books of my own and was unlikely to meet with your
works in the libraries I should have access to, I copied out
St. Paul, St. John, Love's Consolation, and others from both
volumes and keep them by me.

What I am saying now I might, it is true, have written
any time these many years back, but partly I hesitated,
partly I was not sure you were yet living; lately however I
saw in the Athenaeum a review of your historical work newly
published and since have made up my mind to write to you
—which, to be sure, is an impertinence if you like to think it
so, but I seemed to owe you something or a great deal, and
then I knew what I should feel myself in your position—if I
had written and published works the extreme beauty of
which the author himself the most keenly feels and they
had fallen out of sight at once and been (you will not mind
my saying it, as it is, I suppose, plainly true) almost wholly
unknown; then, I say, I should feel a certain comfort to be
told they had been deeply appreciated by some one person,
a stranger, at all events and had not been published quite in
vain. Many beautiful works have been almost unknown and
then have gained fame at last, as Mr. Wells' poem of Joseph,
which is said to be very fine, and his friend Keats' own, but
many more must have been lost sight of altogether. I do not
know of course whether your books are going to have a re-
vival, it seems not likely, but not for want of deserving. It is
not that I think a man is really the less happy because he has
missed the renown which is his due, but still when this happens it is an evil in itself and a thing which ought not to be
and that I deplore, for the good work's sake rather than the
author's.

Your poems had a medieval colouring like Wm. Morris's
and the Rossetti's and others but none seemed to me to have
it so unaffectedly. I thought the tenderness of Love's Consolation no one living could surpass nor the richness of colouring
in the 'wolfsbane' and the other passages (it is a mistake, I
think, and you meant henbane) in that and Mark and Rosalys
nor the brightness of the appleorchard landscape in Mother
and Daughter. And the Tale of Dauphiny and 'It is the time
to tell of fatal love' (I forget the title) in the other book are
purer in style, as it seems to me, and quite as fine in colouring

and drawing as Morris' stories in the *Paradise*, so far as I have read them, fine as those are. And if I were making up a book of English poetry I should put your ode to Summer next to Keats' on Autumn and the Nightingale and Grecian Urn. I do not think anywhere two stanzas so crowded with the pathos of nature and landscape could be found (except perhaps there are some in Wordsworth) as the little song of the Feathers of the Willow: a tune to it came to me quite naturally. The extreme delight I felt when I read the line 'Her eyes like lilies shaken by the bees' was more than any single line in poetry ever gave me and now that I am older I could not be so strongly moved by it if I were to read it for the first time. I have said all this, and could if there were any use say more, as a sort of duty of charity to make up, so far as one voice can do, for the disappointment you must, at least at times, I think, have felt over your rich and exquisite work almost thrown away. You will therefore feel no offence though you may surprise at my writing.

I am, Very Rev. Sir, your obedient servant

GERARD M. HOPKINS S.J.

(I am, you see, in 'Christ's Company').

TO R. W. DIXON

Stonyhurst, Blackburn. June 13 1878.

VERY REVEREND AND DEAR SIR, Pax Christi,—I am very glad now to think I followed my impulse and wrote to you, since my writing could affect you so much and draw out so kind an answer.

I suppose it is me that you remember at Highgate: I did get a prize for an English poem, I do not remember when; it may have been while you were there. In those days I knew poor Philip Worsley the poet; he had been at school at Highgate himself; and spent some time at Elgin House (I suppose as Dr. Dyne's guest) when I was a boarder there; indeed he read over and made criticisms on my successful poem: I recollect that he knew you (perhaps you may have made the acquaintance then, but all these facts I recall detachedly, and cannot group them) and said you would praise Keats by the hour—which might well be: Keats' genius was so astonishing, unequalled at his age and scarcely surpassed at any, that one may surmise whether if he had lived he would not have rivalled Shakspere.

When I spoke of fame I was not thinking of the harm it does to men as artists: it may do them harm, as you say, but so, I think, may the want of it, if 'Fame is the spur that the clear spirit doth raise To shun delights and live laborious days'—a spur very hard to find a substitute for or to do without. But I meant that it is a great danger in itself, as dangerous as wealth every bit, I should think, and as hard to enter the kingdom of heaven with. And even if it does not lead men to break the divine law, yet it gives them 'itching ears' and makes them live on public breath. (You have yourself said something of this—about 'seeking for praise in all the tides of air' in an ode, that 'on Departing Youth', I think) Mr. Coventry Patmore, whose fame again is very deeply below his great merit, seems to have said something very finely about the loss of fame in his lately published odes (*The Hidden Eros*)—I speak from an extract in a review.

What I do regret is the loss of recognition belonging to the work itself. For as to every moral act, being right or wrong, there belongs, of the nature of things, reward or punishment, so to every form perceived by the mind belongs, of the nature of things, admiration or the reverse. And the world is full of things and events, phenomena of all sorts, that go without notice, go unwitnessed. I think you have felt this, for you say, I remember, in one of the odes: 'What though the white clouds soar Unmarked from the horizon-shore?' or something like that. And if we regret this want of witness in brute nature much more in the things done with lost pains and disappointed hopes by man. But since there is always the risk of it, it is a great error of judgment to have lived for what may fail us. So that if Mr. Burne Jones works for a man who is to arise ages hence he works for what the burning of his pictures or the death of his admirer may for ever cut off. However he in particular has surely many vehement admirers living and even men who have the ear of the public—detractors too no doubt, but who has not? that comes with admiration.

I am happy to think you have an admirer in Mr. Rossetti (Gabriel Rossetti, I suppose): indeed if he read you it could not be otherwise. And I take the same for granted of Mr. Burne Jones.

Let me recommend you, if you have not seen them, my friend Dr. Bridges' poems—not his first little volume of roundels and so forth, now so much in fashion, for I have not read it and he is ashamed of it and does not wish to be known by it, but a set of sonnets, a tiny anonymous work no bigger than a short pamphlet of two dozen pages, they are called *The Growth of Love* and are to be continued some day. They are strict in form and affect Miltonic rhythms (which are caviare to the general, so that his critics, I believe, think him rough) and seem to me, but I am prepossessed, very beautiful—dignified, both manly and tender, and with a vein of quaintness. In imagery he is not rich but excels in phrasing, in sequence of phrase and sequence of feeling on feeling. Milton is the great master of sequence of phrase. By sequence of feeling I mean a dramatic quality by which what goes before seems to necessitate and beget what comes after, at least after you have heard it it does—your own poems illustrate it, as 'Yes, one time in the church I think you mean' or 'It makes me mad' and 'It makes me very sad to think of all the bitterness he had'. This little work is published by Pickering and costs only a shilling, I think.

June 15—This letter has run to a greater length than the little time at my disposal makes justifiable.—It is sad to think what disappointment must many times over have filled your heart for the darling children of your mind. Nevertheless fame whether won or lost is a thing which lies in the award of a random, reckless, incompetent, and unjust judge, the public, the multitude. The only just judge, the only just literary critic, is Christ, who prizes, is proud of, and admires, more than any man, more than the receiver himself can, the gifts of his own making. And the only real good which fame and another's praise does is to convey to us, by a channel not at all above suspicion but from circumstances in this case much less to be suspected than the channel of our own minds, some token of the judgment which a perfectly just, heedful, and wise mind, namely Christ's, passes upon our doings. Now such a token may be conveyed as well by one as by many. Therefore, believing I was able to pass a fair judgment as people go, it seemed in the circumstances a charity to tell you what I thought. For disappointment and humiliations embitter the heart and make an aching in the very bones. As far as I am concerned I say with conviction and put it on record again that you have great reason to thank God who has given you so astonishingly clear an inward eye to see what is in visible nature and in the heart such a deep insight into what is earnest, tender, and pathetic in human life and feeling as your poems display.

Believe me, dear sir, very sincerely yours

GERARD M. HOPKINS S.J.

My address will be after next month 111 Mount Street, Grosvenor Square, London W., where I am to be stationed. But a letter to Stonyhurst would find me.

TO ROBERT BRIDGES

[Postmark, London, W., 8 August 1878.]

I will come tomorrow as near after one as Bedford Square is near here, I mean I shall start at one and wish I had said so at once. I cannot come today, because 4.45 is within a quarter of an hour of our dinner time. After two tomorrow do not wait: something will have kept me at home. It must only be a call, as next Sunday's sermon must be learnt better than last's.

I was very little nervous at the beginning and not at all after. It was pure forgetting and flurry. The delivery was not good, but I hope to get a good one in time. I shall welcome any criticisms which are not controversy. I am glad you did not like the music and sorry you did not like the mass.

G.M.H.

Edgell lives in the street and comes to church here regularly.

TO ROBERT BRIDGES

St. Joseph's, Bedford Leigh, near Manchester. Oct. 22 1879 (you will be surprised at this hand: I employ it sometimes with steel pens).

DEAREST BRIDGES,—One thing you say in your last is enough to make me quite sad and I see that I shall have to write at some length in order to deal with it. You ask whether I really think there is any good in your going on writing poetry. The reason of this question I suppose to be that I seemed little satisfied with what you then sent and suggested many amendments in the sonnet on Hector. I do still think 'nor he the charms' and its context obscure and cumbersome. The other I thought very beautiful (I said so), full of feeling and felicities, as 'The breathing Summer's sloth, the scented Fall' and 'sweet jeopardy'; only I called one part obscure. I find it so after your explanation: it is the 8th line that is most in fault, for the rest would bear your meaning if that did. To my mind you cannot be understood unless you write something like 'Last' did something-or-other 'and last had hope in thrall'. The present line is so vague, it might conceivably mean so many things, it stamps the mind with nothing determinate. But you are to know, indeed very likely you experience the same thing, I see your work to its very least advantage when it comes to me on purpose to be criticised. It is at once an unfinished thing, in my eyes, and any shortcoming or blemish that in print I should either not notice or else easily digest with the excellence of the context becomes a rawness and a blot, to be removed before my mind can even sit down to receive an impression of the whole or form a final judgment about it. It is just as if I had written it myself and were dissatisfied, as you know that in the process of composition one almost always is, before things reach their final form. And things you shewed me at Bedford Square in MS and I did not so much care for then, when I came to see them in print I read in a new light and felt very differently about them. Before that they are too near the eye; then they fall into focus. Oct. 23—Therefore in your book almost everything seems perfect and final and exercises its due effect and the exceptions prove the rule, such as the pieces in sprung rhythm, or some of them, and that is just because they *are* experimental and seem submitted to revision, and also the song, truly beautiful as it is, 'I have loved flowers'; but I was not satisfied with the music and mentally altered it: now it comes to me like a thing put by for repairs. And while on repairs and before going further I will say that I think it wd. be better to write 'One irrevocable day'. 'That . . . day' is ambiguous: you mean *ille dies*, the particular day which in fact did etc; I took it for *is dies*, a day such that, whenever it shall come, it is doomed to etc. You see, perfects in dependent sentences, like *held* there, need not be historical pasts; they may also be subjunctives of present or any date, and so I took it.

But now in general. And first to visit the workhouse. Oct. 25—You seem to want to be told over again that you have genius and are a poet and your verses beautiful. You have been told so, not only by me but very spontaneously by Gosse, Marzials, and others; I was going to say Canon Dixon, only, as he was acknowledging your book, it was not so spontaneous as Gosse's case. You want perhaps to be told more in particular. I am not the best to tell you, being biassed by love, and yet I am too. I think then no one can admire beauty of the body more than I do, and it is of course a comfort to find beauty in a friend or a friend in beauty. But this kind of beauty is dangerous. Then comes the beauty of the mind, such as genius, and this greater than the beauty of the body and not to call dangerous. And more beautiful than the beauty of the mind is beauty of character, the 'handsome heart'. Now every beauty is not a wit or genius nor has every wit or genius character. For though even bodily beauty, even the beauty of blooming health, is from the soul, in the sense, as we Aristotelian Catholics say, that the soul is the form of the body, yet the soul may have no other beauty, so to speak, than that which it expresses in the symmetry of the body— barring those blurs in the cast which wd. not be found in the die or the mould. This needs no illustration, as all know it. But what is more to be remarked is that in like manner the soul may have no further beauty than that which is seen in the mind, that there may be genius uninformed by character.

I sometimes wonder at this in a man like Tennyson: his gift of utterance is truly golden, but go further home and you come to thoughts commonplace and wanting in nobility (it seems hard to say it but I think you know what I mean). In Burns there is generally recognized on the other hand a richness and beauty of manly character which lends worth to some of his smallest fragments, but there is a great want in his utterance; it is never really beautiful, he had no eye for pure beauty, he gets no nearer than the fresh picturesque expressed in fervent and flowing language (the most strictly beautiful lines of his that I remember are those in Tam O'Shanter: 'But pleasures are like poppies spread' sqq. and those are not). Between a fineness of nature which wd. put him in the first rank of writers and a poverty of language which puts him in the lowest rank of poets, he takes to my mind, when all is balanced and cast up, about a middle place. If I were not your friend I shd. wish to be the friend of the man that wrote your poems. They shew the eye for pure beauty and they shew, my dearest, besides, the character which is much more rare and precious. Did time allow I shd. find a pleasure in dwelling on the instances, but I cannot now. Since I must not flatter or exaggerate I do not claim that you have such a volume of imagery as Tennyson, Swinburne, or Morris, though the feeling for beauty you have seems to me pure and exquisite; but in point of character, of sincerity or earnestness, of manliness, of tenderness, of humour, melancholy, human feeling, you have what they have not and seem scarcely to think worth having (about Morris I am not sure: his early poems had a deep feeling). I may then well say, like St. Paul, *aemulor te Dei aemulatione*. To have a turn for sincerity has not made you sincere nor a turn for earnest / in earnest; Sterne had a turn for compassion, but he was not compassionate; a man may have natural courage, a turn for courage, and yet play the coward.

I must now answer the rest of your letter. The Ship is very striking and beautiful in your manner. Only who is to take the advice? parents? I shd. like something more like 'And let him deep in memory's hold have stored'. However I am not to make amendments of this sort. The other is beautiful too, but not quite satisfactory in point of finish. The image of the saplings is perhaps not so pointed as some other might have been. (By the by I see nothing to object to in the *rhythm* of 'The careless ecstasy of leafy May'; so far as run goes it runs well enough. I should not alter the line 'Ride o'er the seas' etc.).

I hardly know what you allude to at Oxford, it is better that I should not. I used indeed to fear when I went up about this time last year that people wd. repeat against me what they remembered to my disadvantage. But if they did I never heard of it. I saw little of University men: when you were up it was an exceptional occasion, which brought me into contact with them. My work lay in St. Clement's, at the Barracks, and so on. However it is perhaps well I am gone; I did not quite hit it off with Fr. Parkinson and was not happy. I was fond of my people, but they had not as a body the charming and cheering heartiness of these Lancashire Catholics, which is so deeply comforting; they were far from having it. And I believe they criticised what went on in our church a great deal too freely, which is d—d impertinence of the sheep towards the shepherd, and if it had come markedly before me I shd. have given them my mind.

I doubt whether I shall ever get to Liverpool, but if I settle there I will avail myself of your kind offer. Tomorrow I am going to Wigan (St. John's) for eight days. Today is Nov. 18.

I cannot stop to defend the rhymes in the Bugler.[2] The words 'came down to us after a boon he on My late being there begged of me' mean 'came into Oxford to our Church in quest of (or to get) a blessing which, on a late occasion of my being up at Cowley Barracks, he had requested of me': there is no difficulty here, I think. But the line 'Silk-ashed' etc in the Sacrifice[3] is too hard and must be changed to 'In silk-ash kept from cooling.' I meant to compare grey hairs to the flakes of silky ash which may be seen round wood embers burnt in a clear fire and covering a 'core of heat', as Tennyson calls it. But *core* there is very ambiguous, as your remark shews. 'Your offer, with despatch, of' is said like 'Your name and college': it is 'Come, your offer of all this (the matured mind), and without delay either!' (This should now explode.) Read the last tercet 'What Death dare lift the latch

of, What Hell hopes soon the snatch of, Your offer, with despatch, of!'

It was embarassment [*sic*] made Grace odd that night, I
have no doubts: you think she only cares for learned music
and she thinks so of you. No question she admires Handel.
She stands in dread of your judgment probably.

I sent her your hymn. I mentioned it and she begged to
see it. She said it was not original-sounding but it was very
sweet: she wd. not be pleased if she knew I repeated her
criticism. If I could have found her the music to 'O earlier
shall the rose buds blow' she would have thought it original-
sounding as well as sweet. Yet it was youthful too. I return
the hymn.

Do you like Weber? For personal preference and fellow
feeling I like him of all musicians best after Purcell. I feel as
if I cd. have composed his music in another sphere. I do not
feel that of Handel or Mozart or Beethoven. Moreover I
do not think his great genius is appreciated. I shd. like to
read his life. He was a good man, I believe, with no hateful
affectation of playing the fool and behaving like a blackguard.

I cannot undertake to find a motto for the ring.

Remember me very kindly to Mrs. Molesworth And when
is your brother's book coming? Believe me your loving friend
                    GERARD HOPKINS S.J. Nov. 18 1879

TO ROBERT BRIDGES

Manresa House, Roehampton, S. W. June 5 '82.
DEAREST BRIDGES,—My heart warmed towards that
little Bertie Molesworth (I do not mean by this that he is so
very small), so that if you were to bring him again I shd. be
glad to see him. (But I am afraid he felt dull. He is shy I
dare say.) However I expect he is no longer with you. It
cannot be denied nevertheless that the presence of a third
person is a restraint upon confidential talk.

Davis the gardener was discontented that I would not let
you buy his peaches: he wd. have let you have them on reasonable terms, he said.

I have been studying the cuckoo's song. I find it to vary

much. In the first place cuckoos do not always sing (or the same cuckoo does not always sing) at the same pitch or in the same key: there are, so to say, alto cuckoos and tenor cuckoos. In particular they sing lower in flying and the interval is then also least, it being an effort to them to strike the higher note, which is therefore more variable than the other. When they perch they sing wrong at first, I mean they correct their first try, raising the upper note. The interval varies as much as from less than a minor third to nearly as much as a common fourth and this last is the tune when the bird is in loud and good song.

About the book I will not write.

Your affectionate friend

GERARD M. HOPKINS S.J.

TO R. W. DIXON

The Holy Name, Oxford Rd., Manchester. Aug. 12 1883.

MY DEAR FRIEND,—I am here filling a gap and take the opportunity of letting you know that two days before our 'Great Academies', that is the speechday with which our Stonyhurst scholastic year ends, Coventry Patmore came to visit us and stayed three or four days. The Rector gave me charge of him and I saw a good deal of him and had a good deal of talk. He knew and expressed great admiration of Bridges' Muse upon the strength of extracts in reviews only, not having till that time been able to get the poems from his bookseller; but of you he knew nothing, not even your name. I brought him all I had of yours in MS and he read it all. He told me he was very slow in taking in a new poet, even the meaning, much more the effect and spirit: he said 'I feel myself in presence of a new mind, a new spirit, but beyond that at a first reading I am not yet accustomed to the strange atmosphere'. This he said after a little reading of the MS. Then he became much taken up with *Love's Consolation* and that made the most impression. He was in fact completely won by it and pointed out passages with the insight of the predestined reader. In the end he told me when I next wrote to you to express to you 'the immense pleasure the reading of your poems had given him'; he was amazed and sorry he had never known anything of them before. I furnished him with titles and publisher and told him to expect *Mano's* coming out. He would have it that Morris must have borrowed from you, but I told him I thought it was a case of parallel growth. His conversation was of course full of interest. He is fastidious and searching in his criticism. Of his friend Aubrey de Vere he said, assenting to a remark of mine, 'He has all the gifts that make a poet excepting only that last degree of individuality which is the most essential of all'. Of Browning, whom he can no longer bring himself to read, he said something the same only severer. I suppose I am more tolerant or more inclined to admire than he is, but in listening to him I had that malignant satisfaction which lies in hearing one's worst surmises confirmed—the joy Mrs. Candour's audience must have felt when she discussed Mrs. Vermilion and Miss Evergreen.

I expect on Thursday to go to my father's at Hampstead and in a week's time to Holland for a week. I suppose I shall be back at Stonyhurst by the beginning of next month. I am reappointed for the ensuing year, I am happy to say.

Believe me your affectionate friend

GERARD HOPKINS S.J.

I shall see Bridges at Hampstead, I expect.

By the by Patmore has a very great admiration for Dorset Barnes.

TO ROBERT BRIDGES

University College, 85 & 86, Stephens Green, Dublin. March 7 1884

MY DEAREST BRIDGES,—Remark the above address: it is a new departure or a new arrival and at all events a new abode. I dare say you know nothing of it, but the fact is that, though unworthy of and unfit for the post, I have been elected Fellow of the Royal University of Ireland in the department of classics. I have a salary of £400 a year, but when I first contemplated the six examinations I have yearly to conduct, five of them running, and to the Matriculation there came up last year 750 candidates, I thought that Stephen's Green (the biggest square in Europe) paved with gold would not pay for it. It is an honour and an opening and has many bright sides, but at present it has also some dark ones and this in particular that I am not at all strong, not strong enough for the requirements, and do not see at all how I am to become so. But to talk of weather or health and especially to complain of them is poor work.

The house we are in, the College, is a sort of ruin and for purposes of study very nearly naked. And I have more money to buy books than room to put them in.

I have been warmly welcomed and most kindly treated. But Dublin itself is a joyless place and I think in my heart as smoky as London is: I had fancied it quite different. The Phoenix Park is fine, but inconveniently far off. There are a few fine buildings.

It is only a few days since I sent the MS book to Mr. Patmore (and in packing I mislaid, I hope not lost, your copy of the poem 'Wild air, world-mothering air', so that I had to send that unfinished): he acknowledged it this morning.

I enclose a poem of Tennyson's which you may not have seen. It has something in it like your Spring Odes and also some expressions like my sonnet on Spring.

I shall also enclose, if I can find, two triolets I wrote for the Stonyhurst Magazine; for the third was not good, and they spoilt what point it had by changing the title. These two under correction I like, but have fears that you will suspend them from a hooked nose: if you do, still I should maintain they were as good as yours beginning 'All women born'.

Believe me your affectionate friend

GERARD HOPKINS S.J.

There was an Irish row over my election.

TO ROBERT BRIDGES

University College, 85 & 86, Stephens Green, Dublin. April 30 1884

DEAREST BRIDGES,—The secret out: I too am engaged[4] on examination papers and must therefore be very brief.

First I am not the least surprised, not that I suspected anything but that nothing about marriage surprises me ever.

Next I am glad: I say every one should marry, and do not see why you did not, years ago, except that

Thirdly you were waiting for Miss Waterhouse to turn up,* which having happened and being to complete your happiness I am very glad of it and feel sure she must be both good and charming. For I have reasons not altogether a priori for judging she is both. Of course I wish you both great joy and am your (the both of yiz) affectionate friend

GERARD M. HOPKINS S.J.

I am, I believe, recovering from a deep fit of nervous prostration (I suppose I ought to call it): I did not know but I was dying.

---

* Indeed to be born.

TO ROBERT BRIDGES

Furbough House, near Galway. July 18 1884.

DEAREST BRIDGES,—I must let you have a line now, I see, and write more hereafter. I ought to have answered you before, but indeed I hardly thought you were in earnest in proposing I should be your best man, pleasant and honourable as the position would be. But to show no other reasons why not, at the time you name I should be about beginning my examination work and it would be altogether impossible for me to be out of Ireland. However you do not want for friends better fitted to do the work than I.

I am here on holiday. I have been through Connemara, the fine scenery of which is less known than it should be. Yesterday I went to see the cliffs of Moher on the coast of Clare, which to describe would be long and difficult. In returning across the Bay we were in some considerable danger of our lives. Furbough House stands amidst beautiful woods, an Eden in a wilderness of rocks and treeless waste. The whole neighbourhood is most singular.

The weakness I am suffering from—it is that only, nervous weakness (or perhaps I ought not to say nervous at all, for I am not in any unusual way nervous in the common understanding of the word)—continues and I see no ground for thinking I can, for a long time to come, get notably better of it, but I may reasonably hope that this pleasant holiday may set me up a little for a while. Your enquiries are very kind: there is no reason to be disquieted about me, though weakness is a very painful trial in itself. If I could have regular hard exercise it would be better for me.

The reason of course why I like men to marry is that a single life is a difficult, not altogether a natural life; to make it easily manageable special provision, such as we have, is needed, and most people cannot have this.

I shall begin my annual eight days' retreat in a few days and then return to Dublin.

Coventry Patmore has kept your MS book a long time, as though it were to give himself the opportunity of repentance for not admiring all the poems, and indeed appears to look on his condition as one of guilt and near to reprobation—which is very odd of him. And I believe it will be of no avail and that like Esau and Antiochus he will not get the grace and is in a fair way to die in his sins.

I find that 2557 is divisible by nothing till you reach 20, beyond which I have not tried: what then can the length of the stanza be? and what is the subject of the poem?

Believe me your affectionate friend

GERARD M. HOPKINS S.J.

Write University *College*, Stephen's Green: the number is unnecessary.

TO ROBERT BRIDGES

University College, 85 & 86, Stephen's Green, Dublin. Aug. 21 1884

DEAREST BRIDGES,—I must let you have a line to acknowledge, with many thanks, the receipt of the MS book and two or three very kind letters. I guessed whose was the elegant and legible hand on two of the addresses. As for the piece of a new garment, I came to the conclusion it was put in to bigout the enclosure. I also concluded that that new garment was a pair of wedding trousers. Circumstances may drive me to use my piece as a penwiper.

It is so near your wedding that I do not know I ought to write of anything else. I could not ask to be present at it; and indeed, much as I desire to see you and your wife and her mother and Yattendon itself, perhaps that would not be so good a day for this after all as some other. Only unhappily I do not see when that other is to be. However it is a fine buoyant saying, Non omnium rerum sol occidit.

I had an interesting letter from Mr. Patmore all in praise of you.

Several things in your letters call for reply, but not now. If you do not like 'I yield, you do come sometimes,'[5] (though I cannot myself feel the weakness you complain of it in it, and it has the advantage of being plain) will 'I yield, you foot me sometimes' do? 'Own my heart' is merely 'my own heart', transposed for rhythm's sake and then *tamquam exquisitius*, as Hermann would say. 'Reave' is for rob, plunder, carry off.

I find that in correcting 'Margaret'[6] I wrote '*world* of wanwood' by mistake for '*worlds*', as the sense requires.

Our society cannot be blamed for not valuing what it never knew of. The following are all the people I have let see my poems (not counting occasional pieces): some of them however, as you did, have shewn them to others. (1) The editor and subeditor of our *Month* had the *Deutschland* and later the *Eurydice* offered them—(2) my father and mother and two sisters saw these, one or both of them, and I have sent them a few things besides in letters—(3) You—(4) Canon Dixon—(5) Mr. Patmore—(6) Something got out about the *Deutschland* and Fr. Cyprian Splaine, now of Stonyhurst, wrote to me to send it him and perhaps other poems of mine: I did so and he shewed it to others. They perhaps read it, but he afterwards acknowledged to me that in my handwriting he found it unreadable; I do not think he meant illegible—(7) On the other hand Fr. Francis Bacon, a fellownovice of mine, and an admirer of my sermons saw all and expressed a strong admiration for them which was certainly sincere. They are therefore, one may say, unknown. It always seems to me that poetry is unprofessional, but that is what I have said to myself, not others to me. No doubt if I kept producing I should have to ask myself what I meant to do with it all; but I have long been at a standstill, and so the things lie. It would be less tedious talking than writing: now at all events I must stop.

I must tell you a humorous touch of Irish Malvolio or Bully Bottom, so distinctively Irish that I cannot rank it: it amuses me in bed. A Tipperary lad, one of our people, lately from his noviceship, was at the wicket and another bowling to him. He thought there was no one within hearing, but from behind the wicket he was overheard after a good stroke to cry out 'Arrah, sweet myself!'

I must write once more against the 3rd.

Believe me always your affectionate friend

GERARD M. HOPKINS S.J.

Aug. 24 1884.

TO R. W. DIXON

Milltown Park, Milltown. Oct. 25 1884.

MY DEAR FRIEND,—I am heartily ashamed of myself that I never answered your most kind and comforting letter received on Galway Bay in the summer. Neither do I answer it now, but only say that I am, thank God, much better since then and now drowned in the last and worst of five examinations. I have 557 papers on hand: let those who have been thro' the like say what that means. At this most inopportune time Mr. Tom Arnold has asked me to write a short notice of you for the forthcoming new edition of his handbook of English Literature and somehow or other I must do it. Therefore please fill up the following and send it me without delay here (where I am come for quiet).

Add any particular you like, but I do not say they or even all the above can appear, so short is the space at my disposal.

I am your affectionate friend

GERARD M. HOPKINS S.J.

TO KATE HOPKINS

University College, Stephen's Green. Dublin. Dec. 9 1884

ME DEAR MISS HOPKINS,—Im intoirely ashamed o

meself. Sure its a wonder I could lave your iligant corspon-
dance so long onanswered. But now Im just afther conthroiv-
ing a jewl of a convaniance be way of a standhen desk and
tis a moighty incurgement towards the writin of letters in-
toirelee. Tis whoy ye hear from me this evenin.

It bates me where to commince, the way Id say anything
yed be interistud to hear of. More be token yell be plased
tintimate to me mother Im intirely obleeged to her for her
genteel offers. But as titchin warm clothen tis undher a mis-
apprehinsion shes labourin. Sure twas not the inclimunsee of
the saysons I was complainin of at all at all. Twas the pover-
tee of books and such like educational convaniences.

And now, Miss Hopkins darlin, yell chartably exkees me
writin more in the rale Irish be raison I was never rared to ut
and thats why I do be so slow with my pinmanship, bad luck
to ut (savin your respects), but for ivery word I delineate I
disremember two, and thats how ut is with me.

(The above very fair).

The weather is wild and yet mild.

I have a kind of charge of a greenhouse.

I am hoping to hear Dvorak's Stabat Mater at Trinity College tomorrow. I think you heard it.

I have an invitation for Xmas to Lord Emly's.

A dear old French Father, very clever and learned and a
great photographer, who at first wanted me to take to pho-
tography with him, which indeed in summer would be pleasant enough, finding that once I used to draw, got me to bring
him the few remains I still have, cows and horses in chalk
done in Wales too long ago to think of, and admired them to
that degree that he is urgent with me to go on drawing at all
hazards; but I do not see how that could be now, so late: if
anybody had said the same 10 years ago it might have been
different.

You spoke in your last of meeting Baillie. He was always
the kindest and best of friends and I always look upon myself
in the light of a blackguard when I think of my behaviour to
him and of his to me. In this case however he has not written
since you met him and I hope to be beforehand with him.

Tis a quare thing I didn't finish this letter yet. Ill shlip me kyard in betune the sheets the way yell know Im not desaivin ye. Believe me your loving brother

GERARD.

Dec. 13 1884

TO ALEXANDER BAILLIE

University College, Stephen's Green, Dublin. April 24 1885

MY DEAREST BAILLIE,—I will this evening begin writing to you and God grant it may not be with this as it was with the last letter I wrote to an Oxford friend, that the should-be receiver was dead before it was ended. (There is no bad omen in this, as you will on reflexion—REMARK: *reflexion:* I USED TO WRITE *reflection* TILL YOU POINTED OUT THE MISTAKE: YOU DID SO TWICE, FOR I HAD, THROUGH HUMAN FRAILTY AND INADVERTENCE, LAPSED—see.) I mean poor Geldart, whose death, as it was in Monday last's *Pall Mall,* you must have heard of. I suppose it was suicide, his mind, for he was a selftormentor, having been unhinged, as it had been once or twice before, by a struggle he had gone through. Poor Nash's death, not long before, was certainly suicide and certainly too done in insanity, for he had been sleepless for ten nights: of this too you will have heard. It much comforts me and seems providential that I had renewed my friendship with Geldart some weeks before it was too late. I yesterday wrote to his widow. Three of my intimate friends at Oxford have thus drowned themselves, a good many more of my acquaintances and contemporaries have died by their own hands in other ways: it must be, and the fact brings it home to me, a dreadful feature of our days. I should say that Geldart had lent me his autobiography called (I wish it had another name) *A Son of Belial.* It is an amusing and a sad book—but perhaps you have seen it. I am in it and Addis, Coles, Jeune, MacInnon, Nash, Jowett, Liddon, and lots more thinly disguised, though some I do not recognise. You are not there.

May 8—For one thing I was sorry when I got your late delightful letter. Since my sister told me of her meeting you I had been meaning to write and be first with you—but now I

am slow even in answering. Some time since, I began to over-
haul my old letters, accumulations of actually ever since I
was at school, destroying all but a very few, and growing ever
lother to destroy, but also to read, so that at last I left off
reading; and there they lie and my old notebooks and beginnings of things, ever so many, which it seems to me might
well have been done, ruins and wrecks; but on this theme I
will not enlarge by pen and ink. However there were many
of your letters among them and overflowing with kindness
(but not towards Hannah and MacFarlane; however you
need not distress yourself so much about them; I agree with
you in the main, and believe I used to remonstrate sometimes
of old on their behalf, because they were good fellows and
the persistency of their attentions was a most real compliment
—a sort of compliment that as one gets older and writes the
senile parenthetic style I am maundering in now one values a
great deal higher—but still I can distinctly remember, though
I shall not recall, real provocation they gave you; and you
never did more than have a humourous fling at them; but to
return) and for those letters I was deeply grateful and keep
it constantly before me that I was undeserving of them; but
still it was a cruel thing of you now to tell me that my own
very first letter to you begins with 'Yes, you are a fool'. The
context, I suppose, the sequel, I mean, does something to
mitigate, but mitigate as you may I wish it were not said.
But I have to regret so much! and what is it to withdraw a
thing long after the event? Almost meaningless.

As I have told you before, the first thing not that you said
to me but that I can remember your saying was some joke
about a watering hose which lay on the grass plot in the
Outer Quad: a small spray was scattering from it. I stood
watching it and you, coming in from a walk, waving your
stick at it quoted or parodied either 'Busy curious thirsting
fly' or the Dying Christian to his Soul. You never could remember this after and IN FINE (an expression which, it has
always appeared to me, could never take root in our garden
and yet we could never make up our minds to throw back
again over the wall into the French one where it came from)
I am more sure that it was said than that you said it.

I think this is from a literary point of view (not from a

moral) the worst letter I ever wrote to you, and it shall not run much longer. You will wonder I have been so long over it. This is part of my disease, so to call it. The melancholy I have all my life been subject to has become of late years not indeed more intense in its fits but rather more distributed, constant, and crippling. One, the lightest but a very inconvenient form of it, is daily anxiety about work to be done, which makes me break off or never finish all that lies outside that work. It is useless to write more on this: when I am at the worst, though my judgment is never affected, my state is much like madness. I see no ground for thinking I shall ever get over it or ever succeed in doing anything that is not forced on me to do of any consequence.

I forget what the verses were I shewed you and you 'did not criticise.' It is putting friendship unwisely to a strain to shew verses, neither did I do it much. Those verses were afterwards burnt and I wrote no more for seven years; then, it being suggested to write something I did so and have at intervals since, but the intervals are now long ones and the whole amount produced is small. And I make no attempt to publish.

You said, and it was profoundly true then, that Mr. Gladstone ought to be beheaded on Tower Hill and buried in Westminster Abbey. Ought he now to be buried in Westminster Abbey? As I am accustomed to speak too strongly of him I will not further commit myself in writing.

Much could be said about Ireland and my work and all, but it would be tedious; especially as I hope we may meet soon. I seem glad you keep up your Oriental studies. Believe me always your affectionate friend

GERARD M. HOPKINS S.J.

May 17 '85 and still winter.

TO ROBERT BRIDGES

University College, St. Stephen's Green, Dublin. Sept. 1 1885.

DEAREST BRIDGES,—I have just returned from an absurd adventure, which when I resigned myself to it I could not help enjoying. A hairbrained fellow took me down to

Kingstown and on board his yacht and, whereas I meant to return to town by six that evening, would not let me go either that night or this morning till past midday. I was afraid it would be compromising, but it was fun while it lasted.

I have been in England. I was with my people first at Hampstead, then at Midhurst in Sussex in a lovely landscape: they are there yet. And from there I went to Hastings to Mr. Patmore's for a few days. I managed to see several old friends and to make new ones, amongst which Mr. W. H. Cummings the tenor singer and composer, who wrote the Life of Purcell: he shewed me some of his Purcell treasures and others and is going to send me several things. I liked him very much but the time of my being with him was cut short. I did not attempt to see you: I did not know that visitors wd. at that time be very welcome and it wd. have been difficult to me in any case to come. I am very sorry to hear of Mrs. Bridges' disappointment: somehow I had feared that would happen.

I shall shortly have some sonnets to send you, five or more. Four of these came like inspirations unbidden and against my will. And in the life I lead now, which is one of a continually jaded and harassed mind, if in any leisure I try to do anything I make no way—nor with my work, alas! but so it must be.

Mr. Patmore lent me Barnes' poems—3 volumes, not all, for indeed he is prolific. I hold your contemptuous opinion an unhappy mistake: he is a perfect artist and of a most spontaneous inspiration; it is as if Dorset life and Dorset landscape had taken flesh and tongue in the man. I feel the defect or limitation or whatever we are to call it that offended you: he lacks fire; but who is perfect all round? If one defect is fatal what writer could we read?

An old question of yours I have hitherto neglected to answer, am I thinking of writing on metre? I suppose thinking too much and doing too little. I do greatly desire to treat that subject; might perhaps get something together this year; but I can scarcely believe that on that or on anything else anything of mine will ever see the light—of publicity nor even of day. For it is widely true, the fine pleasure is not to do a thing but to feel that you could and the mortification that goes to the heart is to feel it is the power that fails you: *qui occidere nolunt Posse volunt;* it is the refusal of a thing that we like to have. So with me, if I could but get on, if I could but produce work I should not mind its being buried, silenced, and going no further; but it kills me to be time's eunuch and never to beget. After all I do not despair, things might change, anything may be; only there is no great appearance of it. Now because I have had a holiday though not strong I have some buoyancy; soon I am afraid I shall be ground down to a state like this last spring's and summer's, when my spirits were so crushed that madness seemed to be making approaches—and nobody was to blame, except myself partly for not managing myself better and contriving a change.

Believe me, with kind wishes to Mrs. Bridges, your affectionate friend

GERARD M. HOPKINS S.J.

Sept. 8 '85.

This day 15 years ago I took my first vows.

I hope Mrs. Molesworth is well. Where is she now?

Is your brother John going to bring out a second volume?

If I had not reread your letter I shd. have left it unanswered. The expression 'The Mass is good' is, I feel sure, never used in these islands. But the meaning in the circumstances is pretty plain and must be just what you take it to be. To satisfy the obligation of hearing mass on Sundays and the 'Festivals of Obligation' one must be present from at least the Offertory to the Priest's Communion. The question is well threshed out: for laxer and for stricter opinions see the Moral Theologians passim; whose name is Legion, but St. Alphonsus Liguori will do for all (Treatise *de Praeceptis Ecclesiæ* or *De Decem Praeceptis Decalogi*). However the phrase would not easily be understood by your readers or hearers. I hope to see those plays. Are the choral parts written strictly to the music? I never saw good poetry made to music unless that music itself had first been made to words.

TO COVENTRY PATMORE

[University College, St. Stephen's Green, Dublin.] June 4 1886

MY DEAR MR. PATMORE,—I have been meaning and meaning to write to you, to return the volumes of Barnes' poems you lent me and for other reasons, and partly my approaching examination work restrained me, when last night there reached me from Bell's the beautiful new edition of your works. I call it beautiful and think it is the best form upon the whole for poetry and works of pure literature that I know of and I thank you for your kindness in sending it. And I hope the bush or the bottle may do what little in a bush or bottle lies to recommend the liquor to the born and the unborn. But how slowly does the fame of excellence spread! And crooked eclipses and other obscure causes fight against its rise and progress.

Your poems are a good deed done for the Catholic Church and another for England, for the British Empire, which now trembles in the balance held in the hand of unwisdom. I remark that those Englishmen who wish prosperity to the Empire (which is not all Englishmen or Britons, strange to say) speak of the Empire's mission to extend freedom and civilisation in India and elsewhere. The greater the scale of politics the weightier the influence of a great name and a high ideal. It is a terrible element of weakness that now we are not well provided with the name and ideal which would recommend and justify our Empire. 'Freedom': it is perfectly true that British freedom is the best, the only successful freedom, but that is because, with whatever drawbacks, those who have developed that freedom have done so with the aid of law and obedience to law. The cry then shd. be Law and Freedom, Freedom and Law. But that does not please: it must be Freedom only. And to that cry there is the telling answer: No freedom you can give us is equal to the freedom of letting us alone: take yourselves out of India, let us first be free of you. Then there is civilisation. It shd. have been Catholic truth. That is the great end of Empires before God, to be Catholic and draw nations into their Catholicism. But our Empire is less and less Christian as it grows.

There remains that part of civilisation which is outside Christianity or which is not essentially Christian. The best is gone, still something worth having is left. How far can the civilisation England offers be attractive and valuable and be offered and insisted on as an attraction and a thing of value to India for instance? Of course those who live in our civilisation and belong to it praise it: it is not hard, as Socrates said, among the Athenians to praise the Athenians; but how will it be represented by critics bent on making the worst of it or even not bent on making the best of it? It is good to be in Ireland to hear how enemies, and those rhetoricians, can treat the things that are unquestioned at home. I know that to mere injustice and slander innocence and excellence themselves stand condemned, but since there is always in mankind some love of truth and admiration for good (only that the truth must be striking and the good on a great scale) what marked and striking excellence has England to shew to make her civilisation attractive? Her literature is one of her excellences and attractions and I believe that criticism will tend to make this more and more felt; but there must be more of that literature, a continued supply and in quality excellent. This is why I hold that fine works of art, and especially if, like yours, that are not only ideal in form but deal with high matter as well, are really a great power in the world, an element of strength even to an empire. But now time and tediousness forbid me to write more on this.

It has struck me since I was at Hastings that, if it is not impertinent of me to say it, Miss Patmore might gain by taking some lessons from some painter. It is true she does what no painter can either do or teach but it is also true there are other things she might with advantage learn. For in fact everyone is the better for teaching: it is universally true. It struck me that she was hampered by want of some mechanical knowledge, as in the use of washes for background, and she tends, I think, to use bodycolour in a way which would be considered vicious. This has naturally arisen from her circumstances; for in the delicate detail in which she so wonderfully excells the use of bodycolour is legitimate and even necessary and naturally she extended a practice with which she was familiar to a new field. I will send Barnes's poems back in a few days.

Believe me your sincere friend

GERARD M. HOPKINS S.J.

Please give my kindest remembrances to Mrs. Patmore and the Miss Patmores. I hope all are well and Piff is not killing himself with his sensibilities.
June 6.

TO ROBERT BRIDGES

University College, Stephen's Green, Dublin. Oct. 13 1886. DEAREST BRIDGES,—Fr. Mat Russell of ours (he is Sir Charles Russell's brother), who edits a little half-religious publication the *Irish Monthly*, wrote to me lately for an opinion of some Latin verses furnished him; and this led to two things. The first was my suddenly turning a lot of Shakspere's songs into elegiacs and hendecasyllables (my Latin muse having been wholly mum for years) and sending him one copy (and the rest I believe I can and shall get published in the Trinity *Hermathena* by means of Mr. Tyrrell). The other was that he proposed to me to introduce your poems to the fewish but not despicable readers of his little periodical. Now this I must do, as soon as it shall become possible; but you must therefore send me (not for this purpose *Prometheus*, which I have, but) those pamphlets copies of which I think I left at Stonyhurst. It is no doubt wasteful work giving me presentation copies; but the above is my most permanent abode and the nest likely to be best feathered. Yours

GERARD M. HOPKINS S.J.

By the bye, I say it deliberately and before God, I would have you and Canon Dixon and all true poets remember that fame, the being known, though in itself one of the most dangerous things to man, is nevertheless the true and appointed air, element, and setting of genius and its works. What are works of art for? to educate, to be standards. Education is meant for the many, standards are for public use. To produce then is of little use unless what we produce is known, if known widely known, the wider known the better, for it is by being known it works, it influences, it does its duty, it does good. We must then try to be known, aim at it, take means to it. And this without puffing in the process or pride in the success. But still. Besides, we are Englishmen. A great work by an Englishman is like a great battle won by England. It is an unfading bay tree. It will even be admired by and praised by and do good to those who hate England (as England is most perilously hated), who do not wish even to be benefited by her. It is then even a patriotic duty τῇ ποιήσει ἐνεργεῖν[7] and to secure the fame and permanence of the work. Art and its fame do not really matter, spiritually they are nothing, virtue is the only good; but it is only by bringing in the infinite that to a just judgment they can be made to look infinitesimal or small or less than vastly great; and in this ordinary view of them I apply to them, and it is the true rule for dealing with them, what Christ our Lord said of virtue, Let your light shine before men that they may see your good works (say, of art) and glorify yr. Father in heaven (that is, acknowledge that they have an absolute excellence in them and are steps in a scale of infinite and inexhaustible excellence).

Let me hear that you got all my letters. One, begun I think in Wales and sent from here, was addressed to Judge Fry's at Bristol, the next to Yattendon and had (I believe it was that one) a torn drawing in it. Well of course you must have got that one, but the one to Bristol with the long address you may not. Earlier ones are I think accounted for.

Did I ever send you St. Patrick's 'Breastplate' or prayer? I do now at all events. Read it and say if it is not one of the most remarkable compositions of man.

TO ROBERT BRIDGES

University College, St. Stephen's Green, Dublin. March 29 '87
DEAR BRIDGES,—I found your letter on coming back to town last night from Monasterevan, quite too late for return of post. However for the curiosity of the thing I answer your queries.

The irises of the present writer's eyes are small and dull,

of a greenish brown; hazel I suppose; slightly darker at the outer rims.

His hair (see enclosed sample, carriage paid) is lightish brown, but not equable nor the same in all lights; being quite fair near the roots and upon the temples, elsewhere darker (the very short bits are from the temple next the ear, the longer snip from the forehead), and shewing quite fair in the sun and even a little tawny. It has a gloss. On the temples it sometimes appears to me white. I have a few white hairs, but not there.

It is very pleasant and flattering thought that Wooldridge is painting my portrait, but is it (and was yours) wholly from memory? I am of late become much wrinkled round the eyes and generally haggard-looking, and if my counterfeit presentment is to be I shd. be glad it were of my youth.

And if Wooldridge is still with you tell him not to trouble to answer that letter at all nor to make the enquiries, which I have made elsewhere (besides which I feel pretty sure the matter never struck Rockstro nor perhaps anyone else and that I have the key to the history of modern music in what my enquiry points to, viz. that modern harmony could not arise till the old system and its tuning was got rid of and that it was goodness, not dulness, of ear which delayed its growth). Presently I hope to write to him again, not lengthily, and may enclose something.

I shd. have felt better for the delicious bog air of Monasterevan were it not that I had a sleepless night of it last night.

The young lady of my Elegy[8] was tossed in the earthquake. She and her mother ran down lightly clad and spent the next day under an umbrella (against sun, not rain). She was greatly terrified and begged and prayed her father to fetch her home, which I fancy he has not yet done.

I am yours affectionately

GERARD M. HOPKINS, S.J.

If I can manage to read the Feast of Bacchus it must be in the ensuing Easter holidays. You shall hear in a day or two.

TO COVENTRY PATMORE

Glenaveena, Howth. Whitsunday [20 May] 1888

DEAR MR. PATMORE,—This is to express the hope that your attack of quinsy has passed or is passing off and to say that my paper on the *Angel* is really in hand and when finished will be printed without difficulty: there is more difficulty about getting it finished. If it is to be printed at all however it is a pity it cannot be somewhere where it would have more readers. It treats of the matters your letter touches on. But about the 'tyke' you did not altogether understand me. If I had said you had less than anyone else of the Bohemian, though that is not the same thing, the meaning would have been plainer. As there is something of the 'old Adam' in all but the holiest men and in them at least enough to make them understand it in others, so there is an old Adam of barbarism, boyishness, wildness, rawness, rankness, the disreputable, the unrefined in the refined and educated. It is that that I meant by tykishness (a tyke is a stray sly unowned dog) and said you have none of; and I did also think that you were without all sympathy for it and must survey it when you met with it wholly from without. Ancient Pistol is the typical tyke, he and all his crew are tykes, and the tykish element undergoing dilution in Falstaff and Prince Hall appears to vanish, but of course really exists, in Henry V as king. I thought it was well to have ever so little of it and therefore it was perhaps a happy thing that you were entrapped into the vice of immoderate smoking, for to know one yields to a vice must help to humanise and make tolerant.

Since I wrote last I have had a piece of good luck which also has something to do with you. I made another attempt on my tune to the Crocus. I set it in strict counterpoint (or as strict as the case allowed of) as a madrigal in canon at the octave, a most difficult task, and after much labour sent it to my friend Sir Robert Stewart to correct. He gave it a very good mark, but suggested some changes in the rhythm chiefly. I have made them, but to touch a composition of this sort is like touching a house of cards: one piece pulls down another, so the alterations cost a good deal of trouble more. And this is only the first verse: the two others are still to do. When all is done it ought to be sung by an unaccompanied choir. I hope in the end it may be: the attempt was daring (like verse in intricate metre) and Sir Robert's verdict amounted to saying that it was successful.

I am very sincerely yours

GERARD M. HOPKINS.

TO ROBERT BRIDGES

Univ. Coll., Stephen's Green, Dublin. Oct. 19 '88

DEAREST BRIDGES,—You remark, I am glad to find, a 'lambness' in my last letter: now in the present I shall have somewhat as schoolboys say, to 'lamb in'. But first of various matters.

My little Paper on *Statistics and Free Will* obeyed the general law and did not appear; so I win that wager, if you remember. The editor made some objections which involved recasting it: I have partly done so, and when it is all recast he will no doubt find others. But meantime I get into print in a way I would not. My father wrote a little book on Numbers, the numbers one to ten, a sketchy thing, raising points of interest in a vast, an infinite subject: the *Saturday* lately had a paper on this book, making great game of it from end to end (of it and the article), including something I had contributed to it; however I was not named. Last week same Review has an article 'The American Poet', a comment on Gosse, who lately said, it seems, there *is* no American poet—great poet, he means, or poet proper perhaps. It ends 'After all, the whole affair is a fluke. Great poets are the results of exquisitely rare and incalculable combinations of causes, and nobody would be to blame if there were not a great poet for another century. This country does not seem likely to have another in a hurry [take that], nor have we observed him mewing his mighty youth in France, Germany, Italy, or Spain. Perhaps he is at school in Bolivia at this moment, or he may be at Johns Hopkins University, Baltimore, and his Christian name may be "Gifted"'. It is an allusion to that same 'Gifted Hopkins' the humorist 'who died of his own jocosity' that, if you remember, was meant the time before. But if Lang wrote this paper too, then, putting together that very fact that he then did *not* mean me with the fact that Gosse (you told me) admires my muse and the one that being imprudent he may have said so and others, I do not know but I say to myself, O my soul, perhaps This Is Fame. But I don't want it and beg you will not expose me to it; which you can easily forbear from doing now that you disapprove of my γένος as vicious, and surely you shd. not vitiate taste. And at any rate I shall never cease to deplore that unhappy letter of mine you read sitting leagues and parasangs of country lanes next to Lang that morning: how could I foresee it was so dangerous to write to a remote world's-end place like Yattendon? But indeed you have told me there is plenty of intellectual life there.

Next, music. I am glad to find it is only there we are so far apart. But the contrary is true: there we agree well enough and the rift is elsewhere. I agree to your musical strictures and almost invite your rebukes and if I do not do so heartily it is because a perfect organisation for crippling me exists and the one for 'encouragemental purposes' (modern English) is not laid down yet. I agree that for contrapuntal writing we shd. read the great masters and study the rules, both. The great masters unhappily I cannot read (unless very little), but the rules I do carefully study, and just on account of the great formality of the art of music it happens that mere adherence to them, without study of examples from the masters, produces—given faculty—results of some interest and value. (I like not that last sentence: it is too much in the manner of the magazines I read and too far entirely from Doughty and the Mighty Dead.) And my madrigal in canon, so far as it has gone, is strict and Sir Robert Stewart (a demon for rule) says it is correct and that it might even have been freer. But, as you say, you have not seen it and now that I have no piano I cannot go on with it. This morning I gave in what I believe is the last batch of examination-work for this autumn (and if all were seen, fallen leaves of my poor life between all the leaves of it), and but for that want I might prance on ivory this very afternoon. I have had to get glasses, by the bye: just now I cannot be happy either

with or without them. The oculist says my sight is very
good and my eye perfectly healthy but that like Jane Night-
work I am old. And, strange to say, I have taken to drawing
again. Perverse Fortune or something perverse (try me):
why did I not take to it before? And now enough, for I must
whet myself, strop myself, be very bitter, and will secrete and
distil a good deal beforehand.

However with no more stropping than the palm of my
hand and chopping at a hair, no but at the 'broth of goldish
flue' (how well now does the pleasing modern author come
in in his own illustration and support!), I can deal with one
matter, the sonnet on St. Alphonsus. I am obliged for your
criticisms, 'contents of which noted', indeed acted on. I have
improved the sestet (in itself I do not call the first version
'cheeky', the imagery as applied to God Almighty being so
familiar in the Scripture and the Fathers: however I have
not kept it). But now I cannot quite understand nor so far
as I understand agree with the difficulty you raise about the
continents and so on. It is true continents are partly made
by 'trickling increment'; but what is on the whole truest and
most strikes us about them and mountains is that they are
made what now we see them by trickling *de*crements, by
detrition, weathering, and the like.* And at any rate whatever is markedly featured in stone or what is like stone is
most naturally said to be hewn, and to *shape*, itself, means
in old English to hew and the Hebrew *bara* / to create, even,
properly means to hew. But life and living things are not
naturally said to be hewn: they grow, and their growth is by
trickling increment.

I will not now interpret the thought of the sestet. It is
however, so far as I can see, both exact and pregnant.

I am altogether at a loss to see your objection to *exploit*
and to *so we say*. You will allow—would, I shd. think, urge
on me—that where the ὄνομα κύριον[9] has nothing flat or

_____

* By the bye, some geologists say the last end of all continents and dry land altogether is to be washed into the sea
and that when all are gone 'water will be the world', as in the
Flood, and will still be deep and have to spare.

poor about it it is the best word to use in poetry as in prose, better I mean than its paraphrase. Now *exploit* is the right word, it is κύριον, there is no other for the thing meant but *achievement*, which is not better, and it is a handsome word in itself: why then should I not say it? Surely I should. By 'regular indoors work' I understand you to mean a drawing finished at home with the eye no longer on the object, something poorly thrown in to fill up a blank the right filling of which is forgotten. But 'so we say' is just what I have to say and want to say (it was made out of doors in the Phoenix Park with my mind's eye on the first presentment of thought): I mean 'This is what we commonly say, but we are wrong'. The line now stands 'Glory is a flame off exploit, so we say' and I think it must so stand.

I am warming myself at the flame of a little exploit of my own done last night. I could not have believed in such a success nor that life had this pleasure to bestow. Somebody had tried to take me in and I warned him I wd. take him in at our next meeting. Accordingly I wrote him a letter from 'the son of a respected livery and bait stables in Parteen [suburb of Limerick] oftentimes employed by your Honoured Father' asking for an introduction to one of the Dublin newspapers 'as Reporter, occasional paregraphs or sporting inteligence'. The sentence I think best of was one in which I said I (or he) could 'give any color which may be desired to reports of speeches or Proceedings subject to the Interests of truth which must always be the paremount consideration'. It succeeded beyond my wildest hopes and action is going to be taken. The letter is even to be printed in the *Nation* as a warning to those who are continually applying in the like strain; but before this takes place I must step in.

It is as you say about Addis. But why should you be glad? Why at any rate should you burst upon me that you are glad, when you know that I cannot be glad?

It seems there is something in you interposed between what shall we say? the Christian and the man of the world which hurts, which is to me like biting on a cinder in bread. Take the simplest view of this matter: he has made shipwreck, I am afraid he must even be in straits: he cannot support himself by his learned writings; I suppose he will have to teach. But this is the least. I hope at all events he will not pretend to marry, and especially no one he has known in his priestly life. Marriage is honourable and so is the courtship that leads to marriage, but the philanderings of men vowed to God are not honourable nor the marriages they end in. I feel the same deep affection for him as ever, but the respect is gone. I would write to him if I had his address, which, I am sorry to say, is still or was lately somewhere at Sydenham; for after bidding farewell to his flock he had not the grace to go away.

This is enough for the time and I will put off the lambing to another season. With kindest remembrances to Mrs. Bridges and Mrs. Molesworth, I am your affectionate friend

GERARD M. HOPKINS.

Oct. 20 '88.

TO HIS FATHER

University College, St. Stephen's Green, Dublin.

May 3 1889

MY DEAREST FATHER,—I am laid up in bed with some fever, rheumatic fever I suppose, but I am getting round. This is the first day I took to bed altogether: it would have been better to do so before. The pains are only slight, but I wish that Charlton Scott and Isidore de Lara would agree to plant a garden, a garden of sleep in my bed, as I am sleepy by day and sleepless by night and do not rightly sleep at all. I saw a doctor yesterday, who treated my complaint as a fleabite, a treatment which begets confidence but not gratitude.

I hope to hear better news of Mary, whose complaint, I am afraid, is far more obstinate than mine. I suppose it is neuralgia and a general nervous sinking. Give her my best love and wishes.

With best love to all, I am your affectionate son

GERARD.

TO HIS MOTHER

Written at F. Gerard's dictation.

University College, St. Stephen's Green, Dublin.

May 8. 89

MY DEAREST MOTHER,—My fever is a sort of typhoid: it is not severe, and my mind has never for a moment wandered. It would give me little pain were it not that while it was incubating I exposed my head to a cold wind, and took neuralgia which torments me now. Thank you for your letters and the flowers which duly revived in water: they are on my table now.

I wonder that none of you understood the allusion to the Garden of Sleep. It is a sentimental song which I thought you must be sick and tired of in England as it has now come over to us. Charlton or Clement Scott is the Author of the words. By every post he receives enquiries as to his meaning which he cannot give except that the Garden of Sleep is a poppy-grown churchyard in the Corner of the Cliff. He gives a text from Ruskin to the effect that all pure natures admire bright colours, referring to the poppies. Accordingly with his genius and his purity he must be a good catch. The Composer is Isidore de Lara who is represented with Byronic look[,] heavy moustaches and furred cloak. He sings his own songs. The piece is not without merit; but when you have heard it as often as I have taken beef tea and chicken jelly, you will have had enough of it.

I had a good deal of sleep last night. The nurse is first rate and every condition is present that could make a serious thing trifling. The only complaint I have to make is that food and medicine keep coming in like cricket balls. I have in fact every attention possible.

Best love to all—I am your affectionate son

GERARD.
per T. W.

VII

RELIGION

*Art and fame do not really matter, spiritually they
are nothing, virtue is the only good.*

TO ALEXANDER BAILLIE

[? Oak Hill, Hampstead, 10–12 Sept. 1865]

DEAR BAILLIE,—I read yr. letter with very great pleasure, though certainly my delay in answering does not look
like it. All I need say in direct reply is on the subject of mis-
apprehension. As you had a temptation to mislead me so
you must almost know I purposely affected to misapprehend,
not very much, but a little: I can best express what I did by
saying I minimised the implications of what you said and took
the words with the narrowest literality. I knew a great change
had taken place but not so soon as it appears I ought to have
done, and I was not so blind to yr. hints as you thought, for
twice I remember determining to write down something you
had said: the first time I neglected to do this till I had forgotten the words and the other time I cannot find that I did
so; however I meant to do it. I only name this to shew I was
alive to and interested in what you said.—In letter-writing it
is eminently true that it is *le premier pas qui coûte* (what
does it mean?), and therefore, as I know now I have once
begun I can go on, I shall put this letter by, as it is Sunday
and I want to do some reading.

Tuesday, Sept. 12. My fear was once that my extravagances (and perhaps also my pugnacity) might indispose you towards my opinions and I might stand in the way of truth. I hope you will logically put them out of the way as also things wh. can only be deplored and wh. must especially shock you in the *Dublin Review* and the *Church Times* and all other writings or men who have more of the effervescence and enthusiasm given by noble principles than of their moral and essential parts. I am writing more unreservedly and effusively than, except seldom, I could do; but as the mood is on me I will not gag it. You will no doubt with caution follow the developments of the Catholic principle wh. has approved itself to you, and I wd. not press anything out of place. But I may for once speak, as far as I am competent to understand them and, having recognised them—in a conscious and deliberate shape—longer than you, to say anything about them to another, of the difference the apprehension of the Catholic truths one after another makes in one's views of everything, beyond all others those of course of the blessed sacrament of the altar. You will no doubt understand what I mean by saying that the *sordidness* of things, wh. one is compelled perpetually to feel is perhaps, taking ἓν ἀνθ᾽ ἑνός,[1] the most unmixedly painful thing one knows of: and this is (objectively) intensified and (subjectively) destroyed by Catholicism. If people cd. all know this, to take no higher ground, no other inducement wd. to very many minds be needed to lead them to Catholicism and no opposite inducement cd. dissuade them fr. it. I ought perhaps not to say this as you cd. have said it just as well, but it is a view I have had in my thoughts lately, and I can speak of it as confirmed or excited by certain things possibly more detailed and definite than the subjects wh. it is likely have been more especially present to your mind. In whatever I have said in this letter—and generally—pray pardon any assumption, wh. I am afraid I must often have offended you with in old times when yr. opinions were not altogether fixed in shape, it being, though very wrong, a natural consequence fr. time to time of the irrepressible sense of holding the truth however unworthy one really was to hold it.

I have heard fr. Addis: it is wonderful how good he is. I

am teeming with thoughts, but I shall not say more about them, as it is time you had an answer to yr. letter and as they are in connection chiefly with a subject wh. you have one of yr. deep objections to, metaphysics. I am amused to find how very far the advance of thought or science is fr. being on every side an encroachment on Christianity. I think I see them retiring fr. old positions before it in important parts. I shall write again. See in this month's *Union R.* a *critique* on a certain Mrs. Seton—interesting.—Yr. affectionate friend,

G.M.H.

TO E. H. COLERIDGE[2]

[Balliol College, Oxford]

DEAR COLERIDGE,—I never wrote to congratulate you on your best essay wh. I meant to do. I was sincerely proud of you, and I had half thought beforehand it might be so.

I have thought often since you were here of what you said about the particular shape in wh. the doctrine of eternal punishment presented itself with offence to you. You said you know yr. repugnance was to view the issues of eternity as depending on anything so trivial and inadequate as life is. I do understand the point of view. But I think the answer wh. I have then comes at once—that in fact the argument tells the other way, because it is incredible and intolerable if there is nothing wh. is the reverse of trivial and will correct and avenge the triviality of this life. To myself all this trivialness is one of the strongest reasons for the opposite belief and is always in action more or less. Of course it is plain too that the belief in the future of theology destroys the triviality in proportion to its intensity. I think certainly that strong beliefs make ordinary goings on look more ridiculously trivial than they wd. otherwise, but then the trivialness is one to wh. oneself does not belong and fr. wh. one longs to bring other people. However this is to the same effect as what I said before; but I have thought of something wh. will weigh perhaps more as not being merely a reversal of yr. argument. I think that the trivialness of life is, and personally to each one, ought to be seen to be, done away with by the Incarnation—or, I shd. say the difficulty wh. the trivialness of life presents ought to be. It is one adorable point of the incredible condescension of the Incarnation (the greatness of which no saint can have ever hoped to realise) that our Lord submitted not only to the pains of life, the fasting, scourging, crucifixion etc. or the insults, as the mocking, blindfolding, spitting etc, but also to the mean and trivial accidents of humanity. It leads one naturally to rhetorical antithesis to think for instance that after making the world He shd. consent to be taught carpentering, and, being the eternal Reason, to be catechised in the theology of the Rabbins. It seems therefore that if the Incarnation cd. *versari inter* trivial men and trivial things it is not surprising that our reception or non-reception of its benefits shd. be also amidst trivialities.

Buchanan (Buchannan?) had no further message for you than that he was here. I see too that Ball is up. Believe me always yr. affectionate friend,

GERARD HOPKINS.

Jan. 22, 1866.

TO THE REV. DR. JOHN H. NEWMAN

REVEREND SIR,—I address you with great hesitation knowing that you are in the midst of yr. own engagements and because you must be much exposed to applications from all sides. I am anxious to become a Catholic, and I thought that you might possibly be able to see me for a short time when I pass through Birmingham in a few days, I believe on Friday. But I feel most strongly the injustice of intruding on yr. engagements or convenience and therefore, if that is the case, I shall think it a favour if you will kindly let me know that you are unable to see me. I do not want to be helped to any conclusions of belief, for I am thankful to say my mind is made up, but the necessity of becoming a Catholic (although I had long foreseen where the only consistent position wd. lie) coming upon me suddenly has put me into painful confusion of mind about my immediate duty in my circumstances. I wished also to know what it wd. be morally my duty to hold on certain formally open points, because the same reasoning which makes the Tractarian ground contradictory wd. almost lead one also to shrink from what Mr.

Oakley calls a minimising Catholicism. I say this much to take fr. you any hesitation in not allowing me to come to Birmingham if duties shd. stand in the way: you will understand that by God's mercy I am clear as to the sole authority of the Church of Rome. While much in doubt therefore as to my right to trouble you by this application, I wd. not deny at the same time that I shd. hope not to detain you long. I may perhaps in some way introduce myself by reminding you of an intimate college friend of mine, William Addis, who once had the pleasure of spending an hour with you at the Oratory; I think also he has written to you since: I have little doubt that in not a very long time he will become a Catholic. If I shd. be so happy as to hear before Friday that you cd. spare time to see me, I shd. hope to be at Birmingham that day and sleep there, or if you had any convenient time in the two or three weeks after that I shd. like to come over fr. Rochdale where I shall be staying at Dr. Molesworth's. But in ending I wd. again say that I beg you will have no hesitation, as I have no doubt you will not, in declining to see me if you think best.

Believe me, Reverend Sir, your obedient servant,

GERARD M. HOPKINS.

Oak Hill, Hampstead, N.W. Aug. 28, 1866.

TO ROBERT BRIDGES

DEAR BRIDGES,—I had not forgotten about Mr. Street. I called there today, but he was out: you shall hear however as soon as possible. At Mayer's too I was unsuccessful, for they had, it seemed to me, not much of the altar service of any kind and no bottles at all, only cruets, which were not to the purpose! I am not sure now where to apply but I will try and find out and, unless you want the bottle ordered or got more immediately than I can be sure of doing it, it will give me pleasure to go about it. Am I to design the stopper? if you wish it and it shd. turn out after all that my design wd. cost too much I cd. always fall back on the Maltese cross, wh. has no objection, I suppose, except that it is so common.

Dr. Newman was most kind, I mean in the very best sense,

for his manner is not that of solicitous kindness but genial and almost, so to speak, unserious. And if I may say so, he was so sensible. He asked questions which made it clear for me how to act; I will tell you presently what that is: he made sure I was acting deliberately and wished to hear my arguments; when I had given them and said I cd. see no way out of them, he laughed and said 'Nor can I': and he told me I must come to the church to accept and believe—as I hope I do. He thought there appeared no reason, if it had not been for matters at home of course, why I shd. not be received at once, but in no way did he urge me on, rather the other way. More than once when I offered to go he was good enough to make me stay talking. Amongst other things he said that he always answered those who thought the learned had no excuse in invincible ignorance, that on the contrary they had that excuse the most of all people. It is needless to say he spoke with interest and kindness and appreciation of all that Tractarians reverence. This much pleased me, namely a bird's-eye view of Oxford in his room the frame of which he had had lettered *Fili hominis, putasne vivent ossa ista? Domine Deus, tu nosti.* This speaks for itself. He told me what books to get and then left me at lunch-time to Mr. John Walford—discovered at football. Mr. Walford gave me lunch in the refectory and shewed all the school and the oratory, then walked back and took me to St. Chad's cathedral. He told me to remember him very kindly indeed to you and to say how glad he shd. be to see you on yr. way to Oxford, if you liked it. You have much common interest fr. Eton etc, and of course he wd. avoid all religious subjects, I am sure.

I am to go over fr. Oxford to the Oratory for my reception next term—early in the term I must make it, and since a Retreat is advisable for a convert. Dr. Newman was so very good as to offer me to come there at Xtmas, which wd. be the earliest opportunity for it. He thought it both expedient and likely that I shd. finish my time at Oxford, and next term at all events I shall be there, since I shall announce my conversion to my parents by letter at the time of my reception. And now I have even almost ceased to feel anxiety.—Sept. 22.

You were surprised and sorry, you said, and possibly hurt

that I wd. not tell you of my conversion till my going to Birmingham made it impossible any longer to conceal it. I was never sorry for one minute: it wd. have been culpably dishonourable and ungrateful, as I said before, not to have done one's best to conceal it: but I do not mean that, but this—the happiness it has been the means of bringing me I cd. not have conceived: I can never thank you enough for yr. kindness at that time. Notwithstanding my anxiety, which on the day we filled the aquarium was very great indeed, it gives me more delight to think of the time at Rochdale than any other time whatever that I can remember. I did not see Mrs. Molesworth at the last: will you give her for me my very greatest thanks for her kindness? Dr. Molesworth I did say Goodbye to. I am most distressed to think that the news of my conversion, if they hear it, may give them pain and alarm for you, but you must remember that when I came to Rochdale I did not look upon my reception as to be so soon as it really was to be. You see the point of what was on my mind at the vicarage was chiefly this, that my wishes about you cd. not be gained except at your own and their trouble and grief. This will make it plain how I feel that wherever I go I must either do no good or else harm.

Walford believed that Dolben had been mobbed in Birmingham. He went in his habit without sandals, barefoot. I do not know whether it is more funny or affecting to think of.

My father and mother are still abroad and are or will soon be at Dinan in Brittany, where it happens that Urquhart now is, coaching Morris. I hope they will meet. My mother, my brother says, has some prejudice about Urquhart, I conceive because he is looked upon as leading me over to Rome.

I heard first fr. Dr. Newman of Mr. Riddell's death. He was always most kind to me. He was so good that one scarcely can regret his loss, but for our college it is very sad and disastrous.

I did leave something behind, my sponge, wd. you be so kind as to bring it if you can, though I am afraid I cd. not ask for anything more inconvenient.

I am now going to see Mr. Street and I can find out fr. him, you know, any detail about the bottle. You shall hear this evening, if I have seen him.

Believe me, dear Bridges, with the utmost gratitude your very affectionate friend,

GERARD HOPKINS.

Oak Hill, Hampstead, Sept. 24, 1866.

TO THE REV. E. W. URQUHART[3]

DEAR URQUHART,—It was certainly wrong of me to be so much in a hurry about you. The difference between your stake and mine is very great and besides you have had this subject so long before you that it has no doubt come to turn on a great many points and got much complexity, whereas to me it was pretty simple—now of course I think, very simple. In fact as I told you my conversion when it came was all in a minute. Again I cd. not say that your talk influenced me in that direction: to see or hear 'Romanising' things wd. throw me back on the English Church as a rule. In fact it is almost implied by what I have told you that for a good time past I have been uninfluenced by anybody, especially fr. the Catholic side. I shall not enter into the points or point you raise except to say this: I cannot at all allow what you say about Dr. Newman. On the contrary I always think it is of all the errors about the Church the most fatal to Tractarians—very naturally. The report you speak of has been contradicted and, if it had not, all our experience goes to show that Dr. Newman is like no one else for the frequency and wrongness of the rumours he is the subject of. How many times has he been going to return to the Church of England? How many people has he not told to stick where they were? Why Mr. Lyford of Shoreditch, a man who is able to judge, firmly believes that he will come back and that he restrains Romanising Tractarians. Now of course I have small means of knowing which wd. satisfy you, but all the times I have heard Catholic opinion on the subject it is just the opposite thing which I have understood. You speak of him and Oxenham together: now the *Dublin* in reviewing Dr. Newman's letter said 'We cannot but think Dr. Newman has been rather hard' on the authors of the Marian sayings quoted by Dr. Pusey; Oxenham and Ffoulkes it calls heretics —and the *Dublin* is an extreme paper and represents, as Dr.

Newman says, nobody but itself. Oxenham is most different. I quite agree with what you say about him, but have you the slightest drawing towards his point of view? He minimises— does he not?—and concedes, and certainly that seems to me to be altogether the wrong thing. You must not therefore consider this idea of yours unchallenged in your reviews of your position.—Accordingly I shall wish to be sanguine but not impatient, and of course to force one's convictions is only harmful.

Strange to say you not only saw my father and mother but talked to them. It was at the Menhir de St. Samson. You had a young man with you (Morris, I suppose). There was a young man sketching the stone at the time. Afterwards you bowed to my father at passing him in a *boulevart*.

I will go to your lodgings.

Challis I have not told, nor Mr. Liddon. That is a deeply painful thought. I got no letter from him at Challis' conversion as you supposed. How kind of him to think of me, but how very sad!

Believe me yr. affectionate friend,

GERARD HOPKINS.

Hampstead. St. Francis, Oct. 4, 1866.

Kind remembrances to Morris.

TO THE REV. DR. JOHN H. NEWMAN

VERY REVEREND FATHER,—I have been up at Oxford just long enough to have heard fr. my father and mother in return for my letter announcing my conversion. Their answers are terrible: I cannot read them twice. If you will pray for them and me just now I shall be deeply thankful. But what I am writing for is this—they urge me with the utmost entreaties to wait till I have taken my degree—more than half a year. Of course it is impossible, and since it is impossible to wait as long as they wish it seems to me useless to wait at all. Wd. you therefore wish me to come to Birmingham at once, on Thursday, Friday, or Saturday? You will understand why I have any hesitation at all, namely because if immediately after their letters urging a long delay I am received without any, it will be another blow and look like intentional cruelty. I did not know till last night the rule about *communicatio in sacris*—at least as binding catechumens, but I now see the alternative thrown open, either to live without Church and sacraments or else, in order to avoid the Catholic Church, to have to attend constantly the services of that very Church. This brings the matter to an absurdity and makes me think that any delay, whatever relief it may be to my parents, is impossible. I am asking you then whether I shall at all costs be received at once.

Strange to say of four conversions mine is the earliest and yet my reception will be last. I think I said that my friend William Garrett was converted and received shortly after hearing of my conversion; just before term began another friend, Alexander Wood, wrote to me in perplexity, and when I wrote back to his surprise telling him I was a convert he made up his own mind the next morning and is being received today; by a strange chance he met Addis in town and Addis, who had put off all thought of change for a year, was by God's mercy at once determined to see a priest and was received at Bayswater the same evening—Saturday. All our minds you see were ready to go at a touch and it cannot but be that the same is the case with many here. Addis' loss will be deep grief to Dr. Pusey I think: he has known him so long and stayed with him at Chale in a retreat.

I shall ask F. William Neville to open and answer this in your absence.

Monsignor Eyre seemed to say that I ought not to make my confession by means of a paper as I have been used to do. Will you kindly say whether you wd. prefer it so or not?

Believe me, dear Father, your affectionate son in Christ,

                              GERARD M. HOPKINS.
18 New Inn Hall Street, Oxford.—St. Theresa [15 October], 1866.

P. S. And if you shd. bid me be received at once will you kindly name the day? The liberality of the college authorities will throw no hindrance in the way.

TO HIS FATHER

Oct. 16. [1866]

MY DEAR FATHER,—I must begin with a practical immediate point. The Church strictly forbids all communion in sacred things with non-Catholics. I have only just learnt this, but it prevents me going to chapel, and so yesterday I had to inform the Dean of Chapel. Today the Master sent for me and said he cd. not grant me leave of absence without an application from you. As the College last term passed a resolution admitting Catholics and took a Catholic into residence it has no right to alter its principle in my case. I wish you therefore not to give yourself the pain of making this application, even if you were willing: I am of age moreover and am alone concerned. If you refuse to make the application, the Master explains that he shall lay my case before the common-room. In this case there is very little doubt indeed that the Fellows wd. take the reasonable course and give me leave of absence fr. chapel, and if not, I am quite contented: but in fact I am satisfied as to the course our Fellows will take and the Master will at the last hesitate to lay the matter before them perhaps even. I want you therefore to write at once, if you will,—not to the Master who has no right to ask what he does, but to me, with a refusal: no harm will follow.

The following is the position of things with me. You ask me to suspend my judgment for a long time, or at the very least more than half a year, in other words to stand still for a time. Now to stand still is not possible, thus: I must either obey the Church or disobey. If I disobey, I am not suspending judgment but deciding, namely to take backward steps fr. the grounds I have already come to. To stand still if it were possible might be justifiable, but to go back nothing can justify. I must therefore obey the Church by ceasing to attend any service of the Church of England. If I am to wait then I must either be altogether without services and sacraments, which you will of course know is impossible, or else I must attend the services of the Church—still being unreceived. But what can be more contradictory than, in order to avoid joining the Church, attending the services of that very Church? Three of my friends, whose conversions were later than mine, Garrett, Addis, and Wood, have already been received, but this is by the way. Only one thing remains to be done: I cannot fight against God Who calls me to His Church: if I were to delay and die in the meantime I shd. have no plea why my soul was not forfeit. I have no power in fact to stir a finger: it is God Who makes the decision and not I.

But you do not understand what is involved in asking me to delay and how little good you wd. get from it. I shall hold as a Catholic what I have long held as an Anglican, that literal truth of our Lord's words by which I learn that the least fragment of the consecrated elements in the Blessed Sacrament of the Altar is the whole Body of Christ born of the Blessed Virgin, before which the whole host of saints and angels as it lies on the altar trembles with adoration. This belief once got is the life of the soul and when I doubted it I shd. become an atheist the next day. But, as Monsignor Eyre says, it is a gross superstition unless guaranteed by infallibility. I cannot hold this doctrine confessedly except as a Tractarian or a Catholic: the Tractarian ground I have seen broken to pieces under my feet. What end then can be served by a delay in wh. I shd. go on believing this doctrine as long as I believed in God and shd. be by the fact of my belief drawn by a lasting strain towards the Catholic Church?

About my hastiness I wish to say this. If the question which is the Church of Christ? cd. only be settled by laborious search, a year and ten years and a lifetime are too little, when the vastness of the subject of theology is taken into account. But God must have made his Church such as to attract and convince the poor and unlearned as well as the learned. And surely it is true, though it will sound pride to say it, that the judgment of one who has seen both sides for a week is better than his who has seen only one for a lifetime. I am surprised you shd. say fancy and aesthetic tastes have led me to my present state of mind: these wd. be better satisfied in the Church of England, for bad taste is always meeting one in the accessories of Catholicism. My conversion is due to the following reasons mainly (I have put them down without order)—(i) simple and strictly drawn arguments partly my own, partly others', (ii) common sense, (iii) reading the Bible, especially the Holy Gospels, where texts like 'Thou art Peter' (the evasions proposed for this alone are enough to make one a Catholic) and the manifest position of St. Peter among the Apostles so pursued me that at one time I thought it best to stop thinking of them, (iv) an increasing knowledge of the Catholic system (at first under the form of Tractarianism, later in its genuine place), which only wants to be known in order to be loved—its consolations, its marvellous ideal of holiness, the faith and devotion of its children, its multiplicity, its array of saints and martyrs, its consistency and unity, its glowing prayers, the daring majesty of its claims, etc etc. You speak of the claims of the Church of England, but it is to me the strange thing that the Church of England makes no claims: it is true that Tractarians make them for her and find them faintly or only in a few instances borne out for them by her liturgy, and are strongly assailed for their extravagances while they do it. Then about applying to Mr. Liddon and the Bp. of Oxford. Mr. Liddon writes begging me to pause: it wd. take too long to explain how I did not apply to him at first and why it wd. have been useless. If Dr. Pusey is in Oxford tomorrow I will see him, if it is any satisfaction to you. The Bishop is too much engaged to listen to individual difficulties and those who do apply to him may get such answers as young Mr. Lane Fox did, who gave up £30,000 a year just lately to become a Catholic. He wrote back about a cob which he wanted to sell to the Dean of some place and wh. Lane Fox was to put his own price on and ride over for the Bishop to the place of sale. In fact Dr. Pusey and Mr. Liddon were the only two men in the world who cd. avail to detain me: the fact that they were Anglicans kept me one, for arguments for the Church of England I had long ago felt there were none that wd. hold water, and when that influence gave way everything was gone.

You are so kind as not to forbid me your house, to which I have no claim, on condition, if I understand, that I promise not to try to convert my brothers and sisters. Before I can promise this I must get permission, wh. I have no doubt will be given. Of course this promise will not apply after they come of age. Whether after my reception you will still speak as you do now I cannot tell.

You ask me if I have had no thought of the estrangement. I have had months to think of everything. Our Lord's last care on the cross was to commend His mother to His Church and His Church to His mother in the person of St. John. If even now you wd. put yourselves into that position wh. Christ so unmistakeably gives us and ask the Mother of sorrows to remember her three hours' compassion at the cross, the piercing of the sword prophecied by Simeon, and her seven dolours, and her spouse Joseph, the lily of chastity, to remember the flight into Egypt, the searching for his Foster-Son at twelve years old, and his last ecstacy with Christ at his death-bed, the prayers of this Holy Family wd. in a few days put an end to estrangements for ever. If you shrink fr. doing this, though the Gospels cry aloud to you to do it, at least for once—if you like, only once—approach Christ in a new way in which you will at all events feel that you are exactly in unison with me, that is, not vaguely, but casting yourselves into His sacred broken Heart and His five adorable Wounds. Those who do not pray to Him in His Passion pray to God but scarcely to Christ. I have the right to propose this, for I have tried both ways, and if you will not give one trial to this way you will see you are prolonging the estrangement and not I.

After saying this I feel lighter-hearted, though I still can by no means make my pen write what I shd. wish. I am your loving son,

GERARD M. HOPKINS.
23 New Inn Hall Street. Oct. 17, 1866.

P.S. I am most anxious that you shd. not think of my future. It is likely that the positions you wd. like to see me in wd. have no attraction for me, and surely the happiness of my prospects depends on the happiness to me and not on intrinsic advantages. It is possible even to be very sad and very happy at once and the time that I was with Bridges, when my anxiety came to its height, was I believe the happiest fortnight of my life. My only strong wish is to be independent.

If you are really willing to make the application to the Master, well and good; but I do not want you to put yourself to pain. I have written a remonstrance to him.

Many thanks to Arthur for his letter.

TO THE REV. H. P. LIDDON

DEAR MR. LIDDON,—It may seem useless returning to what is quite past but there is one thing I wanted to say before and ought, to have done any good, to have said before which I shall say now. The two last letters you wrote and also a note from Dr. Pusey I got on Saturday night, in time to stop the last step if anything could, but my mind was made up. I wish to thank you for your kindness and even for the trouble you took to prevent my reception, for of course to you it was the right thing to do.

It wd. be most unreasonable to wish to put my conversion in such a light to you as to make it seem a justifiable thing, but I do want to prevent its being rationalised (as while an Anglican one always rationalised particular conversions) in such a way as to empty it of any influence it might have on any of my acquaintance, and therefore I am sorry I did not write before. You think I lay claim to a personal illumination which dispenses with the need of thought or knowledge on the points at issue. I have never been so unwise as to think of such a claim. There is a distinction to be made: in the sense that every case of taking truth instead of error is an illumination of course I have been illuminated, but I have never said anything to the effect that a wide subject involving history and theology or any turning-point question in it has been thrown into light for me by a supernatural or even unusual access of grace. If you will not think it an irreverent way of speaking, I can hardly believe anyone ever became a Catholic because two and two make four more fully than I have. I certainly said my conversion was sudden when it came, though the conviction which I wd. not acknowledge to myself was not sudden but old and always present, but this was quite natural: I had thought it my duty to resist the doubts of the English Church wh. were always assailing me, and this resistance was in the form of refusing to answer certain plain questions which I cd. not but be aware of or of answering them perversely. When at last I consented to listen to them it was not surprising that one minute shd. be enough to answer such questions as these—If there are Catholics who are not Roman Catholics, can the Church of Rome hold such people under sentence of loss of their souls and yet remain part of the Catholic Church? formally they are under this sentence, as is clearly expressed e.g. in the form of reconciling converts—or this: a Church committing itself to heresy falls out of the Catholic Church: can a Church enjoin sin and not fall out? for the Church is the guardian of faith and morals both: but the Church of Rome enjoins sin by enjoining submission under terrible penalties and this submission is *ex hypothesi* schism: to say schism is not a deadly sin as Dr. Pusey does is useless, for a true Church cannot command any sin however small. There was also the obvious question Can the one Church be three Churches at war (two out of the three claiming each to be the whole meanwhile)? The latter is a point of common-sense, but as common-sense is open to discussion I will speak only of the others, which are direct reasoning. Where the issues are so simple you must permit me to say that to search the Fathers or Church history for parallels is to throw reason overboard and to prefer confusion. Now there is only one thing which can suspend the free use of reason (though in fact you have not told me it was my duty to suspend it) and that is the infallible authority of the Church. Of course if the infallible Church says there are three Churches, the Roman, Eastern, and Anglican, *causa finita est,* it is sin to have a doubt, and indeed it is meaningless to talk of a question to be examined at all unless we are also going to examine the question with the Calvinists or even Mormons. But not only has the collective church never said this but the theory has not been known even to individual Churches in it before how long a time? Not at the time of the separation of East and West certainly, for both East and West claim to be the whole Church. Not fr. the Reformation, for Anglican divines (you will know whether all do or do not; many at all events do) regarded the Lutheran, etc bodies as helping to make up the Church. Not even fr.

the Tractarian movement, for Dr. Newman cd. at one time
without being out of harmony speak of the Church of Rome
as a Church insane. Has then the view that the whole infallible Church is made up of these three Churches, singly
fallible but as yet orthodox, been believed by a body of men
in the whole Church for more than 20 years? Of course as
the view of individuals I do not know its age or history but
individual views do not concern the Church; it is only with
some sort of collective voice or consent that Churches begin
to be compromised. I must have decided as I have done if I
had waited till after my Degree for a leisure time of thought,
but since the only claim the Church of England made on my
allegiance was by a theory of 20 years prevalence among a
minority of her clergy, it is not wonderful that the claims of
the Catholic Church broke down my efforts to wait that time
many months beforehand.

The above questions had not perhaps all the definiteness
then with which I put them now but still they were quite
clear.

Should you therefore ever again be speaking of our conversions I hope I may ask you as far as I am concerned (and
the others wd. say the same) not to lay them to any belief in
a personal illumination of the kind you spoke of, for I have
had no such belief. My conversion was only sudden or quick
because at last I consented to answer simple questions wh. I
had refused to answer before and of which in fact I had for
months known the answers. It is right for me to say this and
I ought to have said it before. I hope I have not said anything
more hardly than the truth needed.

Believe me, dear Mr. Liddon, always gratefully and affectionately yours,

GERARD M. HOPKINS.

Do not trouble yourself to write again: this needs no answer and I know how precious your time is.

Nov. 7, 1866.—23 New Inn Hall Street.

P.S. The Papal Supremacy on wh. you lay so much stress
I did not of course believe as an Anglican and do of course

believe as a Catholic, but it was one of the things I took up
in the change of the position and was no element in my decision.

TO ROBERT BRIDGES

Catholic Church, St. Giles's, Oxford Jan. 19 1879

DEAREST BRIDGES,—In introducing yours and Mr. Dixon's Muses to each other I find myself crossed. I have just
heard from him. He says his publishers are Smith, Elder, and
Co. and as he says nothing about being out of print (indeed
that would imply a run and a demand) no doubt you can still
get his books, now you know where. He says *he* cannot get
yours. Perhaps you told me the impression was sold—of the
pamphlet, the G. of L. I mean. But if so you must have some
copies. Could you not forward one 'with the author's compli-
ments' to the Rev. R. W. Dixon, Hayton Vicarage, Carlisle?
or else through me? I wish you would, and it is your own
interest, for a poet is a public in himself.

Now Mr. Dixon having asked me whether I did not myself
write, bearing in mind my prize poems at Highgate (where,
I dare say I told you, I first knew him) I told him yes and
what, and thereon he asks to see them, and so he shall when
I have them to send. Which reminds me that I hope you for-
warded the *Deutschland* as directed.

When we met in London we never but once, and then
only for a few minutes before parting, spoke on any important subject, but always on literature. This I regret very
much. If it had ended in nothing or consisted in nothing but
your letting me know your thoughts, that is some of them, it
would have been a great advantage to me. And if now by
pen and ink you choose to communicate anything I shall be
very glad. I should also like to say one thing. You understand
of course that I desire to see you a Catholic or, if not that, a
Christian or, if not that, at least a believer in the true God
(for you told me something of your views about the deity,
which were not as they should be). Now you no doubt take
for granted that your already being or your ever coming to be
any of these things turns on the working of your own mind,
influenced or uninfluenced by the minds and reasonings of

others as the case may be, and on that only. You might on reflection expect me to suggest that it also might and ought to
turn on something further, in fact on prayer, and that suggestion I believe I did once make. Still under the circumstances it is one which it is not altogether consistent to make
or adopt. But I have another counsel open to no objection
and yet I think it will be unexpected. I lay great stress on it.
It is to give alms. It may be either in money or in other
shapes, the objects for which, without knowledge of several
hospitals, can never be wanting. I daresay indeed you do give
alms, still I should say give more: I should be bold to say /
give, up to the point of sensible inconvenience. *Fieri non
potest ut idem sentiant qui aquam et qui vinum bibant:* the
difference of mind and being between the man who finds
comfort all round him unbroken unless by constraints which
are none of his own seeking and the man who is pinched by
his own charity is too great for forecasting, it must be felt: I
do not say the difference between being pinched and being
at one's ease, that one may easily conceive and most people
know, willynilly, by experience, but the difference between
paying heavily for a virtue and not paying at all. It changes
the whole man, if anything can; not his mind only but the
will and everything. For here something applies like the
French bishop's question to his clergy whenever one of them
came to tell him that he had intellectual difficulties and must
withdraw from the exercise of his priestly functions—*What
is her name?* in some such way a man may be far from belief in Christ or God or all he should believe, really and truly
so; still the question to be asked would be (not *who is she?*
for that to him is neither here nor there) but *what good have
you done?* I am now talking pure christianity, as you may
remember, but also I am talking pure sense, as you must see.
Now you may have done much good, but yet it may not be
enough: I will say, it is not enough. I say this, you understand, on general grounds; I am not judging from particular
knowledge, which I have no means to do and it would be
very wrong and indiscreet.

Jan. 23—I feel it is very bold, as it is uncalled for, of me to
have written the above. Still, if we care for fine verses how
much more for a noble life!

I enclose some lines by my father, called forth by the proposal to fell the trees in Well Walk (where Keats and other interesting people lived) and printed in some local paper. See what you think of them. And return them, please.

Believe me your affectionate friend

GERARD M. HOPKINS, S.J.

I forget if I ever told you that Addis had left the Oratory and become mission priest at Sydenham.

Our position here is quiet but we make a certain number of converts both from Town and Gown. Mrs. Paravicini, whose husband is Fellow of Balliol (he was my contemporary and is very kind) and her brother is Robert Williams, may be considered as belonging to both; she is a very sweet good creature. Small as Oxford compared to London is, it is far harder to set the Isis on fire than the Thames.

If you have any poetry to send I shall be very glad. If rough copy, I can mentally allow for the last touches.

It has occurred to me that your Pompeian bell may have been intended for a dog, cat, or other domestic animal and τοῖς ὄμμασιν ὑποτέταγμαι[4] might mean that the sound was to guide you where to look for the bearer. We have a belled cat in this house. And sheep bells and cattle bells serve this among others, indeed I suppose it is their first end. I do not see that it can have anything to do with the evil eye: the words wd. rather mean / I help the evil eye / than / I help against it.

I have been holding back this letter as if it wd. mellow with keeping, but it is no good. Jan. 24.

SERMONS

Christ our Hero

FOR SUNDAY EVENING NOV. 23 1879 AT BEDFORD LEIGH—
Luke ii. 33. *Et erat pater ejus et mater mirantes super his quae dicebantur de illo* (text taken at random)

ST. JOSEPH though he often carried our Lord Jesus Christ in his arms and the Blessed Virgin though she gave him birth and suckled him at her breast, though they seldom either of

them had the holy child out of their sight and knew more of
him far than all others, yet when they heard what Holy
Simeon a stranger had to say of him the Scripture says they
wondered. Not indeed that they were surprised and had
thought to hear something different but that they gave their
minds up to admiration and dwelt with reverent wonder on
all God's doings about the child their sacred charge. Brethren, see what a thing it is to hear about our Lord Jesus
Christ, to think of him and dwell upon him; it did good to
these two holiest people, the Blessed Virgin and St. Joseph,
even with him in the house God thought fit to give them
lights by the mouth of strangers. It cannot but do good to
us, who have not got him before our eyes to look at. And
though we do have him before our eyes masked in the
Sacred Host, at mass and Benediction and within our lips
receive him at communion, yet to hear of him and dwell on
the thought of him will do us good.

Our Lord Jesus Christ, my brethren, is our hero, a hero all
the world wants. You know how books of tales are written,
that put one man before the reader and shew him off handsome for the most part and brave and call him My Hero or
Our Hero. Often mothers make a hero of a son; girls of a
sweetheart and good wives of a husband. Soldiers make a
hero of a great general, a party of its leader, a nation of any
great man that brings it glory, whether king, warrior, statesman, thinker, poet, or whatever it shall be. But Christ, he is
the hero. He too is the hero of a book or books, of the divine
Gospels. He is a warrior and a conqueror; of whom it is written he went forth conquering and to conquer. He is a king,
Jesus of Nazareth king of the Jews, though when he came to
his own kingdom his own did not receive him, and now, his
people having cast him off, we Gentiles are his inheritance.
He is a statesman, that drew up the New Testament in his
blood and founded the Roman Catholic Church that cannot
fail. He is a thinker, that taught us divine mysteries. He is
an orator and poet, as in his eloquent words and parables
appears. He is all the world's hero, the desire of nations. But
besides he is the hero of single souls; his mother's hero, not
out of motherly foolish fondness but because he was, as the
angel told her, great and the son of the Most High and all

that he did and said and was done and said about him she laid up in her heart. He is the true-love and the bridegroom of men's souls: the virgins follow him whithersoever he goes; the martyrs follow him through a sea of blood, through great tribulation; all his servants take up their cross and follow him. And those even that do not follow him, yet they look wistfully after him, own him a hero, and wish they dared answer to his call. Children as soon as they can understand ought to be told about him, that they may make him the hero of their young hearts. But there are Catholic parents that shamefully neglect their duty: the grown children of Catholics are found that scarcely know or do not know his name. Will such parents say they left instruction to the priest or the schoolmaster? Why, if they sent them very early to the school they might make that excuse, but when they do not what will they say then? It is at the father's or the mother's mouth first the little one should learn. But the parents may be gossipping or drinking and the children have not heard of their lord and saviour. Those of you, my brethren, who are young and yet unmarried resolve that when you marry, if God should bless you with children, this shall not be but that you will have more pity, will have pity upon your own.

There met in Jesus Christ all things that can make man lovely and loveable. In his body he was most beautiful. This is known first by the tradition in the Church that it was so and by holy writers agreeing to suit those words to him/ Thou art beautiful in mould above the sons of men: we have even accounts of him written in early times. They tell us that he was moderately tall, well built and slender in frame, his features straight and beautiful, his hair inclining to auburn, parted in the midst, curling and clustering about the ears and neck as the leaves of a filbert, so they speak, upon the nut. He wore also a forked beard and this as well as the locks upon his head were never touched by razor or shears; neither, his health being perfect, could a hair ever fall to the ground. The account I have been quoting (it is from memory, for I cannot now lay my hand upon it) we do not indeed for certain know to be correct, but it has been current in the Church and many generations have drawn our Lord accordingly either in their own minds or in his images. Another proof of his beauty may be drawn from the words *proficiebat sapientia et aetate et gratia apud Deum et homines* (Luc. ii 52)/he went forward in wisdom and bodily frame and favour with God and men; that is/ he pleased both God and men daily more and more by his growth of mind and body. But he could not have pleased by growth of body unless the body was strong, healthy, and beautiful that grew. But the best proof of all is this, that his body was the special work of the Holy Ghost. He was not born in nature's course, no man was his father; had he been born as others are he must have inherited some defect of figure or of constitution, from which no man born as fallen men are born is wholly free unless God interfere to keep him so. But his body was framed directly from heaven by the power of the Holy Ghost, of whom it would be unworthy to leave any the least botch or failing in his work. So the first Adam was moulded by God himself and Eve built up by God too out of Adam's rib and they could not but be pieces, both, of faultless workmanship: the same then and much more must Christ have been. His constitution too was tempered perfectly, he had neither disease nor the seeds of any: weariness he felt when he was wearied, hunger when he fasted, thirst when he had long gone without drink, but to the touch of sickness he was a stranger. I leave it to you, brethren, then to picture him, in whom the fulness of the godhead dwelt bodily, in his bearing how majestic, how strong and yet how lovely and lissome in his limbs, in his look how earnest, grave but kind. In his Passion all this strength was spent, this lissomness crippled, this beauty wrecked, this majesty beaten down. But now it is more than all restored, and for myself I make no secret I look forward with eager desire to seeing the matchless beauty of Christ's body in the heavenly light.

I come to his mind. He was the greatest genius that ever lived. You know what genius is, brethren—beauty and perfection in the mind. For perfection in the bodily frame distinguishes a man among other men his fellows: so may the mind be distinguished for its beauty above other minds and that is genius. Then when this genius is duly taught and trained, that is wisdom; for without training genius is imperfect and again wisdom is imperfect without genius. But Christ, we read, advanced in wisdom and in favour with God and men: now this wisdom, in which he excelled all men, had to be founded on an unrivalled genius. Christ then was the greatest genius that ever lived. You must not say, Christ needed no such thing as genius; his wisdom came from heaven, for he was God. To say so is to speak like the heretic Apollinaris, who said that Christ had indeed a human body but no soul, he needed no mind and soul, for his godhead, the Word of God, thát stood for mind and soul in him. No, but Christ was perfect man and must have mind as well as body and that mind was, no question, of the rarest excellence and beauty; it was genius. As Christ lived and breathed and moved in a true and not a phantom human body and in that laboured, suffered, was crucified, died, and was buried; as he merited by acts of his human will; so he reasoned and planned and invented by acts of his own human genius, genius made perfect by wisdom of its own, not the divine wisdom only.

A witness to his genius we have in those men who being sent to arrest him came back empty handed, spellbound by his eloquence, saying/ Never man spoke like this man.

A better proof we have in his own words, his sermon on the mount, his parables, and all his sayings recorded in the Gospel. My brethren, we are so accustomed to them that they do not strike us as they do a stranger that hears them first, else we too should say/ Never man etc. No stories or parables are like Christ's, so bright, so pithy, so touching; no proverbs or sayings are such jewellery: they stand off from other men's thoughts like stars, like lilies in the sun; nowhere in literature is there anything to match the Sermon on the Mount: if there is let men bring it forward. Time does not allow me to call your minds to proofs or instances. Besides Christ's sayings in the Gospels a dozen or so more have been kept by tradition and are to be found in the works of the Fathers and early writers and one even in the Scripture itself: It is more blessed etc. When these sayings are gathered together, though one cannot feel sure of every one, yet reading all in one view they make me say/ These must be Christ's, never man etc. One is: Never rejoice but when you look upon your brother in love. Another is: My mystery is for me and for the children of my house.

And if you wish for another still greater proof of his genius and wisdom look at this Catholic Church that he founded, its ranks and constitution, its rites and sacraments.

Now in the third place, far higher than beauty of the body, higher than genius and wisdom the beauty of the mind, comes the beauty of his character, his character as man. For the most part his very enemies, those that do not believe in him, allow that a character so noble was never seen in human mould. Plato the heathen, the greatest of the Greek philosophers, foretold of him: he drew by his wisdom a picture of the just man in his justice crucified and it was fulfilled in Christ. Poor was his station, laborious his life, bitter his ending: through poverty, through labour, through crucifixion his majesty of nature more shines. No heart as his was ever so tender, but tenderness was not all: this heart so tender was as brave, it could be stern. He found the thought of his Passion past bearing, yet he went through with it. He was feared when he chose: he took a whip and singlehanded cleared the temple. The thought of his gentleness towards children, towards the afflicted, towards sinners, is often dwelt on; that of his courage less. But for my part I like to feel that I should have feared him. We hear also of his love, as for John and Lazarus; and even love at first sight, as of the young man that had kept all the commandments from his childhood. But he warned or rebuked his best friends when need was, as Peter, Martha, and even his mother. For, as St. John says, he was full both of grace and of truth.

But, brethren, from all that might be said of his character I single out one point and beg you to notice that. He loved to praise, he loved to reward. He knew what was in man, he best knew men's faults and yet he was the warmest in their praise. When he worked a miracle he would grace it with/ Thy faith hath saved thee, that it might almost seem the receiver's work, not his. He said of Nathaniel that he was an Israelite without guile; he that searches hearts said this, and yet what praise that was to give! He called the two sons of Zebedee Sons of Thunder, kind and stately and honourable name! We read of nothing thunderlike that they did except,

what was sinful, to wish fire down from heaven on some sinners but they deserved the name or he would not have given
it, and he has given it them for all time. Of John the Baptist
he said that his greater was not born of women. He said to
Peter/ Thou art Rock/ and rewarded a moment's acknowledgment of him with the lasting headship of his Church. He de-
fended Magdalen and took means that the story of her generosity should be told for ever. And though he bids *us* say we
are unprofitable servants, yet he himself will say to each of
us/Good and faithful servant, well done.

And this man whose picture I have tried to draw for you,
brethren, is your God. He was your maker in time past; hereafter he will be your judge. Make him your hero now. Take
some time to think of him; praise him in your hearts. You can
over your work or on your road praise him, saying over and
over again/Glory be to Christ's body; Glory to the body of
the Word made flesh; Glory to the body suckled at the
Blessed Virgin's breasts; Glory to Christ's body in its beauty;
Glory to Christ's body in its weariness; Glory to Christ's body
in its Passion, death and burial; Glory to Christ's body risen;
Glory to Christ's body in the Blessed Sacrament; Glory to
Christ's soul; Glory to his genius and wisdom; Glory to his
unsearchable thoughts; Glory to his saving words; Glory to
his sacred heart; Glory to its courage and manliness; Glory to
its meekness and mercy; Glory to its every heartbeat, to its
joys and sorrows, wishes, fears; Glory in all things to Jesus
Christ.

The Fall of Man

FOR SUNDAY EVENING JAN. 25 1880, SEPTUAGESIMA SUNDAY,
AT ST. FRANCIS XAVIER'S, LIVERPOOL—ON *the Fall of God's
First Kingdom*—'EVERY KINGDOM DIVIDED AGAINST ITSELF
SHALL BE MADE DESOLATE AND EVERY CITY (COMMON-
WEALTH) OR HOUSE DIVIDED AGAINST ITSELF SHALL NOT
STAND (Matt. xii 25.)'

I am to speak tonight of the fall of God's first kingdom, of
the Fall of Man. Those of you who have heard this month's
evening sermons will understand how this comes now in due
course. God entered in the beginning into a contract with

man that they two should make one commonwealth for their common good, which was that God might be glorified in man and man in God; God was the sovereign in this commonwealth and kingdom and man the subject; God by his providence, his laws and appointments and man by his obedience and execution of them undertook to bring this good about; both parties were bound by justice and in justice lived, which in man was called original justice, but lasted/ not long. It ended with the Fall, of which I am now to speak.

Before God was king of man he was king of angels and before man fell angels had fallen. Then man was made that he might fill the place of angels. But Satan, who had fallen through pride and selflove, resolved that through pride and selflove man should be brought to fall and that, whereas a breach had been made in God's kingdom in heaven, God's kingdom on earth should be broken utterly to pieces. And as he could not do it by force he would do it by fraud. Now the wise assailant attacks the weakest spot, therefore Satan tempted Eve the woman.

He chose his disguise, he spoke by the serpent's mouth; he watched his time, he found Eve alone. And here some say she should have been warned when she heard a dumb beast speaking reason. But of this we cannot be sure: St. Basil says that all the birds and beasts spoke in Paradise: not of course that they were not dumb and irrational creatures by nature then as now, but if a black spirit could speak by them so could a white and it may be that the angels made use of them as instruments to sing God's praises and to entertain man. Neither would Satan needlessly alarm the woman, rather than that he would invisibly have uttered voices in the air. But when she heard what the serpent said, *then* she should have taken alarm. So then to listen to a serpent speaking might be no blame; but how came Eve to be alone? for God had said of Adam/ *It is not good for man to be alone: let us make him a helpmate like himself/*; and Eve was without the helpmate not like only but stronger than herself. She was deceived and Adam, as St. Paul tells us, was not nor would have been. Then why was Eve alone?

Now, I know, my brethren, that the Scripture does not tell us this and we cannot with certainty answer the question, but yet it is useful to ask it because it throws a great light on what God's first kingdom was and how it came to fall. Take notice then that, besides those things which we must do whether we like or no, which we cannot help doing, such as breathe, eat, and sleep, there are three sorts of things that we may lawfully do, that are right in us, that we are within our rights in doing. The first are *our bounden duties,* as to hear mass on Sunday: these God commands. The second are *what God sanctions* but does not command nor in any special way approve, as to amuse ourselves. The third are what God does not command but especially approves when done, as to hear mass on a weekday: these are called *works of supererogation.* All these are good, not only the things God commands and the things he specially approves and accepts but also the things he only sanctions, for he sanctions nothing but what is good, that is to say/ nothing but what is in itself harmless and which his sanction then makes positively good, and when a man says/ *I do this because I like it and God allows me/* he submits himself to God as truly as if it were a duty and he said/ *I do this because God wills it and commands me.* But though all are good they are not equally good; far from that. In the things God sanctions and we do for our own pleasure the whole good, the only good, comes from God's sanction and our submission to his sovereign will; for that he may reward us, but not for anything else: for the rest, we were doing our own pleasure and our own pleasure is our work's reward. But when we do what God commands or what God specially approves, then he is ready to reward us not only for our submission of ourselves to his sovereign will but also for the work done, for the pains taken; for we were doing *his* pleasure, not our own. Now you will easily understand, indeed you know, that it is the mark of a truly good will to do the good God approves of but does not bind us to, to do, in other words, works of supererogation: it shews that good is loved of itself and freely. And it is the mark of a cold heart, of a poor will, I will not say a bad one, to do nothing that God especially approves, only what he commands or else sanctions: it shews that there is little love of good for good's sake. And though no one can be lost but for sin, yet those who do the least good they lawfully can are very likely indeed to fall into doing *less than that least* and so to sin. Now if this applies to us now/ very strongly does it apply to man unfallen. For Adam and Eve though they were in God's kingdom not sovereign but subject, yet they were king and queen of all this earth, they were like vassal princes to a sovereign prince, God's honour was more in their hands than it is in any one of ours; we are but ourselves, they represented mankind, they represented the commons in God's commonwealth; if I dishonour God today one of you may make up by honouring him, but if they left him unhonoured who was to honour him? the beasts and birds and fishes? When Adam obeyed God/ mankind was obeying its sovereign; when Adam offered God of his own free will unbidden sacrifice/ mankind was all engrossed in a work of supererogation, in giving God fresh glory; when Adam was doing his own pleasure/ mankind was in its duty indeed but God's honour was not growing, the commonwealth was idle. Now, brethren, with this thought turn to Eve's temptation and look for what shall appear there.

Eve was alone. It was no sin to be alone, she was in her duty, God had given her freedom and she was wandering free, God had made her independent of her husband and she need not be at his side. Only God had made her for Adam's companion; it was her office, her work, the reason of her being to companion him and she was not doing it. There is no sin, but there is no delicacy of duty, no zeal for the sovereign's honour, no generosity, no supererogation. And Adam, he too was alone. He had been commanded to dress and keep Paradise. What flower, what fruitful tree, what living thing was there in Paradise so lovely as Eve, so fruitful as the mother of all flesh, that needed or could repay his tendance and his keeping as she? There was no sin; yet at the one fatal moment when of all the world care was wanted care was not forthcoming, the thing best worth keeping was unkept. And Eve stood by the forbidden tree, which God had bidden them not to eat of, which *she* said God had bidden them not even touch; she neither sinned nor was tempted to sin by standing near it, yet she would go to the very bounds and utmost border of her duty. To do so was not dangerous of itself, as it would be to us. When some child, one of Eve's poor daughters, stands by a peach-tree, eying the blush of colour on the fruit, fingering the velvet bloom upon it, breathing the rich smell, and in imagination tasting the sweet juice, the nearness, the mere neighbourhood is enough to undo her, she looks and is tempted, she touches and is tempted more, she takes and tastes. But in Eve there was nothing of this; she was not mastered by concupiscence, *she* mastered *it*. There she stood, beautiful, innocent, with her original justice *and with nothing else,* nothing to stain it, but nothing to heighten and brighten it: she felt no cravings, for she was mistress of herself and would not let them rise; she felt no generous promptings, no liftings of the heart to give God glory, for she was mistress of herself and gave them no encouragement. Such was Eve before her fall.

Now, brethren, fancy, as you may, that rich tree all laden with its shining fragrant fruit and swaying down from one of its boughs, as the pythons and great snakes of the East do now, waiting for their prey to pass and then to crush it, swaying like a long spray of vine or the bine of a great creeper, not terrible but beauteous, lissome, marked with quaint streaks and eyes or flushed with rainbow colours, the Old Serpent. We must suppose he offered her the fruit, as though it were the homage and the tribute of the brute to man, of the subject to his queen, presented it with his mouth or swept it from the boughs down before her feet; and she declined it. Then came those studied words of double meaning the Scripture tells us of: *What! and has God forbidden you to eat of the fruit of Paradise?*—Now mark her answer: you would expect her to reply: No, but of this one fruit only: he has given us free leave for all the trees of Paradise excepting one—but hear her: *Of the fruit of the trees in Paradise we do eat*—no mention of God's bounty here, it is all their freedom, what they do: 'we do eat'—*but the fruit of the tree in the midst of Paradise*—as though she would say/ of the best fruit of all—*God has commanded us not to eat of, nor so much as touch it, or we shall die: then* she remembers God when it is question of a stern and threatening law. She gave her tempter the clew to his temptation—that God her sovereign was a tyrant, a sullen lawgiver; that God her lord and landlord was envious and grudging, a rack-rent; that God her father, the author of her being, was a shadow of death. The serpent took the hint and bettered it. Well was he called subtle: he does not put her suggestion into words and make it blacker; she would have been shocked, she would have recoiled; he gives the thing another turn, as much as to say: Why yes, God would be all this if you took his law according to the letter. No no; what does 'death' mean? you will not *die:* you will die to ignorance, if you will, and wake to wisdom: *God knows, on the day you eat of it your eyes will be opened and you will be as gods, knowing good and evil.* And with these words he dealt three blows at once against God's kingdom—at God as a lawgiver and judge, at God as an owner or proprietor, at God as a father; at God as a lawgiver and judge, for the Serpent said/ God has made this the tree of the knowledge of good and evil, that is/ which shall decide for him whether to call you good or evil, good if you keep from it, evil if you touch it: be your own lawgivers and judges of good and evil; be as God yourselves, be divinely independent, why not? make it *good* to try the tree, *evil* to leave it untasted; at God as a proprietor, for as owner of man and the earth and all therein and sovereign of the commonwealth God had given the other trees of Paradise to his subjects but reserved this one to the crown: the Serpent advised them to trespass boldly on these rights and seize crown-property; and at God as a father, for God like a fatherly providence found them food and forbad them poison: the Serpent told them the deadly poison was lifegiving food. It was enough: Eve would judge for herself. She *saw that the tree was good to eat,* that it was *not* poison, it was the food of life—and here was the pride of life; *that it was beautiful to the eyes,* a becoming object to covet and possess—and here was the desire of the eyes; *and that it was delightful to behold,* that is/ sweet and enjoyable in imagination even and forecast, how much more in the eating and the reality!—and here was the desire of the flesh; she freely yielded herself to the three concupiscences; *she took and eat* of this devil's-sacrament; she rebelled, she sinned, she fell.

She fell, but still God's kingdom was not fallen yet, because it turned upon the man's obedience, not the woman's. Then came the meeting between the husband and the wife and she learnt that she was deceived and undone. Then her husband must share her lot for better and worse; this selfish and fallen woman would drag her husband in her fall, as she had had no thought of God's honour in her innocence, so in her sin she had no charity for her husband: she had so little love for him that she said, if he loved her he must share her lot. Most dearly he loved her, and she stood before him now lovely and her beauty heightened by distress, a thing never seen before in Paradise, herself a Tree of Knowledge of Good and Evil and offering him its fruit; herself a Tree of Life, the mother of all flesh to be. For he thought his hope of offspring would go with her. He was wrong: God, who gave back to Abraham for his obedience his all but sacrificed son, would have given back to Adam for his obedience his fallen wife; but he did not pause to make an act of hope. He listened to her voice. He left his heavenly father and clave to his wife and they two were in one fallen flesh; for her he took the stolen goods and harboured the forfeit person of the thief, rebelling against God, the world's great landlord, owner of earth and man, who had bestowed upon him Paradise, who had bestowed upon him the body of his wife; for her he eat the fatal fruit, making a new contract, a new commonwealth with Eve alone, and rebelling against God his lawgiver and judge. With that the contract with God was broken, the commonwealth undone, the kingdom divided and brought to desolation. God was left upon his rights but his tenant had refused him payment, God was left a father but his children were turned to children of wrath. Then followed the disinheriting of the disobedient son; then followed the first and most terrible of evictions, when Cherubim swayed the fiery sword and man was turned from Paradise; then followed the judgment of death and the execution of the sentence which we feel yet. *Wretched men that we are, who shall deliver us from this body of death?—The grace of God through Jesus Christ our Lord* (Rom. vii 24, 25.). *For the wages of sin are death, but the grace of God is eternal life in Christ Jesus our Lord* (ib. vi 23.), a blessing etc.

The Paraclete

FOR SUNDAY APRIL 25TH, THE 4TH AFTER EASTER, AT ST. FRAN-
CIS XAVIER'S, LIVERPOOL, ON THE GOSPEL JOHN xvi 5–14.
AND IN PARTICULAR 8–11. (*arguet mundum de peccato et
de justitia et de judicio*' etc)

Notes (for it seems that written sermons do no good)—This
Gospel and those for the other Sundays after Easter taken
from Christ's discourses *before* Easter, before his Passion, and
in particular from the discourse delivered at the Last Supper.
They are out of their season and why. Cannot give them the
proper attention when engrossed with the Passion. But when
he should be gone, Christ said, the Holy Ghost would remind
them of what he had said: that time is now and, very suit-
ably, at the earliest opportunity after Easter.

(However the Rector wishes me to write)

Brethren, you see that this Gospel I have just read is taken
from that discourse which Christ our Lord made to his disciples the night before he suffered. So is the Gospel for last
Sunday, so is the Gospel for next Sunday. The words we read
in these Gospels were spoken *before* Easter, on the night before the Passion, and we read them *after* Easter. They come
then out of their season. But this cannot be helped; it is reasonable, it is wise and right. During Lent, during Passiontide,
it is the Church's wish that the minds of Christians should be
full of the Passion, should be engrossed with Christ's suffer-
ings: the mind cannot pay full and proper heed to two
thoughts at once, cannot be in two moods at once, and so it
cannot, if it is fixed on Christ's sorrows and what he underwent, be free to dwell on Christ's wisdom and the words he
said. That must be put off, it has been wisely put off till after
Easter and yet not long after, but at the first suitable opportunity to Christ's words the Church returns and so you hear
them in last Sunday's and today's and next Sunday's Gospels.
But indeed Christ's own words on that same occasion explain
all: This, he says (xiv 26.), I have said to you while with
you, but when the Holy Ghost is come, *he* shall teach you all
my meaning and remind you of all I have said. That time is

now come: Christ is gone to heaven, the Holy Ghost has been sent and is, and has long been, at his work of teaching the Church Christ's meaning and reminding it of Christ's words. Therefore it comes about that with the assistance of the same Holy Ghost I must this morning endeavour to bring out Christ's meaning in that Gospel which is this day appointed to be read.

And that, brethren, is no easy task; for in this same Gospel of today are found words reckoned by writers on Holy Scripture to be among the very darkest and most mysterious that the sacred page contains. But since many enlightened minds and many learned pens have in the course of Catholic ages been busied upon them, it is now to be supposed that this darkness and mystery is in part cleared up and that with their help we need not go far astray. Bend then, my brethren, your ears and minds to follow and understand, for it is the Church that has appointed the words to be read and not for nothing, not for us to stare or sleep over them but to heed them and take their meaning; besides that it seems to me a contemptible and unmanly thing, for men whose minds are naturally clear, to give up at the first hearing of a hard passage in the Scripture and in the holiest of all kinds of learning to care to know no more than children know.

Here then are the mysterious words which we are to consider: *And when he,* that is the Holy Ghost, whom our Lord in this place calls the Paraclete, *has come he will convince the world of sin and of justice and of judgment,* and he adds a reason to each; *of sin,* he says, *because* so and so, *of justice because* so and so, *and of judgment because* so and so. This is what needs explanation and in explaining it/ by these steps I shall go: first I shall say what a Paraclete is and how both Christ and the Holy Ghost are Paracletes; then I shall shew what a Paraclete has to do with those three things, sin and justice and judgment; lastly I shall shew why Christ as a Paraclete would not do alone, why it was better for him to go and another Paraclete to come, why Christ's struggle with the world taken by itself looked like a failure when the Holy Ghost's struggling with the world is a success. And in so speaking the meaning of the text will, I hope, have by degrees grown plain.

THE FIRST IS TO SAY WHAT A PARACLETE MEANS. As when the Holy Ghost came at Whitsunday upon the Apostles there was heard a rush of air before the tongues of fire were seen/ so when we hear this name of Paraclete our ears and minds are filled with a confused murmuring of some mystery which we know to have to do with the Holy Ghost. For God the Holy Ghost is the Paraclete but what is a Paraclete? often it is translated Comforter, but a Paraclete does more than comfort. The word is Greek; there is no one English word for it and no one Latin word, Comforter is not enough. A Paraclete is one who comforts, who cheers, who encourages, who persuades, who exhorts, who stirs up, who urges forward, who calls on; what the spur and word of command is to a horse, what clapping of hands is to a speaker, what a trumpet is to the soldier, that a Paraclete is to the soul: *one who calls us on*, that is what it means, a Paraclete is one who calls us on to good. One sight is before my mind, it is homely but it comes home: you have seen at cricket how when one of the batsmen at the wicket has made a hit and wants to score a run, the other doubts, hangs back, or is ready to run in again, how eagerly the first will cry/ Come on, come on!—a Paraclete is just that, something that cheers the spirit of man, with signals and with cries, all zealous that he should do something and full of assurance that if he will he can, calling him on, springing to meet him half way, crying to his ears or to his heart: This way to do God's will, this way to save your soul, come on, come on!

If this is to be a Paraclete, one who cries to the heart/ Come on, no wonder Christ is a Paraclete. For he was one, he said so himself; though the Holy Ghost bears the name, yet Christ is a Paraclete too: *I will send you*, he says, *another Paraclete*, meaning that he himself was a Paraclete, the first Paraclete, the Holy Ghost the second. And did he not cry men on? Not only by words, as by his marvellous teaching and preaching; not only by standards and signals, as by his splendid miracles; but best of all by deeds, by his own example: he led the way, went before his troops, was himself the vanguard, was the forlorn hope, bore the brunt of battle alone, died upon the field, on Calvary hill, and bought the victory by his blood. He cried men on; he said to his disciples,

Peter and Andrew, James and John, Matthew at the custom-house, and the rest: Follow me; they did so; he warned all: He that would come after me let him deny himself and take up his cross and follow me; but when they would not follow he let them go and took all the war upon himself. *I have told you,* he said to those who came to arrest him, *that I am Jesus of Nazareth; if therefore you seek me let these go their way.* For though Christ cheered them on they feared to follow, though the Captain led the way the soldiers fell back; he was not for that time a successful Paraclete: *all,* it says, *they all forsook him and fled.* Not that they wanted will; *the spirit was willing: Let us go too,* said Thomas, *that we may die with him;* Peter was ready to follow him to prison and to death; *but the flesh was weak:* Peter denied him in his Passion, Thomas in his resurrection, and all of them, *all forsook him and fled.* I say these things, brethren, to shew you that God himself may be the Paraclete, God himself may cheer men on and they too be willing to follow and yet *not* follow, not come on; something may still be wanting; and therefore Christ said: *It is for your own good that I should go; for if I do not go away the Paraclete will not come to you, whereas if I go I shall send him to you.* The second Paraclete was to do what the first did not, he was to cheer men on *and they to follow;* therefore he is called, and Christ is not called, *the* Paraclete.

(2) I have said, brethren, what a Paraclete is and shewn that God the Son as well as God the Holy Ghost is a Paraclete. Next I am to say WHAT A PARACLETE HAS TO DO WITH THOSE THREE THINGS—SIN AND JUSTICE AND JUDGMENT.

If a Paraclete is one who cheers us on to good it must be good that is hard, good that left to ourselves we should hardly reach or not reach at all; it must be in the face of hardships, difficulties, resistance, enemies, that he cheers us on. For now, after the Fall, good in this world is hard, it is surrounded by difficulties, the way to it lies through thorns, the flesh is against it, the world is against it, the Devil is against it: therefore if a Paraclete cheers men on to good it will be to good that is hard. Now one way and another all that makes good hard is/ or comes from/ sin. So that a Paraclete must cheer us on to good *in the face of sin.* And one question out of three is soon answered: we see well enough what a Paraclete has to do with sin.

But a Paraclete has also to do with justice. And how?—Why, justice is that very good to which the Paraclete cheers men on. Justice in the Scripture means goodness. If a Paraclete cheers men on to goodness/ that is to say he cheers them on to justice. And yet, mark you, cheering men on against sin is not the same as cheering men on to justice, though now the two things go together. For if there were no sin in the world and yet man as dull in mind and heart as he is now/ a Paraclete might well be needed still to stir him up and set him on, to shew him what justice was and how great its beauty, before man would rouse himself to pursue it. And again if there were no true goodness in the world, nothing, I mean, that would make men just before God, yet if his law still bound them, forbidding sin, they would need a Paraclete to cheer them in resisting sin. However now the Paraclete does both at once, cheers us on to follow justice and to stand against sin. So much then of what a Paraclete has to do with sin and with justice.

There remains what a Paraclete has to do with judgment. Though the Paraclete's voice cry to men to come on to justice and cry to them to stand firm against sin, this will not do alone; the bare word will not do, nay the bare example will not do; there must be some bait before them and some spur and sting behind. This bait and this spur are the thought of God's judgments. There is the bait or prize of hope, the crown in heaven for the just, and there is the spur of fear, the fire of hell for the sinner. And the Paraclete waves before them that golden prize and plies their hearts with that smarting spur. And thus, brethren, it is clearly brought out that a Paraclete has to do, has everything to do, with sin, with justice, and with judgment.

(3) And now lastly we are to hear why it was good that Christ the first Paraclete should go and the Holy Ghost the second Paraclete, *the* Paraclete, should come and why this second Paraclete was to accomplish that task in the world which the first had not, *in his lifetime,* succeeded in accomplishing. This task was to convince the world of sin, of justice, and of judgment. The reason why Christ did not and the

Holy Ghost does is not certainly that God the Son is less powerful than God the Holy Ghost: *the Father*, says the Athanasian Creed, *is almighty, the Son almighty, and the Holy Ghost almighty, and they are not three almighties but one almighty;* their almightiness, their might, their power is one and the same thing. Neither is the reason that though Christ as God is almighty as man he is weak. No, *for the Father*, we read, *had put all things into his hands.* To understand it let us look at what this convincing the world of sin, justice, and judgment means.

When then it is said that the Paraclete *will convince the world* of three things it is meant that he will convict the world of its being wrong about these things, will convince it of himself being right about them, will take it to task about them, reprove it, and so bring the force and truth of his reproof home to it as to leave it no answer to make. He will take it to task upon three heads and leave it no answer. Now did Christ do this, did he leave the world no answer?—Certainly not. To all that Christ taught and did the world's answer was to put him to death and when he rose from the dead the world's answer for a time was that his disciples had stolen his corpse away—for a time; that is to say/ till the Holy Ghost came.

The world to which Christ spoke was, you know, not the world at large, not the Roman empire, much less the other kingdoms of the earth; he spoke only, as he said himself, to the House of Israel. And he did not convince the world he spoke to, he did not convince Israel. Neither indeed has the Holy Ghost convinced them yet, but then they are not the world he speaks to; they are but a very little part of it. To Christ they were the only world he spoke to and he did not convince them of his being in the right, did not convict them of their being in the wrong, on sin or on justice or on judgment. He spoke to them first of sin: he sent the Baptist before him to preach the baptism of repentance, then he came himself saying, as we read (Matt. iv 17.): *Repent, for the kingdom of heaven is at hand.* Did they repent? remember that when we say the world we mean most people, not a few: did most of the Jews, did the world of them repent?—They added to their sins by unbelief, they crowned their unbelief by crucifying him, the very prophet and Paraclete that thus reproved them.

Again he spoke to them of justice. He preached the Sermon on the Mount; he set before the world of them a new standard of goodness and of holiness; a justice higher than that, he said, of their Scribes and Pharisees; a justice indeed without which he said they could not enter into the kingdom of heaven, could not be saved. And not by words only but by his own example; he *did* and taught, he went about doing good, he challenged them himself to prove a fault aganst him: *Which of you,* he asked, *convinces or convicts me of sin?* They could not prove but they could accuse, they could not convict and yet they would condemn: they called him glutton and winebibber, sabbathbreaker, false prophet, blasphemer, deserving of death, no matter by what name, *a malefactor* any road, crying without shame to the Roman governor when he asked for a particular charge: *If he were not* A MALEFACTOR *we would not have brought him to thee.* And they prevailed: as a malefactor he was judged, between thieves he was crucified, *cum iniquis reputatus est/* he was counted among evildoers, Jesus Christ the just. So they were not convicted about sin nor about justice, they were not left without an answer, Crucify him/ was their answer, and they crucified him.

Of judgment it is the same. He warned them of God's judgments: unless they repented, he said, they should all perish; unless they believed in him they should die in their sins; the fallen angel was their father, his desires they would do and of course would share his fall; Depart, they would hear said to them, cursed, into everlasting fire, prepared for the Devil and his angels. Their answer was still the same: *he* was the sinner, the blasphemer, and cursed by God; it was *he* that was on the Devil's side and cast out devils by Beelzebub prince of the devils; it was *he* that by God's own law deserved to die—and should die too, by stoning or somehow: they failed to stone him, get him crucified they did. The world was not convinced about judgment nor put to silence; *he* was put to silence, put to trial, put to death, got rid of. And, mark you, brethren, it was not like a martyrdom now: the tyrant when he has done his worst upon the martyr knows that he has but cut off one Christian or ten or a thousand, there are others yet that he cannot reach; he may reck his rage on Christians, he cannot rid the world of Christianity. But when Christ the shepherd was struck down the sheep were scattered and without him would not have reunited; when the head was off the body would go to pieces; when Christ died all his words and works came to the ground, all seemed over for ever and the world his enemy's triumph looked that day complete.

But they did not know that their seeming triumph was total defeat, that his seeming defeat was glorious victory. For it was not the world Christ had come to fight but the ruler of this world the Devil. The world he came not to condemn but to save: *God did not send his son into the world,* Christ said, *to judge (or condemn) the world but that by him, the world might be saved.* Only while he preached to them, trying to save them, they were judged by their way of receiving him; therefore he said *Now it is the trial of the world, now the ruler of the world is to be cast out; and I though taken off the earth, got rid of from the earth, shall draw all things to me.* This then had happened: the rulers of this world, the devils, had crucified the Lord of Glory and at the instant of his death they saw themselves defeated, condemned, cast out, their empire of sin over the souls of men undone and the reins of power on all things drawn into the hand of the crucified victim. They felt it with unutterable dismay and despair but the world did not at that time feel it; the hellish head was crushed but the earthly members were not aware of a wound. They were therefore not convinced or convicted of their sin, of Christ's justice, or of God's judgments.

Christ was gone and in 50 days the Holy Ghost the new Paraclete came. He lost no time, but from nine o'clock in the morning of the first Whitsunday began his untiring agelong ever conquering task of convincing the world about sin and justice and judgment. But first he would play the Paraclete among the disciples before he went out to convince and convert the world. First he cheered *them,* but he cheered them on not like Christ by his example from without but by his presence, his power, his breath and fire and inspiration from within; not by drawing but by driving; not by shewing them what to do but by himself within them doing it. His mighty breath ran with roaring in their ears, his fire flamed in tongues upon their foreheads, and their hearts and lips were filled with himself, with the Holy Ghost. And they went forth and he went forth in them to convince the world. Hear a sample of how he convinces it. St. Peter spoke to the multitude, a crowd well representing the world, for there were men there, it is said, from every nation under heaven. At the end of his speaking 3000 souls were added to the Church. Three thousand were at one stroke convinced: here was a beginning of the world's being convinced and converted indeed. Hear too how it was done. First he told them that Jesus of Nazareth, a man marked by miracles with the stamp of God's approval, they had put to death: here then they were convinced of *their sin* because they had not believed in Christ. Then he said that this same Jesus God had raised again, that he had gone up to heaven, and that it was he who had that very day poured out the Holy Ghost: here then they were convinced of *Christ's justice*, because he had gone to the Father and could be seen no more. Lastly he bid them save themselves from that wicked generation, and they obeyed: they were then convinced that the world they had belonged to was doing the Devil's work and condemned like him; they were convinced what *God's judgment* on the world was, because its prince was Satan, and he was already judged.

And now, brethren, time fails me. Else I should shew you how the Holy Ghost has followed and will follow up this first beginning, convincing and converting nation after nation and age after age till the whole earth is hereafter to be covered, if only for a time, still to be covered, with the knowledge of the Lord. I should shew too the manner of his convincing the world, the thousand thousand tongues he speaks by and his countless ways of working, drawing much more than I have drawn from my mysterious text, but I must forbear: yet by silence or by speech to him be glory who with the Father and the Son lives and reigns for ever and ever. Amen.

TO R. W. DIXON

Manresa House, Roehampton, S. W. Dec. 1 1881

(the very day 300 years ago of Father Campion's martyrdom).

MY DEAR FRIEND,—I am heartily glad you did not make
away with, as you say you thought of doing, so warm and
precious a letter as your last. It reached me on the first break
or day of repose in our month's retreat; I began answering it
on the second, but could not finish; and this is the third and
last of them.

When a man has given himself to God's service, when he
has denied himself and followed Christ, he has fitted himself
to receive and does receive from God a special guidance, a
more particular providence. This guidance is conveyed partly
by the action of other men, as his appointed superiors, and
partly by direct lights and inspirations. If I wait for such
guidance, through whatever channel conveyed, about anything, about my poetry for instance, I do more wisely in every
way than if I try to serve my own seeming interests in the
matter. Now if you value what I write, if I do myself, much
more does our Lord. And if he chooses to avail himself of
what I leave at his disposal he can do so with a felicity and
with a success which I could never command. And if he does
not, then two things follow; one that the reward I shall nevertheless receive from him will be all the greater; the other
that then I shall know how much a thing contrary to his will
and even to my own best interests I should have done if I
had taken things into my own hands and forced on publication. This is my principle and this in the main has been my
practice: leading the sort of life I do here it seems easy, but
when one mixes with the world and meets on every side its
secret solicitations, to live by faith is harder, is very hard; nevertheless by God's help I shall always do so.

Our Society values, as you say, and has contributed to
literature, to culture; but only as a means to an end. Its history and its experience shew that literature proper, as poetry,
has seldom been found to be to that end a very serviceable

means. We have had for three centuries often the flower of
the youth of a country in numbers enter our body: among
these how many poets, how many artists of all sorts, there
must have been! But there have been very few Jesuit poets
and, where they have been, I believe it would be found on
examination that there was something exceptional in their circumstances or, so to say, counter-balancing in their career.
For genius attracts fame and individual fame St. Ignatius
looked on as the most dangerous and dazzling of all attractions. There was a certain Fr. Beschi who in Southern Hindu-
stan composed an epic which has become one of the Tamul
classics and is spoken of with unbounded admiration by those
who can read it. But this was in India, far from home, and
one can well understand that fame among Hindu pundits
need not turn the head of an Italian. In England we had Fr.
Southwell a poet, a minor poet but still a poet; but he wrote
amidst a terrible persecution and died a martyr, with circumstances of horrible barbarity: this is the counterpoise in
his career. Then what a genius was Campion himself! was
not he a poet? perhaps a great one, if he had chosen. His History of Ireland, written in hiding and hurrying from place to
place, Mr. Simpson in his Life says, and the samples prove it,
shews an eloquence like Shakspere's; and in fact Shakspere
made use of the book. He had all and more than all the rhetoric of that golden age and was probably the most vigorous
mind and eloquent tongue engaged in theological strife then
in England, perhaps in Europe. It seems in time he might
have done anything. But his eloquence died on the air, his
genius was quenched in his blood after one year's employment in his country. Music is more professional than poetry
perhaps and Jesuits have composed and well, but none has
any fame to speak of. We had one painter who reached excellence, I forget his name, he was a lay-brother; but then he
only painted flower pieces. You see then what is against me,
but since, as Solomon says, there is a time for everything,
there is nothing that does not some day come to be, it may
be that the time will come for my verses. I remember, by the
by, once taking up a little book of the life of St. Stanislaus
told or commented on under emblems; it was much in the
style of Herbert and his school and about that date; it was

by some Polish Jesuit. I was astonished at their beauty and brilliancy, but the author is quite obscure. Brilliancy does not suit us. Bourdaloue is reckoned our greatest orator: he is severe in style. Suarez is our most famous theologian: he is a man of vast volume of mind, but without originality or brilliancy; he treats everything satisfactorily, but you never remember a phrase of his, the manner is nothing. Molina is the man who *made* our theology: he was a genius and even in his driest dialectic I have remarked a certain fervour like a poet's. But in the great controversy on the Aids of Grace, the most dangerous crisis, as I suppose, which our Society ever went through till its suppression, though it was from his book that it had arisen, he took, I think, little part. The same sort of thing may be noticed in our saints. St. Ignatius himself was certainly, every one who reads his life will allow, one of the most extraordinary men that ever lived; but after the establishment of the Order he lived in Rome so ordinary, so hidden a life, that when after his death they began to move in the process of his canonisation one of the Cardinals, who had known him in his later life and in that way only, said that he had never remarked anything in him more than in any edifying priest. St. Stanislaus Kostka's life and vocation is a bright romance—till he entered the noviceship, where after 10 months he died, and at the same time its interest ceases. Much the same may be said of St. Aloysius Gonzaga. The Blessed John Berchmans was beatified for his most exact observance of the rule; he said of himself and the text is famous among us, Common life is the greatest of my mortifications; Gregory XVI (I think) when the first steps were to be taken said of him too: at that rate you will have to canonize all the Roman College. I quote these cases to prove that show and brilliancy do not suit us, that we cultivate the commonplace outwardly and wish the beauty of the king's daughter the soul to be from within.

I could say much more on all this, but it is enough and I must go on to other things. Our retreat ended on the 8th. The 'hoity toity' passage I have not seen; indeed I have never even had your book in my hands except one day when waiting to see Bridges in his sickness I found it on the table and was just going to open it—but to the best of my remembrance

I did not then open it either. I have for some years past had
to put aside serious study. It is true if I had been where your
book was easy of access I should have looked at it, perhaps
read it all, but in Liverpool I never once entered the public
library. However if, as I hope, the time for reading history
should ever come I shall try to read this one. You said once
you did not pretend not to have a side and that you must
write as an Anglican: this is of course and you could not hon-
estly be an Anglican and not write as one. Do you know Cobbett's *Reformation?* Cobbett was a most honest man but not
an honest Anglican; I shd. rather say that he was an honest
thinker and an honest speaker but not an honest actor-out
of his convictions but is a conspicuous 'bell in a bellcot' and
'signpost on a road'. The book is written with the greatest
violence of language; I must own that to me the strength
seems not at all too strong; but from the point of view of ex-
pediency it is far too much so, it has overshot its mark, and
those for whom it is meant will not read it. I much wish some
learned Catholic would re-edit it and bring it up to date. The
most valuable and striking part of it to me is the doctrine
about the origin of pauperism; I shd. much myself like to follow this out. My Liverpool and Glasgow experience laid upon
my mind a conviction, a truly crushing conviction, of the
misery of town life to the poor and more than to the poor, of
the misery of the poor in general, of the degradation even of
our race, of the hollowness of this century's civilisation: it
made even life a burden to me to have daily thrust upon me
the things I saw.

I have found to my dismay what I suspected before, that
my sister only sent you the music to two stanzas of your Song,
whereas I made it for six. How she came to make so dreadful an oversight I cannot tell: the music changes and she had
remarked on the change. But I must get her to send the rest
and then you will be able to judge of the whole. I do not
believe that my airs—if I can compare them with the work
of an accomplished musician—would really be found to be
like Mr. Metcalf's—to judge by the two pieces of his that
you sent me.

I should tell you that I by no means objected to the couplet 'Rattled her keys', I admired it as a happy medley: I thought the fusion or rather the pieing was less happy in the opening of the poem.

About the sonnet-writing I never meant to override your own judgment. I have put the objections to licentious forms and I believe they hold. But though many sonnets in English may in point of form be great departures from and degenerations of the type, put aside the reference to the type, and they may in themselves be fine poems of 14 lines. Still that fact, that the poet has tied himself within 14 lines and calls the piece a sonnet, lays him open to objection.

I must hold that you and Morris belong to one school, and that though you should neither of you have read a line of the other's. I suppose the same models, the same masters, the same tastes, the same keepings, above all, make the school. It will always be possible to find differences, marked differences, between original minds; it will be necessarily so. So the species in nature are essentially distinct, nevertheless they are grouped into genera: they have one form in common, mounted on that they have a form that differences them. I used to call it the school of Rossetti: it is in literature the school of the Prae-raphaelites. Of course that phase is in part past, neither do these things admit of hard and fast lines; still consider yourself, that you know Rossetti and Burne Jones, Rossetti through his sympathy for you and Burne Jones —was it the same or your sympathy for him? This modern medieval school is descended from the Romantic school (Romantic is a bad word) of Keats, Leigh Hunt, Hood, indeed of Scott early in the century. That was one school; another was that of the Lake poets and also of Shelley and Landor; the third was the sentimental school, of Byron, Moore, Mrs. Hemans, and Haynes Bailey.[5] Schools are very difficult to class; the best guide, I think, are keepings. Keats' school chooses medieval keepings, not pure nor drawn from the middle ages direct but as brought down through that Elizabethan tradition of Shakspere and his contemporaries which died out in such men as Herbert and Herrick. They were also great realists and observers of nature. The Lake poets and all that school represent, as it seems to me, the mean or standard of

English style and diction, which culminated in Milton but was never very continuous or vigorously transmitted, and in fact none of these men unless perhaps Landor were great masters of style, though their diction is generally pure, lucid, and unarchaic. They were faithful but not rich observers of nature. Their keepings are their weak point, a sort of colourless classical keepings: when Wordsworth wants to describe a city or a cloudscape which reminds him of a city it is some ordinary rhetorical stage-effect of domes, palaces, and temples. Byron's school had a deep feeling but the most untrustworthy and barbarous eye, for nature; a diction markedly modern; and their keepings any gaud or a lot of Oriental rubbish. I suppose Crabbe to have been in form a descendant of the school of Pope with a strong and modern realistic eye; Rogers something between Pope's school and that of Wordsworth and Landor; and Campbell between this last and Byron's, with a good deal of Popery too, and a perfect master of style. Now since this time Tennyson and his school seem to me to have struck a mean or compromise between Keats and the medievalists on the one hand and Wordsworth and the Lake School on the other (Tennyson has some jarring notes of Byron in *Lady Clare Vere de Vere, Locksley Hall* and elsewhere). The Lake School expires in Keble and Faber and Cardinal Newman. The Brownings may be reckoned to the Romantics. Swinburne is a strange phenomenon: his poetry seems a powerful effort at establishing a new standard of poetical diction, of the rhetoric of poetry; but to waive every other objection it is essentially archaic, biblical a good deal, and so on: now that is a thing that can never last; a perfect style must be of its age. In virtue of this archaism and on other grounds he must rank with the medievalists.

This is a long ramble on literary matters, on which I did not want to enter.

At Torquay Bridges made at last a sudden and wonderful recovery: so I am told, for he has not written. He then went abroad with a common friend of ours, Muirhead, and is, I suppose, likely to be abroad for the winter. And I am afraid when he returns I shall not see him; for I may now be called away at any time.

Earnestly thanking you for your kindness and wishing you all that is best I remain your affectionate friend

GERARD M. HOPKINS S.J.

Dec. 16 1881.

TO ROBERT BRIDGES

Manresa House, Roehampton, S. W. June 10 1882.

DEAREST BRIDGES,—It was a needless and tedious frenzy (no, the phrase is *not* like Flatman's 'serene and rapturous joys' to which poor Purcell had to drudge the music): another train came up on that train's tail, and indeed it was a dull duncery that overhung us both not to see that its being Ascot day ensured countless more trains and not fewer. There was a lovely and passionate scene (for about the space of the trump) between me and a tallish gentleman (I daresay he was a cardsharper) in your carriage who was by way of being you; I smiled, I murmured with my lips at him, I waved farewells, but he would not give in, till with burning shame (though the whole thing was, as I say, like the duels of archangels) I saw suddenly what I was doing.

I wish our procession, since you were to see it, had been better: I find it is agreed it was heavy and dead. Now a Corpus Christi procession shd. be stately indeed, but it shd. be brisk and joyous. But I grieve more, I am vexed, that you had not a book to follow the words sung: the office is by St. Thomas and contains all his hymns, I think. These hymns, though they have the imperfect rhetoric and weakness in idiom of all medieval Latin verse (except, say, the Dies Irae: I do not mean weakness in classical idiom—that does not matter—but want of feeling for or command of *any* idiom), are nevertheless remarkable works of genius and would have given meaning to the whole, even to the music, much more to the rite.

It is long since such things had any significance for you. But what is strange and unpleasant is that you sometimes speak as if they had in reality none for me and you were only waiting with a certain disgust till I too should be disgusted with myself enough to throw off the mask. You said something of the sort walking on the Cowley Road when we were last at Oxford together—in '79 it must have been. Yet I can hardly think you do not think I am in earnest. And let me say, to take no higher ground, that without earnestness there is nothing sound or beautiful in character and that a cynical vein much indulged coarsens everything in us. Not that you do overindulge this vein in other matters: why then does it bulk out in that diseased and varicose way in this?

Believe me your affectionate friend

GERARD HOPKINS S.J.

June 11—Since writing the above I have luckily come across the enclosed, which contains some of the hymns.

Remember me very kindly to Mrs. Molesworth, who is, I hope better. Also to Mr. Woolrych. Must meet him next time I am at—but I shall never be there by the by now.

I am just starting for Brentford.

ON ST. IGNATIUS'S SPIRITUAL EXERCISES

The Principle or Foundation

AN ADDRESS BASED ON THE OPENING OF THE SPIRITUAL EXER-
CISES OF ST. IGNATIUS LOYOLA

The Principle or Foundation—

Homo creatus est—CREATION THE MAKING OUT OF NOTHING, bringing from nothing into being: once there was nothing, then lo, this huge world was there. How great a work of power!

The loaf is made with flour; the house with bricks; the plough, the cannon, the locomotive, the warship/ of iron—all of things that were before, of matter; but the world, with the flour, the grain, the wheatear, the seed, the ground, the sun, the rain; with the bricks, the clay, the earth; with the iron and the mine, the fuel and the furnace, was made from nothing. And they are MADE IN TIME AND WITH LABOUR, the world in no time with a word. MAN CANNOT CREATE a single speck, God creates all that is besides himself.

But MEN OF GENIUS ARE SAID TO CREATE, a painting, a poem, a tale, a tune, a policy; not indeed the colours and the canvas, not the words or notes, but the design, the character, the air, the plan. How then?—from themselves, from their own minds. And they themselves, their minds and all, are creatures of God: if the tree created much more the flower and the fruit.

To know what creation is LOOK AT THE SIZE OF THE WORLD. Speed of light: it would fly six or seven times round the earth while the clock ticks once. Yet it takes *thousands of years* to reach us from the Milky Way, which is made up of stars swarming together (though as far from one another as we are from some of them), running into one, and looking like a soft mist, and each of them a million times as big as the earth perhaps (the sun is about that). And there is not the least reason to think that is anything like the size of the whole world. And all arose at a word! So that the greatest of all works in the world, nay the world itself, was easier made than the least little thing that man or any other creature makes in the world.

Why did God create?—Not for sport, not for nothing. Every sensible man has a purpose in all he does, every workman has a use for every object he makes. Much more has God a purpose, an end, a meaning in his work. He meant the world to give him praise, reverence, and service; *to give him glory*. It is like a garden, a field he sows: what should it bear him? praise, reverence, and service; it should yield him glory. It is an estate he farms: what should it bring him in? Praise, reverence, and service; it should repay him glory. It is a leasehold he lets out: what should its rent be? Praise, reverence, and service; its rent is his glory. It is a bird he teaches to sing, a pipe, a harp he plays on: what should it sing to him? etc. It is a glass he looks in: what should it shew him? With praise, reverence, and service it should shew him his own glory. It is a book he has written, of the riches of his knowledge, teaching endless truths, full lessons of wisdom, a poem of beauty: what is it about? His praise, the reverence due to him, the way to serve him; it tells him of his glory. It is a censer fuming: what is the sweet incense? His praise, his reverence, his service; it rises to his glory. It is an altar and a victim on it lying in his sight: why is it offered? To his praise, honour, and service: it is a sacrifice to his glory.

The creation does praise God, does reflect honour on him, is of service to him, and yet the praises fall short; the honour is like none, less than a buttercup to a king; the service is of no service to him. In other words *he does not need it.* He has infinite glory without it and what is infinite can be made no bigger. Nevertheless he takes it: he wishes it, asks it, he commands it, he enforces it, he gets it.

The sun and the stars shining glorify God. They stand where he placed them, they move where he bid them. 'The heavens declare the glory of God'. They glorify God, *but they do not know it.* The birds sing to him, the thunder speaks of his terror, the lion is like his strength, the sea is like his greatness, the honey like his sweetness; they are something like him, they make him known, they tell of him, they give him glory, but they do not know they do, they do not know him, they never can, they are brute things that only think of food or think of nothing. This then is poor praise, faint reverence, slight service, dull glory. Nevertheless what they can *they always do.*

But AMIDST THEM ALL IS MAN, man and the angels: we will speak of man. Man was created. Like the rest then to praise, reverence, and serve God; to give him glory. He does so, even by his being, beyond all visible creatures: 'What a piece of work is man!' (Expand by 'Domine, Dominus, quam admirabile etc. . . . Quid est homo. . . . Minuisti eum paulo minus ab angelis'.) But man can know God, *can mean to give him glory.* This then was why he was made, to give God glory and to mean to give it; to praise God frée ly, wíllingly to reverence him, gládly to serve him. Man was made to give, and mean to give, God glory.

I WAS MADE FOR THIS, each one of us was made for this. Does man then do it? Never mind others now nor the race of man: DO I DO IT?—If I sin I do not: how can I dishonour God and honour him? wilfully dishonour him and yet be meaning to honour him? choose to disobey him and mean to serve him? No, we have not answered God's purposes, we have not reached the end of our being. Are we God's orchard or God's vineyard? We have yielded rotten fruit, sour grapes, or none. Are we his cornfield sown? we have not come to ear

or are mildewed in the ear. Are we his farm? it is a losing one
to him. Are we his tenants? we have refused him rent. Are we
his singing bird? we will not learn to sing. Are we his pipe or
harp? we are out of tune, we grate upon his ear. Are we his
glass to look in? we are deep in dust or our silver gone or we
are broken or, worst of all, we misshape his face and make
God's image hideous. Are we his book? we are blotted, we
are scribbled over with foulness and blasphemy. Are we his
censer? we breathe stench and not sweetness. Are we his sacrifice? we are like the sacrifice of Balac, of Core, and of Cain.
If we have sinned we are all this.

But what we have not done yet we can do now, what we
have done badly hitherto we can do well henceforward, we
can repent our sins and BEGIN TO GIVE GOD GLORY. The moment we do this we reach the end of our being, we do and
are what we were made for, we make it worth God's while
to have created us. This is a comforting thought: we need not
wait in fear till death; any day, any minute we bless God for
our being or for anything, for food, for sunlight, we do and
are what we were meant for, made for—things that give and
mean to give God glory. This is a thing to live for. Then make
haste so to live.

For IF YOU ARE IN SIN YOU ARE GOD'S ENEMY, you cannot
love or praise him. You may say you are far from hating God;
but if you live in sin you are among God's enemies, you are
under Satan's standard and enlisted there; you may not like
it, no wonder; you may wish to be elsewhere; but there you
are, an enemy to God. It is indeed better to praise him than
blaspheme, but the praise is not a hearty praise; it cannot be.
You cannot mean your praise if while praise is on the lips
there is no reverence in the mind; there can be no reverence
in the mind if there is no obedience, no submission, no service.
And there can be no obeying God while you disobey him,
no service while you sin. Turn then, brethren, now and give
God glory. You do say grace at meals and thank and praise
God for your daily bread, so far so good, but thank and praise
him now for everything. When a man is in God's grace and
free from mortal sin, then everything that he does, so long
as there is no sin in it, gives God glory and what does not give
him glory has some, however little, sin in it. It is not only

prayer that gives God glory but work. Smiting on an anvil, sawing a beam, white-washing a wall, driving horses, sweeping, scouring, everything gives God some glory if being in his grace you do it as your duty. To go to communion worthily gives God great glory, but to take food in thankfulness and temperance gives him glory too. To lift up the hands in prayer gives God glory, but a man with a dungfork in his hand, a woman with a sloppail, give him glory too. He is so great that all things give him glory if you mean they should. So then, my brethren, live.

The Principle or Foundation

'Homo creatus est'—Aug. 20 1880: during this retreat, which I am making at Liverpool, I have been thinking about creation and this thought has led the way naturally through the exercises hitherto. I put down some thoughts.—We may learn that all things are created by consideration of the world without or of ourselves the world within. The former is the consideration commonly dwelt on, but the latter takes on the mind more hold. I find myself both as man and as myself something most determined and distinctive, at pitch, more distinctive and higher pitched than anything else I see; I find myself with my pleasures and pains, my powers and my experiences, my deserts and guilt, my shame and sense of beauty, my dangers, hopes, fears, and all my fate, more important to myself than anything I see. And when I ask where does all this throng and stack of being, so rich, so distinctive, so important, come from/ nothing I see can answer me. And this whether I speak of human nature or of my individuality, my selfbeing. For human nature, being more highly pitched, selved, and distinctive than anything in the world, can have been developed, evolved, condensed, from the vastness of the world not anyhow or by the working of common powers but only by one of finer or higher pitch and determination than itself and certainly than any that elsewhere we see, for this power had to force forward the starting or stubborn elements to the one pitch required. And this is much more true when we consider the mind; when I consider my selfbeing, my consciousness and feeling of myself, that taste of myself,[6] of *I* and *me* above and in all things, which is more distinctive than the taste of ale or alum, more distinctive than the smell of walnutleaf or camphor, and is incommunicable by any means to another man (as when I was a child I used to ask myself: What must it be to be someone else?). Nothing else in nature comes near this unspeakable stress of pitch, distinctiveness, and selving, this selfbeing of my own. Nothing explains it or resembles it, except so far as this, that other men to themselves have the same feeling. But this only multiplies the phenomena to be explained so far as the cases are like and do resemble. But to me there is no resemblance: searching nature I taste *self* but at one tankard, that of my own being. The development, refinement, condensation of nothing shews any sign of being able to match this to me or give me another taste of it, a taste even resembling it.

One may dwell on this further. We say that any two things however unlike are in something like. This is the one exception: when I compare myself, my being-myself, with anything else whatever, all things alike, all in the same degree rebuff me with blank unlikeness; so that my knowledge of it, which is so intense, is from itself alone, they in no way help me to understand it. And even those things with which I in some sort identify myself, as my country or family, and those things which I own and call mine, as my clothes and so on, all presuppose the stricter sense of *self* and *me* and *mine* and are from that derivative.

From what then do I with all my being and above all that taste of self, that selfbeing, come? Am I due (1) to chance? (2) to myself, as selfexistent? (3) to some extrinsic power?

(1) Chance in name no one acknowledges as a cause or principle or explanation of being. But to call things positive facts and refuse further explanation is to explain them by chance. What then is chance proper, not chance as we use it for causes unknown or causes beside a present purpose?— Chance applies only to things possible; what must be does not come by chance and what cannot be by no chance comes. Chance then is the ἐνέργεια, the stress, of the intrinsic possibility which things have. A chance is an event come about by its own intrinsic possibility. And as mere possibility, passive power, is not power proper and has no activity it cannot of

itself come to stress, cannot instress itself. And in fact chance existence is a selfexistence. Chance is incredible or impossible by this *a priori* consideration, but more strikingly is it incredible from experience. It is never verified and the more examined the less is it verified, the more is it out of the question. For if it is a chance for anything at any given instant to exist and exist as so-and-so it is so for the next. These chances are equal and in any finite time it is infinitely unlikely that it should continue being and being what it was, for there are infinite instants. It is incredible then that its continued existence should be due to chance. If you say that its being is the mental flush of a string of broken existences at very small average intervals, this is incredible because monstrous. Moreover its nature should quite change, for its parts might chance elsewhere and the parts of other things here, and the variation will be infinite. The most plausible, if anything is plausible here, is that virgin matter is due to chance, other things not. But as this does not affect the present case it may be let alone. No man then can believe that his being is due to chance.

(2) Can I then be selfexistent and even in some way necessary?—This is clearly not true of my body and that crowd of being in me spoken of above, but may it be true of some part of it or something in it, *aliquid ejus,* the soul, the mind and its consciousness?

The mind and all my being is finite. This is plain in its outward and inward operations. In its outward, for there is a resistance in the body and things outside the body which it cannot overcome; there is a degree of effort, pain, weariness to which it yields. And in the inward; it has a finite insight, memory, grasp of apprehension, power of calculation, invention, force of will.

Nothing finite can exist of itself. For being finite it is limited and determined in time and space, as the mind is limited and determined to particular dates of time and place by the body. And apart from the body it is determined. I say apart from the body because it may be maintained that the mind has no bound from space nor even from time, for it may exist after death and may have existed before birth. Nevertheless it is finite in its own being, as said above, and determined. Its faculties compared one with another and compared with those of other minds are determined; they might be more, they might be less, they might be otherwise; they are then determined and distinctive. It is plain it has more perfection, more being. Nevertheless the being it has got has a great perfection, a great stress, and is more distinctive and higher selved, than anything else I see, except other such minds, in nature. Now to be determined and distinctive is a perfection, either self-bestowed or bestowed from without. In anything finite it cannot be self-bestowed; nothing finite can determine its own being, I mean its being as a whole; nothing finite can determine what itself shall, in the world of being, be. For to determine is a perfection, greater than and certainly never less than, the perfection of being determined. It is a function of a nature, even if it should be the whole function, the naturing, the selving of that nature. It always in nature's order is after the nature it is of. Nothing finite then can either begin to exist or eternally have existed of itself, because nothing can in the order of time or even of nature act before it exists or exercise function and determination before it has a nature to 'function' and determine, to selve and instress, with; how much less then when the very determination is what the determiner itself is to be and the selving what its self shall be like! And this is above all true of that inmost self of mine which has been said to be and to be felt to be, to taste, more distinctive than the taste of clove or alum, the smell of walnutleaf or hart'shorn, more distinctive, more selved, than all things else and needing in proportion a more exquisite determining, selfmaking, power.

But is it as a last alternative possible that, though neither my body nor the faculties and functions of my soul exist of themselves, there should be one thing in the soul or mind, as if compounded or selved-up with these, which does? a most spiritual principle in some manner the form of the mind as the mind or the soul is said to be of the body; so that my mind would be one selving or pitch of a great universal mind, working in other minds too besides mine, and even in all other things, according to their natures and powers and becoming conscious in man. And this would be that very/ distinctive self that was spoken of. Here we touch the *intellectus agens* of the Averrhoists and the doctrine of the Hegelians and others.

Whether anything of this sort can be true or not, alike I find that I myself can not be selfexistent. I may treat the question from the side of my being, which is said to be compounded, selved-up, or identified with this universal mind, or from the side of the universal mind itself. And first from my side.

The universal mind being identified not only with me but also with all other minds cannot be the means of communicating what is individual in me to them nor in them to me. I have and every other has, as said above, my own knowledge and powers, pleasures, pains, merit, guilt, shame, dangers, fortunes, fates: we are not chargeable for one another. But these things and above all my shame, my guilt, my fate are the very things in feeling, in tasting, which I most taste that selftaste which nothing in the world can match. The universal cannot taste this taste of self as I taste it, for it is not to it, let us say/ to him, that the guilt or shame, the fatal consequence, the fate, comes home; either not at all or not altogether. If not at all, then he is altogether outside of my self, my personality/ one may call it, my *me*. If not altogether, if for instance there is something done or willed which I am wholly chargeable with and answerable for and he only so far as I am a part of him, a function or selving of his, then only so far is he answerable and chargeable, and this difference may make the difference of mortal and venial sin and of a happy or unhappy fate. Put it thus: suppose my little finger could have a being of its own, a personal being, without ceasing to be my finger and my using it and feeling in it; if now I hold it in the candleflame the pain of the burning, though the selfsame feeling of pain, experienced by me in my finger and by my finger in itself, will be nevertheless unlike in us two, for to my finger it is the scorching of its whole self, but to me the scorching only of one finger. And beyond this, taking it morally, if I have freely put my finger into the flame and the finger is unwilling, but unable to resist, then I am guilty of my folly and self-mutilation, but my finger is innocent; if on the other hand my finger is willing, then it is more guilty than I, for to me the loss of a finger is but mutilation, but to my finger itself it 's selfmurder. Or if again it were selfsacrifice the sacrifice would be nobler in the finger, to which it was a holocaust, than in me, in whom it was the consuming of a part only. Though then I most intimately share my finger's feeling of pain, for indeed it is to me and to it one and the same, I do not share its feeling of self at all and share little, if I share any, of its guilt or merit, fortune and fate. So then the universal mind is outside of my inmost self and not within it; nor does it share my state, my moral standing, or my fate. And for all that this universal being may be at work in mine it leaves me finite: *I* am selfexistent none the more for any part the selfexistent plays in me.

And the same conclusion follows if I look at the matter from the other side, that of the universal mind or being itself. For (1) the universal being too must have its self, its distinctive being, and distinctive more than mine. For if this is what I find myself to have above all other things I see, except only my peers in nature, other men, this self, in its taste to me so distinctive, how much more this greater being! Now if it, or he, has the same intimate feeling, consciousness, of all that goes on in me as I have of what goes on in my finger, so that even I were to him like a part or member, or not to speak of parts or members in what is infinite, as a feature or a selving, yet as my self was outside mine so must this infinite being's self be outside of mine as clearly as mine is outside of his: he must be able to think, mean, and say *I* and *me* as much as I am and when he says them he does not mean me who write this. Then too if, as said above, he does (or not in the same degree) bear my guilt or merit or feel my shame, neither do I his: if e.g. it is ambition in him to want to be identified with or compounded or selved-up with all things, that is not my case nor my ambition, for I am compounded only with him and that by no choice of mine; if it is charity in him so to impart him self to all, that is not my case nor my merit either. And more generally (2) his *inlaw*, the law of his being is unlike mine, as the Ten of Hearts is unlike any one of the hearts in it: it is many or made of many, each of them is one. In fact his very composition with me, being a sample of his composition with other things, all things, makes him unlike me or any other one thing. If X is compounded with A, B, C, D, etc so as to give AX, BX, CX, DX etc, then X has its being in a series, which is its inlaw, but A and B or AX and BX have not. And if it has besides a simple being X besides the series, that makes the matter no better. Whether then the universal mind by *me* and *myself* means his Being X or his Being in the shape of the series AX, BX etc he has another self than mine, which is, say, CX; either way self tastes differently to him and to me.

For, to speak generally, whatever can with truth be called a self—not merely in logic or grammar, as if one said Nothingness itself—, such as individuals and persons must be, is not a mere centre or point of reference for consciousness or action attributed to it, everything else, all that it is conscious of or acts on being its object only and outside it. Part of this world of objects, this object-world, is also part of the very self in question, as in man's case his own body, which each man not only feels in and acts with but also feels and acts on. If the centre of reference spoken of has concentric circles round it, one of these, the inmost, say, is its own, is óf it, the rest are tó it only. Within a certain bounding line all will be self, outside of it nothing: with it self begins from one side and ends from the other. I look through my eye and the window and the air; the eye is my eye and of me and me, the windowpane is my windowpane but not of me nor me. A self then will consist of a centre *and* a surrounding area or circumference, of a point of reference *and* a belonging field, the latter set out, as surveyors etc say, from the former; of two elements, which we may call the inset and the outsetting or the display. Now this applies to the universal mind or being too: it will have its inset and its outsetting; only that the outsetting includes all things, with all of which it is in some way, by turns, in a series, or however it is identified. But then this is an altogether different outsetting from what each of those very things to its own particular self has. And since self consists in the relation the inset and the outsetting bear to one another, the universal has a relation different from everything else and everything else from everything else, including the universal, so that the self of the universal is not the self of anything else. In other words the universal is not really identified with everything else nor with anything else, which was supposed; that is/ there is no such universal.

(In shewing there is no universal a true self which is 'fetched' or 'pitched' or 'selved' in every other self, I do not deny that there is a universal really, and not only logically, thus fetched in the universals, but either it is selfless and they Selves, as may be the case in Man, or else it may be a true Self and they like its members only and not true Selves, something like which I am inclined to believe the species and individual in the brutes, or at least that the specific form, the form of the whole species, is nearer being a true Self than the individual. But these universals are finite only.

In the case of such a universal as humanity these questions would arise: *first* of the attributes—say the merit or guilt—of each member, each individual by and to itself; *next* those of the universal collectively, the average morality; *thirdly* those of each member considered as a pitch of the universal and so of the universal morality and the degree in which each agrees or disagrees with, avows or disavows this average morality.

Neither do I deny that God is so deeply present to everything ('Tu autem, O bone omnipotens, eras superior summo meo et interior intimo meo') that it would be impossible for him but for his infinity not to be identified with them or, from the other side, impossible but for his infinity so to be present to them. This is oddly expressed, I see; I mean/ a being so intimately present as God is to other things would be identified with them were it not for God's infinity or were it not for God's infinity he could not be so intimately present to things.

There is another proof that the universal being cannot be selved in or identified with all other things. Either the universal is selved not only in this world of things but in all possible ones or only in this one. If in all possible worlds then there is no difference between possible and actual and all possible and 'incompossible', incompatible, frames of being exist together or *are* together, for what coexist with a third thing (or are as true as a third thing) coexist with (or are as true as) one another. But this is absurd. Only then is this. Then this world must have been determined by the universal being out of all possible worlds, for, as shewn above, it could

not determine its own being or determine itself into being. If
so the universal exercises choice, is selfdetermining. But this
is a great proof of self. It has then a self independent of its
supposed selving in other things or, in other words it is not
selved in or identified with other things.

No thing then, including myself, is in any sense selfexistent
except this great being.

(3) The third alternative then follows, that I am due to an
extrinsic power.

(Remark that the assumption in no. 2 is to assume in oneself a hypostatic union.)—Aug. 12 1882.

The Contemplation to Obtain Love

The last mystery meditated on in the Spiritual Exercises is
our Lord's Ascension. This contemplation is that which comes
next in order, namely the sending of the Holy Ghost; it is the
contemplation of the Holy Ghost sent to us through creatures.
Observe then it is on love and the Holy Ghost is called Love
('Fons vivus, ignis, *caritas*'); shewn 'in operibus', the works
of God's finger ('Digitus paternae dexterae'); consisting 'in
communicatione' etc, and the Holy Ghost as he is the bond
and mutual love of Father and Son, so of God and man; that
the Holy Ghost is uncreated grace and the sharing by man
of the divine nature and the bestowal of himself by God on
man ('Altissimi donum Dei'): hence we are to consider
'quantum . . . Dominus desideret dare seipsum mihi in quantum potest'; hence also the repetition in pt. 2 of 'dans'. Remark also how after the benefits of creation and Redemption
he does not add, he means *us* to add, that of sanctification.
Again in Pt. 2 'templum', in 3. 'operatur' as above, in 4. 'a
sole . . . radii, a fonte aquae' ('*Fons* vivus, *ignis*') (Dec. 8
1881). All things therefore are charged with love, are
charged with God and if we know how to touch them give
off sparks and take fire, yield drops and flow, ring and tell of
him.[7]

'Faciens me templum, cum creatus sim ad similitudinem
et imaginem'—The word Temple at first sight hides the
thought, which is, I think, that God rests in man as in a place,

a *locus*, bed, vessel, expressly made to receive him as a jewel in a case hollowed to fit it, as the hand in the glove or the milk in the breast (Dec. 8 1881). And God *in forma servi* rests *in servo*, that is/ Christ as a solid in his member as a hollow or shell, both things being the image of God; which can only be perfectly when the member is in all things conformed to Christ. This too best brings out the nature of the man himself, as the lettering on a sail or device upon a flag are best seen when it fills

TO ROBERT BRIDGES

Stonyhurst College, Blackburn. Feb. 3 1883.

DEAREST BRIDGES,—I cd. not venture to ask that our library should subscribe half a sovereign for an *édition de luxe* of a new book by an almost unknown author; still less could I expect, nor shd. I like, you to present me, that is our library, with a copy. Here then is a downright deadlock and there is nothing for it but for me to wait for the second edition and then, like Brewer in the *Mutual Friend*, 'see how things look'.

Many thanks for the anthems. I remember now that I heard the first at Magdalen. Did you remark that the first 9 notes of the Hallelelujah are, with a slight change, the beginning of *Cease your funning*?

This is a terrible business about my sonnet 'Have fair fallen',[8] for I find that I still 'make myself misunderstood'. *Have* is not a plural at all, far from it. It is the singular imperative (or optative if you like) of the past, a thing possible and actual both in logic and grammar, but naturally a rare one. As in the second person we say 'Have done' or in making appointments 'Have had your dinner beforehand', so one can say in the third person not only 'Fair fall' of what is present or future but also 'Have fair fallen' of what is past. The same thought (which plays a great part in my own mind and action) is more clearly expressed in the last stanza but one of the *Eurydice*, where you remarked it.

I quite understand what you mean about gentlemen and 'damfools'; it is a very striking thing and I could say much on the subject. I shall not say that much, but I say this: if a gentleman feels that to be what we call a gentleman is a thing essentially higher than without being a gentleman to be ever so great an artist or thinker or if, to put it another way, an artist or thinker feels that were he to become in those ways ever so great he wd. still essentially be lower than a gentleman that was no artist and no thinker—and yet to be a gentleman is but on the brim of morals and rather a thing of manners than of morals properly—then how much more must art and philosophy and manners and breeding and everything else in the world be below the least degree of true virtue. This is that chastity of mind which seems to lie at the very heart and be the parent of all other good, the seeing at once what is best, the holding to that, and then of not allowing anything else whatever to be even heard pleading to the contrary. Christ's life and character are such as appeal to all the world's admiration, but there is one insight St. Paul gives us of it which is very secret and seems to me more touching and constraining than everything else is: This mind he says, was in Christ Jesus—he means as man: being in the form of God—that is, finding, as in the first instant of his incarnation he did, his human nature informed by the godhead—he thought it nevertheless no snatching-matter for him to be equal with God, but annihilated himself, taking the form of servant; that is, he could not but see what he was, God, but he would see it as if he did not see it, and be it as if he were not and instead of snatching at once at what all the time was his, or was himself, he emptied or exhausted himself so far as that was possible, of godhead and behaved only as God's slave, as his creature, as man, which also he was, and then being in the guise of man humbled himself to death, the death of the cross. It is this holding of himself back, and not snatching at the truest and highest good, the good that was his right, nay his possession from a past eternity in his other nature, his own being and self, which seems to me the root of all his holiness and the imitation of this the root of all moral good in other men. I agree then, and vehemently, that a gentleman, if there is such a thing on earth, is in the position to despise the poet, were he Dante or Shakspere, and the painter, were he Angelo or Apelles, for anything in him that shewed him *not* to be a gentleman. He is in the position to do it, I say, but if he is a gentleman perhaps this is what he will not do. Which leads me to another remark.

The quality of a gentleman is so very fine a thing that it seems to me one should not be at all hasty in concluding that one possesses it. People assume that they have it, take it quite for granted, and claim the acknowledgment from others: now I should say that this also is 'no snatching-matter'. And the more a man feels what it means and is—and to feel this is certainly some part of it—the more backward he will be to think he can have realised in himself anything so perfect. It is true, there is nothing like the truth and 'the good that does itself not know scarce is'; so the perfect gentleman will know that he is the perfect gentleman. But few can be in the position to know that and, being imperfect gentlemen, it will perhaps be a point of their gentlemanliness, for a gentleman is modest, to feel that they are not perfect gentlemen.

By the by if the English race had done nothing else, yet if they left the world the notion of a gentleman, they would have done a great service to mankind.

As a fact poets and men of art are, I am sorry to say, by no means necessarily or commonly gentlemen. For gentlemen do not pander to lust or other basenesses nor, as you say, give themselves airs and affectations nor do other things to be found in modern works. And this adds a charm to everything Canon Dixon writes, that you feel he is a gentleman and thinks like one. But now I have prosed my prose and long enough.

Believe me your affectionate friend
GERARD M. HOPKINS S.J.
Feb. 10 1883.

I am rueful and remorseful about P.F. But what else could come of handmade Dutch paper? I regret that Daniel made his offer. And I hope the 2nd edition will be this one's Jacob.

TO ROBERT BRIDGES

Stonyhurst, Blackburn. Oct. 24 1883.
DEAREST BRIDGES,—Thank you first for very kindly

copying out the poem on the Blessed Virgin and then for your letter.

You always do misunderstand me on matters like that prayer for Mrs. Waterhouse. I was not thinking of you and her, not, I mean, as using the prayers in that book or of your opinions as mirrored in them, but of the buyers of the book and the public it was meant for; which public I suppose you and Mrs. W. to know the mind and need of better than I do and therefore to be right in admitting one thing and excluding another: now in that public I regret, and surely I may, that it can no longer be trusted to bear, to stomach, the clear expression of or the taking for granted even very elementary Christian doctrines. I did not realise this well enough, did not realise that distinct Christianity damages the sale and so the usefulness of a well meant book; but now that I do what ought I to be but sorry?

But by the way you say something I want to remark on: 'Even such a doctrine as the Incarnation may be believed by people like yourself', as a mystery, till it is formulated, but as soon as it is it seems dragged down to the world of pros and cons, and '*as its mystery goes,* so does its hold on their minds'. You do not mean by mystery what a Catholic does. You mean an interesting uncertainty, the uncertainty ceasing interest ceases also. This happens in some things; to you in religion. But a Catholic by mystery means an incomprehensible certainty: without certainty, without formulation there is no interest (of course a doctrine is valuable for other things than its interest, its interestingness, but I am speaking now of that); the clearer the formulation the greater the interest. At bottom the source of interest is the same in both cases, in your mind and in ours; it is the unknown, the reserve of truth beyond what the mind reaches and still feels to be behind. But the interest a Catholic feels is, if I may say so, of a far finer kind than yours. Yours turns out to be a curiosity only; curiosity satisfied, the trick found out (to be a little profane), the answer heard, it vanishes at once. But you know there are some solutions to, say, chess problems so beautifully ingenious, some resolutions of suspensions so lovely in music that even the feeling of interest is keenest when they are known and over, and for some time survives the discovery.

How must it then be when the very answer is the most tantalising statement of the problem and the truth you are to rest in the most pointed putting of the difficulty! For if the Trinity, as Francis Newman somewhere says, is to be explained by grammar and by tropes, why then he could furnish explanations for himself; but then where wd. be the mystery? the true mystery, the incomprehensible one. At that pass one should point blank believe or disbelieve: he disbelieved, his brother at the same pass believed. There are three persons, each God and each the same, the one, the only God: to some people this is a 'dogma', a word they almost chew, that is an equation in theology, the dull algebra of schoolmen; to others it is news of their dearest friend or friends, leaving them all their lives balancing whether they have three heavenly friends or one—not that they have any doubt on the subject, but that their knowledge leaves their minds swinging; poised, but on the quiver. And this might be the ecstasy of interest, one would think. So too of the Incarnation, a mystery less incomprehensible, it is true: to you it comes to: Christ is in some sense God, in some sense he is not God—and your interest is in the uncertainty; to the Catholic it is: Christ is in every sense God and in every sense man, and the interest is in the locked and inseparable combination, or rather it is in the person in whom the combination has its place. Therefore we speak of the events of Christ's life as the mystery of the Nativity, the mystery of the Crucifixion and so on of a host; the mystery being always the same, that the child in the manger is God, the culprit on the gallows God, and so on. Otherwise birth and death are not mysteries, nor is it any great mystery that a just man should be crucified, but that God should fascinates—with the interest of awe, of pity, of shame, of every harrowing feeling. But I have said enough.

Oct. 25—Austin Dobson's triolet I knew well by quotation: I dare say it is the best the Rondeliers have done. The stupid fellow, to change it! Makes me think the worse of him. But yours may be carried, I think, a step farther: the fine subtlety of 'Said my ear to my eye' is not broad enough for a skit. I should put it into his own mouth and entitle it[9]

The expectations I raised in Mr. Patmore about Mano were my own and got from you: I had not then seen it. Afterwards however, when I had, I wrote to him that if he got it he wd. not be disappointed; whereas he is. I have not got it by me now and will not at present say more of it than this, that crowded as it is with beauties of the noblest sort, the deepest pathos and tragedy, besides a few touches of humour, finely conceived character, interest, romance, landscape, imagery, and unflagging music, still I am much of Mr. Patmore's mind: it either has not or else I have hitherto missed finding a leading thought to thread the beauties on—or almost worse, that I see one but it breaks and is unsatisfactory, namely that Mano is a kind of Adam and falls and also a kind of Second Adam and is crucified. I will write more hereafter.

I had not meant Mr. Patmore to know I wrote poetry, but since it has come naturally and unavoidably about there is no more to be said and you may therefore send me your book and I will point it and make a few corrections. You were right to leave out the marks: they were not consistent for one thing and are always offensive. Still there must be some. Either I must invent a notation applied throughout as in music or else I must only mark where the reader is likely to mistake, and for the present this is what I shall do.

I have a great deal more I could say, but must conclude.

I am your affectionate friend

GERARD HOPKINS S.J.

I may presently but will not just yet avail myself of your kind offer of the loose Purcells.

I have yet heard nothing particular about Grace. She will settle down and be happy: she is too simple-minded and too sweet-natured to let herself be soured or enfeebled by a grief. She may even come to care for someone else, though no doubt she does not believe she ever could.

NOTES ON POEMS

Many commentators, starting with Robert Bridges, have been consulted for the following notes. See 'Suggested Readings'.

I. POEMS

HEAVEN-HAVEN

7. *swell:* a long relatively low wave or an unbroken series of such waves.

THE HABIT OF PERFECTION

6. *shut:* a device used in shutting or closing, a bolt, a bar. 11. *ruck and reel:* jumble and tumult. 12. *coils:* ensnares. 13. *hutch:* cupboard. 24. *unhouse and house:* bring the Eucharist from the tabernacle and put it back. 27–28: *cf.* Matthew VI, 28–29.

THE WRECK OF THE DEUTSCHLAND

St. 1.8. *thy finger:* referring to grace, Hopkins wrote, '. . . . this is truly God's finger touching the very vein of personality, which nothing else can reach.' St. 2.5. when he heard of the wreck or, more likely, an earlier experience either at the time of his conversion or during an important Jesuit retreat. St. 3.2. *hurtle:* clashing conflict. St. 3.4. *that spell:* that time (noun) or that spell out (verb). St. 3.5. *Host:* God. St. 4: Disintegration and transiency are suggested by the figure of sand in an hourglass, stability and growth by the well fed by underground rivulets. St. 4.3. *mined:* as in undermined. St. 4.4. *combs:* as the sand sifts to its fall. St. 4.6. *roped . . . vein:* fed by a streamlet. St. 4.7. *fells:* hilly moors or mountains. St. 4.7. *voel:* Welsh for bare hill; also the name of a hill near the college Hopkins attended in Wales. St. 4.8. *gospel . . . gift:* grace. St. 5.5. *dappled-with-damson:* pied with violet. St. 5.7. *instressed, stressed:* 'God's nature, though a mystery, can and must "come to stress" in us, be impressed upon our being, through an "illumination" or an act of faith; it must then be dwelt upon, actualized and kept at stress by our own readiness to respond to further grace (as in 1.8.); moreover the truth of all this must be *stressed*, emphasized.' (Gardner) St. 6.2. The 'stress felt,' Redemptive grace, springs from Man's Fall (*felix culpa*). Since the Incarnation, its message, carried by the physical universe, predominates, and yet is difficult to accept. St. 7.1. refers to 'the stress felt' in St. 6. St. 7.7. *Though felt before:* even before the Incarnation and Redemption, as in the cases of certain Old Testament figures. St. 8.3. *sloe:* the fruit of the blackthorn with its astringent bittersweet flesh. St. 8.6. *Brim, in a flash, full:* tmesis for brimfull in a flash. St. 9.3 *dogged in den:* obstinately determined in its hideout. St. 10.5–6: apocalyptically as in the case of St. Paul or slowly and gradually as in the case of St. Augustine. St. 11.2. *flange:* the rim or edge of a railway wheel. St. 11.6. *Dust!:* a daring ellipsis in which a whole sentence is reduced to a single word. St. 11.8. *cringe:* to cause to cringe, cower. St. 11.8. *blear:* depriving of luster. St. 12.3. *tell:* count. St. 12.7. *bay:* the architectural figure may be suggested: a large partially enclosed space. St. 12.8. *reeve:* fasten, secure. St. 14.3. *combs:* crests, ridges. St. 14.4. *Kentish Knock:* a sandbar near the mouth of the Thames. St. 14.5. *bows:* the forward parts of the ship. St. 14.6. *beam:* the supports of the deck. St. 14.7. *whorl:* the screw propeller. (Gardner) St. 14.8. *wind:* in the nautical sense of to turn, to move; to guide a course, make a turn about for some goal. (Schoder) St. 15.8. *shrouds:* rigging but also their burial garments. St. 16.5. *dreadnought:* a coinage. St. 16.5. *thew:* sinew, strength, vitality, muscular power. St. 16.7. *cobbled:* rough, coarse. St. 16.8. *burl:* mottled whirling. St. 17.8. *told:* as Peters remarks the word *towered* suggests that the homophone *tolled* is also implied. St. 18.5. *after:* in the sense of pursuit after. St. 18.6–8. the paradox of the tragedy of suffering and the exultant realization that the nun had chosen correctly. St. 19.3. *inboard seas:* the seas rushing inside the ship's bulwarks or hull. *hawling:* combining the senes of hauling (changing the course of the ship) and howling. St. 19.4. *rash:* a wind-driven storm (Scotch). St. 19.6. *fetch:* stratagem; a dying gasp; but also a phantom double of a living person appearing as an omen of death (Christ). St. 19.8. *tops:* topsail or tops'l. St. 20.1. *first of five:* the tall nun was the religious superior. St. 20.3. *Deutschland . . . name:* because it is both the name of the ship and of Germany. St. 20.5. Both the virginal St. Gertrude and Luther are associated with the same German town. St. 21.5. *Orion:* Christ as the Hunter, the Pursuer. St. 21.6. *unchancelling:* throwing them out of sanctuary (chancel); also as Peters has suggested, not ruled by mere chance. St. 22.1. *finding:* suffering is the avenue for finding Christ; also device, emblem. *sake:* see under 'Practical Criticism' letter to Bridges May 26, 1879. St. 22.3. *Mark . . . make:* the first *mark* is probably verbal and imperative; man caused Christ's wounds. St. 22.7. *stigma:* stigmata, the wounds of Christ. *cinquefoil:* a rose having leaves of five divisions each. St. 23.1. *father Francis:* St. Francis of Assisi who founded the religious order to which the nuns belonged and who suffered the stigmata. St. 23.4. *Lovescape:* the pattern of the five wounds of the stigmata. St. 23.5. *seraph-arrival:* St. Francis is traditionally known as the Seraphic Father. St. 24.2. *Wales:* at the time of the shipwreck Hopkins was at St. Beuno's in Wales. St.

24.6. *catches and quails:* gasps and cowers. St. 25.2. *Breathe . . . Breath:* inspire me, O Holy Spirit. St. 25.4. *Breathe . . . Death:* Inspire me, O Christ. St. 25.6. cf. Matthew VII, 25. St. 25.7. *crown:* of martyrdom, of heaven. St. 26.8. cf. I Corinthians II, 9. St. 27.2. *jading:* cf. jade, a broken-down fatigued horse. St. 27.8. *burly:* cf. hurly-burly. St. 29.2. cf. Luke XI, 34. St. 29.3–4. Martin suggests that she saw 'Shape' in what seemed 'unshapeable,' saw meaning in what was apparently meaningless tragedy. St. 29.8. *Tarpeian-fast:* she was as stable as the Tarpeian rock in Rome. St. 30.3. *What . . . night:* the wreck had taken place on December 7th; on December 8th the feast of the Immaculate Conception is celebrated. St. 31.8. *shipwrack:* a coinage. St. 32.2. *Yore-flood:* the reference may be to the opening of Genesis or, since the art image appears in the next stanza, to the Great Deluge. St. 32.5. *motionable:* rather than suggesting instability this may imply that God can be moved by prayer and sacrifice. St. 32.8. *bodes:* foreshadows by means of signs. St. 33.3–4. *for . . . dark:* God's mercy descends lovingly pursuing the lingerer, even beyond the deathbed and into Purgatory. St. 33.5. *vein:* rich source. St. 33.8. *fetched:* (obs.) 'reached'; *i.e.* Christ, the giant, reached the 'uttermost mark'. (Gardner) St. 34.2. *Double-naturèd:* both God and Man. St. 34.3. *maiden-furled:* furled in the Blessed Virgin. St. 34.4. *Miracle-in-Mary-of-flame:* tmesis for Miracle of flame in Mary. St. 35.1. *door:* the shipwreck took place in the mouth of the Thames. St. 35.3. *roads:* a place where ships may ride at anchor, a roadstead. St. 35.5. *easter:* the noun coined into a verb. *dayspring:* the beginning of a new era or order of things. *crimson-cresseted:* a cresset is a torch, lantern, or beacon.

PENMAEN POOL

Place names in the poem are Welsh. 17. *Charles's Wain:* the Big Dipper made up of seven principal stars.

GOD'S GRANDEUR

1. *charged:* the electrical image is not irrelevant. 2. *shook foil:* glinting from gold or silver, etc. foil; or from a sword. 3–4. *like . . . crushed:* olive press; or the more cosmic processes of the formation of oil. 4. *reck his rod:* regard God's power, authority, or synecdoche for land or as in Isaiah II, 1, 'And there shall come forth a rod out of the stem of Jesse.'

THE STARLIGHT NIGHT

4. *delves:* pits, dens. 5. *quickgold:* coined by analogy with quicksilver. 6. *whitebeam:* a tree having leaves with white undersurfaces. *abeles:* white poplars. 7. the stars are like the feathers of frightened doves in a farmyard. 11. *sallows:* willows. 12–13. cf. Matthew XIII, 30. 13. *piece-bright paling:* enclosure bright with stars. 14. *hallows:* holy ones, saints.

SPRING

4. *timber:* the homophone *timbre* is also suggested. 5. *like . . . sing:* an example of synesthesia. 11–14. *Have . . . winning:* the subject is 'Christ, lord,' the imperative verbs are 'have, get,' the object is 'mind and Mayday' with numerous appositives.

THE LANTERN OUT OF DOORS

9–10. *wind . . . after:* '. . . I mean that the eye winds/only in the sense that its focus or point of sight winds and that coincides with a point of the object and winds with that. For the object, a lantern passing further and further away and bearing now east, now west of one right line, is truly and properly described as winding.' (Letter to Bridges) 13. *kind:* Christ's kind foot follows but also his foot follows his kind.

THE SEA AND THE SKYLARK

2. *trench:* make a deep impression. 5. *hear . . . ascend:* synesthesia. 6–8. *His . . . spend:* for an exegesis see under 'Practical Criticism' the letter to Bridges Nov. 26, 1882. 9–11. How these two put to shame this shallow and frail town! How our sordid turbid era, if it were pure, would ring out! 13. *make and making:* our nature and what we make.

THE WINDHOVER

The difficulties of this sonnet begin with the title. It is uncertain whether 'To Christ our Lord' is part of the title or a dedication. 1. *I caught:* elliptical for I caught sight of. *minion:* in the older sense of darling, favorite. *king-:* Hopkins separates in order to force the reader to proceed immediately to the following line. 2. *dapple-dawn-drawn:* etched against the dappled dawn or, preferably, drawn forth from. 3. *rung upon the rein:* a term in the manège of a horse and also a term in falconry. 6. *skate's heel:* the image is of ice skating. 9. *air:* mien, bearing. 10. *Buckle:* the word has two quite different sets of meanings: 1). fasten, bring together, enclose, prepare for action, apply intensively and with vigor, strive, etc. or 2). give way, crumple, collapse, bend, yield. 12. *sillion:* furrow; critics have suggested that either the sillion shines or the plough shines.

PIED BEAUTY

A curtal sonnet. 2. *brinded:* pied, dappled. 4. *Fresh-firecoal chestnut-falls:* fallen chestnuts like fiery coals. 6. *trim:* in the archaic sense, ready for service or use. 7. *counter:* not easily classified. *spare:* possibly in the sense of austere.

HURRAHING IN HARVEST

1. *barbarous:* bearded, barbed. *stooks:* shocks of grain. 4. *meal-drift:* a coinage suggesting cirrocumulus clouds. 6. *glean:* the har-

vesting image. 10. *as . . . very-violet-sweet:* the hills have the rugged quality of a stalwart stallion but they are also sweet with violets. 13. *wings:* possibly verbal.

THE CAGED SKYLARK

1. *scanted:* narrowly imprisoned. 3. *fells:* downs, moors, wild fields. 5. *turf:* according to an old custom, within the cage. 6. *spells:* charms, incantations; periods of time. 13. *meadow-down:* the delicate grass, etc.; also direction. 13–14. The meadow-down no more feels the encumbrance of the rainbow upon it than does man feel his risen body.

IN THE VALLEY OF THE ELWY

6–7. *as . . . spring:* as the mothering wing will make a hood over a bevy of eggs or as mild nights will make a hood over the new morsels of spring. 9. *combes:* valleys, ravines. 10. *air:* look, appearance, bearing.

THE LOSS OF THE EURYDICE

6. *furled:* in the sand and sea. 7–8. *flockbells . . . forefalls:* the bells of the flocks which were on the airy edges of the uplands. 12. *lade:* load, cargo. 16. *bole:* trunk. 23. *Boreas:* north wind. 29. *Carisbrook keep:* the fortress or stronghold at Carisbrook; most of the place names in the poem are from the Isle of Wight. 34. *royals:* sails. 37. *fell:* fierce, cruel. 48. *champ-white:* gnashing, trampling. 61. *afterdraught gullies:* the whirlpool caused by the sinking ship engulfs and swallows. 68. *rivelling:* rending, pulling, tugging; wrinkling. 99. *riving:* sundering, tearing away. 101–3. *That . . . one:* During the Middle Ages the English had such faith that they thought of the Milky Way as pointing the direction to the great shrine of Mary at Walsingham and Duns Scotus who was especially devoted to her, etc. 105–6. *O . . . one:* It is well for a mother who has lost a son or for a wife who has lost a husband or for a sweetheart who wanted to be reunited to her loved one to weep (or to have wept). 111–20. *'Holiest . . . eternal:* O holiest, loveliest, bravest Hero who saves, save my hero. And may you have heard the prayer, that you hear me making, at the time of the awful tragedy, may you have granted grace on that day when grace was needed. It is not that souls can be redeemed from hell but since we do not know the fate of souls until the Day of Judgment it is well to pray.

THE MAY MAGNIFICAT

5. *Candlemas, Lady Day:* February 2nd, March 25th. 21. *bugle blue:* a plant with blue flowers. 25. *sizing:* growing greater. 39. *thorp:* hamlet. 40. *silver-surfèd cherry:* the cherry trees covered with a foam of silver. 41. *azuring-over greybell:* the grey-blue changing to sky-blue.

BINSEY POPLARS

Binsey is near Oxford. 14–15. just as one prick of an eyeball will make it blind. 21. *únselve:* cause it to lose its inscape.

DUNS SCOTUS'S OXFORD

2. *rook-racked:* crow-infested; castellated. 4. *coped:* country and town attained an equipoise. 5. *brickish:* possibly a reference to the polluted river skirting Oxford. 7. *confounded:* spoiled, corrupted. 14. *Who . . . spot:* Scotus who in a famous defense of the Immaculate Conception enflamed France with devotion.

HENRY PURCELL

For a detailed exegesis see under 'Practical Criticism' the letter to Bridges Jan. 4, 1883. 1. *Have fair fallen:* 'This is a terrible business about my sonnet "Have fair fallen", for I find that I still "make myself misunderstood". *Have* is not a plural at all, far from it. It is the singular imperative (or optative if you like) of the past, a thing possible and actual both in logic and grammar, but naturally a rare one. As in the second person we say "Have done" or in making appointments "Have had your dinner beforehand", so one can say in the third person not only "Fair fall" of what is present or future but also "Have fair fallen" of what is past. The same thought (which plays a great part in my own mind and action) is more clearly expressed in the last stanza but one of the *Eurydice,* where you remarked it.' (Letter to Bridges)

PEACE

This curtal sonnet has many inversions ('Your round me roaming end, and under be my boughs' etc.) 4. *yield:* grant. 7. *reaving:* taking, seizing. 9. *plumes:* preens.

THE BUGLER'S FIRST COMMUNION

12. *Low-latched . . . housel:* humbly in the Eucharistic wafer which is as light as a leaf. 15. *vaunt- and tauntless:* vauntless and tauntless. 18. ellipsis; supply 'that' between ranks and sally. 36–37. '*and . . . lift':* let disappointment not kill those sweet hopes whose least quickenings lift me. 46. *brandle:* shake, shock, cause to totter.

MORNING MIDDAY AND EVENING SACRIFICE

2. *wimpled:* curved, rippled. 6. *fuming:* passing away, transient. 8. *thew:* sinew, muscular power. 17–21: For an explanation see under 'Personal Letters' to Bridges Nov. 18, 1879.

ANDROMEDA

The sonnet uses the Greek legend as an analogy for the Church facing special dangers in the 19th century but to be rescued by Christ.

THE CANDLE INDOORS

4. *Or . . . eye:* the fine lines of light from the candle subserviently obsequious to the movements of the eye. 8. *aggrándise:* make greater. 12–13: *cf.* Matthew VII, 3, 'And why beholdest thou the mote that is in thy brother's eye, but considerest not the beam that is in thine own eye?' 13–14: *cf.* Matthew V, 13, 'Ye are the salt of the earth: but if the salt have lost his savour, wherewith shall it be salted?'

THE HANDSOME HEART

For the background of this poem see under 'Practical Criticism' letter to Bridges Aug. 14, 1897. 4. The image of a compass is suggested. 5. *carriers:* homing pigeons. 7. *self-instressed:* 'impelled by its own inner impulse or natural dynamism.' (Schoder) 14. *strain:* inherent quality or disposition.

FELIX RANDAL

1. *farrier:* a smith who shoes horses. 6. *anointed:* the Sacrament of Extreme Unction. 7. *reprieve and ransom:* confession and the Eucharist. 8. *all road:* in whatever way. 13. *random:* stonemasonry in which the stones are not laid in regular courses. 14. *fettle:* shape, prepare, get ready.

SPRING AND FALL

1. *Márgarét:* coinage indicating a diminutive of endearment. 2. *Goldengrove:* coinage for autumnal woods. *unleaving:* losing its leaves; also persistently. 8. *wanwood:* woods that have lost their color. *leafmeal:* coinage suggesting leaves ground up under foot; also by analogy with piecemeal, leave by leaf. 9. *will weep:* grammatically futuritive, rhythmically volitional. 11. *springs:* the ever-renewed rebirths; also sources, wellsprings. 13. *ghost:* spirit, soul in the older sense as of a living person.

INVERSNAID

The setting is Scotland. 1. *burn:* brook. 3. *coop and in comb:* in confined places and in valleys. 4. *flutes:* makes music and/or splays into flutings. 6. *twindles:* a complex coinage. 7. *féll-frówning:* savagely frowning. 9. *degged:* dampened, sprinkled. 10. *braes:* banks, slopes. 11. *heathpacks, flitches:* patches of heath, slices or strips.

'AS KINGFISHERS CATCH FIRE, DRAGONFLIES DRÁW FLÁME'

3. *tucked:* tugged, plucked. *tells:* says, utters, reveals, expresses. 4. *Bow . . . tongue:* the bow and the tongue are technical parts of a bell. 7. *selves:* reveals its selfhood or inscape. 9. *justices:* used verbally. 11–14. *cf.* 'All the world's a stage' AYLI II, vii, 139.

RIBBLESDALE

The Ribble is a stream near Stonyhurst College where Hopkins was stationed. 2. *louchèd:* slouched (Brit. dial.). 10. *dogged:* obstinate. 12. *reave:* plunder, pillage, despoil. 13. *reck:* heed, regard.

THE LEADEN ECHO AND THE GOLDEN ECHO

4. *Dówn:* goes with *frowning;* warding off; but also, deeply wrinkled. 12. *ruck:* wrinkle, pucker. *winding sheets:* shrouds. 21. *Tall:* handsome, comely. 29. *To its own best being:* the glorified body in its resurrected and eternal state. 31. *lovelocks:* longlocks or curls of hair hanging over the shoulder. 38–39. *Nay . . . slept:* ' "Nay, what we had lighthanded" etc. means "Nay more: the seed that we so carelessly and freely flung into the dull furrow, and then forgot it, will have come to ear meantime" etc.' (Letter to Bridges) 42. *so fashed, so cogged, so cumbered:* so troubled, so weighed down, so deceived.

THE BLESSED VIRGIN COMPARED TO THE AIR WE BREATHE

5. *frailest-flixed:* frailest furred, downed, haired. 42. *almoner:* one who gives out alms on behalf of or in the name of another. 48. *ghostly:* spiritual. 79. *sapphire-shot: cf.* shot silk. 103. *So . . . old: cf.* Old Testament. 106. *daystar:* the sun, Christ. 119. *froward:* obstinate, wilful, wayward.

TO WHAT SERVES MORTAL BEAUTY?

2. *O-seal-that-so ' feature:* Hopkins's intention is suggested by an earlier version, 'face feature-perfect'. 6–8. *Those . . . Rome:* How could Pope Gregory have singled out from multitudinous Rome those handsome lads once upon a time who were captured at sea as a result of war? According to legend Pope Gregory going through the Roman market noticed a group of captives for sale as slaves and asked who they were. 'Angles', said his companions. 'No, not Angles, Angels,' said the Pope. As a result he sent Augustine to convert England.

SPELT FROM SIBYL'S LEAVES

1. *attuneable:* susceptible to being brought into harmony or being blended. 3. *hornlight:* the light of the horned moon or the soft yellow evening glow as of light from an old horn lantern (Schoder) or the last 'horny rays' of the setting sun (Gardner). 4. *earl-stars:* rising-stars (from O.E.). 6. *throughther:* syncope for 'through-other' (Gardner). *páshed:* beaten, smashed. 7. *round me:* counsel, whisper, address. 11. *párt, pen páck:* verbs. 12. *reckon:* consider, enumerate, count over. *reck:* heed, know. 13. *wáre:* suggests both 'be aware of' and 'beware of'. *tell:* matter, be of importance. 14. *sheathe- and shelterless:* sheatheless and shelterless.

(THE SOLDIER)

6–7. *It . . . smart:* The heart imagines, assumes, supposes, and holds precious the artist on the basis of his art and would like to find everything as genuinely sincere as its external attractiveness suggests; so also it considers that the external appearance of a soldier is the expression of all the finest military spirit. 10. *reeve:* fasten, etc.

(CARRION COMFORT)

With this the series of 'terrible sonnets' begins. 5–6 *rude . . . rock:* Why would you make me suffer with the rocking (verbal force) of your powerful right foot? 10. *coil:* trouble, tumult.

'NO WORST, THERE IS NONE. PITCHED PAST PITCH OF GRIEF'

2. *forepangs:* earlier paroxysms of extreme pain. 6. *on . . . sing:* cf. 'With an anvil-ding/ And with fire in him forge thy will' (*The Wreck of the Deutschland.* St. 10.1–2.). 8. *fell:* savage, cruel. *force:* perforce. 12. *durance:* archaic for endurance. 13. *under . . . whirlwind:* ellipsis for 'under a comfort [that] serves in a whirlwind'.

'TO SEEM THE STRANGER LIES MY LOT, MY LIFE'

7–8. *I . . . rife:* I who am weary of being merely an idle being on the sidelines where wars (of Irish conflict with the English) are rampant. 9–10. *third/ Remove:* Since Hopkins was very devoted to Wales the reference may be geographical: in Ireland he is at a third remove from England. 14. *leaves . . . began:* leaves me a lonely person who only began, or Peters and Gardner suggest a substantive as in designating a failure as an 'also-ran'.

'I WAKE AND FEEL THE FELL OF DARK, NOT DAY'

1. *fell:* past tense of fall; also the cruel fierceness; also possibly the covering over of darkness. 14. *but worse:* the condition of the lost is even worse than his own condition.

'PATIENCE, HARD THING! THE HARD THING BUT TO PRAY'

2–4. Patience in turn requires the facing of conflict, injury, weariness, deprivation, defeat, and obedience. 8. *purple eyes:* referring to the berries of the ivy (Patience). 10. *dearer:* more earnestly. 14. *combs:* honeycombs.

'MY OWN HEART LET ME MORE HAVE PITY ON; LET'

5–8. *I . . . wet:* I cast about for comfort which I can no more get by groping around my comfortless world than blind eyes in their dark world can find daylight or than thirst can find its satisfaction in a world of salt water. 9. *Jackself:* mildly pejorative for the ordinary everyday self. 11. *size:* used verbally: to grow great, increase. 13–14. *as . . . mile:* joy's smile, which cannot be forced, lights up a lovely mile as the skies unexpectedly will do between mountains.

TOM'S GARLAND

For a lengthy exegesis see under 'Practical Criticism' the letter to Bridges Feb. 10, 1888.

HARRY PLOUGHMAN

1. *Hard as hurdle arms:* ellipsis for arms as hard as the arms of a hurdle. *flue:* down, fluff. 3. *rope-over thigh; knee-nave:* muscled thigh; kneecap. 6–10. Each limb's hill-like brawn and muscle finds his rank, as at a roll call, and demonstrates in flesh his deed, etc. 13. *quail:* recoil. 14. *wind- lilylocks -laced:* tmesis for wind-laced lilylocks. 16. *Churlsgrace:* the grace of a peasant. 17–19. 'How his churl's grace governs the movement of his booted (in bluff hide) feet, as they are matched in a race with the wet shining furrow overturned by the share.' (Note by Bridges)

THAT NATURE IS A HERACLITEAN FIRE AND OF THE COMFORT OF THE RESURRECTION

1. *chevy:* chase, race. 4. *shivelights and shadowtackle:* the fragmented light and outlines of the elms. 6–7: in pool and in rut the peel (subject) parches (verb) the squandering ooze (object) to squeezed dough, then to crust, then to dust. 7. *stanches:* stops or checks. 8. *masks and manmarks:* footprints and other evidences of man. 11. *firedint:* fire + imprint. 14. *disseveral:* a coinage suggesting man's apartness from the rest of creation. 23. *Jack:* ordinary fellow; *patch:* dolt, fool, ninny.

ST. ALPHONSUS RODRIGUEZ

3. *tongue:* used verbally. 8. *hurtle:* clashing. 13. *world without event:* creative variation of 'world without end'. 14. *Majorca:* St. Alphonsus was attached to the Jesuit College at Palma in Majorca.

'THOU ART INDEED JUST, LORD, IF I CONTEND'

1–3 are a creative translation of the epigraph which is from Jer. XII, 1, 'Righteous art thou, O Lord, when I plead with thee: . . . Wherefore doth the way of the wicked prosper?' etc. 9. *brakes:* thickets. 11. *Fretty chervil:* the fern-like herb characterized by its finely divided and often curled leaves.

TO R. B.

6. *combs:* Gardner has suggested two meanings: straightens out, sets in order; stores and matures, as in a honeycomb. 13–14. The halting and almost prosaic diminuendo expresses perfectly his apologia.

NOTES ON PROSE

The following notes are largely drawn from the many annotations by the editors of Hopkins's prose works. 'Suggested Readings' should be consulted for more detailed information.

II. OBSERVATION OF NATURE: INSCAPE

[1] (p. 95) After this entry Hopkins usually omits the end stop at the close of a paragraph in the Journal.

[2] (p. 95) The brackets are those of Hopkins.

[3] (p. 101) Hopkins's usual spelling.

[4] (p. 110) Hopkins's usual spelling.

[5] (p. 113) A Stonyhurst word for a holiday.

III. POETIC THEORY

[1] (p. 125) Alexander William Mowbray Baillie was born in Edinburgh in 1843 and went to Balliol where his friendship with Hopkins began. Later he was called to the Bar, but because of ill health he also travelled for a time and in many letters corresponded with Hopkins about such subjects as Egyptian archaeology and philology. Some sixty letters from Hopkins to him have been printed in *Further Letters*.

[2] (p. 142) The brackets are those of Hopkins.

[3] (p. 142) *The Wreck of the Deutschland*, stanza 12.

[4] (p. 144) Ibid., stanza 2.

[5] (p. 145) Hopkins started his correspondence with Dixon in 1878, and he later contributed an article on him to Thomas Arnold's *A Manual of English Literature*; the following paragraphs from it are largely biographical:

'Richard Watson Dixon, now vicar of Warkworth and hon. canon of Carlisle, was born at Islington, near London, in 1833, and educated at King Edward's School, Birmingham, and Pembroke College, Oxford. At Oxford he became the friend and colleague of William Morris, Burne-Jones, and others of the mediaevalist school, to which, as a poet, he belongs. The chance reading of his earlier poems also won for him the friendship of D. G. Rossetti.

'He is engaged on a history of the Church of England on a great scale; of this three volumes have appeared. In verse he has published—in 1859, *Christ's Company, and other Poems*; in 1863, *Historical Odes* (on Marlborough, Wellington, Sir John Franklin, &c.);

in 1883, *Mano* (his greatest work, a romance-epic in *terza-rima*: Mano is a Norman knight put to death A.D. 1000, and the story, darkly and affectingly tragic, turns upon the date); in 1884, *Odes and Eclogues.*'

6 (p. 147) Both examples are from *Paradise Regained.*

7 (p. 150) The image is in Hopkins's *The Lantern out of Doors.*

8 (p. 150) The close of this letter has been lost.

9 (p. 150) These are poems by Dixon.

10 (p. 153) A slip for 'Henry'.

11 (p. 161) *Spring and Fall.*

12 (p. 167) A slip for 'Spenser'.

13 (p. 170) 'those around', or 'the followers of'.

14 (p. 170) A slip for 'Spenser'.

15 (p. 173) *The Leaden Echo and the Golden Echo.*

16 (p. 178) 'the land of Zeus whose pastures march with Syria, we have quitted in exile'; 'receive as suppliants this company of womankind with the reverent spirit of the land'; 'engendering breath'; 'but the thronging swarm of wanton men of Aegyptus. . . .'

17 (p. 185) This was written for the manuscript book of his poems which Bridges kept.

IV. PRACTICAL CRITICISM

1 (p. 190) Edward Bond was born in the same year as Hopkins, 1844, and was his contemporary at Oxford.

2 (p. 192) Marzials.

3 (p. 192) Edmund Gosse.

4 (p. 193) Theodore Watts-Dunton.

5 (p. 201) Music for *Morning Midday and Evening Sacrifice.*

6 (p. 203) *The Leaden Echo and the Golden Echo.*

7 (p. 204) *The Sea and the Skylark.*

8 (p. 207) *God's Grandeur.*

9 (p. 220) Aeschylus's *Agamemnon:* 'beautiful statues'.

10 (p. 233) On Milton's prosody.

11 (p. 234) *Tom's Garland.*

12 (p. 236) The close of the letter is missing; the succeeding paragraph is a postscript which had been added at the head of the first page.

V. THE OTHER ARTS

1 (p. 242) Tennyson's *The Daisy.*

2 (p. 254) François Joseph Fétis (1784–1871) is known for his *Biographie universelle des musiciens,* but his *Instruments de Musique* is probably referred to here.

3 (p. 255) A reference to the story by Anne Isabella Thackeray.

4 (p. 260) In the manuscript there is a gap here.

5 (p. 267) His sister Grace Hopkins.

[6] (p. 267) *Hurrahing in Harvest.*

[7] (p. 267) Probably *Felix Randal* and *At the Wedding.*

[8] (p. 268) See the article by Bridges on Harry Ellis Wooldridge (1845–1917) in *D.N.B.*

[9] (p. 271) *Spring and Fall.*

[10] (p. 272) The first part of this letter has been lost.

[11] (p. 274) Sir John Stainer (1840–1901) was Professor of Music at Oxford, 1889–99.

[12] (p. 275) Bridges deleted the name in this and the following letters.

[13] (p. 275) John Frederick Bridges's *Counterpoint* or *Double Counterpoint and Canon.*

[14] (p. 276) By Bridges.

[15] (p. 277) Sir Robert Prescott Stewart (1852–94) was a well-known composer, organist, teacher, and conductor in Dublin.

[16] (p. 277) The Rev. Sir Frederick Arthur Gore Ouseley (1825–89) was Professor of Music at Oxford.

[17] (p. 279) This paragraph may belong to another letter.

[18] (p. 283) Dixon dedicated the book to Hopkins and included *Morning Midday and Evening Sacrifice.*

[19] (p. 286) It is not certain whether the following paragraphs belong to this letter.

[20] (p. 291) Here Hopkins inserted a little sketch.

[21] (p. 296) Hopkins started but did not complete a poem titled *On the Portrait of Two Beautiful Young People: A Brother and Sister.*

VI. PERSONAL LETTERS

[1] (p. 297) *ad infinitum.*

[2] (p. 317) *The Bugler's First Communion.*

[3] (p. 317) *Morning Midday and Evening Sacrifice.*

[4] (p. 321) Here the page turns.

[5] (p. 324) The references in this paragraph are to his poem *Peace.*

[6] (p. 324) An alternative title for *Spring and Fall.*

[7] (p. 335) 'To be active producing poetry.'

[8] (p. 336) His uncompleted poem *On the Portrait of Two Beautiful Young People: A Brother and Sister.*

[9] (p. 340) Proper name for a thing; exact word. The term is from Aristotle's *Poetics.*

VII. RELIGION

[1] (p. 345) Plato's *Republic:* 'One thing set against another'.

[2] (p. 346) E. H. Coleridge (1846–1920), son of Derwent Coleridge, went to Balliol (1866–70) and is noted for his work on Byron and Coleridge.

[3] (p. 351) Edward William Urquhart (1839–1916) distinguished himself at Balliol (1857–61) and was ordained in the Church of England.

4 (p. 363) Perhaps: 'I am subordinate to the eyes.'

5 (p. 389) A slip for 'Bayly'.

6 (p. 396) See the sonnet beginning 'I wake and feel the fell of dark, not day'.

7 (p. 404) See *God's Grandeur*.

8 (p. 405) *Henry Purcell*.

9 (p. 409) Apparently the deletion was made by Bridges.

SUGGESTED READINGS

BY HOPKINS:

Correspondence of Gerard Manley Hopkins and R. W. Dixon. Ed. Claude Colleer Abbott. Oxford. Second edition. 1956.

Further Letters of Hopkins. Ed. Claude Colleer Abbott. Oxford. Second edition. 1956.

Journals and Papers of Gerard Manley Hopkins. Ed. Humphry House, completed by Graham Storey. Oxford. 1959.

Letters of Gerard Manley Hopkins to Robert Bridges. Ed. Claude Colleer Abbott. Oxford. Second edition. 1955.

Poems of Gerard Manley Hopkins. Ed. W. H. Gardner. Oxford. Third edition 1948. Reprinted with additions and corrections. 1961.

Sermons and Devotional Writings of Gerard Manley Hopkins. Ed. Christopher Devlin, S.J. Oxford. 1959.

ABOUT HOPKINS:

Boyle, Robert, S.J. *Metaphor in Hopkins*. North Carolina. 1961.

Downes, David A. *Gerard Manley Hopkins: A Study of His Ignatian Spirit*. Bookman Associates. 1959.

Gardner, W. H. *Gerard Manley Hopkins: A Study of Poetic Idiosyncrasy in Relation to Poetic Tradition*. Two volumes. Second edition. Oxford. 1962.

Heuser, Alan. *The Shaping Vision of Gerard Manley Hopkins*. Oxford. 1958.

Keating, John E. *The Wreck of the Deutschland: An Essay and Commentary*. Kent State University Research Series VI. 1963.

Kenyon critics. *Gerard Manley Hopkins*. New Directions. 1945.

Leavis, F. R. 'Gerard Manley Hopkins' in *New Bearings in English Poetry*. Ann Arbor Paperbacks. 1960.

Martin, Philip M. *Mastery and Mercy: A Study of Two Religious Poems: The Wreck of the Deutschland, by G. M. Hopkins and Ash Wednesday, by T. S. Eliot*. Oxford. 1957.

Peters, W. M. A., S.J. *Gerard Manley Hopkins: A Critical Essay towards the Understanding of his Poetry*. Oxford. 1948.

Pick, John. *Gerard Manley Hopkins: Priest and Poet.* Oxford. 1942.

————. "Gerard Manley Hopkins" in *The Victorian Poets: A Guide to Research* (Ed. Frederic E. Faverty). Harvard. 1956.

Ritz, Jean-Georges. *Robert Bridges and Gerard Manley Hopkins: A Literary Friendship.* Oxford. 1960.

Weyand, Norman, S.J. (Ed.) *Immortal Diamond: Studies in Gerard Manley Hopkins.* Sheed and Ward. 1949.

INDEX OF FIRST LINES OF POEMS

INDEX